4.

Unwin Education Books: 6

THE PHILOSOPHY OF EDUCATION:
AN INTRODUCTION

Unwin Education Books

Unwin Education Books
Series Editor: Ivor Morrish

The Philosophy of Education

An Introduction

HARRY SCHOFIELD

M.A. (Cantab.), M.Ed.

Head of the Education Department
St Katharine's College of Education, Liverpool

London
GEORGE ALLEN & UNWIN
Boston   Sydney

12076

First published in 1972
Eleventh impression 1982

© George Allen & Unwin (Publishers) Ltd 1972

ISBN 0 04 370039 X *Hardback*
     0 04 370040 3 *Paperback*

Printed in Great Britain by
Biddles Ltd, Guildford, Surrey

To my wife Olive ~~[redacted]~~
for her wonderful patience and understanding *and the odd shag!*

Acknowledgements

Acknowledgement is due to the following publishers for permission to reproduce copyright material from the works listed below:

George Allen and Unwin: *A History of Western Philosophy*, Bertrand Russell: *Ethics and Education*, R. S. Peters.

George G. Harrap: *An Essay on the Content of Education*, E. James (now Lord James of Rusholme): *Groundwork of Educational Theory*, James S. Ross.

Harvard University Press: *Social Class Influences upon Learning*, Allison Davis.

John Wiley: *Authority and Freedom in Education; An Introduction to the Philosophy of Education*, Paul Nash.

Manchester University Press: *Aims in Education; the Philosophical Approach*, edited T. H. B. Hollins. The passage quoted is from 'Against Utilitarianism', A. C. MacIntyre.

Routledge and Kegan Paul (also Philosophical Library, New York, and Humanities Press, New York): *An Introduction to the Philosophy of Education*, D. J. O'Connor.

The Concept of Education, edited R. S. Peters. The passage quoted is from 'Indoctrination', J. P. White.

Plato's Theory of Education, R. C. Lodge.

Contents

Author's Preface

During the last few years, there has been an increasing number of books produced on the philosophy of education. Many of these are the work of experts in this particular field, and are admirably suited to those students who have some knowledge of general philosophy, or who have no such knowledge but do possess a mind which takes easily to philosophy.

Unfortunately, many students in Colleges of Education do not fall into either of these categories. For them, the admirable books are rather forbidding, and convince the reader that 'philosophy is not for him'.

This book has been planned and written for just this type of student. It aims to show that to find philosophy difficult in such circumstances is neither extraordinary nor a sign that the average student cannot learn to study philosophy successfully.

The book starts from scratch. It attempts to answer simply the two major questions: 'What is philosophy?' and 'What is philosophy of education?' From this simple start, we proceed slowly to discover the areas which philosophy examines, all the while explaining and illustrating basic terms. It is ignorance of these which, in many cases, acts as a barrier between the student and a successful study of philosophy.

Gradually, the reader is introduced to the techniques of linguistic analysis and concept analysis in such a way as to show that these two techniques are not as difficult as their names suggest. To the inexperienced, all such names are terrifying. Closer acquaintance will remove any such fears.

Not all readers will have the same educational background and experience, so that references throughout the book which are familiar to some may be totally new to others. To ensure that the latter will not be at a disadvantage, copious notes are provided at the end of each chapter explaining references to the classical world, medieval universities, literary works, etc. Any terms introduced from other educational disciplines, e.g. psychology and sociology, are similarly explained.

We ask only that the reader be willing to exercise patience, especially in the early stages of the book, and that he be prepared to go slowly and, if necessary, to retrace his steps in places. To provide further assistance, and to stress that all concepts within education are closely interrelated, frequent cross-references are provided. These prepare the way for related ideas yet to be dealt with and, in the later stages, serve as reminders of ideas previously examined.

It is our firm conviction that philosophy is not the province of the privileged few. Those who are prepared to tackle it slowly and confidently will, we feel, be pleasantly surprised at the progress which they make.

H.S.

Liverpool

Chapter 1

The Meaning and Function of Philosophy and Educational Philosophy

The word 'philosophy' frequently causes a feeling of apprehension in the average man and even in the average student. Both believe that it deals with mysterious matters far removed from everyday life and that it traffics in ideas which only the brilliant few are capable of understanding. Such apprehension causes the average man (and the average student) to close his mind firmly against philosophy.

THE ORIGIN OF THE WORD 'PHILOSOPHY' AND A DEFINITION

The word 'philosophy' comes from the Ancient Greek noun φιλοσοφία (*philosophia*) which literally means 'love of wisdom'. The word 'wisdom' is somewhat old-fashioned nowadays and the expression 'love of wisdom' causes little less apprehension than the word 'philosophy' itself. It suggests abstract and even other-worldly ideas and that strange area of philosophical investigation – metaphysics. The word 'metaphysics' comes from the Greek expression '*ta meta physica*' – 'things beyond the physical realm' – and again we feel mysterious associations which suggest that philosophy is beyond us.

Moreover, if we turn to the writings of Bertrand Russell, one of the most lucid exponents of philosophy, and read his definition of the word 'philosophy', we are more certain than ever that our fears about its difficulty were well founded. Russell (1) writes:

'"Philosophy", as I shall try to understand the word, is something intermediate between theology and science. Like theology, it consists of speculations on matters as to which definite knowledge has, so far, been unascertainable; but like science, it appeals to human reason rather than to authority, whether that of tradition or that of revelation. All DEFINITE knowledge, so I should contend, belongs to science; all DOGMA as to what surpasses definite knowledge belongs to theology. But between theology and science there is a no-man's-land exposed to attack by both sides; this no-man's-land is philosophy.'

We shall have need to refer on many occasions throughout this book to the terms 'speculation', 'reason' and 'types of knowledge', but our overall impression of the quotation is that it offers little comfort and merely tells us that philosophy deals with vague matters, which is what we suspected before turning to Russell for help and comfort.

Furthermore, Scheffler (2) suggests that it is not only the average man who shies away from philosophy and believes that it offers little help to him. Scheffler says that in the past and still to some extent in the present *professional* philosophers and *professional* educators come together as 'relative strangers in an academic landscape'. The professional educator cannot see how the general philosopher, who can give no definite answers even to general problems in the same way that science can give definite answers, can throw light on educational problems. The sole purpose of this book is to show that philosophy *can* help not only professional educators, but also practising teachers, however experienced or inexperienced they may be in their chosen profession. It is never too early or too late to enlist the help of philosophy.

In the first place, nothing is ever achieved in life by running away from problems and situations which overawe us. The child who states emphatically that he hates cabbage without ever having tasted it, denies himself the opportunity of ever coming to like it. In addition, every time cabbage forms part of the family meal, there is a tense atmosphere caused by the parents insisting that he must eat cabbage because it is good for him, and the child, with mounting frustration, flatly denying that he will eat cabbage. Consequently, for the child cabbage comes to be associated with his parents' anger, just as Pavlov's dog associated the ringing of a bell with the appearance of food (3), and a perfectly harmless vegetable becomes highly emotionally-toned for that particular child.

Similarly, those who visit psychiatrists are often there for no other reason than that they regularly fail to face up to problems and consequently become afraid of all problems. They try to push the fear out of their conscious mind, but they do not prevent the fear from continuing to work destruction. When they can endure the mental agony no longer, they resort to the psychiatrist. He brings them face to face with their fears and prevents their running away. Only in this way can the fears be destroyed.

Like the child, we shied away from the word 'philosophy' and like the psychiatrist's patient we ran away from Russell's definition of philosophy. It is now time that we faced the situation, to decide whether in fact it is as bad as we feared. If we read what Russell writes directly after the passage quoted, he says that the term 'philosophy' can be used and indeed has been used 'in a number of ways'. Immediately we realize that the terrifying 'no-man's-land' idea may not be the only one available. Furthermore, he writes that the term may be used in a wider or a narrower sense. These two ideas tempt us to think that possibly the term may be used in a simpler way. Assuming that it can, and because we have already seen that philosophy concerns itself with speculation, we will define philosophy as 'the process of asking questions' and see where this definition leads us.

THE PROCESS OF ASKING QUESTIONS

We have now come from a very complex definition to a very simple one, and it is possible that we have oversimplified matters in the transition. We can think of some questions that merely arouse the original fear in our minds, such as the one asked elsewhere by Russell. He says that a philosophical question may be 'Is there a china tea-pot between earth and Mars revolving in elliptical orbit?'

Again, the thought occurs to us that many people besides philosophers ask questions, and we wonder if all philosophical questions must be like the example which Russell gives to us. It will help at this point if we return to our original definition (by translation) of 'philosophy' as 'love of wisdom'. Since we are attempting to simplify matters, let us substitute the more everyday word 'knowledge' for 'wisdom'. A moment's thought tells us that, young as we are, we have acquired a tremendous store of knowledge (or wisdom), that the process began in infancy and largely consisted of asking questions. We did not approach philosophers for the answers, but, *by asking questions* of our parents, teachers, friends, *we obtained knowledge*. Nor was the knowledge which we acquired in this way, i.e. by asking questions, 'metaphysical' or unrelated to daily life. But there were times when we asked difficult questions, such as 'Where was I before I was born?' or 'How was I born?', which caused the people we asked no small difficulty. Without being taught to ask questions, we formed of our own accord a connection between wanting to know and asking questions. It is a simple matter now to suggest that the philosopher, wanting to know the answers to certain problems, asks a certain type of question.

Our apparently naïve and over-simplified definition of philosophy as 'the process of asking questions' has a famous precedent. No less a person than Plato's teacher Socrates used the question and answer technique, which came to be known as the Socratic method, in his search for true knowledge. The questions which he asked and the answers he received, and the conclusions which he came to, are recorded in the philosophical dialogues of Plato.

Moreover, Socrates asked questions in order to clarify people's ideas, to 'rid their minds of error', as he called it. He believed that too many people accepted ideas at secondhand without ever questioning them. Once they had acquired them, they applied them automatically, without any real understanding of them, and in some cases gained an unjustified reputation for wisdom. Socrates, on the other hand, said that he himself was the wisest man in the world because he did not pretend to know what he did not know. His wisdom consisted of recognizing his own limitations. By asking questions, he attempted to rid his own mind and the minds of other people of preconceived ideas, which were often a barrier to understanding. We shall find, throughout this book, that once we begin to ask questions we are frequently forced to abandon many preconceptions, often those which we hold most dear. It is not comfort to either intending or practising teachers to know that we are just as prone to these preconceived ideas as anyone else. In view of what we have said already it is clear that philosophy, at least in the form of asking questions, can be practically useful to us.

Some of Socrates' questions are of the metaphysical kind. When he asks 'What is justice?', he is being just as metaphysical as Pontius Pilate when he asked Christ 'What is truth?' At other times, the questions he asks are everyday ones, such as that directed at Cephalus (4): 'But has your property, Cephalus, been chiefly inherited or acquired?' There is certainly nothing mysterious or other-worldly here.

However, we must notice now one of the greatest weaknesses of the Socratic method, namely that it is easy to ask 'loaded' questions. 'Loaded' questions are those which compel the person whom we are questioning to give the answer which we require to suit our purposes. In a court of law such questions are called leading questions, and no judge will allow counsel to use them when interrogating a witness, because they make the witness, who can answer only 'Yes' or 'No', condemn himself out of his own mouth. The questions of the prosecutor 'lead' him to the answer which the prosecutor needs to clinch his case.

It is easy to see, then, that philosophical questions asked in the quest for true knowledge must not be loaded but impartial. They must not reflect the preconceived ideas and bias of the person asking them. The questioner must keep an open mind throughout his investigation and be scrupulously fair in the questions he asks.

One of Socrates' victims becomes very indignant when he realizes that the questions asked of him are loaded (5): 'This is scandalous, Socrates. You understand my doctrine in the sense in which you can damage it most easily.' In the present century, Ryle (6) warns against the same thing when he says that he becomes most angry in his writings when he sees in other people the assumptions, prejudices, and bias which he realizes he himself has.

Emmet (7) says that questions which make 'illegitimate assumptions', which 'beg the question', are the most frequent sources of error in the history of philosophy. This is a further indication that even great minds can become victims of this fault. It also warns us, who are not great minds, that we must be extra careful when we ask questions. Teachers are particularly prone to ask loaded questions when tackling philosophical problems, because in their daily routine they frequently use a loaded question to make a pupil give them the correct answer, as an alternative to providing him with the information. When the matter is of fact, the method is legitimate, because facts are certain. But, philosophy often asks questions in the realm of beliefs, and loaded questions here are illegitimate. We may find when we begin to ask questions about educational problems that we expose false doctrines and destroy them. If this is done, it must be as the result of asking fair questions.

In order to chart the no man's land which Russell said was philosophy, we must determine not only what sort of questions the philosopher is entitled to ask, but also the areas in which he can legitimately ask them. We hinted at this when we said that not only philosophers ask questions. In other words, not all questions are philosophical questions.

THEORETICAL AND EMPIRICAL QUESTIONS

Some questions can be answered in the laboratory, while others cannot. The former are empirical questions, and Russell, in his definition, suggested that this sort of question belongs to science, the area of *definite* knowledge. The other type of question was described by Russell as speculative. We also refer to these as theoretical questions and again we use a Greek word which was used in a philosophical context by Aristotle (8). The Greek noun θεωρία (*theoria*), as used by Aristotle, referred to a state of contemplation or speculation. This theoretical state was the supreme state of happiness, and one cannot measure happiness in the laboratory. Similarly, Plato's Guardians (9) 'contemplated the good' (rather similar to studying philosophy). Again, one cannot measure the good in the laboratory.

Speculative or theoretical or contemplative questions, then, are not scientific, since they cannot produce in the laboratory answers on which certain knowledge or definite knowledge is based. These questions may belong to the realm of theology, as Russell indicates, but they may equally belong to philosophy. This point will become clearer in a moment. Speculative or theoretical or contemplative questions require us to 'sit down and think', in order to obtain an answer.

The word 'empirical' is derived from the Greek noun *empeiria*, meaning 'experience'. Thus, empirical questions can be answered by our own direct experience. We can test the rightness or the wrongness of the answer. To answer empirical questions, we must 'get up and do'. We can illustrate these two types of questions by very simple examples.

Let us assume that I am sitting on the beach and somebody asks me, 'Is the sea warm today?' If I have already been in for a swim, I can give him a certain answer based directly on my own first-hand experience. If he sees that I am wearing swimming trunks and that my skin is still wet, he can assume that the experience on which I base my answer is recent experience and therefore reliable. If the same person asks me the same question when I have not been in for a swim, it is probable that my answer would be, 'I'm sorry. I cannot tell you, because I have not been in.'

However, let us assume that I am undecided whether to go in the water or not, because I am not certain that it will be warm enough for my liking. I then pose the question 'Is the sea warm today?' to myself. It is possible to arrive at a theoretical answer. I can summon all the evidence which I know is relevant, such as what time of year it is, what time of day it is, whether the sun is out or not, and how long it has been out. All these pieces of evidence help me to come to a conclusion about the temperature of the sea. But there is still an 'element of doubt'. Perhaps I have got my facts wrong about the temperature of the sea at certain times of the year or of the day. I can be 'pretty sure' of my facts but not 'absolutely' sure. The only sure way to remove the lingering doubt is 'to get up and do', to go and put my hand in the water. In these circumstances, it is probably quicker, and certainly more effective, to go and test the water in the first instance, than it is to sit and theorize about its warmth.

But as I sit on the beach, instead of asking myself 'Is the sea warm today?', I might well ask myself 'Where did the sea come from originally?' A certain theoretical line of reasoning may lead me to ask further questions: 'Is there a God?', 'Did God create the sea?' I have now asked myself four questions as I sit on the beach. I can answer the first one, which is a very ordinary, everyday sort of question, either by speculation (sitting and thinking), or empirically (getting up and doing). In the case of the remaining three questions, I cannot go and do; I can only sit and think, contemplate, speculate, theorize. I can avail myself of experience in my theoretical answers, but not of direct experience. To have learned the theories of philosophers and theologians is a sort of experience, but not the same sort as that experience where I went and put my hand in the water. In answering the last three questions I must avail myself of ideas. After considering my own theories and those of other people that I recall, I may arrive at an answer which satisfies me, or I may not. In neither instance is there any final arbiter, any conclusive evidence equivalent to testing the warmth of the sea with my hand.

From the above examples it becomes clear why Russell assigns all DEFINITE knowledge to science. Science can test its answers empirically, by 'going and doing' in the laboratory, by setting up experiments. At the end of the performance, science can give tangible proof. It can say, 'There, see for yourself, if you do not believe me'. The theologian and the philosopher cannot do this. The answers to the problems of science lie in the 'physical' world, the answers to theological and philosophical problems lie in the 'metaphysical' world, that world which is 'beyond the physical'.

It seems at this point that we were justified in our apprehensions about philosophy when we thought that it dealt with mysterious matters far removed from everyday life. Even after we have defined it as 'the process of asking questions', it seems that we come back to the same sphere of metaphysics, of intangibles (things which we cannot touch or understand by sense impression), of abstract ideas. Moreover, it seems that the questions which philosophy asks are not very different from those asked by theology. '*Theos*' is the Greek word meaning 'God'. Consequently when I asked the question, 'Is there a God?', I can be said to be asking a theological question. When I ask, 'Where did the sea come from?' I am asking a philosophical question. The answer may be that God created the sea, but my original question was not about the existence of God, the essence or attributes of God, or anything to do with religious problems.

To return to our three areas in which questions are asked, theology, science and philosophy, it is often said that science gives definite and precise answers to questions, whereas theology and philosophy do not. We can see now that this is inevitable. Science gives different types of answers from theology and philosophy only because it asks basically different questions. The questions of science are empirical, those of theology and philosophy are speculative. If theology and philosophy ceased to ask speculative questions and began to ask empirical ones, they would cease to be theology and philosophy. Similarly, if science abandoned its method of asking questions and adopted the method of theology and philosophy, it would cease to be science. This is not a condemnation of philosophy and theology but an appreciation that they are not the same as science.

We have now shown briefly that philosophy asks its questions outside the realm of theology as well as outside the realm of science. But it is not necessary to regard this area strictly as a 'no man's land'. The term 'no man's land' implies a waste land in which no one is interested and in which no one holds territorial rights. But philosophy has more right to a place in areas where questions are asked than any other field of inquiry.

THE ANCIENT AND MODERN TASKS OF PHILOSOPHY

If we go back to the days before Plato, when the Ionian philosophers (10) asked their questions we find that originally all questions were philosophical. The Ionians asked about the nature of the universe and where it came from, about the existence of a god and what he did, about the origin of man and what was the relationship between this tiny speck, man, and the immense universe. Thus the philosopher asked questions in those early days which later became the property of different fields of knowledge and inquiry. As man's knowledge developed, certain people specialized in one sphere of investigation, while others specialized in another. After the rise of modern science in the seventeenth century, the lines of demarcation between areas of investigation became more obvious and more permanent. The development of instruments for measuring made for a very big advance in the methods of giving precise answers to questions; there was no comparable development in the realms of philosophy and theology.

The Greeks were very fond of 'creation myths', especially the type where Mother Earth produced races of gigantic offspring. If we make our own creation myth at this point, it will help us to understand not only how all the other disciplines developed from philosophy, but also how philosophy functions.

At different times, philosophy brought forth offspring. These were called 'science', 'theology', 'history', 'mathematics', and each of these 'children of philosophy' gathered a store of knowledge of his own. Ultimately, when their store of knowledge was great, Philosophy called her children to her and asked them to show her what knowledge they had discovered. Being older and wiser than her children, she was able to derive great meaning from what knowledge each provided. She herself acquired no factual knowledge, but, by putting side by side all the knowledge that her children brought to her, she was able to develop an overall understanding, to look at all the variables. Sometimes there were gaps in the overall pattern. On such occasions, Philosophy did not produce knowledge of her own, or criticize her offspring for providing her with insufficient information. Instead she made suggestions that would fill in the gaps, and interpretations that would provide greater coherence in the picture.

This 'overall picture' which philosophy develops after reviewing all the available data from other disciplines, is produced by the synoptic or speculative function of philosophy. The synoptic Gospels are the Gospels which, when placed side by side and looked at simultaneously (the Greek word means 'looking at together'), are seen to contain much of the same material. Just as the theologian looks at the content of the synoptic Gospels, so philosophy looks at the different disciplines side by side. Brubacher (11) reminds us that philosophy may begin an investigation at the level of common sense and 'that stolid first cousin of common sense, tradition'. We recall that Socrates, too, questioned tradition and that many times his first questions were of an everyday, common sense kind. By asking Cephalus if his wealth was inherited or acquired, he took the first step towards answering the much greater question, 'What is justice?'

However, philosophers find that common sense and tradition are like 'raw data' to the psychologist, i.e. not sufficiently precise to enable him to arrive at meaningful answers. Thus, when a psychologist collects 'marks' (to give a single example) in an experiment, he subsequently applies statistical techniques to these marks (raw scores) and produces 'processed figures', which give greater accuracy to his findings. The raw data of common sense is in the same category as the raw score marks. Tradition, too, is imprecise, because it may be an untidy collection of data in no really coherent form. Philosophy sifts and refines this, simply by processing the facts of history and science, which themselves examine tradition.

Out of the synoptic role of philosophy, where the data from different areas is set side by side, develops the critical role, which is concerned with the derivation of meaning from the data. If philosophy were merely to arrange the material, so that all the variables could be seen together, it would be like the psychologist who prepares his data for the statistical process he has chosen, but never completes the process, never obtains results.

The combination of the synoptic and critical approaches of philosophy leads logically to the 'normative role'. A 'norm' is a standard or goal, and philosophy, especially when it is applied to educational problems, is frequently concerned with establishing standards and formulating goals. As a result of its present survey of the past, it sees where the past is useful and where it can be approved and where it needs to be improved. From there, it looks to the future and helps to establish guide lines, norms, aims, standards.

We are now in a position to pause and see where our definition of philosophy as a 'process of asking questions' has led us. We have, at the same time, given some answer to our second question, namely, 'In what area does philosophy operate and what type of questions does it ask?' First, it asks questions which are outside the narrower scope of the similar process, theology. It also asks those *speculative* questions to which there is no *empirical* answer, and which are, therefore, not strictly within the realm of science. It may use the findings of both theology and science to help arrive at the final answer to a question, but it will not give as that final answer either a *scientific* or a *theological* answer.

Nor will this answer, when finally given, necessarily be a simple answer such as those produced by science. The application of the philosophical method is not like the application of a formula which always provides a precise solution. At worst, philosophy, after conducting its investigation, will produce an awareness of all the aspects of the problem, and provide those using the method with all possible clarity with the common theory underlying a variety of practices, with a rationally-based, coordinated structure. Where science refuses to accept authorities and their pronouncements at face value and tests them by experiment (empirically), philosophy, likewise, refuses to accept without analysis what authorities say. Instead of the experiment of the scientist, the philosopher uses reason.

Wilson (12) reminds us of the difficulty of the word 'certainty', which is closely associated with the demand for a simple, ready answer, when he says that there are very few things which teachers can regard as one hundred per cent certain. If we confined our teaching to those things which *are* one hundred per cent certain, we would be unemployed most of the time. If there is doubt about the certainty of 'facts', there is even more doubt about the certainty of beliefs. We shall see, in a later chapter, that this is a problem inherent in teaching religion. Instead of refusing to teach beliefs and 'facts' which cannot be proved absolutely, Wilson advocates that we teach them 'rationally', that is, by producing 'generally acceptable evidence' in support of the 'facts' or beliefs. It is not sufficient to teach them because we believe them, or because they are said to be 'good for children'. The children themselves must be shown the evidence which makes what is taught acceptable. Philosophy seeks objectivity (an unbiased view which accords with acceptable evidence) rather than accepting subjectivity (seeing things from a personal point of view).

This is a further reminder that the human mind is full of preconceptions. The scientist when he formulates hypotheses looks at the evidence. If this supports the hypotheses, he makes a statement of fact based on the findings. No reputable scientist would twist the facts (or data) from his experiment so that they supported his hypothesis. Yet frequently, and not always consciously, we do exactly this. We start off with an idea or a belief and refuse to take heed of anything which contradicts that idea or belief. Such a process is often the foundation on which bigotry is built. Many people had tried to write history before Tacitus (13). He was sufficiently aware of the danger of recording history in the light of preconceptions that he stated that his aim was to record the deeds of Rome and her people 'without partisanship and bias'. Had these faults not been apparent in the works of previous writers of history, there would have been little point in making the statement at all. We can illustrate what is meant by appeal to reason, rather than to preconceptions, by a simple example. If we ask the question, 'Is Russia a more aggressive nation than the United States?' we ought to get an answer from a pro-Russian, a pro-American and a complete neutral, based on the evidence available. Each would first define what he meant by the term 'aggressive', and then, after gathering together the evidence and laying it side by side (the speculative or synoptic approach), he would sift and analyse it rationally (the critical approach) before coming to an answer. If there were no bias, complete objectivity instead of subjectivity, it would be possible to reach an answer acceptable to all three people. It would not matter whether the answer was 'Yes', 'No', or 'in the light of evidence available, no definite answer can be given'. It is most unlikely that this would happen, since the question would be answered in vastly different ways by the pro-American and the pro-Russian.

It is even probable that the so-called complete neutral would produce an answer biased (even if only slightly) in one direction or the other.

Wilson warns us of the danger of asking such questions as 'What is education?' Some people may take the question as a request for a definition of education, and we shall deal with this problem in Chapter 2. Others might think, as Thrasymachus thought when asked by Socrates 'What is justice?', that a sociological answer was required. Others might merely see the question as a chance to air some personal (subjective) opinion, possibly in a very dogmatic way. Using philosophical investigation, we shall find that dogmatism is often produced as a substitute for evidence and reason. Moreover, if we remember what we said earlier about loaded questions, we could so load further questions that we could steer the person questioned towards whichever of the three alternatives we wished to choose, irrespective of the first answer that he gave. This was precisely the method of Socrates.

PHILOSOPHY AND PHILOSOPHIZING

We have said a great deal so far about philosophy and about philosophers. We have even referred to some philosophers by name. We have seen that they asked questions because philosophy is 'a process of asking particular questions in particular areas'. But if we say that philosophy is a process of asking questions, can we 'philosophize' without asking questions ourselves? Is it possible to say that we are asking philosophical questions when we ask, 'What did philosopher x say on subject y?' Kant (14) would have given a very firm 'NO' to this question, as we shall see later in this chapter Scheffler does. Kant wrote: 'You will not learn from me philosophy, but how to philosophize; not thoughts to repeat, but how to think.' If we ourselves ask philosophical questions in an attempt to solve philosophical problems, then we philosophize. If we ask ourselves what answers did thinkers of the past produce when they asked philosophical questions to solve philosophical problems, we do not philosophize. If we adopt the second alternative, we use what might be called the 'historico-philosophical' approach by asking what conclusion philosophers came to throughout history. We accept only that answer which appears to suit our needs. But if we philosophize, we have to commit ourselves, to attempt to reach a conclusion for ourselves. Scheffler (15) says that there is nothing new or revolutionary about this distinction, but that it is all too often neglected, especially by educational philosophers in their writings.

Now, we are not saying that what thinkers of the past have said when giving answers to philosophical questions is not important, though we do well to remind ourselves that Wittgenstein (about whom we shall say more later) claims that the total of past philosophizing has led to no solution of major problems. Indeed, in later chapters we shall have reason to look at some of the ideas of philosophers from the past. But this will only be part of the process; either before or after mentioning their ideas we shall ask our own questions.

It is not presumptuous to say that, valuable as past philosophizing is, the answers it produces may not always be directly relevant to current problems. The variables may have changed, thus changing the problem, however slightly. Secondly, those who are training to teach must realize at the start that there will be many times when they have to make up their own minds on important educational issues which impinge on them as teachers. They will have to commit themselves one way or another. To begin one's teaching career seeking ready-made answers from the past is no preparation for the making of personal decisions.

PHILOSOPHICAL ANALYSIS. THE PROBLEM OF LANGUAGE

We can call the process of asking questions for ourselves in an effort to produce solutions to philosophical problems the 'analytical' approach, since we have already said that philosophy sifts and analyses evidence. The analytical approach starts from a contemporary problem.

In the context of modern philosophy, three terms are frequently used: 'philosophical analysis', 'linguistic analysis', and 'concept analysis'. The second and third terms are really more precise expressions of the first. Strict interpretation of the terms shows that linguistic analysis examines statements to see if they have any real meaning, while concept analysis analyses certain terms (words) which represent ideas (or concepts). 'History' is a concept. If we examine Henry Ford's statement, 'History is bunk', we apply linguistic analysis. If we merely write down the term 'history' and attempt to decide what it means, we, strictly speaking, use concept analysis. However, in examining Ford's statement, we have to analyse the concept 'history' before we can analyse the total statement 'History is bunk'.

Because philosophical or linguistic or concept analysis is normally associated with twentieth-century philosophy, it is sometimes thought to be a twentieth-century invention. In fact, the awareness that such analysis was necessary dates back at least to the time of Leibniz (16). He realized that when two people attempt to communicate they often fail, either because they use the same words to mean different things, or because they use different words to mean the same thing. In neither case is there any 'essential' difference between them. Deadlock results from misuse and misunderstanding of words. Let us take a simple illustration, to show how two people put the same word into a sentence and seem to say something different. A layman often says, 'If he had any intelligence he would not behave in that foolish way'. The psychologist says 'The idiot and the imbecile have low intelligence'. Yet our layman used the word 'intelligence' when speaking of a 'normal' man performing a foolish act, and implied that the act showed that he possessed *no* intelligence. Again, our layman says, 'The success of the Beatles is proof that they have personality'. The psychologist says that everyone has a 'personality', but that not all 'personalities' are the same. Again, these statements seem to be contradictory, but they are not. The lay statement does not define clearly the concept of 'personality'.

Leibniz felt that the solution to this sort of problem could be achieved only by developing a 'universal symbolism', which he called *Characteristica Universalis*. The idea was not unlike the idea of developing Esperanto as a world language. But for Leibniz, this universal symbolism was mathematical in nature. Once established, it would ensure that philosophical problems could be solved exactly like mathematical problems. If there were ever a dispute between two philosophers, they would behave exactly like two accountants and say, 'To resolve our difficulty let us sit down and calculate'.

The apparent failure of philosophy to reach conclusive answers to essential problems led twentieth-century philosophers to seek a fresh approach. Both Warnock and Wittgenstein wanted to bring words back from their metaphysical use to their everyday use. Again, we see the common-sense beginnings of philosophical analysis. Warnock wished to take a concept and the problems which surround it, and worry away at it until a solution was reached. Moore, too, advocated a return to the everyday, common-sense use of language as the first step to clearing away the fog created by philosophy in the past.

Thus all three philosophers show an awareness that the long history of philosophy has not apparently brought us any nearer to solving vital problems, and that part of the blame may rest with a failure to use language effectively to communicate philosophical ideas and findings. Colin Wilson (17) has written that we use words in an attempt to 'digest' our experiences, and that at times we suffer from indigestion. At such times analytical philosophy is taken as a kind of 'Alka-Seltzer'!

Later in his career, Wittgenstein said that the misunderstanding arose not from any fault of language itself, but because people tended to think that there was only one set of language rules. This is as wrong as to think that there is only one set of rules covering all forms of sport. Just as there are separate rules for the games of cricket and golf, so there are different sets of rules for the language used in everyday life and language used as a means of communicating philosophical ideas.

Emmet (18) warns against what he calls 'the bewitchment of language'. In particular, we must realize that words can be used 'rationally' and they can be used 'emotively'. If we think back a little way in this present chapter, we will remember that we said that we could get three different answers to the question 'Is Russia more aggressive than the United States?' The reason for this is that anyone except a complete neutral would be 'emotionally involved' on one side or the other. Emotive language and subjectivity go together; rational language and objectivity go together. Rational language is impartial; emotive language always reveals bias and preconceived ideas.

Because this book is so closely connected with particular uses of language ,and ways of examining language, it is worth while to pause for a moment and to consider how easily misunderstanding can arise when words are used to describe events which we have not experienced.

We often show a few-months-old baby an object of a particular colour and shape and at the same time say, 'Teddy'. We pair the toy and the word, as Pavlov paired the bell and the meat and as the child whom we described as 'disliking cabbage', paired 'cabbage' and 'parental displeasure.' Eventually the sight of the toy is sufficient to make the child say the word 'Teddy'. He first uses the word while he is looking at the toy.

Later, however, he 'develops a concept' (or idea) of 'Teddy'. Then he is able to say the word 'Teddy' without the toy being there for him to see. Later still, his vocabulary increases and enables him to talk about 'actions' outside the house, as, for example, 'Daddy gone work'. Because at a certain time daddy is not at home, the child's experience tells him that he is outside the home and that he has gone to work. The child has experienced seeing his daddy go out and hearing his mother say 'Daddy gone work'. The early language of the child is based on his direct experience of things and actions which are explained to him in words by his parents.

Once the child begins formal schooling, his experience widens. His vocabulary grows. But he is still very much dependent on what he sees as a basis for his expressions. Moreover the language which he hears and uses is very much above the level of difficulty of the naming of particular objects. It is also very much more complex than the simple sentence, 'Daddy gone work'. Someone is not talking to him individually all the time. Because of this, it is very easy to 'talk above the head' of the child, to use words in a way which is very familiar to us, but which is very difficult, if not impossible, for the child to understand. In a well-known experiment, nine-year-old children heard the story of King Alfred and the cakes. Later, they were asked questions on what they had heard. One of these questions involved the use of the word 'ruler' which had no 'relevant' meaning for some of the children. Their experience told them that a ruler was 'a piece of wood used for measuring'. They did not understand the abstract use of the word, which was synonymous with the word 'king'.

Later still, when the child begins to learn foreign languages, the same difficulty occurs. The Latin word '*ludus*', he is told, means a 'school'. But the Roman school was not exactly like the school in which he is learning Latin. When he learns French, he has to appreciate that the same 'speech-pattern' is not always used in French and English to express the same idea. Thus 'He must be good', in English, is not expressed in French as '*Il doit être bon*', but as '*Il est nécessaire qu'il soit sage*'.

It is not necessary to go outside the English language to produce misunderstandings of words and expressions. Bernstein (19) has produced a theory which is precisely relevant to our present problem of misunderstandings arising from the use of language in philosophy. Bernstein argues that there are two languages in English, 'public language' and 'formal language'. Public language is a basic method of communicating. It is the language used by Alf Garnet in the famous television programme ''Til death us do part'. The characteristics of the public language are limited vocabulary, short, simple sentences with little use of subordinate clauses, rigid structure which allows no sensitivity, the use of dogmatism and a raised voice in place of reason to win an argument. The content, too, is limited to those things which the speaker experiences at first hand, such as last Saturday's football match or the winner of the three-thirty. It includes such ungrammatical expressions as 'Me and 'im is goin'', and 'We was sat down minding us own business'.

Formal speech is what used to be known as the 'King's English'. It is the speech which is accepted as grammatically correct. It is as flexible as public speech is rigid, as complex as public speech is simple, as rational and sensitive as public speech is irrational and insensitive. Moreover, for our purpose here it is the language of communication in formal education.

Now, a child entering school, after hearing nothing but public language for five years, is suddenly subjected daily to formal language. He is completely bewildered by it. It does not mean anything to him. How can he 'give reasons' for what he says, when for five years his experience has been limited to people avoiding giving reasons for what they say, and winning arguments by the use of verbal and even physical violence, because they know no other way and because the language they use admits of no other way?

In exactly the same way, the layman and the philosopher employ two different languages. The same vocabulary may be used but not to convey the same ideas. We have already seen that this happens when the psychologist and the layman use the words 'intelligence' and 'personality'. Different sets of rules apply.

Emmet argues that because of this, Spencer (20) was wrong to insist that every word has an 'essential meaning'. If this were true, we would determine the meaning of a word by examining it in a number of sentences and seeing what factor was common to its use in all the sentences examined.

What would be the common ground for the word 'intelligence' in the expressions 'If he had any intelligence he would not behave like that', 'Idiots and imbeciles have low intelligence', 'Intelligence tests measure intelligence', and 'Spearman says that intelligence consists of a g factor and an s factor'? Scientists may communicate easily with other scientists who share their knowledge of and expertise in science. Philosophers may communicate with philosophers who share their knowledge of and expertise in philosophy or they may not. But it is even more difficult for either party to communicate successfully with laymen who have not been initiated into the knowledge and language of science and philosophy.

Earlier in this chapter, we saw that Scheffler feels that general philosophers, that is those philosophers who seek to solve general problems by the use of philosophical methods and educational philosophers who attempt to solve educational problems by using philosophical methods, are 'aliens' in an academic landscape. But why should they be? Is not the general philosopher, who asks, 'What is the universe?', doing exactly the same as the political philosopher who asks, 'What is the state?', and the educational philosopher who asks, 'What is education?' If error can result from applying the wrong language rules in the first and second instances, it can equally arise in the third instance for the same reasons. Therefore, if it is relevant to apply philosophical, or linguistic, or concept analysis in general philosophy, why is it less relevant to apply the same technique in political and educational philosophy? All three have the term 'philosophy' in common.

If the reader thinks for a moment, he will recall a large number of statements that he has heard concerning education. Not the least common is the 'sweeping generalization' or the 'pontification'. Many of these are expressed in emotive language, and are designed to appeal via 'bewitchment' rather than via 'rational evidence'. Such statements are as dangerous as loaded questions, because they lack objectivity. They contain large elements of subjectivity and bias. Consider for a moment the following statement, made in the United States of America in the nineteenth century, by Horace Mann, addressing his annual report to his State Board of Education:

'I believe in the existence of a great, immortal, immutable principle of natural law . . . which proves the absolute right to an education of every human being.'

We have already said that, strictly speaking, linguistic analysis would examine the whole sentence to see if it has any meaning, and that concept analysis would examine the concepts themselves, to see if they have any meaning. If we look at this sentence, we shall see that, unless the concepts have meaning, the sentence cannot possibly have meaning. If 2 and 3 in the expression $2+3 = 5$ do not mean what we normally understand by 2 and 3, then they cannot equal 5, and the whole statement is meaningless because two of the main items are meaningless.

Analysing Mann's impassioned or 'bewitching' statement, we would ask, 'On what evidence does he *believe*?' 'What is "natural law"?' 'If "natural law" has some precise meaning, what does "principle" mean in relation to this meaning?' 'How does this principle of natural law "*prove*"?' 'What does "an education" mean?'

It is easy to say that the statement was 'typical of those days a century and a half ago', and that such statements could not be made today. To show the error of such thinking, here is a sentence from a long attempt in 1942 by the National Society for the Study of Education in America to define 'education':

'Education should be thought of as the process of man's reciprocal adjustment to nature, to his fellows, and to the ultimate nature of the cosmos.'

There is a marked similarity between these two statements, especially between the expressions 'immortal, immutable principle of natural law', and 'the ultimate nature of the cosmos'. Both are 'bewitching' expressions, both suggest something vast and 'metaphysical'. But, if we were asked *precisely what we understood* by either of these expressions, we would find it most difficult, to say the least, to give a reply.

One of the members of the pre-war Brains Trust on B.B.C. radio, Professor C. E. M. Joad, when asked to answer questions sent in by listeners, almost inevitably prefaced his remarks with, 'It all depends on what you mean by . . .' This came to be regarded as an amusing catch-phrase, a pleasant diversion, but it is essentially an indication of the spirit of philosophical or linguistic or concept analysis. In the two examples quoted above, it does 'all depend' on what is meant by 'immortal, immutable principle of natural law', and 'ultimate nature of the cosmos'.

Scheffler (21) says that educational ideas can be expressed as 'definitions', 'metaphors', 'slogans', while O'Connor (22) says that slogans, which are frequently repeated, become mistaken for facts, and even mistaken for aims of education. In a later chapter, we shall see that 'value-judgments' can also become mistaken for facts by the uncritical.

James (23) shows how error can arise from failure to realize that 'it all depends on what you mean by . . .', when he stresses that the term 'academic' is frequently thought of as expressing something extremely undesirable in education, merely because people seldom stop to examine the consequences of this belief. He argues that it is the same line of thinking which wrongly believes that the 'factory' is closer to 'reality' than is the 'school'. Similarly, 'theory' is despised as being something totally divorced from 'practice'. If a theory is put forward, these people argue, it is as useless as a practice is useful. These statements are frequently unsupported by evidence, repeated frequently and emotionally, and accepted by many as being statements of fact beyond dispute.

It has been argued that linguistic analysis is just as 'practically useless' as were the arguments of the Schoolmen (24) in the later Middle Ages. Everything that they discussed had to have a 'theological form' and a 'philosophical bearing'. Monroe (25) writes that the type of question debated might be: 'How many angels could stand on a pin-head?'

It is only possible for linguistic analysis to be useless in this way if we think no further than the words which we analyse. But if we remember that words are only ways of expressing ideas, then we realize that when we analyse the words we are really trying to clarify ideas. If I attempt to apply linguisitc analysis to the statement 'Comprehensive education is neither good nor bad', I am not performing the same sort of exercise as I perform when I try to solve the *Daily Telegraph* crossword. The latter is a mental exercise undertaken for pleasure; it has no purpose over and above this. But when, as a teacher, I examine the statement about comprehensive education, I am not merely looking *at* words, I am looking *for* ideas, and, moreover, ideas which affect me as a parent and a teacher, and my child as one who has to be educated. Far from being 'hair-splitting' and 'word-quib-bling', the analysis is of very great importance for me and for other people.

NEED TO AVOID NARROWNESS OF OUTLOOK

We have already suggested that the attitude that the factory is closer than the school to reality indicates not only a failure to define 'reality' but also a very narrow attitude. It suggests that only those things which are directly and obviously useful are worth heeding.

Unfortunately, teachers and potential teachers are not always free from narrowness of outlook. There is a great temptation to look upon teaching as something compartmentalized and undertaken by people who wear particular labels. Our educational system is divided into institutions which ought to be parts of an evolutionary process, just as Piaget's stages of thought development ought to be parts of an evolutionary process. Unfortunately they are not always looked upon in this way. Because Piaget says, to take one example, that the stage of thought development between the ages of four and seven years is 'intuitive', and has certain characteristics and that the age from 7-8 to 11-12 is 'concrete operational', and has certain characteristics, some people think that these two periods are 'self-contained'. In much the same way, we regard the different 'levels of education' as self-contained. I am a teacher in an infants school. This is my label and I live in a little, water-tight compartment safe from any necessity to think about comprehensive education and selection for secondary education. Such things are the concern of people who wear the label 'secondary school teacher'. The student training to teach in secondary schools is often most indignant when he is required to study 'the pre-school child'. He claims that he came to college to learn how to teach adolescents. For him, the pre-school child is the concern of the infants school teacher. Such a study is relevant for her, but totally irrelevant for him.

The dangers of this attitude can be shown by considering the once prevailing attitude to social class. Not many years ago, it was considered extremely patronizing (26) to talk about people belonging to a certain 'social class'. It was the attitude of the 'haves' looking down on the 'have-nots'. Consequently, people used to shy away from the mention of social class as we shied away from philosophy, and as the child shied away from cabbage, and the neurotic from reality.

More recently, we have been made painfully aware how much damage this irrational, emotional thinking did to individual children. In an age which did not talk about social class and which did not respect individual differences in children, many children who, to take one example already mentioned, had no other language than public language and could not benefit from their teaching, were beaten daily in order to 'make them learn'. An age which thought that 'social class' was not 'a drawing-room' term only added to the harm which belonging to a certain class had already done. The importance of the change of attitude is indicated by Jarret (27), who claims that the most important discovery affecting teacher education during recent years is the fact that a 'staggering number' of our pupils who come from 'economically and culturally underprivileged' homes derive very little benefit from formal education.

We are not suggesting that every time an infants school teacher says that comprehensive education is nothing to do with her, or a secondary school teacher says that to study the pre-school child is for him totally irrelevant, they will do as much harm as those people who suppressed by social disapproval any study of social class. But, the narrow attitude in one area often produces narrowness of attitude in another. Apparently harmless narrowness may, one day, result in the doing of real harm. History is full of the consequences of narrowness of thought, from exposing sickly infants on a mountainside to die in ancient Sparta, to putting lunatics in Bedlam in more recent times in our own country. The narrow mind can so easily become the completely closed mind. Once this happens, we even cease to analyse the problems which directly affect us, and accept the easiest, ready-made solution. A character in one of Terence's plays says: 'I am a human being. I consider all human affairs to be my concern.' Similarly the teacher should consider all educational problems to be his concern, irrespective of the particular institutional level at which he teaches.

THE APPROACH TO CONCEPTS IN THE REMAINING CHAPTERS;
LOGICAL GEOGRAPHY

Throughout the remainder of this book we shall be analysing key educational concepts. These will appear in groups of three (trilogies), as a reminder that no educational concept can be considered in isolation. Between trilogies there will be a link chapter, which will take up the threads of the previous trilogy and relate what has been said to what is about to be said in the next trilogy.

We cannot undertake to analyse every educational concept, since this would be too long a process. We shall select those which more obviously affect teachers, remembering all the time that what philosophy teaches us can produce a greater understanding of the classroom and greater skill inside it.

It must not be thought that there is anything significant in the order in which the individual concepts and the trilogies are arranged. It seemed sensible to start with the concept 'education', since this is the largest and most complex concept of all. But we could, equally well, have started with 'culture', 'curriculum', or 'liberal education'. If we think what happens when we throw a stone into a still pond, we shall understand why the order of concepts is relatively unimportant. If we throw a stone into a pond, it makes a circular ripple, which in turn makes other ripples, and these all move outwards from the centre towards the bank. The bank, being the perimeter of the pond, contains all the ripples and does not allow them to overflow. If we throw in a stone marked 'education', it will produce ripples which may end at a perimeter marked 'culture'. If we throw in a stone marked 'curriculum', it may make ripples which move to a bank marked 'education'. In both cases, the first ripple affects all the others.

More important than the order of concepts is what we actually do to the concepts themselves. We assign to each what the philosopher calls a 'logical geography'. There are two counties in England known as Lancashire and Yorkshire. One is famous for its cotton manufacture, and a damp climate; the other for a drier climate and its woollen trade. They both possess cricket teams which engage in a dour struggle with each other twice a year in the 'Roses Matches'. There is a little town called Todmorden. It is said that the town of Todmorden has some streets with houses whose back doors are in Yorkshire and whose front doors are in Lancashire. But there is a very distinct line which separates the two counties, the official county boundary. However difficult it is to decide whether one is in Lancashire or Yorkshire in certain borderline places, there is always the ultimate arbiter – the county boundary line.

Similarly, it is difficult at times to determine where one concept begins and another ends in educational contexts. We shall find this when we discuss 'education and training', 'training and drill'. We shall find that some concepts contain other and lesser concepts within them, but that the smaller concept can never become the larger concept. Each has its own 'logical geography', which is exactly like saying that the counties of Lancashire and Yorkshire have an official county boundary between them.

In view of what we have said throughout this chapter, we shall not expect, in every case or necessarily in any instance, to end each chapter with a ready-processed answer which can be applied by all teachers like a formula in specific situations. Each chapter will raise a problem. It will be our task, using linguistic (or concept) analysis, to examine the problem carefully, to pick out the salient points for consideration, to assemble the evidence and to attempt clarification. At times, we shall appear, like Socrates, to be understanding an idea only in the way that destroys it. If we do appear to be behaving in this way, we must be sure that we are doing so in the light of 'generally acceptable evidence', not as a result of reading our own preconceived ideas into the problem. We may ask very searching questions which probe weak points, but we must never ask loaded or leading questions. We must modify hypotheses, if necessary, in the light of evidence, not twist the evidence to support our hypotheses. We shall try to ensure, in each case, not that we ask questions, but that we ask *the right questions*. We may have occasion to consider the views of other philosophers of the past and present. This will both introduce us to their ideas gradually, and also serve to show that we are not merely putting forward 'subjective opinions in a vacuum'. But we shall not be seeking answers tailor made for present problems by earlier thinkers.

To sum up, we shall be attempting to do four main things throughout the remainder of this book. First, we shall aim to rediscover meanings which particular educational terms possess but which have become blurred through frequent careless usage. (28) The meanings which we seek will be those which can be rationally justified, rather than the stylized and conventional ones which people uncritically and often unhesitatingly accept.

Secondly (and this point is closely associated with our first one), we must examine all concepts objectively, reminding ourselves constantly that, because we are attempting to philosophize, there is no automatic guarantee that we have rid our minds of all preconceived ideas. It may be that in the early stages, we do little more than reveal to ourselves such bias and prejudice in exactly the same way that we saw the neurotic is brought face to face with his fears. Like Socrates, once we have exposed these barriers to objectivity, we have taken the first step towards ridding the mind of error.

Thirdly, we must scrupulously expose inconsistencies and accept nothing solely because an 'authority' says that it is so. We wrote earlier of Leibniz and his recognition of the need for a universal symbolism. Leibniz, described by Russell as one of the greatest intellects of all time, discovered inconsistencies in Aristotelian logic which had escaped every eye until that time. The reason was that the name of Aristotle carried such authority that no one ever thought of looking for errors in his ideas. Even Leibniz had such respect for Aristotle that he refrained from publishing the errors that he had found. Nevertheless, the errors were there. All too often, dogmatic statements are accepted in education because they are made by those who are, or are considered to be, 'authorities'. Authorities are no more free from the demands to justify their claims than are lesser mortals like ourselves. It is the duty of an efficient sentry to challenge all who approach the camp, irrespective of rank.

Some of the ideas that we examine may enjoy great popularity and may be tenaciously held. This was the fate of many of the traditionally-held beliefs that Socrates challenged. Many of his victims enjoyed great reputations for wisdom in their day, but none escaped on the grounds of reputation alone. To arrive at real problems and to formulate real questions, we may frequently be compelled to sweep away pseudo-problems and pseudo-questions.

Finally, such a process of investigation will require a more exact appreciation of the relationship between 'thought', 'language' and 'reality'. If we do not have this at the start, we shall need to tread warily until we have developed it. But once we acquire it, we shall find our investigation much more rewarding. We must guard, too, against sheer destructiveness. We are no more aiming to expose every idea of every thinker as false than we are aiming to show that none of our own ideas has any validity or that they are all the product of bias and preconception. Few things in life are ever simple cases of distinguishing black from white, and clear-cut, absolute solutions are not the stock-in-trade of philosophy.

It is hoped that every reader, when he reaches the end of the book, will be able to look back with satisfaction on the course his study has taken. In some cases, what he formerly believed and accepted will have been rejected, but in others the bases on which his beliefs and convictions and values are founded will have been broadened and strengthened.

NOTES AND REFERENCES FOR CHAPTER I

1 *A History of Western Philosophy*, Bertrand Russell (Allen & Unwin, 1946). Introduction. This is a famous work of reference which deals with philosophy from its pre-Platonic days, in ancient Greece, to the present day. Many of the ideas which it sets out are difficult, and the beginner should use the book only for obtaining a little information on basic points or

about specific philosophers. Prolonged reading, before one is ready for such an undertaking, may well result in the fear of philosophy, mentioned at the start of this chapter, being magnified.

2 *The Language of Education*, Israel Scheffler (Thomas & Co. 1960). This is a much smaller book than *A History of Western Philosophy*, and has an excellent introductory chapter which explains both the 'historico-philosophical' approach (as we have called it) and linguistic analysis. He refers to the latter specifically in the context of educational philosophy.

3 Pavlov, a Russian physiologist, who carried out experiments in conditioning the reflex in Alsatian dogs. In an attempt to be 'scientific', Pavlov was mainly concerned with things that could be measured. He therefore measured the amount of saliva which dripped from the jaws of a hungry Alsatian when it was shown meat or meat powder. Because emitting saliva (like blinking in humans) is a reflex action, it is not consciously controlled by the dog. It is an automatic response to a stimulus. Pavlov found that, when he had shown the meat to the dog on a number of occasions and had sounded a bell at the same time as he showed the meat to the dog, the sound of the bell, without the sight of the meat, produced the same amount of saliva. The dog had been 'conditioned' to salivate to the bell because it had been paired with the meat, which itself had produced salivation. No 'teaching' was needed for the process. The whole process is known as 'Classical conditioning'.

4 The *Republic* of Plato. The quotation used in this chapter is taken from the translation by J. L. Davies and D. J. Vaughan, 1852, published by MacMillan. Perhaps the best-known translation is by D. M. Cornford, Oxford University Press, 1941. The *Republic* begins with Socrates seeking an answer to the question, 'What is Justice?' Justice is found to be a 'social phenomenon', and the discussion centres on the 'state' and what the 'ideal state' would be. The ideal state would be produced by an ideal education system, which is the thing for which the *Republic* has become famous. For a detailed study of the proposed education system, readers who are interested should consult *Plato's Theory of Education*, R. C. Lodge, Routledge and Kegan Paul, 1947.

5 Also taken from the *Republic* (see 4 above).

6 *The Concept of Mind*, Gilbert Ryle (Hutchinson's University Library 1949). The most famous chapter is possibly 'Knowing How and Knowing That', which has been reproduced several times in edited works, particularly, in *Philosophy and Education*, Israel Scheffler (Allyn & Bacon 1966).

7 *Learning to Philosophize*, E. R. Emmet (Longmans 1964). (Also Penguin.) This work deals with the problem of philosophizing as distinct from understanding the philosophizing of other people. Parts of this work, too, are difficult for the absolute beginner, but those with some experience of philosophy and philosophical problems will find much useful material in it. In particular, the book contains 'philosophical exercises', where the reader is confronted with a situation which requires him to philosophize.

8 A thorough analysis of Aristotle's philosophy is found in Russell's *History of Western Philosophy*. Again it is stressed that the beginner should approach the discussion with care, since parts of it are by no means easy, and the inexperienced can soon become entangled in a puzzling mass of detail.

9 Another reference to the *Republic* of Plato. The Guardians were the ruling class, the *élite*. For them alone Plato proposed a system of Higher Education based on the principles of Science and Mathematics and Dialectic (logic), and finally a return to theoretical studies after practical experience as rulers. This theoretical study was to be 'contemplation of the Good'. A useful modern expression to describe the process might be 'a study of philosophy'.

10 The early Greek philosophers are now referred to by a number of group names. One of these is the 'Ionian Philosophers'. This term denotes their geographical origin, since they came from that part of the ancient world known as Ionia. In addition they are known as the 'pre-Socratic Philosophers'. We might say that this is a 'chronological definition', showing that they all flourished before the time of Plato's master, Socrates. His interpretation of the function of philosophy marked a major development in the subject.

The earliest of these philosophers are again known by a 'geographical group name' – the Milesian school, since they came from the city of Miletus. Thales of Miletus, born in 623 B.C., was the founder of the school. He was included by later generations in the 'Seven Sages of Greece'. He believed that everything was basically the 'world-substance', water. He was also famous for predicting a solar eclipse. Anaximander was a contemporary of Thales and believed that there was a substance outside earth, air, fire, and water, from which everything originated. He is said to have constructed a sundial and a map of the world and to have been the first Greek writer to change from verse to prose. For a remarkable indication of a scientific work in verse, readers should see Lucretius: *On the Nature of Things* in the Penguin translation. The original consisted of six books of hexameter verse (lines of verse each of six metrical feet) written in Latin. The third member of the Milesian School was the philosopher Anaximenes. He was rather later than Anaximander (dates of birth and death are not known accurately at this time). He believed that the 'primary source' of all things was air. Russell says that the 'Milesian School' were commendably 'scientific', for their time, in the investigations which they undertook. These investigations were confined to physical problems and avoided metaphysical issues such as morality.

Later pre-Socratics included the famous Heracleitus. He was at his peak about 500 B.C.; he believed that everything was 'in a state of flux', and that even matter itself was constantly changing.

Parmenides (who figures in one of Plato's dialogues) was born about 510 B.C. and believed that the universe was a single, unchanging, indivisible whole and the only object of knowledge. What is changing and perishable cannot be known, except through 'conjecture' (opinion or even guesswork).

Later still came the 'Atomists', including Leucippus and Democritus. The latter was born in 460 B.C. As well as developing the atomic theory of Leucippus, Democritus wrote on such topics as 'music' and 'morality'.

This brief survey has been undertaken to show how Greek philosophy originated, and the directions of its investigation between the seventh and fifth centuries B.C.

11 *Modern Philosophies of Education*, J. S. Brubacher (3rd edn), (McGraw-Hill 1962).

12 The reference is to a chapter 'Education and Indoctrination' in *Aims in*

Education; the Philosophical Approach, ed. T. H. B. Hollins (Manchester University Press 1964). Further references will be made to this work in our discussion of aims, in Chapter 5 of this book.

13 Publius Cornelius Tacitus (A.D. 55–117), a Roman historian, was famous for three works – *Agricola*, an account of Roman Britain in the first century A.D., with some interesting comments on the English climate; the *Histories*, dealing with the later Roman emperors; and the *Annals*, dealing with the emperors from Tiberius to Nero. Tacitus was really a diehard Republican, who believed that the 'good old days' were over when the Empire was established. Thus, in spite of his claim to write 'without partisanship and bias', he was as much a victim of his own preconceived ideas as we have seen it possible to be in this first chapter. Tacitus had a penetrating assessment of human nature and a biting style. These led him to highlight the bad in men rather than the good. Some of his most famous sayings include: 'They make a wilderness and call it peace'; 'A master ruler if he had never ruled', and 'It is typical of human nature to despise those we have wronged.'

14 Immanuel Kant (see *A History of Western Philosophy,* Chapter 20). Born 1724, died 1804; generally considered to be among the greatest of modern philosophers, though Russell does not accept this. Famous for his *Critique of Pure Reason* (1781) and *Critique of Practical Reason* (1786). See also Chapter 11, Section 4.

15 *The Language of Education*. See also 2 above.

16 Leibniz (see *History of Western Philosophy*, Chapter 11). Born 1646, died 1716. He is described by Russell as one of the supreme intellects of all time. He was concerned with the celebrated philosophical problem of centuries ago, the 'Mind/Matter' debate, i.e. whether the mind and the body were the same substance or different substances. Nowadays we talk of the body and the brain being the same, i.e. composed of physical cells, and think of 'mind' as the activities of the brain in thinking and reasoning. The 'Mind/Matter' controversy was also connected with philosophical concern about the nature of the 'soul'.

17 An article on the most famous modern philosophers, Strawson, Wittgenstein, Moore, and Popper, in the *Daily Telegraph* supplement, November 1, 1968. It is most useful, especially as it explains why there are often no clear-cut solutions to philosophical problems, as there are to mathematical and scientific problems.

18 *Learning to Philosophize*. E. R. Emmet. See also 7 above.

19 Reference to another well-known article – 'Social Class and Linguistic Development; A Theory of Social Learning', Basil Bernstein, in *Education, Economy and Society*, ed. A. H. Halsey, J. Floud, and C. A. Anderson (Free Press 1961). See also notes and references for Chapter 4, Section 23.

20 Herbert Spencer was a nineteenth-century educational thinker whose style can vary between the biting and the pompous. The work which concerns us here is *Education; Intellectual, Moral and Physical*. There is an edition published by Watts & Co. in the Thinker's Library, 1929. Spencer poses the question, 'What knowledge is of most worth?', but in the full knowledge that his reply is going to be 'Science'. He regards science as 'culture' and 'useful', and the classical education of his day as 'empty' and 'ornamental'.

21 Another reference to *The Language of Education*. See 7 and 18 above.

22 *An Introduction to the Philosophy of Education*, D. J. O'Connor (Routledge & Kegan Paul 1957). A small book but not always an easy one for beginners.

in spite of its title. We shall have reason to refer to the work, on another occasion, in connection with 'aims', in our own Chapter 5.

23 *An Essay on the Content of Education*, E. James now Lord James of Rusholme, and Vice-chancellor, University of York (Harrap 1949). The book is a small one and makes excellent reading, since it begins with a consideration of the historical development of the curriculum, continues with problems which this development has caused, and then considers the philosophical basis of the curriculum. This is very much the same idea as Peters' Three Criteria for Education. See also Chapter 7.

24 The Schoolmen. A name given to a group of thinkers in the later Middle Ages. See also notes and references for Chapter 11, Section 8.

25 *A Text-book in the History of Education*, P. Monroe (Macmillan 1925).

26 In *The Struggle for Education*, B. MacArthur and R. Bourne (Schoolmaster Publishing Co.) a cartoon from 1883 is reproduced with the caption: 'Fears were often expressed that the lower classes were being educated "beyond their station".'

27 *In Education for Teaching*, No. 77, Autumn 1968

28 Cf. Bertrand Russell, *An Outline of Philosophy* (N.Y., Meridian Books Inc., 1960); 'What passes for knowledge in everyday life suffers from three defects: it is cocksure, vague and self-contradictory. The first step towards philosophy consists in becoming aware of these defects, not in order to rest content with a lazy scepticism, but in order to substitute an amended kind of knowledge which shall be tentative, precise and self-consistent.'

The First Trilogy

EDUCATION
TRAINING
CHILD-CENTREDNESS

Chapter 2

The Concept 'Education'

DEFINITIONS AND THEIR FUNCTION

In the daily task of teaching, we frequently use definitions. These distinguish one object or idea from other objects and ideas by describing their particular characteristics or functions. Once the name of the object is associated with a definition, the word can be used meaningfully. Because the people with whom we communicate also know the association between the name of the object or idea and the definition, they understand what we mean when we use the word in question.

Sometimes two objects are so dissimilar that it is quite impossible to confuse them. No one, for example, would find any similarity between a 'shoe' and a 'house', unless he was thinking of 'The old woman who lived in a shoe', but this is most unlikely in most contexts. A shoe and a house are totally different objects with totally different characteristics. The only thing common to both is that they are 'forms of protection against the weather'.

There is another way of learning to distinguish between objects, that is by observing them regularly. We associate a certain shape, size, and structure with a certain word which names the object in question. We have so often seen a pin and a needle that whenever we see one, we never mistake it for the other. Moreover, if someone uses the word 'pin', we have a clear idea of what they mean. We would never think of a 'needle' when we hear the word 'pin'. In such cases, we do not need a definition to distinguish one object from the other. We do not so much think of a definition of 'pin' or 'needle' when the word is spoken as have a 'mental picture' of the object.

When we try to define a 'needle' and a 'pin', so that we can explain the difference between them to someone who has never seen either, we find the task difficult. It is the more frustrating because we know *exactly* what each one looks like, but we do not find it easy to 'put the differences into words'. A similar situation arises when we attempt to describe by definition the difference between a 'car' and a 'bus'. It is because it is so difficult to explain in words what a car is and what a bus is that we use 'visual aids' when we attempt to show very young children the difference between them. We are now in a position to say that education falls into the 'needle/pin' or the 'bus/car' category, especially for teachers. It has been, and will continue to be, so much an essential part of their day-to-day lives that they are appalled when asked to define 'education' and find that they cannot. Later in this chapter, we shall see that even educational 'experts' find great difficulty in defining education. Peters (1) tells us that modern philosophers have abandoned the attempt. We shall see (in Chapter 3) that it can be as difficult in certain circumstances to distinguish 'education' from 'training' by using a definition, as it was to distinguish between a 'pin' and a 'needle'. But before we look at these problems, we must look further into the reasons why some definitions cause more difficulty than others.

We have said that we often use visual aids to make our definitions clearer. But there are times when this is not possible, because we are describing something which cannot be seen or which, when seen, is very much like something else. As an example of the first type we can quote an 'erg', and as an example of the second type we can quote an 'adverb'. We cannot *see* an 'erg' because it is a 'concept', which is very much like saying that it is an 'idea'. Similarly, we cannot *see* intelligence, although we can see intelligent behaviour. We now realize that education is also a concept. It may be a process; it is certainly not a physical object.

When we turn to the 'adverb', it is possible to *show* one, but this helps very little. 'Quickly' is an adverb and we can show the word on its own. We can also put it in a sentence: 'The holidays passed quickly.' But it is only one word among several in the sentence. We can see other words which are not adverbs as well as the single word which is an adverb.

We can immediately distinguish between an 'adverb' and an 'erg', by a most elementary form of definition. 'An adverb is a part of speech; an erg is a unit of work.' We would be very stupid indeed if we confused a 'unit of work' and a 'part of speech'. The need for a definition is not to distinguish between an 'adverb' and an 'erg' but between, say, an 'adverb' and a 'noun', since a noun is also a part of speech, or between an 'erg' and a 'horse-power', which is also a unit of work.

The next step in these cases is to 'extend the definition' and define in terms of function what ergs and adverbs do. This gives information which is not given by saying what it *is*. This extension gives us: 'An adverb is a part of speech, which modifies or limits the action of a verb', and 'An erg is a unit of work, specifically the amount of work needed to raise one gram through one centimetre in one second'. This will prevent confusion with other parts of speech which cannot be defined in the same way as an adverb, and with other units of work which must not be confused with an 'erg'.

ATTEMPTS TO DEFINE 'EDUCATION'

We can now turn to some definitions of 'education'. The reader, as he progresses, should try to determine for himself which of these definitions, if any, are of the simple type ('an adverb is a part of speech') or a simple type expanded, by saying what education does ('An adverb is a part of speech which modifies or limits the action of verb'). The first definition, historically, in our list comes from Plato (2):

'By education I mean that training which is given by suitable habits to the first instincts of virtue in children, when pleasure and pain are rightly implanted in non-rational souls. The particular training in respect of pleasure and pain, which leads you to hate and love what you ought to hate and love, is called "education".'

This is not only an 'expanded' definition, but, as we have already been led to believe by our ideas about 'logical geography', a questionable one. For the moment, we can ask ourselves have not 'education' and 'training' got their own 'logical boundaries', like counties in England with their 'geographical boundaries'? We shall have more to say about this in Chapter 3.

We also note a similarity between the beginning of Plato's definition of 'education' and the definition of 'philosophy' by Russell at the beginning of Chapter 1. Russell writes: 'Philosophy, *as I shall try to understand the word* . . .' Plato writes: 'By education *I mean* . . .'

The reader should keep this point in mind because we shall return to it in a few moments, when we talk about 'descriptive' definitions and 'stipulative' definitions. There is no need to be apprehensive about these new terms, since they are easily explained in everyday language. Finally, we can note that Plato's definition of education has a 'moral emphasis', since it talks about 'good' and 'bad', 'pleasure' and 'pain'.

Milton (3) defined education as follows: 'I call, therefore, a complete and generous education that which fits a man to perform justly, skilfully and magnanimously, all the offices, both public and private, of peace and war.'

This definition seems to cover much more ground than Plato did. It uses less words but it is less precise. It takes far longer to list the areas of study which Milton's idea of education entailed than to write the definition itself. They were: Greek, Latin, Italian, Hebrew, Chaldaic, Syriac, arithmetic, mathematics, geography, physics, astronomy, meteorology, mineralogy, anatomy, physiology, fortification, architecture, engineering, navigation, ethics, economics, politics, law, logic, rhetoric; the scriptures, theology and church history.

The reader who says, 'What Milton is saying is that, if you know everything, you can do everything', is exactly right. Both Milton and Comenius (4) believed that the 'educated man' should be a 'know-all'. Indeed, the word they used, *pansophia*, comes from two Greek words: *pan*, meaning 'all' and *sophia* (which we have already met in *philosophia*) meaning 'wisdom', or 'knowledge'. It must be remembered that, in those days, the body of available knowledge was much smaller than it is today, since modern science has led to a tremendous expansion of knowledge. Nevertheless, what Milton required was a mammoth task, as we shall see when we discuss the 'curriculum' (Chapter 7).

Lodge (5) writes that there are two uses of the word 'education', one 'wider', one 'narrower'. Again, we note the similarity between this and what Russell said about the uses of philosophy. He gives the wider definition as:

'Education is equivalent to "experience", the experience of a living organism interacting with its normal environment.'

His narrower definition is:

'Experience or nature, is still the teacher, but in the specific social institution known as "schooling" it is guided by the teacher.'

We should note, in the first definition, that Lodge says that education 'is equivalent to', rather than education 'is'. We shall have reason to return to this point later.

It was fashionable at one time to use 'etymological' definitions. These were definitions of a word in terms of the word from which it was derived (usually Greek or Latin). We did this when we said, in Chapter 1, that the term 'philosophy' is derived from a Greek noun meaning 'love of wisdom', or 'love of knowledge'. Ducasse (6) gives the following etymological definition of 'education': 'Etymologically, to educate is to lead out or bring out.' This is our first instance of a definition which states, categorically, 'education *is*'. Unfortunately, this particular theory was sterile, as another school of thought denied that education comes not from *educere*, to lead out,' but from *educare*, which means 'to form or train'. If we realize that the two greatest opponents in educational thinking, the 'formalists' (who believed that education was a discipline and that children learn what is good for them, are seen and not heard, and are *made* into specific people by their education) and the 'naturalists' (who believed that education should merely 'let the child develop'), both claim that they are right in terms of 'etymological definition', we see how futile it is and was at the time to give this definition further thought.

Later, Ducasse expands the above definition and says that education takes place through 'instruction', 'training', and 'indoctrination'. We shall consider all three terms in later chapters. For the moment we must ask ourselves is it reasonable to suggest that 'education' should 'indoctrinate'?

In Chapter 1, we saw a definition of education which was both vague and emotionally-toned. It was vague because we were able to say on too many occasions, 'It all depends on what you mean by'. Below is another definition by Horne (7). It will be seen that this one shows the same faults as the previous one:

'Education is the eternal process of superior adjustment of the physically and mentally developed, free, conscious, human being to God, as manifested in the intellectual, emotional and volitional environment of man.'

The reader should ask himself which terms he would ask to be clarified before he was willing to say whether the definition is acceptable or not. We see, too, that this is also a *definite* statement that education '*is*', not a suggestion that it 'might be', as we saw in the definitions by Russell (of 'philosophy') and by Plato (of 'education').

We have seen a number of definitions of 'education'. They have differed in length, in character, and in degree of definiteness. They have been, on the whole, much more complex than our definition which said, 'an adverb is a part of speech', and also more complex than the expanded definition of an adverb. As our last example of a definition of education, we have chosen a brief one by Langford (8):

'Education is an activity which aims at practical results in contrast with activities which aim at theoretical results.'

This is an '*is*' statement (9), but it is much simpler than some we have seen. Although we have to think what 'practical' and 'theoretical' results are, we can immediately think of 'science' as aiming at theoretical results. (We even talk of 'scientific theory'.) 'Activity' seems to imply a 'process', and we can agree with both terms, since in education teachers and learners are active. However, Langford goes on to liken education to other activities which aim at practical results, such as 'politics', 'manufacturing', and 'farming' and contrasts it with activities which aim at theoretical results such as 'physics' and 'psychology'. This rather dashes our hopes. If politics, manufacturing, farming, and education are all 'practical' activities, which aim at 'practical' results, we want to know how any one differs from any other one. We are back where we started when we defined an adverb as 'a part of speech', which did nothing, as it stood, to distinguish an adverb from other parts of speech. We may now begin to see that Peters is justified when he says that the task of *defining* 'education' is extremely difficult. We may also understand why modern philosophers have abandoned the attempt. From the definitions we have seen, it is clear that we would accept some rather than others, or some claims in some and some ideas in others. But, reminding ourselves that all our minds are full of preconceived ideas, it is possible that it is these and not the merits of the definition which would determine our choice.

DIFFERENT TYPES OF DEFINITION: DESCRIPTIVE AND STIPULATIVE DEFINITIONS

Scheffler (10) is very helpful at this point. He says that one of the difficulties we face when we use definitions is that there is more than one sort. This is like Wittgenstein's saying that there is not *one* set of language rules but many sets. We do not need to consider all the types which Scheffler names, but we must compare two types, to help us see why the definitions we have quoted are different. The types which are important are DESCRIPTIVE definitions and STIPULATIVE definitions.

Descriptive definitions are familiar to us all. They are often called 'dictionary definitions'. We gave a descriptive or dictionary definition of an 'adverb' and an 'erg' a little while ago. A descriptive definition is one that has been formulated in the past, has become standard, and is accepted as explaining adequately what something is.

However, if we return to Socrates in the *Republic*, we find that he was anxious to discover 'What is justice?' He put forward a number of STIPULATIVE definitions, one of which was that 'Justice is doing just acts'. What Socrates was really saying was: 'We don't have a *descriptive* definition which is acceptable. The descriptive definition *determines* what we shall think. We want to *think freely*. Therefore, let us STIPULATE what we shall consider justice to be, and use this as our starting point.'

The reader will now recognize that we ourselves used a stipulative definition of philosophy, when, to free our minds from fears, we stipulated that we would think of it as 'the process of asking questions'. We did not finally accept the precise wording of the stipulative definition, but we did find that philosophy involves asking questions. It took us a good deal further than the definition of philosophy as 'a no man's land between theology and science'. This, too, was a stipulative definition, since Russell stated, 'Philosophy, *as I shall understand it* . . .'

We can now suggest that those definitions of education which begin, 'Education IS . . .' are descriptive definitions and those which begin, 'Education may be thought of as . . .' may well be stipulative definitions which people have mistaken for descriptive ones. A stipulative definition must be placed in its context, so that we can see what ideas developed from it and whether it finally gained acceptance as a descriptive definition.

We need to remind ourselves of one more danger before leaving descriptive and stipulative definitions, definitions which describe something, and those which stipulate what *we wish to be understood for the moment*. The danger is that a stipulative definition may be 'disguised'. A teacher in a 'progressive' school may say to a friend who teaches in a 'traditional', or 'formal', school, 'In *our* school, children learn by discovery.' This is really like saying that the people who are responsible for the decisions about teaching method 'in our school' believe that learning may be defined as 'the acquiring of information for oneself by an act of discovery'. When the teacher tells her friend this, she is really 'stipulating' that this is what learning 'means'. Her friend may define learning as 'the acquiring of information as the result of being instructed'.

We should now be in a much better position to understand how misunderstandings arise and have arisen in the past, whether people have been talking about highly metaphysical points such as 'How creation began', or about 'What is education?' Unless we recognize the difference between the descriptive definition and the prescriptive or stipulative definition, which 'prescribes' or 'stipulates' how we shall think of 'creation' or 'education', we shall be like someone trying to play cricket according to the rules of golf.

At the beginning of this chapter, we suggested that it was easier to define in some areas than in others. Peters makes the same statement and says that, while it is easy to define terms such as 'geometry' and 'triangularity', it is neither easy nor desirable to define 'education'. Education, he feels, forms a 'family' of ideas united by a complicated network of similarities, which overlap and criss-cross. We have already suggested that 'education' and 'training' are connected, for a number of reasons: perhaps because we feel that education must involve training, or because we think that education and training both include teaching and instruction. The one thing that these terms have in common may be that both are 'educational'. We can say that 'teaching', 'training', and 'instruction' are 'educational', but not that they are 'education'. We can say that the thing that Lancashire and Yorkshire have in common is that they are both counties and both parts of England. But, they have their separate and distinctive characteristics and are separated by boundaries.

CRITERIA FOR THE PROCESS OF EDUCATION

Peters proposes, in place of a definition of education, three 'criteria'. *Kriterion* is a Greek word meaning a 'standard', something against which to compare or match. A criterion is a guide, as distinct from a precise measure. We can say that something 'comes close to the criterion' and is therefore acceptable. We cannot be as precise as we are when we say that two pieces of wood are 'exactly the same length'. By establishing three 'criteria', Peters is saying that, if we are in doubt whether or not a process is 'education', we can match it against our three standards and see how close to their demands it comes.

In the same way, we establish criteria for selecting teachers. We determine the standards beforehand, and see how the applicants for teacher training courses match up to or compare with these demands. We may decide on any number of criteria. It is unwise to limit ourselves to one. For example, we may decide that four criteria are necessary for selecting people to train as teachers, for example, 'high intelligence', 'stable personality', 'good academic qualifications', a 'genuine interest in teaching as a career'. There is less likelihood of our making a mistake if we use all four standards than if we choose only one. High intelligence does not automatically guarantee the other three.

Criteria must always be *relevant*. It used to be the custom to accept into Oxford and Cambridge those whose parents were able to pay the necessary fees. This is not the same as saying that the people who *ought* to be admitted to Oxford and Cambridge are the cleverest people, because they will benefit most from going there. Wealth and high academic ability are two very different criteria. If we think of the reason for the existence of Oxford and Cambridge, we can see that high ability is a *relevant* criterion for selecting candidates and that wealth is an *irrelevant criterion*.

The three criteria which Peters puts forward for education are:

1 Education implies the transmission of what is worthwhile to those who become committed to it.
2 Education must involve knowledge and understanding and some sort of 'cognitive perspective' which is not inert.
3 Education at least rules out some procedures of transmission on the grounds that they lack wittingness and voluntariness on the part of the learner.

It will be profitable to look briefly at each of these standards and see how they will relate both to our concern with 'education' in this chapter, and our concern with other 'educational concepts' or 'educational ideas' in other chapters.

The first standard requires something to be transmitted or passed on. We can accept that education does pass things on from one generation to the next. When we ask what is worthwhile, we think of what is valuable, of 'values', of 'culture', both of which we shall examine in later chapters.

In the second criterion or standard, the important words are 'inert' and 'cognitive perspective'. There is a connection between the two. When we first talked of the role of philosophy, we said that it aims to obtain an overall view, to take a broad view, to consider all the variables, to keep problems in perspective. This is really what cognitive perspective means: the ability to see all the aspects of situations. 'Inertia' in science is the opposite of movement; it implies 'dead weight'. We can have knowledge which we understand, and we can make use of such knowledge, or we can have knowledge which we cannot use, because we do not understand it. Thus 'cognitive perspective' is linked with the term 'understanding'.

In the third criterion, we see that 'methods' are involved. If education is to transmit or pass on knowledge from one generation to another, a 'method of handing on' must be involved. Some methods are acceptable, others are not. We saw earlier in this chapter that Ducasse suggested that the methods of education were 'instruction', 'training', 'indoctrination'. At the time, we asked ourselves if 'indoctrination' was really an acceptable method. We shall ask ourselves the same question and analyse the problem in greater detail in Chapter 9. For the moment, we can say that a process of indoctrination does not match up to the third criterion of Peters, because it denies the learner 'voluntariness' and 'wittingness'. (Instead of 'wittingness' we can say 'an awareness of what is happening'.)

It is clear that deciding on criteria or standards against which to match an activity to determine if it merits the title 'education', does not simplify the situation as much as using a definition does. A *good* definition settles issues without raising others. But we saw that definitions of 'education' always seemed to raise at least as many issues as they settled. We also said that criteria were standards, *not* exact measures. Because of this, we ought not to be surprised to find that the criteria leave questions to be asked; these we shall leave to be answered in subsequent chapters. For example, the first criterion raises the problem 'Who decides what is worthwhile?' We shall consider this in relation to the 'curriculum' and 'culture'. We may also ask, if indoctrination is ruled out as a method of passing on knowledge from one generation to another, because it denies the learner awareness and the right to ask questions, whether all methods which *do* allow awareness and the asking of questions are equally effective. This problem will be examined when we look at the idea of 'child-centred' education (in Chapter 4) and 'liberal education' (in Chapter 8). For the moment, the questions are important as reminding us of the point we made (in Chapter 1) that we cannot think of educational concepts or ideas in isolation, and of Peters' analogy between 'educational concepts' and a 'united family'.

The criteria are also interesting for the way in which they are expressed. The first one uses the word 'implies' after 'education', and we shall find this expression useful when we consider aims (in Chapter 5). To say that 'education *implies*' (criterion) is very different from saying that 'Education *is*' (descriptive definition). The criterion suggests one characteristic of education, but leaves room for others to be included.

The second criterion is worded more definitely and categorically. The term *must* indicates that, *unless* the process involves knowledge and understanding and an overall view, it *cannot* qualify for the title 'education'.

Finally, after speaking of a process which transmits and of the content of what is to be transmitted, the third criterion provides a standard of comparison for methods of transmission. It does not dogmatically state that there is any *one* method of handing on knowledge and values. Nor does it categorically state that indoctrination shall not be an educational method of handing on knowledge. Instead, it really establishes two criteria for acceptable methods. Such methods must allow 'awareness' and 'voluntariness' in the learner.

Education, then, is a process. It must have both a content and a method. The content is 'knowledge' and 'what is worthwhile' (values), and the method must allow the learner to understand what he is being taught. Just as we arrived at a clear understanding of philosophy by starting from a simple, stipulative definition, which allowed us room to manœuvre, so, by accepting criteria for education, we have come to discover 'essential characteristics' of education, something of what it *is*, something of what it *is not*. We have not allowed ourselves to be misled by emotional language and we have not allowed our minds to be fogged by using a large number of words which beg the question. We have made suggestions instead of being dogmatic and we have tried to provide reasons for preferring criteria to a definition.

DEFINITION AND CRITERIA COMPARED FOR EFFECTIVENESS

We made two important points in Chapter 1: firstly, that the philosophy of education, using the method of linguistic analysis, was not merely concerned with words, but with the ideas which the words represented; secondly, that findings in the philosophy of education (which can be called 'theoretical') have *practical* implications. We do not always appreciate this; it often comes as a surprise to us to realize that we can cause tremendous damage by the careless use of words. Let us take a simple example.

In company with a friend, I decide to attempt to define 'tolerance'. It appears to be a harmless exercise, and not at all likely to harm *people*. I put forward this definition:

'Tolerance is always accepting the right of any individual to speak and act without interference.'

At first glance it seems that I have put forward a very liberal definition and it could be described as 'very democratic'. But, on closer analysis, it becomes apparent that anyone acting on this definition could produce complete irresponsibility and anarchy. Saying and doing what one wishes without interference can be justified only if the words and actions do not interfere with the freedom of anyone else.

As a result of implementing the ideas in this definition, I can do people an injustice in two ways; firstly, by labelling as 'intolerant' those who do not accept my definition of 'tolerance'; secondly, by encouraging those who do accept my definition to harm people, because my definition leads not to tolerance but to anarchy.

Again, it would be much more sensible to adopt criteria or standards against which to match or compare forms of behaviour, to see how well they measure up to the demands of the standards. Criteria for 'tolerance' might include:

1 Willingness to listen to the speech and to assess the actions of all people, objectively and rationally.
2 Willingness to assess, again rationally and objectively, the consequences of such speech and actions, both for those who speak and act, and for those who are affected by such speech and actions.
3 Willingness, at the same time, to assess the consequences of our own speech (especially where it criticizes others) and our own actions.

Only when we cease to think of 'tolerance' and 'education' as words, or even as ideas, and begin to think of them as processes affecting people do we realize how important it is to make perfectly clear, in our own minds, what is meant by the processes. For this reason also it is important for us to realize, as Peters does, that it is not sufficient merely to establish criteria and leave the matter there. This is why we shall examine many other concepts besides education in this book, so that we shall have considered every aspect of the problem.

EDUCATION AS INITIATION

Peters describes education as 'a process of initiation'. This is like saying that it is an activity rather than that it is a concept or idea. But you cannot have an activity or process or an initiation, in this sense, without involving people. Initiation has a general meaning; it also has specific meanings in education. A closer examination of the concept (or idea) of 'initiation' will help us still further in our attempts to produce clear understanding of the term 'education'.

If we think of a youth in a primitive community being initiated into the tribe, we think of 'acceptance'. When the youth has reached a certain stage of development, he is accepted as an adult. As an outward sign of the recognition of his adulthood by the elders of the tribe, he passes through an initiation ceremony. From that time he enjoys all the privileges enjoyed by other adult members.

But initiation into education is not exactly the same. The first initiation into education in the sense of 'schooling', as defined by Lodge earlier in this chapter, takes place at a certain age. The age is determined by the State, as the elders of the tribe determine at what stage of development they will accept a young man as an adult. After this the two examples of initiation begin to differ.

When we say that a child is 'initiated' into education or culture, we mean that he is 'exposed to' or 'committed to' specific situations. All children are initiated, for example, into the skills of reading, writing, and counting. Not all children, however, benefit equally from the initiation. Some children learn to read, write, and calculate better than others. The skills are the same for all those initiated, but all the initiates are not the same. Some are more intelligent than others; some are more emotionally stable, receive more parental encouragement, possess more determination, and are able to see more clearly the purpose of the initiation. We saw (in Chapter 1) that some children, it has been claimed, are almost incapable of benefiting at all from this process of initiation to which we give the name 'formal education'. This is because of their home background. For, in the home also, all children are initiated into the behaviour patterns of their social class. In some cases, if we match the patterns against the three criteria, we find that what goes on in the home can be called 'education'. In other cases, it is manifestly absurd to suggest that the behaviour patterns of the home fulfil the demands of the criteria of education.

We must now ask what is the purpose of initiation. Is it for the benefit of the individual (since we have seen that in some cases it may not be beneficial to him), or is it for the benefit of society? Throughout the years, there has been this problem whether education is an individual or a social process. The answer is that it cannot be one without the other. In British society, the man who cannot read or write is little use to society. Consequently, he is very little use to himself. He can scarcely earn a livelihood and is forced to live year after year at subsistence level.

On the other hand, initiation must show respect for individuality. Because children are committed to learning the same basic skills, this does not mean that they are all to be poured into the same mould. Nor do free people accept that the State has a right to make them into what it likes. When this happens, we have coercion and indoctrination replacing education. Again the Greek idea of balance and harmony is relevant. It is no more harmonious for the individual to develop through initiation into education at the expense of others and of the State than it is for the State to refuse to allow individual development. So in yet another sphere we see the need for criteria. These will determine what individual development will be socially acceptable and what kind of State direction of education will be acceptable.

The lesson to be drawn from what we have written is that, although it is essential for us to have clear ideas about what constitutes education, we do not automatically ensure that education will be equally beneficial to all those committed to it. This may seem a rather depressing start to a book on the philosophy of education; but we must realize that, if we are not scrupulous in determining what is education and what is not, we may do even more social and individual harm by allowing such constricting activities as indoctrination to pass for education.

In the chapters which follow, we shall analyse other concepts in that 'united family of ideas', to which we give the name of 'education'. We shall undertake this not only to clarify the concepts and the terms which represent them, but also to provide an even clearer idea of what we mean by education. We shall do this by deciding which activities cannot qualify for the title education, as well as by adopting positive criteria against which to measure a process justifying the title.

NOTES AND REFERENCES FOR CHAPTER 2

1 *Ethics and Education* R. S. Peters (George Allen & Unwin 1966).
2 The quotation comes from Plato's second work on education called *The Laws*. At the invitation of the tyrant of Syracuse, Dionysius, Plato tried to implement the ideal system of education which he proposed in the *Republic*. The scheme was a failure. In addition, the defeat of Athens, the great cultural power of Greece, by Sparta, the totalitarian power, in the Peloponnesian War (431–404 B.C.) seemed to herald the end of all the values which Plato cherished. He abandoned his idealistic concept, and in *The Laws* produced an educational system which he described as 'the best in present circumstances'.
3 Taken from *Doctrines of the Great Educators,* R. R. Rusk, 2nd edn (Macmillan 1957), Chap. 6, 'Milton'.
4 Comenius (1592–1670), whose real name was Kominsky, was a Moravian minister. It was fashionable, after the revival of Classical learning in the Renaissance, to latinize one's name. Hence Kominsky became Comenius. His chief educational works were *The Great Didqctic* or 'the art of teaching all things to all men' (see also Milton's idea) and *Orbis Pictus* (the world in pictures), the pioneer book on visual aids. Comenius believed that education should follow the lead of 'nature' and that men should learn everything because one never knew to what task God would call an individual. Education should, therefore, equip every man to perform every task. He advocated a more humane discipline than that in the schools of his day, which he called 'the terror of boys and slaughterhouses of the mind'.
5 *Plato's Theory of Education*, R. C. Lodge (Routledge & Kegan Paul 1947).
6 'What can Philosophy Contribute to Educational Theory?', C. J. Ducasse, in *Selected Readings in the Philosophy of Education*, ed. J. Park (Macmillan 1958), Introduction to Part 1, Chap. 1.
7 'The Philosophical Aspects of Education', H. H. Horne, Chap. 9 of *Selected Readings in the Philosophy of Education* (see 6 above).
8 'Education', G. Langford, The Philosophy of Education Society of Great Britain. *Proceedings of the Annual Conference* (1967).
9 An 'is' statement saying what something *is* differs from an 'ought' statement which says what *ought* to happen. Moral philosophies stress the importance of appreciating this difference.
10 *The Language of Education*, by Israel Scheffler (Thomas & Co. 1960).

Chapter 3

The Concept 'Training'

The concept 'training' is an interesting one. In the first place, there are times when it seems difficult to decide whether a process merits the title 'training' or 'education', as we shall see later. There are other times when it seems difficult to distinguish between 'training' and 'drill'. This illustrates two points already made but which cannot be too frequently emphasized, namely the interrelationships between concepts in a study of education and the need to assign to each concept its 'logical geography', to prevent the confusion of one term with another.

Training is a narrower concept than education. Training may be educational, but it can never be education. In the same way, a person can be saintly without being technically a saint, i.e. in the sense of one who has been canonized. However, this does not prevent people using the term loosely in such expressions as 'He is a perfect saint'.

'TRAINING' QUALIFIED BY DIFFERENT ADJECTIVES

The term 'training' brings to mind certain adjectives which are associated with it. This in itself suggests that it is a narrower and more specific idea than education. The criteria for education demanded broad characteristics. These sometimes implied 'physical elements' in training and at others 'mental elements', and this, too, is an important idea to keep in mind. Until comparatively recently we talked of 'physical training', by which we meant a process which exercised the muscles of the body and kept us fit. 'Military training', also, has a physical rather than a mental emphasis. It is an activity which makes men 'fit for war'. In the days before modern psychology, people talked about 'mental training', and the terms which they linked with this were 'formal discipline' or 'mental discipline', suggesting a 'regimentation of the mind' rather as military training implies a regimentation and disciplining of the body. This was exactly what happened. It was believed that there were different compartments within the brain, each of which controlled a specific mental function. One compartment controlled memory, and was called the 'memory faculty'; another controlled reasoning, and was called the 'reasoning faculty'. Indeed, the whole idea of parts of the brain controlling specific mental activities was known as 'faculty psychology'. The basic idea lingers today in such expressions about old people as, 'He still has all his faculties'. The main meaning of this is that 'his mind is still rational and in control of his actions'. One trained mental faculties by appropriate mental exercises.

Two other adjective/noun combinations involving the term 'training' especially important for our present thinking are 'vocational training' and 'teacher training'. The first is a general term implying a process which fits one for a particular job or profession, the second is a specific term for a process which fits one for competence in the classroom.

Two ideas emerge from these preliminary remarks. The term 'training' implies 'exercising' and 'repetition', and in every case considered training has been *for* something. There is, in each case, a definite end or purpose in view. We do not merely 'train'; we 'train for'. Physical and mental training provide the most obvious examples of training involving exercise. The one exercises the muscles regularly, the other exercises the faculties of the mind regularly. To improve the memory, you exercised the 'memory faculty', by giving children large amounts of material to learn by heart (rote learning). To train the 'reasoning faculty', you taught children a difficult, logical subject, which was frequently Latin. Those who have studied Latin will no doubt appreciate that there is a large element of memorizing and of exercising in Latin, especially when it is badly taught.

We can now return for a moment to consider Plato's definition of education which we saw in Chapter 2, and which caused us to ask if he was justified in using the word 'training' in the sentence, 'I mean by education that *training* given . . .' We are now in a position to suggest that this is not an acceptable definition, because it implies that 'education' and 'training' are here almost synonymous. We could say, 'I take education *to include that training* . . .'; but this is a very different statement.

TRAINING AND INSTRUCTION

What we have said suggests that training is closely associated with instruction. In Chapter 1, we found it natural to talk about 'teaching' and 'teachers' while we were considering the process of education. It seems equally natural to talk about 'instruction' when we think of training. Perhaps the most appropriate illustration, in connection with the types of training we have mentioned, is 'physical training *instructor*'. It sounds less appropriate to speak of the 'physical training teacher'.

Ducasse (1), whose etymological definition of education we discussed (in Chapter 2), also gives an etymological definition of the verb 'to instruct'. To instruct is to build into the mind knowledge of facts, relations, rules or principles of one kind or another. He also gives a definition of the word 'training' as 'the process of imparting to someone the skill to perform some operation or set of operations whether mental or physical, and whether the acquisition of the skill is or is not accompanied by understanding of the principles on which the operation depends'.

This provides us with excellent food for thought. If we think of the three criteria for education, and then attempt to match up what Ducasse says are the characteristics of training against these criteria, we see at once that we shall only confuse education with training if we do not think clearly. Passing on worthwhile activities and values and knowledge is certainly not as narrow as teaching a skill or an operation or a series of operations. In this respect, it is interesting to note that in our technological age an 'operative' is lower in status than a 'technician'.

Again, we cannot possibly confuse education and training if we insist that education must provide those committed to it with knowledge, understanding, and cognitive perspective. Ducasse says that training does not necessarily involve understanding the principles involved.

If we look at the chief feature of instruction as defined by Ducasse, we note that it is 'to build into the mind'. Although he continues with the word 'knowledge', it seems a far cry from building knowledge into the mind to 'handing on' knowledge with the proviso that it shall not be inert, but understood. We can see that in a hot water system with a built-in thermostat, the thermostat performs a very useful function. When the water reaches a certain heat, the thermostat records the fact and switches off the system, so that heat is not applied to the water when there is no need for it. But the thermostat does not work this out for itself. It is merely constructed in such a way that it will perform this particular task. Taken outside the hot water system, it is entirely useless, since its specific construction makes it useful only in one set of circumstances.

DRILL AS A FEATURE OF INSTRUCTION AND TRAINING

We have implied a narrowing down process as we go from 'education' to 'training' to 'instruction'. There is one more term which we must consider, especially in connection with instruction, and that is the term 'drill'. In the army, there are non-commissioned officers who are called 'drill instructors'. These are the individuals who march platoons of men up and down the parade ground, bawling commands at them. The situation is so simple, in terms of learning, that it is merely the 'stimulus-response' learning which the behaviourist psychologists (2) describe. It is significant that when behaviourists talk about 'stimulus-response learning', they are talking about teaching animals – and not always particularly intelligent animals at that. On the command, 'Quick march' (stimulus), the squad of men moves forward (response), and they continue to move forward until the next command is given. The situation is such that, if no other command is given, they will march forward indefinitely; even if they come face to face with a brick wall, they will continue to 'mark time', i.e. their feet will continue to move up and down 'on the spot'. So conditioned are they by the commands of the drill instructor that they are not allowed to think for themselves.

Again, in the army there is the 'arms drill instructor'. He instructs groups of men to perform simple physical exercises 'by numbers'. A typical sequence of 'instruction' in the movement known as 'sloping arms', that is, bringing the rifle from the ground to the shoulder is as follows – 'On the command, "One", you bring the rifle up like this (visual demonstration follows). On the command, "Two", you bring the rifle across the body with the right hand resting the rifle on the left shoulder-so. On the command "Three", the right arm returns to the right side.'

Drill, then, means the 'formation of habits through regular practice of stereotyped exercises'. Although we stressed that 'learning by heart' was not markedly educative, we must not assume that learning the declension of nouns in Latin is such an unthinking process as drill and arms drill. In the former we require the mind to perform 'limited feats'; we do not require it to take no part at all in the activity.

For these reasons Ryle (3) distinguishes between *training* someone to draw, to speak French, or to play cricket and 'drilling' them. In each of the activities which Ryle names, intelligence must be used. If we draw, we have to take into account such important things as perspective. We are trained to know that if we stand at the end of a street and look along it, the street appears to grow narrower at the far end and the height of the houses appears to decrease gradually from the near end to the far end. If we are required to draw this scene, we apply what we have learned about perspective. We do not, however, make everything that we draw taper away as we did with the street and the houses. We have to discriminate between situations which require the application of perspective and those which do not. We cannot do this merely by automatic actions such as those performed in arms drill.

Similarly, when learning French, there may be a certain amount of what the old text-books used to call 'drill exercises'. But this is not to say that the drill exercises are synonymous with learning French. It is significant that it was factors such as the 'drill exercise' which were most roundly condemned when new methods of teaching languages were introduced.

When we are trained (or 'coached') to play cricket, we are taught how to make certain orthodox strokes. The trainer, or coach, bowls to the learner in the nets and teaches him that to a certain type of ball he plays the forward defensive stroke, to another the back defensive stroke, to another the hook shot, to another the cut. But in a game of cricket we do not automatically perform these moves which we have been trained to make. For example, the bowler may bowl a ball wide of the off stump.

Our coach has taught us that this is to be hit with a stroke called the cut. This means that the cut is a more appropriate stroke than the hook. But it does not follow that, if the opposing captain has placed a fielder in such a position that by making a slight error in our shot we risk being caught out, we still make the shot because we have been trained to cut that kind of ball. We would only make the shot automatically if we had been 'drilled'. In the latter case, the ball bowled outside the off stump would be a stimulus similar to the parade-ground command 'Quick march', and the playing of the cut stroke an automatic response, similar to that of beginning to march on hearing the command. What applies to a game like cricket applies even more strikingly to chess, where much more intricate skills are involved. The moves are standard, in that the various pieces can be moved only in certain ways, i.e. a pawn one square forward, or two squares forward as its opening move. This apart, the moves which are produced in combinations result from the intelligent use of known moves.

We have seen that 'training' is always 'training *for*' something, and Peters (4) tells us that it always implies the acquisition of a 'skill' or a 'knack'. Drill therefore may be an essential *part* of training. If it is, it will always be an elementary part; it will be a large part of training only in cases where a low-level skill is being acquired. A skill may begin at the level of drill; it must always end at the level of application. We saw that Ducasse used the expression 'building into the mind' in his definition of 'instruction'. Ryle, speaking of drill, implies that in drill we *inculcate* into the mind, when he uses the term 'inculcated automatisms'. Stopping marching on the command 'Halt' and lifting the rifle off the ground on the command 'One' are both instances of 'inculcated automatisms'. They are automatic responses to a particular stimulus. Far from requiring intelligence, they dispense with the need for the application of intelligence.

Ryle continues by saying that 'skills', 'tastes', 'scruples', which we acquire by training, cannot be defined as 'inculcated automatisms'. We have to learn to apply and develop them. Even if we learn to ride a bicycle, we must ride it *somewhere*. The activity cannot take place in a vacuum or be entirely devoid of purpose. The purpose is always determined by 'thinking' and 'deciding'. The person who acquires habits through drill, develops both himself and what he has acquired by learning to apply them.

Consequently, we can return for a moment to the problem of whether or not 'rote learning' is educational or merely drill. In the days of mental discipline and faculty psychology, rote learning of, for example, Latin declensions and conjugations was a drill. The main purpose of it was to increase the memory power. Thus, when it had improved the memory power, it was thought to have fulfilled its purpose. Similarly, arithmetical tables can be used to exercise the mind, and even so distinguished a thinker as Plato suggested that dull minds should study arithmetic, since arithmetic sharpened the wits.

Rote learning of Latin grammar or arithmetical tables *can*, however, be the first step in a larger process. It can be the 'inculcation of automatisms' necessary for efficiency in reading Latin literature or of solving mathematical problems. Ultimately, both Latin and mathematics may develop 'cognitive perspective' in the learner. By this stage, he has advanced far beyond the initial level of drill.

This is why the term 'knowing how' used by Ryle (5) is so important. He contrasts 'knowing how' with 'knowing that'. We know 'how' to play the piano; we know 'that' certain things are true. It is interesting to recall that people often refer to a skill as 'know-how'. Peters also links the term 'knack' with skill and says that training *for something* involves the acquisition of the appropriate knacks or skills. Ryle would add that the *application* of a knack or a skill requires intelligence.

Ryle also argues that when we say that a person is skilful, we mean that he performs a particular operation *well*, that his work is 'up to standard', it 'matches up' well to certain criteria. But, so does the well-regulated clock. It can be said 'to keep perfect time', in exactly the same way as we can describe a man who is never late for anything as 'absolutely punctual'. The difference between the two is that the clock does not need to have 'awareness' to keep perfect time. It does not have to make decisions, such as whether to make an important 'phone call and be late, or to keep one's standards of punctuality at the expense of making the important 'phone call.

We can now bring together the points that we have made. By drawing a distinction between 'drill' and 'training' we shed further light on training. In the same way, by shedding light on 'training' we came to a better understanding of education. Both training and drill entail repetition. Drill involves the repetition of simple movements or mental operations which result in habits. Training involves the repeated application of skills which have been learned. The skills are not always applied automatically. They require intelligence to be brought to bear on the situation. For this reason Ryle says that training develops 'intelligent capacities' but 'drill produces habits'. Drill dispenses with intelligence; training requires intelligence.

In an interesting statement describing Spartan education, Plutarch (6) writes:

'As for learning, they had just what was absolutely necessary. All the rest of their education was calculated to make them subject to command, to endure labour, to fight and to conquer.'

This is a most important statement for our purposes, since it not only helps to clarify 'education', but also emphasizes what we have been saying in this chapter. Plutarch is really saying that much of Spartan 'education' consisted of 'training' and even of 'drill'. There is even a suggestion of 'indoctrination'. He does not, however, say, 'Spartan *education* was calculated to . . .', but that '*all the rest of their education*' was so calculated.

THE RELATIONSHIP BETWEEN EDUCATION AND TRAINING

It is now time to bring together again the terms 'education' and 'training'. At the beginning of the chapter, we looked at training qualified by certain adjectives. Some of these adjectives have recently been applied to 'education'. We talk of 'physical education' instead of 'physical training'; teacher training colleges have in recent years changed their name to 'colleges of education', and a degree in education has been established. Although we do not talk about 'vocational education' instead of 'vocational training', we shall see (in Chapter 8) that we pair 'vocational training' and 'liberal education'. We do not talk of 'military education' but only of 'military training'. It was 'military training' that formed so large a part of Spartan 'education'.

If the terms 'education' and 'training' are meaningful, then there must be some point in using the term 'physical education' instead of 'physical training' and in contrasting 'teacher education' with 'teacher training'. The difference must be an essential one, not merely a change of name.

Plato (7) was very clear about the difference. He equated education with 'true knowledge', not with 'opinion'. He divided his ideal society into two classes – the ruling class, called the 'Guardians', and the working class, called 'artisans'. The Guardians were capable of acquiring 'true knowledge'; the artisans were capable of acquiring only knacks or skills. The Guardians were to receive education and develop insight into fundamental principles; the artisans were to acquire 'know-how', by which they would enable the State to flourish economically. The Guardians would study what was *intrinsically* valuable; the artisans would learn only what was *extrinsically* valuable – that is, the Guardians would study things *valuable in themselves*, for example art and music; the artisans would acquire only those things which fitted them for a particular job, for example carpentry for the builder, arithmetic for the accountant.

Now, it is sometimes said that what the Guardians received was not education but vocational training. In support of this argument, it is claimed that their education was 'to fit them to rule'. It was therefore as much vocational as the training in techniques and skills which the artisans received. Similarly, it is sometimes argued that the classical education which the public-school pupil receives is really a vocational training for such careers as the diplomatic service and the higher posts in the Civil Service. We can examine these claims in the light of what we have already said about education, training, drill, habits, intelligent capacities, knowing how, and cognitive perspective. All these things help to provide an answer to the question, 'Did Plato's Guardians receive education or vocational training?'

If the Guardians received vocational training, it is essential that there be a knack or skill of 'governing'. We have already established that skill is 'knowing how', and that we can know how to mend a fuse that has burned out (simple skill) or know how to play chess (complex skill). Both these examples, however, apply to 'tangibles'. In order to perform the four 'drill movements' necessary to mend a fuse one need not know why the fuse burned out or understand electricity in general, but playing chess is not quite so simple. Nevertheless, the only difference between mending the fuse and playing chess is that greater use of intelligence is required to apply the more complex skill. But in chess one is ultimately governed by the rules of the game which dictate how the pieces shall be moved.

If we turn now to 'governing', we see at once that it is not like the simple knack or skill of fuse-mending, nor the complex skill of playing chess. 'Governing' has to do with 'the State', an idea which has troubled philosophers throughout the ages. Even when we talk of 'governing people', we are thinking less of affecting their physical bodies than their minds and their emotions. Governing people is not comparable to moving chessmen.

Governing requires, above all other things, something akin to what Peters calls 'cognitive perspective' and what we referred to as the 'synoptic or speculative role' of philosophy. It requires a knowledge of principles and the understanding of human nature. Ethics and morals enter into it; right and wrong are of paramount importance. One must understand and appreciate beliefs and the reasons for the acceptance of those beliefs.

For these reasons we must come to the conclusion that Plato's Guardians received 'education' rather than 'vocational training'. Although they did acquire particular skills, such as the ability to think logically, from their study of the fundamental principles of mathematics and science, supplemented by a study of 'dialectic' (logic), there were 'values' in what they studied over and above these skills. The areas of study may have had practical applications, but fundamentally they were 'intrinsically valuable', i.e. valuable in themselves. There is almost an implication of what recent psychologists have called 'transfer of learning' in the education of the Guardians. 'Transfer of learning' means that the development of logical thinking in one area carries over into another area of study. Thus, if the Guardians learned the fundamentals of mathematics and science, they might more easily understand the fundamentals of government.

The ideal educational system of Plato contained the best features of Athenian education as he knew it. In his famous funeral speech, Pericles (8) describes the Athenians as 'lovers of beauty without effeminacy'. Here he was contrasting the Athenians' enlightened education with the narrow training of the Spartans, which we have already seen described by Plutarch. The bedrock of Athenian education, and consequently of the education of the Guardians, was 'what is worthwhile'.

Further indication of this idea is found in the famous 'Allegory of the Cave' (2). Here Plato likens mankind to prisoners fettered in an underground cave so that they face the wall. Behind them, through the mouth of the cave, the sunlight streams and casts shadows on the wall. This is the only conception of reality that the prisoners have. Dark shadows are there for them to see, but they never see the substance of which the shadow is a reflection. Then, in telling words, he describes the task of education as that of 'turning the eye of the soul to bring it face to face with reality'. This was exactly what he envisaged the education of the Guardians would achieve. Within education, as we have seen, there is nearly always, if not always, an element of training. In Chapter 5, where we shall deal with the aims of education, we shall see that the provision of vocational skills figures prominently among the aims listed by O'Connor. But education can never be equated with training, however complex the skills which training imparts.

In the nineteenth century, the election system which is now an established part of our way of life was introduced. The ordinary man was then given the right to vote and choose his representative in Parliament. The slogan was coined 'We must EDUCATE our masters', and this became the foundation on which the first Education Act of 1870 was founded. Then 'we' referred to the government; 'masters' referred to the people who through their vote could elect or reject the government. Significantly, the word 'educate' rather than 'train' is used. If it were necessary merely to build into the minds of the electorate the skill of filling in a ballot-paper, there would be no need to establish a system of elementary education for all. But reading and writing were not merely training for filling in ballot-papers; they were valuable as means of initiating people who had never before been educated into the culture of their society. Moreover, if the ballot were to be a fair one, they must know something about politics and principles; they must be able to assemble evidence and come to a decision. One *part* of the process was 'training'; the process itself was education.

We compared the public-school boy and his classical education with Plato's Guardians and their education. If we conclude that the second was education and not vocational training, we must also admit that the first is education too. It is not the *direct* means of enabling people to succeed in a certain job, but the *indirect* means. It may include developing 'intelligent capacities', but it does not only have this aim. Over and above any 'applied usefulness' this type of education has a 'spiritual' element using the term as James (10) uses it. It develops a sense of values, sensitivity, and appreciation. Its product was the Guardian of Plato, the Courtier of the Renaissance, the *Hc· ête Homme* of seventeenth-century France, the English gentleman. All these titles imply 'values' rather than 'skills'.

At the school level, we sometimes meet the problem of training or educating citizens. Again there is a similarity between being a 'good citizen' and being a 'good ruler'. It is not something that is understood by acquiring the 'knack' or 'skill' of being a good citizen. It involves at least as much initiation into ideas and beliefs and values as it does direct teaching of modes of behaviour which are characteristic of good citizens. You may train good soldiers, but you educate good citizens.

TEACHER TRAINING AND TEACHER EDUCATION

Since this book is concerned with educational philosophy, and since we said that far from suggesting unrelated theory we should make every effort to underline its practical implications, it is appropriate to close this chapter with 'teacher training' and 'teacher education'. The distinction is not new. In the middle of the last century, the methods of training teachers as applied by Andrew Bell (12) were criticized. Two of the forms that the criticism took are most relevant for us. The first was that he 'scoffed at theory and trusted to classroom practice entirely'. The second one shows the consequences of this attitude to teacher training. It was said that all that Bell's teachers learned from him was 'To tell the tale as t'were told to them'. We are reminded of Ryle's expression 'inculcated automatisms', and of another term which he uses, 'parroting'. What was passed on to the teachers by Bell's system was 'inert'; it produced no understanding and no 'cognitive perspective'.

Yet in the last few years since the Bachelor of Education degree was established and 'teacher training colleges' became 'colleges of education', there were teachers who talked about 'sacrificing' training in classroom competence for the many, to a study of theoretical education by the few.

This is a strangely narrow view indeed. Throughout the last half of the nineteenth century, it was stressed again and again in England, Prussia and Switzerland that teaching was an 'art' rather than a 'skill'. To train someone how to teach (produce 'know-how') was not sufficient. It resulted in *mechanical* teaching, in a narrowing of horizons to those which embraced a certain subject. It implied that there were certain 'tricks of the trade' which the more experienced passed on to the less experienced.

This may be true of training motor mechanics, but it is not true of training teachers. When the motor mechanic puts a new part into an engine, he attaches one unthinking object to another. He can do it only in one particular way, and does it in the same way every time. If he did not, the part would not fit into the engine. But the teacher is an individual and each child taught is an individual. For each the same subject matter may have different meanings, or no meaning at all, or profound meaning. It is absurd to suggest that providing teachers with 'knack' or 'skill' can be called 'teacher training'.

We have said that in applying a skill, the person should, in Ryle's view, develop both the skill and himself. It is open to question whether the motor mechanic achieves this. It is certainly most essential that it should apply in the case of teachers.

'Teacher training' lies within 'teacher education', just as 'training' lies within 'education'. But methods of teaching are not to be acquired as habits through drill and practice on stereotyped exercises. It is an indictment of teacher education that new methods are often so eagerly accepted without the demand for time to assess their possible effectiveness. Teacher training is also likely to inculcate that narrow attitude which we discussed in the first chapter, where the infant school teacher thought that comprehensive education was nothing to do with her, while the secondary school teacher could see no relevance to him in infant development. It is as wrong to think that teachers require only vocational training, as it is to think that what Plato's Guardians received *was* vocational training.

The rapid changes in society make rapidly changing demands on the school system. There is the demand for new material to be included in the curriculum (as we shall see in Chapter 7). At the same time, there is a demand for the old teaching methods to go and to be replaced by more 'progressive' methods. There is the demand that selection procedures for secondary education be abolished and that state nursery schools be established. There is a demand to raise the school-leaving age and to make more and more 'further education' available for more and more people. New phenomena such as polytechnics and technological universities appear in the educational system as we know it. We often hear the accusation that, in spite of the great increase in educational expenditure and of greatly increased educational opportunities, there is still an alarmingly large amount of illiteracy amongst the population. We hear it suggested that soon children will marry while still at school; that parents ought to have greater say in their children's education.

In this list, and the list could be made ten times as long without any difficulty, there is a mixture of factors from both inside and outside the classroom. No classroom can remain unaffected by things which happen outside it. Social factors subtly condition not only *what* we teach but also *how* we teach. To suggest that the most important aspect is a development of 'classroom competence' seems an inadequate reply to the formidable array of problems which we have listed.

It would be absurd to say that there should be no training for classroom competence. This would be equivalent to saying that one could produce a concert pianist without training him to read music. Reading music is an essential piece of know-how, just as ways of teaching reading and methods of interesting children are essential 'know-how' for the teacher.

But no teacher who enters the profession now is going to retire forty years hence and leave the same situation which he found in his first year. It has been suggested that manual workers may have to learn new skills and techniques every five years of their working lives. A changing society which makes demands on its manual workers cannot fail to make demands on its teachers.

Only by providing teacher education can we provide each teacher with a chance to develop cognitive perspective, to see the significance of changes when they come, to assess what is best for particular groups of children in school. We cannot claim that we must *educate* an electorate, *educate* our rulers, and *educate* good citizens and then claim that we should concentrate on *training* teachers, as distinct from *educating* them. Education will include training. Training can never be equated with education, and it can never be the larger concept which contains education. This truth is important for our consideration of aims (Chapter 5).

NOTES AND REFERENCES FOR CHAPTER 3

1 'What can Philosophy Contribute to Educational Theory?', C. J. Ducasse, in *Selected Readings in the Philosophy of Education*, ed. J. Park (Macmillan 1958), Introduction to Part 1, Chap. 1.
2 'Behaviourists' is a term used to describe a school of psychologists concerned, primarily, to answer the question 'How does "learning" take place?'. Frequently, when the non-behaviourist attempts to answer this question, he talks in terms of 'mind', 'intelligence', etc. When Locke concerned himself with this problem in the seventeenth century he talked of the mind as a *tabula rasa* or clean state on which 'experience' wrote different things for different individuals. But the behaviourist condemns such terms as 'subjective' (unscientific), because you cannot measure them in the same way as you can measure drops of saliva, or turns made by white rats running through mazes.

It is on such things as this that the behaviourist concentrates. He believes, like Lord Kelvin, that when you can measure what you are talking about and express it in numbers, you can say that you have knowledge of that thing, but when you cannot measure it and express it in numbers, your knowledge is of a meagre and unsatisfactory kind. The most famous names in the 'Behaviourist School' are:

E. L. Thorndike (1874–1949), famous for his 'theory of connectionism' and 'S(stimulus)R(response) bonds'. E. R. Guthrie, who took Thorndike's theory further, and introduced such terms as 'association shift' and 'contiguous conditioning'. He believed that the last response which the animal in the problem situation made was the crucial one for future performance. C. L. Hull (1884–1952). The concept of 'habit' and 'habit family hierarchy' are central to Hull's theory. He does not accept that behaviour is a simple, single response to a stimulus, but that after a stimulus appears, the animal performs a number of 'fractional antecedent goal responses' before it makes the final response. It is from these fractional responses that some less efficient behavioural forms are eliminated when the learning becomes more efficient. The symbol for these fractional responses is r_g. B. F. Skinner, who is famous for his 'respondent' or 'operant' conditioning, as distinct from the classical conditioning of Pavlov. The successful response to an unknown stimulus is made after a period of random or 'trial-and-error' behaviour. Because this response is 'reinforced', the probability of its being made on subsequent trials in a similar situation is increased. The name of Skinner is associated with 'teaching machines', which developed out of the basic ideas of 'operant conditioning'.

The classic work of reference on 'theories of learning' is a book by that name, written by E. Hilgard, and published by Appleton–Century in 1948. This is, however, an extremely difficult book for the inexperienced. For this reason, readers of the present volume are recommended at this stage to look only at the excellent summaries at the end of the relevant chapters. In this way, they will spare themselves immersion in a mass of complex technical details.

3 'Knowing How and Knowing That', was originally a chapter from Gilbert Ryle's book *The Concept of Mind*. However, it is so important that it has been summarized in numerous books and journals, where it provides inexperienced students with a gentler introduction to high-level philosophical thinking. It can be found in *Philosophy and Education*, ed. I. Scheffler, 2nd edn (Allyn & Bacon 1966), Part IV, Chap. 8.

4 *Ethics and Education*, R. S. Peters (George Allen & Unwin 1966).

5 See also 3 above.

6 Plutarch (A.D. 46–120) was a somewhat unusual writer from the Classical World. He was fundamentally a moralist, who believed that the lives of great people provided moral lessons for subsequent generations (the 'moral concept of history'). His best-known work is the *Parallel Lives*, which consists of twenty-three pairs of biographies of famous Greeks and Romans. In each case the Greek life is compared with its Roman counterpart to show the different concepts of morality held by the Greeks and the Romans. Almost as well known as the work itself is a translation made by Lord North in 1579. In addition, Plutarch wrote the *Moralia*, a collection of ethical, moral and religious writings. This was studied later by such famous people as Montaigne and Francis Bacon.

7 Plato's idea of the difference between 'True Knowledge' and 'Opinion' can be simply illustrated by the following diagram:

	OBJECT OF STUDY	*STATE OF MIND*
Knowledge	The Good	Intelligence
	Ideas	Knowledge
	Mathematical Ideas	Thinking
Opinion	Concrete objects	Belief
	Images	Conjecture

The reader should ask himself what, if any, is the relationship between the basic ideas of Plato shown above and the stages of thought development named by Piaget:

Sensori-motor
Pre-conceptual
Intuitive
Concrete Operational
Formal Operational

8 In the second book of *The History of the Peloponnesian War* by Thucydides (460–400 B.C.) occurs the famous Funeral Speech of Pericles. Pericles was the senior magistrate of Athens and delivered the speech to honour the Athenian war casualties in the life and death struggle with Sparta. One of the reasons why the speech has become so famous is the account which Pericles gives of the way of life of Athens (the cultural state) and Sparta (the totalitarian state). Rather in the manner of Plutarch's *Parallel Lives* (see 6 above), Pericles shows by contrast the vastly different interpretation of the term 'education' by the two sides.

9 *The Republic* of Plato, Book 7, translated by F. M. Cornford (Oxford U.P. 1941).

10 *An Essay on the Content of Education*, E. James (Harrap 1949).

11 Andrew Bell. His name is usually associated with Joseph Lancaster, whenever English education in the nineteenth century is mentioned. Bell believed in what came to be known as the 'Monitorial System' of teaching. By this method, an older pupil, after receiving the most rudimentary instruction, was set to teach younger pupils. This sort of 'on-the-spot' training was severely criticized. To have its equivalent today we would have to envisage A-level candidates in, say, French, teaching French to O-level classes.

Chapter 4

The Concept 'Child-centred'

MANY RELATED IDEAS BUT LITTLE CLARITY

Certain words, such as 'freedom' and 'kindness', gain a ready acceptance by the hearer, because they are pleasant. Other words are repugnant and have the opposite effect on the hearer; 'Concentration camp' and 'cruelty' are examples. The point about all these words is that their effect is on the emotions rather than on the reason. They make an immediate impression, for good or ill, of pleasantness or unpleasantness. The term 'child-centred', often found in the expression 'child-centred education', falls into the first of our two categories along with words like 'freedom' and 'kindness'. Indeed, as we shall see, the ideas of 'freedom' and 'kindness' are implied on many of the occasions when 'child-centred' is used. Our concern, as it is throughout this book, is to measure the effectiveness of concepts not by their emotional appeal, but by how they stand up to rational analysis.

P. S. Wilson (1) tells us that in spite of all that has been written about it, the term 'child-centred' is one of the most obscure in the whole field of educational discussion. This may or may not be true, and we shall be in a better position to judge at the end of the present chapter. What is certain is that the mention of 'child-centred' brings to mind a large number of related terms – 'self-expression', 'project method', 'Dalton Plan', 'Play Way', 'learning by experience', 'learning by discovery' ('Heuristic method'). Moreover, the term 'child-centred' reminds us of certain educational thinkers whose ideas are generally thought to have 'child-centredness' in common. These include Rousseau ('negative' education), Pestalozzi (Anschauung) (2), Froebel ('Play Way'), Montessori (teaching by apparatus), and others (3).

'CHILD-CENTRED' A TERM OF PROTEST

The first thing that we can say is that the term 'child-centred' is a term of protest. Before the time of Rousseau, there had been a number of people (beginning with Montaigne) who had criticized the prevailing education as being unsuitable for many children. But none delivered such an impassioned attack as did Rousseau.

From the time of the Renaissance, education had been 'formal' and 'verbal'. Latin was the content, and the learning of Latin Grammar by drill methods formed a large part of the 'activity of learning'. There was no appreciation of individual differences, only a body of knowledge which an 'authority' (and we shall see in a moment that the authority from time to time changed) decided was good for the learner. Rousseau protested against this type of teaching in the telling words, *'des mots, des mots, encore des mots'* (words, words, and more words).

A later age described the formal method as 'chalk and talk teaching', and unimaginative Latin teaching as 'gerund grinding'. The heart of the protest was that interest was entirely lacking in the learner. He could not understand the adult ideas which were being conveyed to him in abstract terms beyond his limited experience. Consequently, the best that he could achieve was rote learning of the material and the ability to 'parrot' it when required to do so.

Yet the Renaissance itself was a protest movement against the narrow education which the Church had provided in the Middle Ages when, for the majority, education was a preparation for the hereafter, a means of obtaining salvation for the soul by learning the creed and the catechism, and such dogma as the Church determined. For the minority, education was designed to perpetuate the *élite* of the priesthood.

Unfortunately, the gap between the Renaissance scholars such as Erasmus, with their appreciation of that full life which a study of the ancient world revealed, and the average schoolboy with his limited experience and few opportunities for schooling, was so great that it could never be meaningfully reduced.

Subsequent protests included the Reformation, which protested against the claim of the priesthood that they alone could interpret the Scriptures, and the Rationalists, who claimed that the Church was little more than an empty, ritualistic association with no real substance. The Protestants demanded that every man had the right to read the Scriptures for himself, and to have such education as would enable him to achieve this. The idea was excellent, but disputes among the different sects resulted in the basing of the curriculum on the creed of each sect, just as it had been based on the dogma of the Church in the Middle Ages. Similarly the 'Enlightenment' (4) failed to produce an educational content any less narrow than the content which it criticized. The 'authority' of the Enlightenment was 'Reason'.

THE DANGER OF CENTREDNESS; CENTREDNESS AND CENTRATION

We can at this point make a tentative suggestion that child-centredness was a protest against 'content-centredness' or 'curriculum-centredness'. It was a movement which emphasized that the child is more important than subject matter. All children are not alike any more than all adults are alike. Therefore, it is foolish to believe that you can teach the same material by the same method with the same degree of effectiveness to all children.

We recognize in this interpretation a fact which is now accepted not only by modern psychologists but by most teachers. However, any term involving the word 'centred' may be educationally dangerous. Just as one authority fell into the very faults which it criticized in previous authorities, so some of those who said that too much attention centred on content, themselves centred too much attention on the child and on methods of teaching him, to the neglect of 'content'.

If we think for a moment of Piaget's writings, we shall see why the term 'centred' is potentially dangerous. Piaget says that the thinking of a child in the pre-school years is 'egocentric', i.e. the child sees everything in terms of himself. His experience does not allow him to assess things in terms of their effect on other people. Later, when he goes from the infant to the junior school, his thinking is again described as 'centred' and the aim of junior school teaching is to enable him to 'decentre' his thinking. The term 'centred' here implies 'fixation'. Indeed, it is 'irreversible', since, Piaget says, during the junior school years (the time of 'concrete operational' thinking) (5) the child must learn 'reversibility' of thinking. He must, to use a very simple example, appreciate that $2+3 = 5$ is the same as $3+2 = 5$. This involves reversing the direction of his thinking. 'Centration' or irreversibility results in rigidity. At the adult level, rigidity results in such things as bigotry, prejudice, irrationality.

Davis (6) (as we shall see in Chapter 6) states emphatically that teaching is a two-way process. We talk of establishing a 'two-way communication system' between the teacher and the learner: the name given to this is 'rapport'. Herbart (7) reminds us that this rapport is established through the act of teaching, which involves three elements: the teacher, the content of the teaching, and the learner.

We can now see why there is a danger that centredness will result in lack of balance or harmony, in 'centration' and 'fixation'. Subject-centredness stressed the subject to the exclusion of the child; child-centredness can just as easily result in concentration on the child to the exclusion of considering what shall be taught. As James (8) says, it results in the study of teaching methods in a vacuum. To have a teaching method you must have something to teach. You cannot study method without studying content at the same time. Thus child-centredness, like many protests, may well have resulted in an extreme solution instead of a rational and balanced conclusion reached after carefully weighing the evidence for and against. An over-literal interpretation of child-centredness may be no more valuable to education than the state which we describe as 'self-centred' is useful for socialization. Already those who believe that the child-centred philosophy has resulted in a dangerous exaggeration have begun their attack on it (9).

At the beginning of this chapter, we mentioned a number of terms which the expression 'child-centred' brought to mind. At the end of the chapter, we shall try to determine what the real value of the concept 'child-centred' is for present day education. To clarify our thinking still further, we shall examine three ideas which frequently occur in connection with the idea of child-centredness: naturalism (or 'education according to Nature'), learning by experience/discovery (contrasted with 'instruction'), and needs and the 'needs curriculum'. We shall apply the technique of concept analysis to determine to what extent favourable acceptance of the above ideas is rational and how much emotional. We shall be very much concerned with 'evidence', since emotional reaction is subjective, while evidence is necessary for objectivity. Objectivity and rational thinking go hand in hand.

NATURE, NATURALISM, EDUCATION ACCORDING TO NATURE

The term 'Nature' is capable of a number of interpretations. Consequently until its precise meaning has been determined, it is impossible to decide whether the expression 'education according to Nature' has meaning or is merely a catch-phrase or 'emotional rallying-point'.

When the Romans used the expression *secundum Naturam vivere* (to live according to Nature), there were usually two ideas involved, the one dependent on the other. The first was an idea of protest, since Nature was 'pure and simple' compared to city life, which became, like our own, increasingly complex and frustrating. The mind, in an attempt to escape, visualized Nature in its second and related meaning, namely an 'ideal existence' of unspoiled peace and calm which man had destroyed when he built cities and became filled with materialistic ambitions. This escapism pictured the state of Nature as a Golden Age which had passed beyond recall. Similarly, Rousseau, in the eighteenth century, in his prize-winning essay (10) depicted life in a 'natural state' as spontaneous, simple, happy, contented, earnest, and honest. It was exactly the opposite of the *artificial* Parisian life with its divisions between rich and poor, which was destroyed by the French Revolution. This man-made society was superficial, hypocritical, unfeeling, and cruel, as degenerate as the worst type of society in ancient Rome. While Rousseau was prepared to accept 'natural differences' among men, he could see no justification for 'artificial differences', such as 'social class'.

However, it is wrong to suppose that Rousseau was the first educational thinker to advocate 'education according to Nature'. Comenius, born one hundred and twenty years before Rousseau, drew analogies between the way Nature went about her work and the way the educator should go about his. Thus, he said that 'Nature observes a suitable time', 'Nature is not confused in her operations', 'Nature does not hurry but advances slowly', 'Nature prepares the ground carefully in advance'. Education, Comenius implied, must follow the same ways of working. However, Rusk warns of something that we have mentioned frequently in this book: the danger of basing ideas on preconceptions. He says that what Comenius did was not so much to advocate 'following nature' in education, as to draw analogies from Nature to justify certain preconceived ideas of his own.

Many years ago, Ross (11) stressed that 'naturalism' in education was not the same as the naturalism of the physical sciences, nor the naturalism that can be regarded as 'mechanicalism', i.e. the belief that when he learns, man functions like a machine. We saw this idea when we spoke of the Behaviourists, especially Skinner and his teaching machines. Instead, Ross says that naturalism in education stresses the evolutionary character or nature of man. It stresses what he has in common with the animals rather than stressing his spiritual nature (12) and the reasoning faculty that separates man from the animals (13). This emphasis is on instincts, primitive emotions, and unsophisticated judgments. This, in naturalism, becomes idealized as the 'noble savage'. In such terms, stressing the natural characteristics of a child's education or advocating educating a child according to Nature is really saying that education should allow him to develop 'naturally'. We shall see the weakness of this argument in a moment.

Monroe (14) indicates another interpretation of the 'naturalistic trend' in education when he stresses the naturalism of physical science which, says Ross, the naturalist educator neglects. Monroe equates 'naturalistic trends' with the demand for 'realistic education', i.e. education through things not words, which developed with the rise of modern science and led to the doctrine of *Anschauung* or 'sense perception' as the basis of true knowledge, which we have already seen in this chapter.

Finally, before we subject the concept 'nature' and the expression 'education according to Nature' to philosophical analysis, we must return to Rousseau. We have suggested that the word 'nature' can have different meanings, and Rousseau uses it in no less than three different ways (15). By personifying Nature, he comes close to the popular idea of 'Mother Nature' as a way of avoiding reference to God. In this sense, it is often the same as the 'Natural order of things' or 'Natural Law'. Using Nature in this personified sense Rousseau says: 'Fix your eyes on Nature; follow the path she treads.' Later, when he talks about the creed of the Savoyard Vicar, Rousseau stresses a 'natural religion', that is one from which the supernatural element, or God, is excluded.

In the second sense, 'nature' means something closer to natural phenomena, the things around us. This is shown in the statement: 'No other book than the world, no other teacher than things.' Finally, and this for our purposes is the most important of Rousseau's interpretations of the concept 'nature', it means, to use his own words, 'the internal development of our senses'. We shall see in a moment that this may mean no more than what modern psychologists mean when they use the term 'maturation', or readiness to perform certain acts without prior teaching. At a certain age, the infant is ready to crawl, climb stairs, walk. Attempts to teach him before he is ready may retard his natural progress. Modern psychology has developed such ideas as 'reading readiness' and 'number readiness' in primary schools. Modern psychology says only that there is an appropriate time for each child to begin to LEARN such skills as reading and number work. It does not recommend that he is left to acquire them in random fashion. Even Pestalozzi recognized the folly of this when he said that 'education must be taken out of the hands of blind, sportive, nature'.

Hardie (16), a modern analytical writer, declines the attempt to determine what the statement, 'education according to nature', means, because such writers as we have considered are not agreed among themselves about its meaning and because they do not use the expression consistently to convey a single meaning in their individual writings. He dismisses the proposition as we dismissed the proposition: 'Education is a preparation for life', because it is so vague as to be meaningless. What he does examine is a number of statements which develop out of the idea of 'education according to nature', and which are often put forward to explain its meaning. The first of these is: 'Education ought to enable the child to develop according to the laws of his own nature.' The simple interpretation of this statement is that education must enable the child to grow mentally and physically; conversely, education must not retard the physical and mental growth of the child. It would be extremely difficult, Hardie argues, to do either. Nor is it likely that education has ever been conceived as aiming to do either. If we say that this natural process of mental and physical development is 'maturation', we are virtually saying that education must allow maturation to take place. Again, even if education could stop this process, it is a very limited aim to say that education must allow a process to take place which will take place anyway, in the nature of things.

The second statement, which Hardie examines as one designed to explain 'education according to nature', is close to the idea of *Anschauung* to which we have referred twice already. The statement is: 'The only source of true knowledge is direct experience of nature through our own sense impressions.' We can see that this is a 'protest statement', opposing that verbal formal education which we saw stemmed from the Renaissance. However, a moment's thought will show just how naïve the belief is. According to the theory behind the statement, unless I can see, or touch, or smell, or hear something, I have no 'real knowledge' of it. I can have knowledge of a daisy, since I can see it, touch it, smell it. I cannot have knowledge of Africa unless I go there. Even then, how do I know that the place I go to *is* Africa? Someone must tell me.

There can be only two results of this theory. The first is that I shall know only the simplest things which everyone can know; I shall have knowledge of the things around me. Alternatively, I shall know more than this, but the knowledge will take a very long time to acquire, since it will involve, for example, travelling to Africa in order to know Africa. It will also be terribly expensive.

It is much more sensible to admit, with Hospers (17), that there are many sources of what we call 'knowledge'. Hospers names 'propositional knowledge' (including knowledge of concepts), 'knowledge based on authority', 'knowledge by intuition', 'knowledge by faith', 'knowledge by revelation' and 'knowledge obtained as the result of inductive and deductive reasoning'. We need do no more than notice the number of types of knowledge, which Hospers mentions. He does not accept them all as 'knowledge', but this does not mean that people do not interpret 'knowledge' as one or all of these.

For our purposes we need consider only the distinction which Bertrand Russell draws (18) between 'knowledge by acquaintance' and 'knowledge by description'. Hardie says that an example of 'knowledge by acquaintance' is the statement that 'this table is brown' made by someone in the presence of a brown table. For 'knowledge by description' he gives as an example, 'The Prime Minister lives at No. 10 Downing Street'.

We can immediately see that our problem, 'How do I know about Africa?' is solved for us. I learn about Africa not 'by acquaintance' but 'by description'. Somebody, sometime, had direct acquaintance of Africa and at some time communicated this knowledge to others. By the time I receive it, we may never know who was the person who first had first-hand experience of Africa. Unless we accept 'knowledge by description', we shall accept very little. We do not merely have to take the knowledge on trust from a single person. There are many people who know Africa 'by acquaintance', there are books and maps of Africa which can be produced as 'evidence'. It is hardly likely that all these books and maps were designed as part of a monstrous piece of deception. The important thing is to realize that philosophically and practically the kinds of knowledge indicated by 'This table is brown' and 'The Prime Minister lives at No. 10 Downing Street' are not identical. We obtain the two pieces of knowledge by different methods. When we teach, we shall find that our pupils obtain both kinds of knowledge. 'Knowledge by acquaintance' is knowledge which depends on *our own* sense impressions of Nature. 'Knowledge by description' does not depend directly on our own sense impressions of Nature, though it originally depended on someone's direct sense impressions. When we said that 'education is a process of initiation' (in Chapter 1), we were implying that all knowledge could not be as the result of direct personal sense impressions. The race has accumulated a vast amount of knowledge and through education, formal and informal, inside and outside school, initiates people into it via 'knowledge by description'.

If we accept the idea that the only true knowledge comes from our own direct experience of Nature, we not only rule out such areas of knowledge as mathematics, we also devalue the use of language. Language is used frequently to convey ideas where direct experience of Nature through the senses is not possible.

The third proposition that Hardie rejects is: 'The education of the child should be a recapitulation of the stages of development of the race compressed into a much shorter time span.' This idea suffers from the same fault as Comenius's idea of education according to nature. The 'recapitulationists', as we may call them, read into the child's development the development of the race, and then 'idealize' this as the way in which true education functions.

Such a belief resulted in the 'heuristic' method by which the child is supposed to discover knowledge for himself as his primitive ancestors did. Again we are faced with the problem that we met in 'learning by direct experience of nature through sense impressions'. It is an extremely long and laborious process. In addition, there is a good deal of trial and error and arbitrariness. What guarantee is there that every child will make all the essential discoveries, and how can there be any standardization of the knowledge obtained? Such individualism, even if desirable, is scarcely possible in today's educational conditions, with society demanding so many skills from all its members. Again, one of the greatest discoveries of mankind – language – is undervalued. Highly-developed language makes the learning process more rapid and efficient.

If we attempt to sum up the basic strengths and weaknesses of 'education according to nature', it is difficult to find any real value in the idea, except that it is essential that what the child is taught through words must coincide with his own experience. Unless we remember this, the words we use will not only be meaningless to him, they may also be rote-learned and become a definite source of error later on.

But the methods which the naturalists adopt to avoid this danger are extreme ones. The defects of the system outweigh this single advantage. As long ago as Plato, it was recognized that there was a 'bare essential way of life' and a 'comfortable way of life'. By including the idea of 'worthwhileness' in his criteria for education, Peters suggests that the process we call education goes well beyond caring only for the bare necessities of life. The naturalistic emphasis is rather on the rudiments. Much as Plato looked down on the skills acquired by his artisans as their 'education', he appreciated that the art of exact measurement did away with mere manipulation and that guesswork which depends upon sensation. And yet, it is 'manipulation' and 'guesswork' which seem to receive undue emphasis in 'education according to nature'.

Nash (19) admirably expresses the strengths and weakness of the naturalistic approach when he says that the key criteria which determine whether a technique can be acquired for the benefit of the child are the maturity of the child and the nature of the material. Thus, if a child in the infant school wishes to make an elephant with his plasticine, he may be left to perform the task unaided. He knows what an elephant looks like; he has sufficient coordination to manipulate the clay. Whether the finished animal matches up to what *we* think an elephant ought to look like is irrelevant. The child makes it, announces that he has 'made an elephant' and is pleased with the result. If the ten-year-old wishes to make an oak stool, we have a different situation. The material is much more difficult to handle than the plasticine, he has not sufficient manual skill to perform the task unaided. If he tries, he may well injure himself, waste an enormous amount of time and material, and be entirely frustrated by the outcome. There is none of the desirability in the second situation which we saw in the first.

As we shall see later (in Chapter 7) when we discuss 'curriculum' and its relationship with 'culture', the teacher has to act as a 'selecting agent'. He has to determine what knowledge and skills are most necessary for his pupils from the great body of knowledge and skills available. He must make his choice in terms of the stage of development of his pupils, and the 'needs' of children, which in turn become the needs of adults, always in relation to the needs of society.

Finally, the advocates of 'education according to nature' fail to appreciate sufficiently the difference between that broader interpretation of education, which is the sum total of the experiences of any individual, and that narrower concept of education to which the name 'schooling' is often given. Outside school, we learn by experience. Some of these experiences are controlled by the family, such as early opportunities for socialization. Others are what we might call random experiences, such as smoking our first cigarette at an early age. In this respect different individuals have different experiences and learn different lessons from them.

In school, generally speaking, the control of experiences is much greater. It may be the task of the teacher to provide some pupils with necessary experiences which a good home provides but a bad home does not. Society entrusts the teacher with status and authority, and in return expects certain things of the teacher. To this extent, there is greater 'social control' over the experiences which the child receives in school. It is appropriate at this point to consider the next of our three main ideas which develop within the concept 'child-centred'.

INSTRUCTION AND LEARNING BY EXPERIENCE OR DISCOVERY

There is a growing tendency in these days of increasing emphasis on 'progressive' education to regard instruction as a denial of freedom for the learner. Unfortunately, the phrase 'learning by experience' is more of a slogan than a meaningful idea, since instruction and learning by instruction are also experience. (20). We shall, therefore, in this section concentrate our attention on the phrase 'learning by discovery', or what used to be known as the 'heuristic method' from the Greek verb *heuriskein*, 'to find out'.

Instruction is condemned as 'formal', 'denying interest', and 'authoritarian', by the progressives, whose creed is found in the words of Rousseau: 'Present interest, that is the motive force, the only motive force that takes us far and safely.' Few, if any, teachers would deny that both interest and motivation are of paramount importance in teaching, and that, without both, no successful teaching can take place. But it is one thing to make this claim and quite another to assume that instruction makes both interest and motivation in the learner impossible. Instruction is emotionally rejected by the progressives because without analysing the concept, they interpret it as Rousseau's 'deadly sin' of forming the child's mind prematurely. The supporters of learning by discovery believe that 'education' derives from *educere*, 'to lead out', as we saw in the etymological definition by Ducasse in Chapter 2. The 'instruction school' takes the word as being derived from *educare*, 'to form or train'.

Unfortunately, although the basic problem can be expressed, and has often been expressed, in the question, 'Do we learn more effectively if we are told something, or if we learn something for ourselves?', there is no equally simple answer. We must ask, 'At what age?', 'For what ability range?', 'What is to be learned?'

Thus the term 'learning by experience' cannot be limited to activity lessons or activity methods. For this reason we decided to use the term 'learning by discovery' to represent the ideas of the progressive school. For them learning takes place when spontaneous activity leads to a discovery.

Unfortunately, a child may be active without discovering anything. At other times, he may discover something without realizing its significance. The behaviourist claims that 'reinforcement' of the discovery is essential. Consequently, we can say that it is dangerous to claim that learning by discovery is essentially better than being instructed. This does not, however, 'prove' that instruction is always justified.

The first point which we appear to have suggested is that we must avoid extremes. It is as extreme (and futile) to claim that 'We must tell people everything', as it is extreme and futile to claim that we should allow people to find out everything for themselves, or that 'We must never tell people anything'. In these terms instruction and learning by discovery are equally unacceptable.

Dearden (21) goes to the heart of the matter when he suggests that no thinking person can believe that a child is capable of discovering all that he needs to know. Every learning situation in school is 'structured' by the teacher. In the first place, the naturalist gospel ignores the fact that it is not 'natural' for the child to go to school. Moreover, in most of these structured situations, the teacher plays a double role as instructor and unobtrusive guide of the child's activity of learning. To take a simple instance: unless we are to resort to mime, a small number of instructions, or small pieces of information, must be given before any activity resulting in discovery can begin. This suggests not that the teacher must choose one of two roles, the authoritarian (or dominant) role or the retiring (submissive) role, but that the teacher's role has both these elements within it.

There is an old fallacy cherished by advocates of the 'direct method' of language teaching. This was a reaction against the rote-learning of grammar in what was called the 'grammar/translation' method. It was said to be natural for a child to learn a second language in the way he learned the first, namely by hearing it spoken by the teacher.

This is obvious nonsense. We cannot, in the first place, assume that the mental activities of the thirteen-year-old who is beginning to learn French are the same as those of a three-month-old baby hearing the sounds of his mother tongue. Secondly, the learner *needs* to learn his mother tongue in order to survive. He makes his needs known through language. These circumstances do not hold for a second language. Thirdly, Lado (22) tells us that we learn any subsequent language through the habits acquired in learning the mother tongue. When learning the mother tongue, we had no such habits to assist or hinder second language learning.

Gattegno (23) suggests an idea which is almost always overlooked, namely that we cannot teach people anything, but can only 'cause them to learn', and stresses that all second language learning in school is artificial. The learner hears it spoken imperfectly by the teacher or artificially on a record, shut off from the cultural context within which the language is normally used. He does not, therefore, learn French as a young French child learns it. For these reasons, we may be entitled to call these methods less formal or less artificial than some traditional instructional methods. We are certainly not entitled to call them 'natural' methods.

Hardie condemned the vagueness and lack of meaning of the expression 'education according to nature'. 'Learning by discovery' is often equally vague and meaningless. If one states what is to be discovered, the activity of the learner ceases to be natural and spontaneous. It becomes *directed* activity in a structured situation. The structuring may not be repressive, but it is there nevertheless. Once the situation is structured, the teacher knows what he expects the child to discover and hopes that the structuring of the situation will enable the learner to make that discovery. Thus, providing Cuisenaire rods is structuring a learning situation. Within this structuring, some learners may see relationships between the rods on which number concept will later be based. Other children may make no such discoveries, and may merely regard the rods as pleasantly coloured toys.

Similarly, it is dangerous to generalize about instruction (24). In the past instruction may have involved bullying and the denial of interest. It can easily be shown that bad instruction results in the child forming 'verbal habits', acquiring material that he will repeat parrot-fashion without understanding it.

In the last section, we saw the difference between 'learning by acquaintance' and 'learning by description'. The latter can take place only through a 'formal' method of teaching, of which instruction is one. If we go back to the child who wished to make an oak stool, why should it be assumed that if he is instructed in the skills necessary for making the stool, he will automatically become uninterested in the task? Conversely, what assurance is there that the child set to learn by discovery, who discovers nothing or discovers something which he does not recognize as a discovery, will automatically be interested? Skinner and his followers, who advocate teaching by programmes, believe that the greatest rouser of interest is the knowledge that one is succeeding. Consequently, in a simple linear programme (where the material to be learned is presented in a series of 'frames', one after the other), the child is told immediately if his answers to questions on the information in the frame are right or wrong. In addition, the material presented is so small and so simple that it is very difficult for the learner not to give the right answer. This is an extreme form of structuring. Those who advocate learning by discovery appear to believe that trial and error are good. They imply belief in the idea that we learn by our mistakes. Skinner believes that every mistake made is the first step to forming a bad habit. For him, the safest way to learn is by never making a mistake.

If we pursue our line of 'combined methods' further, very few teachers *tell* their pupils everything. A good teacher may instruct for so long; he may give the necessary basic information. Then, at a certain point, he makes his pupils deduce the next step from what they have been told. Are we to assume that, in this situation, the deduction is not a form of discovery? On the other hand, when we teach so-called 'remedial children', we have to tell them everything, at least in the early stages. They have failed to learn for so long that they are unable to discover anything. Failing to discover over a long period of time is frustrating.

Dearden says that the chief feature of instruction is the 'direct imparting of knowledge'. As a result instruction is often concerned with the inculcation of facts. It is arguable that facts ought tò be taught directly, not implied or hinted at. Once we imply or hint, there will always be some child who does not grasp the facts. The danger is that the giving of facts may become an end in itself; it may not always be followed by a structured situation where a problem has to be solved by using the facts acquired. Instruction can thus become associated with rote-learning. Again we must stress that what 'can become' is not inevitably what is.

It is important to realize that instruction uses language for in this lies a danger. We said, in connection with learning by discovery, that some children will make no discoveries. Equally, some children may not learn from instruction because they do not understand the language of instruction.

Bernstein (25) tells us that there are two forms of 'language' within the language we call English. These he defines as 'public speech' and 'formal speech'. The latter is what used to be called the 'King's English'. This meant that it was English accepted as grammatically correct. It is a middle-class language, and the language of instruction as well.

'Public speech' is used to convey meaning irrespective of whether it is accepted as grammatically correct or not. I can say, 'I have seen no one'; this is formal speech. It is grammatically correct. I can also say, 'I ain't seen no one'. This also conveys meaning, but it is not grammatically correct.

Also, I can say to a child about to step out into the road without looking to the right and left, 'Stand still', the child will carry out my command. But I can alternatively take the child by the hand and say, 'Now, you did not look to the right and the left before you stepped on to the road, did you? Well, that is very dangerous. You saw then that you were nearly knocked down by that car. Well, that is why Mummy and Daddy are always warning you that you must look right and left every time you cross the road.'

There are children who throughout the pre-school years are subjected to nothing but the cryptic 'public speech' shown above. The sentences are short, simple, often grammatically incorrect. The ideas expressed are extremely limited, often no more than what is happening or has just happened. The content is one of a small number of alternatives, the result of last Saturday's football match, or grumbles about work and the weather. Reasons are rarely put forward to explain a point. All statements of opinion are expressed dogmatically. The stock reason for something being right is,

'Because I say so'. Arguments are won by the person with the loudest voice.

It is often claimed, and the claim can be supported by evidence, that such children are often unable to understand the formal speech of instruction in school. They are used to concrete things only, not to abstract ideas. They are used to short, simple sentences and cannot follow long, complex ones. But are these children any more likely to learn by discovery? They are used to doing as they are told. A good deal of the speech they hear consists of commands and instructions. We can see now that the more we analyse our two terms 'instruction' and 'learning by discovery', the more difficult it becomes to answer the question which is the better method. What does become clear is that the answer, if reached, will not be as simple and clear cut or as universally true as the question implies.

If we go to the other end of the ability range and think of the academically able child in the secondary school, we find that he has a well developed 'conceptual sense'. He can work in terms of abstract ideas, is capable of manipulating the symbols of language and mathematics. Moreover, he is often able to derive enjoyment from the manipulation itself. He enjoys solving mathematical problems by calculation. The language of instruction is meaningful to him. Given the basic information he is then able to make discoveries for himself in terms of solving complex problems. Yet even with able pupils, such ideas as 'Nuffield Science' are thought to have possibilities. 'Learning by discovery', meaningfully defined, is not ruled out as a possible method of teaching the very able.

An examination of the concepts 'instruction' and 'learning by discovery', reminds us of what Wilson wrote (25) about the question 'What is education?' He stated that in attempting to answer the question we would unearth no hidden treasure, simply because there is none to unearth. What we will discover is a greater awareness of the implications of the question. This is the first step towards a meaningful solution. What applies to the question 'What is education?' applies also to instruction and learning by discovery. The investigation of the two terms, far from yielding a single, simple answer, makes for greater awareness of the danger of using the terms loosely. In such cases, emotional connotations replace logical analysis. Preconceived ideas take the place of objectivity.

The aim of instruction is not merely that certain material shall be committed to memory and 'parroted' at a given moment. We saw, when we considered the concept 'training', that there were various levels of 'knowing how'. Some of these were more complex than others. But we also saw that the aim of training was to develop intelligent capacities rather than habits. Habits are the result of a much narrower concept, 'drill'. Behaviourists believe that habits result from repeating conditioned responses.

So it is with instruction. We can have instruction at the elementary level of learning the physical movements necessary to fire a rifle, or to put together a plastic model. At the higher level we can have instruction in the propositions of advanced mathematics. We can also undergo a 'course of instruction', if we leave one religious sect and join another. This is often regarded by people outside the sect concerned as no more than 'indoctrination'. However, instruction in the beliefs of a religious sect and instruction in higher mathematics ought to have one thing in common. If the instruction is genuine instruction, it ought to provide the learner with the basic information which he needs if he is to have insight into (understanding of) religion or mathematics. The information is provided as the bricklayer is provided with bricks. By correct use of these bricks, the bricklayer builds the house.

Learning by discovery, then, has different meanings at different age levels. The child in the reception class is not nowadays required to make a sudden transition from the informal exploration of play at home, to formal learning by drill at school. But his play or exploration is guided in certain directions by the teacher. The purpose is that all the children shall learn partly by 'haptic perception' (sense of touch). But certain objects, Piaget tells us, are more useful and important than others. The handling, for example, of geometrical solids lays the foundation for ultimately developing geometrical ideas in the final stage of thought development. The child learns the concept of space by moving through space, and the concept of time by seeing that some actions take place after other actions. In a similar way he learns the difficult concept 'causality'. Here, one thing happens 'because' of another.

When he plays with his Cuisenaire rods, he can play with them only because the teacher makes them available. The child would not discover for himself a red rod which was twice as long as a white rod, and so on. Provided that the rods are available, he can 'see' that the red is twice as long as the white. Some children, however, may still require to be told basic information before they can develop number concept. The aim of the whole process is to avoid introducing the child prematurely to the symbolism of numbers. We are providing the child with experience *relevant to what we require him to learn*. This is not the same as providing 'open-ended' experience. The experience which we provide is structured.

Jarman (27) warns that 'non-directive' methods may be far from achieving the results which those who use them desire. We hear that they aim to let the child 'fulfil himself', 'attain his true potential', 'develop insight into life problems'. But what does 'non-directive' mean? If it means 'directed by the child himself', with the teacher 'abdicating' from his role, Bridges warns that the result may be that the child ceases to exist. The teacher adopting the ultimate 'non-directive' role will not interfere in any way for fear of 'forming the child prematurely'. Yet it is difficult to reconcile this point of view with the idea that teaching is a process of two-way communication. In the end the child can only feel that the teacher does not recognize him. The child from the insecure home may crave this very recognition which the non-directive teacher cannot give in terms of his non-directive role.

It seems then, in view of what we have written, that once we define more clearly what we mean by the terms 'instruction' and 'learning by discovery', they are not poles apart. Unless we use an extreme interpretation, or define the terms in the light of preconceived biases and prejudices, they are not two alternative methods. It is not a question of choosing one or the other. At none of the levels we have considered would such a choice be completely appropriate. At the levels considered, it is necessary to have a different proportion of the two approaches. This proportion is decided not in subjective terms, but in the light of psychological evidence, particularly evidence of the way in which children develop mentally and physically. We must appreciate that the child who performs Boyle's experiment is no more doing exactly what Boyle did, than the child who learns French in the secondary school is learning French like an infant native of France learning his mother tongue. We provide the child in science with the apparatus and guide his thinking. He only tries out Boyle's procedure; he does not make Boyle's discovery. Similarly, the child who fills in the last line in the following process of deductive reasoning is not discovering it as Aristotle did:

> All men are mortal,
> All Greeks are men.
> All Greeks are mortal.

Finally, we must accept that activity in learning is not merely physical. We can be active physically without being mentally active. We can be mentally active while sitting at a desk. It is clear from this that the term 'activity methods' often lays more stress on physical than on mental activity. It is a misinterpretation. Similarly, it is a misinterpretation of 'instruction' to equate it with 'chalk and talk'.

The final lesson is that we must examine with the greatest care methods which are described in the form of a slogan, such as 'learning by discovery'. This is necessary because slogans often describe protest methods which go to the other extreme in order to make their point.

We have attempted to assess the merits and defects of both instruction and learning by discovery. We have thought in terms of *children* of different ages and abilities not in terms of a hypothetical child, as in 'child-centredness'. In this way we have tried to give meaning to 'child' as well as to 'centred'.

NEEDS AND THE NEEDS CURRICULUM

'Needs' is a term requiring strict analysis. We can say that the basic biological needs of man are air and food; without these he cannot live. In civilized society, we add shelter and earning a living to these basic needs. The first depends on the second. In primitive societies, shelter does not depend in the same way on earning a living. Primitive people build their own houses, and hunt and fish to feed themselves, not primarily to earn a wage. Because of this we can define 'shelter' and 'earning a living' as 'acquired needs' or 'second-order needs' in civilized man.

Needs can be confused with wants. To determine whether the respective terms are being used correctly (within the boundaries of their 'logical geography') we must examine certain statements in which they appear. Again we are reminded of the value of linguistic analysis directed at statements, and concept analysis which assesses concepts both alone and within statements.

I can say, 'I need air in order to live'. Here is the basic meaning of 'need', to which we have already referred. I can also say 'I need a screwdriver'. This means two things: firstly, that I wish to loosen or tighten a screw; secondly that I do not have a screwdriver in my possession at this moment. 'Need' here means 'have need of' or 'lack'. However, the two 'needs' are not automatically the same. We could picture an extreme situation where one's life depended on the loosening or tightening of a screw. In that case, the need of a screwdriver would be connected with one's survival. Usually it means simply that, in the absence of a screwdriver, some task will remain incomplete.

Again we can say, 'I need more money'. This can be close to the survival need, if we mean that we have insufficient money to buy food and pay rent or mortgage repayments. But it can also mean that I have certain desires which, on my present salary, I cannot afford. The second use is a much looser one.

In this way, 'needs' and 'wants' are confused. When we say that we 'need' more money to buy a bigger car, we are really saying that we *want* a bigger car and are unable to buy it in the absence of more money. It is also possible, when we wish to tighten or loosen a screw, to say, 'I want a screwdriver'. Finally, it is one thing for an ordinary man to say 'I need a good meal' when he is feeling peckish, but quite a different matter to say that a starving man 'needs' a meal.

This confusion between needs and wants is very convenient for industry and commerce. Through advertising, they are able to convince people that 'You need our products'. It is permissible to say that 'it is necessary' to convince people that they 'need' certain goods, in order to maintain full employment. We may even say that our nation 'needs' full employment. We can see here that by 'need' we mean 'it is desirable' or 'it is in keeping with our political beliefs'. We are also coming close to the area of human rights and the idea that every man has the right to earn a living. Looked at from one direction, the establishment of social service benefits has to some extent done away with the 'need' to work in order to earn one's food.

Komisar (28) extends these basic ideas when he writes that there are two main uses of the term 'need'. He admits that the classification is crude, but convenient as a beginning for concept analysis. Moreover, his classification is particularly useful for our purpose, since it shows a definite connection between the terms 'needs' and the 'needs curriculum'. Before we examine Komisar's ideas, however, there are two terms which we must understand: 'prescriptive' and 'descriptive'. If the reader casts his mind back to Chapter 2 where we discussed definitions, he will recall that we said that these fell into two categories. One category was 'descriptive' definitions, i.e. dictionary definitions, such as 'a tiger is a four-legged animal'. The other type were 'stipulative', i.e. they 'stipulate' the meaning we wish terms to have, e.g. 'philosophy is a process of asking questions'. This type can also be called 'prescriptive', since it prescribes the way a term is to be defined.

If we think about grammatical rules for a moment, we shall see that the old form of Latin teaching used prescriptive rules. These told us how we *must* write Latin sentences. But Politzer (29) says that linguists regard rules as descriptive. This means that instead of telling people *how to* speak, they tell us *how* people *do* speak. If we understand this distinction clearly, we can look at Komisar's ideas further.

Komisar says that the word 'need' can be used prescriptively. 'He needs to be warned' is such a use: for we mean that he 'requires' a warning 'for his own good'. The interpretation of the need is in the mind of the person who makes the statement. Thus an anxious mother whose daughter is associating with a married man may say, 'She needs a warning'. From the mother's point of view, the need is glaring and immediate. The daughter, however, may not be aware of the need and indeed may resent the warning and ignore it. This is an important distinction to bear in mind when we think about such statements as 'the curriculum should be determined by the needs of children'. Do we mean 'needs' as they exist and are generally accepted, or what we interpret as 'needs' to tally with our preconceptions? It is all too easy to accept glibly something like 'learning by discovery' as a teaching method and then invent some 'needs' in children to justify it. In the same way, we saw that Comenius called in Nature to justify his ideas about education and teaching.

Komisar calls the second use of 'needs' 'motivational'. Motivation, basically, is whatever it is that makes us do certain things. We may be motivated to learn Japanese, to become a teacher, or to acquire fame. There is still an idea of 'necessity' in the motivational use of 'needs'. But this time we look at the situation from both sides, from the viewpoint of both interested parties. We may say that the adolescent daughter needs a warning; equally truly we may say the daughter needs understanding. This is a need which the parent can supply, just as she can supply the warning. But it is the daughter's state which decides the nature of the need. We may argue that the daughter 'needs' the warning but only 'wants' understanding. However, it is also reasonable to say that some emotional wants are so necessary to emotional stability that they are tantamount to 'needs'.

There are three types of prescriptive need. Their titles may be somewhat confusing, but illustration will make them easily understood. The first type is 'aim-directed', by which we simply mean something like 'Children *need* to go to school'. The whole statement implies something for the future. It is consequently like all aims – directed to future events. It provides a purpose for the activity of going to school. It is possible to say that the child needs to go to school to save his parents from being prosecuted for not sending him. But this is a very narrow sense; it is almost hair-splitting. Much more important is the interpretation that the child needs to go to school to learn skills for work and social competence. We shall see further evidence for this interpretation when we look at two of O'Connor's aims of education in Chapter 5.

Secondly, there is the 'necessity-directed' use of the term, when we say, after the child has gone to school, that he 'needs to learn to write'. Such 'needs' determine curriculum content.

Thirdly, there is the 'deficiency-directed' use of the word. If we say 'each child needs security', we are making a general statement covering all children. We may refer to children, some of whom already have security and others not. The Newsom report (30) says that 'Each child *needs* to find self-respect through his education', which implies that some children do *not* find self-respect. Because they habitually fail to shine academically they are classed as failures and feel insecure. It is the task of the educational reformers to see to it that children have their needs fulfilled by education. At this point the reader may like, as a piece of philosophical thinking for himself, to relate these three types of prescriptive needs to the statements containing the word 'need' which we presented earlier.

In Chapter 2, when we described education as 'initiation', we said that all children did not benefit equally from it. We saw also that education allowed individual development, but only within limits permitted by society. We can now express this idea in terms of 'needs'. Society has needs and children have needs, and one of the tasks of education is to harmonize the two. One of the mistakes of child-centredness is to forget about the needs of society and concentrate solely on the real or imaginary needs of the child. Socrates said that it is the task of the educator to find out each person's *arete*. This Greek word means 'excellence'; we would call it 'strong point' or 'aptitude'. Plato continued by saying that once the aptitude had been discovered, the individual should be given the appropriate training to enable him to benefit *himself and society.*

The above paragraph suggests another and possibly more reliable criterion for 'needs of children' than some of the sentimentalized needs put forward by the naturalist school. One's abilities (31) and aptitudes create certain needs which education must fulfil. Because different pupils have different abilities and aptitudes, they have different needs. By discovering these needs and educating accordingly, the educator can be said to be 'child-centred' (in a justifiable sense). He can also be said to be making possible individual development through initiation into the content of education.

But there is always the danger that emotional thinking will creep in even at this level. James (32) has warned us that we often refuse to accept that brilliant pupils need a special education. But we never deny that 'educationally subnormal' children have special needs. We feel sorry for the educationally subnormal; we often resent brightness and seek, perhaps without realizing what we are doing, to restrict it. It is often argued that in the case of the E.S.N. child the need for a special education is a basic need, that is of a special education to enable him to learn the three Rs. The needs of the bright child, by comparison, are closer to what we have termed 'wants'. However, the weakness of this argument is this; it is nowhere shown that the term 'need' is identical in every child. On the contrary, the evidence which we have assembled in this section suggests that one of the main ideas of child-centredness is that different children have different needs.

We have talked of motivational needs. Also (in Chapter 1) we suggested that philosophy in its synoptic role reviews the findings of many subjects, and we have found that one such subject is psychology. Consequently it is interesting to look at Hull's interpretation of 'motivation' in terms of 'needs' in white rats running mazes, to see what light psychology sheds on the concept 'needs'.

Hull starved the rats and this, he said, set up a need within them, the need to acquire food to still the restlessness which hunger produced. The need became a 'drive', which is tantamount to saying that it became the rat's 'motivation'. A motive is an 'inner drive'. When the rat goes in search of food, Hull says, it does not fulfil the need; really it 'reduces' it. The term 'need reduction' is a central one in Hull's theory of learning.

Similarly, certain psychologists of the *Gestalt* school (33) say that a problem produces inner tension. This tension is emotional, and just as the hunger becomes a drive to activity in the rat, so the tension becomes a drive to activity in the pupil. Thus education, as well as producing problems, also 'reduces needs', if we talk of the situation in Hull's language. Moreover, what we have said about children needing to find self-respect in their education is relevant here. Failure produces tension – inner tension – and, to reduce this tension, the child seeks an area of activity within the school, either inside or outside the classroom, where he can succeed. Other children, unable to succeed either inside or outside the classroom by socially accepted means, resort to delinquency (socially unacceptable means of reducing the tension). In another direction, the slow learner, that is the child who is unable to make normal progress in number work and verbal work (reading and writing), becomes frustrated by his frequent failure to do as well as other children. In his case, tension is the result of frustration. The school seeks to reduce this need by placing the slow learner in a 'remedial stream' where his special needs are catered for along with the needs of other slow learners. He is removed from the group of children whose needs in respect of the basic subjects are not the same as his own.

We have shown some ways in which the term 'needs' can be meaningful. The ways we have analysed have been in 'objective' settings. Because of this, we can relate what we have said about the different needs of different children to the interpretation of 'needs' which we accepted in the term 'needs curriculum'. However, we have seen that subjectivity sometimes replaces objectivity. People develop their ideas not on rational but on emotional grounds. Nowhere is there a greater danger of this happening than in any discussion of needs and the needs curriculum. For example, when the naturalist educator talks about the need for the child to develop 'according to his own nature' and invokes the negative education of Rousseau, there is a danger that 'needs curriculum' will be interpreted as the abolition of the conventional school-determined curriculum and its replacement by activities determined by the children. The interpretation of 'needs curriculum', which we have discussed, plays no part in such a process. To justify an illogical interpretation of 'education', needs which are convenient to the theory are 'read into the child'. But justifying a preconceived theory is not an objective process. It is a procedure which in the past has resulted in a good deal of sentimentalizing of the term 'child-centred'. The results have been educationally harmful. In such circumstances, 'needs and the needs curriculum' becomes an empty slogan instead of an important educational idea with important implications for both teacher and learner. Such sentimentalizing caused the rational educators to condemn a trend which stemmed from it as 'soft pedagogy'. It is for this reason that Komisar urges that if 'need' becomes closely identified with a specific and controversial programme, it loses any utility which it once possessed. Any sound programme must be based on a careful analysis and thorough understanding of the term 'need'.

The child as an individual brings to school his own needs which are classifiable under certain general headings, such as 'social need', 'intellectual need', 'emotional need'; but this is far from being the end of the matter. Although we can classify needs, they are still specific to each child as well as common to many children. No two children are insecure in exactly the same way; no two children have identical problems of 'socialization'.

However, this does not mean that a special curriculum must be devised for each child in terms of each need. The child must be confronted by areas of study which help to fulfil the 'needs' which society imposes on him. He has, in the early years of his education, to learn the 'survival skills' of reading and writing. But because our intellectual performance can be impaired by emotional difficulties, the 'needs' which the child brings to school with him make him react in a specific way to the demands of the curriculum. Some children are unable to read because they have little intellectual ability. For such children, intellectual activity will always be most difficult. Others fail to make intellectual progress because they suffer from 'emotional deficiency'. Until the teacher has decided whether the failure is caused by intellectual or emotional factors, the 'needs' which the child brings with him cannot be matched with the 'needs' which the curriculum embodies. Each child reacts uniquely to the curriculum. It is in this sense that 'child-centred' begins to take on real meaning. The truly 'child-centred' teacher is the one who can, through his knowledge of the individual child and of the curriculum, help each child to derive benefit from that curriculum. 'Child-centredness' can have no such meaning in making up some sort of curriculum on subjective grounds to enable each child to 'perform well'.

For this reason, Pestalozzi was near to the heart of the problem. He said that he wished to 'psychologize' education. He was convinced that there must be some method of teaching the rudiments that made them meaningful to every child, however limited in ability that child might be. He did not accept the negative education of Rousseau but sought a positive solution to the problem of matching the 'needs' imposed by the curriculum to the 'needs' of each individual child in relation to that curriculum. He realized, as did the Newsom Report two centuries later, that education must cater for emotional needs as well as for intellectual needs and that until a child can feel important as a person, there is little to be gained from formal education. He came very close at this point to the idea which we have stated before, that some underprivileged children are unable to benefit from formal education because they cannot understand it. This lack of understanding stems from their own need which the home fails to supply. The need may be the ability to understand formal language. Because they cannot learn, they fail to achieve success; because they fail to achieve success, they lose their self-respect.

CHILD-CENTREDNESS AND AWARENESS

When we considered the difference between 'teacher education' and 'teacher training', we suggested that the latter could be narrowly interpreted as the acquisition of teaching skills. These could be applied mechanically, without any real awareness of the situation in which they were applied. We could teach History in the old 'subject-centred' way without teaching children. We would assume that history was meaningful to the children because it was meaningful to us as adults.

This is what 'lack of awareness' means. Concentration on methods trains us to teach nine-year-olds in a different way from fourteen-year-olds, which is an important point. But how often are we unaware that even nine-year-olds can be poles apart in their needs? 'Nine-year-olds' is a group term which often masks individuality. The *awareness* that we must study our pupils as well as teach our pupils History is something that teacher education, as distinct from teacher training, gives. It also gives meaning to the term 'child-centred'. We do not forget to teach History or decide that we shall dispense with History teaching entirely. The fact that History is in the curriculum shows that it is considered by people of undoubted wisdom to be a 'need'. Instead *we* ask what 'need' each individual child has which enables him to benefit from History or which prevents him from benefiting from History.

Consequently, 'child-centredness' means partly that the teacher becomes aware that he can learn *about* the child, and even learn *from* the child as well as teaching the child. The awareness that will help him to help the child derives from what Allison Davis calls 'cultural background' and 'cultural motivation' (34). It is 'natural' for Merseyside children to watch Association football and to discuss heatedly the merits of Liverpool and Everton. It is not 'natural' for such children to go to school, to learn History and to acquire the middle-class values which the school seeks to communicate. This does not mean that, for Liverpool children at least, we abandon school, or History, or middle-class values. It means that our child-centred approach must bear in mind not the difficulty that we have in teaching them, but the difficulty they have in learning from us.

At the start of this chapter, we quoted P. S. Wilson's statement that the term 'child-centred' is one of the most misunderstood in the whole of education. Throughout this chapter we have tried to look at interpretations which have no meaning as well as at those which have some meaning. At the end of the same article, Wilson makes a number of telling points. He says that the child-centred teacher should not attempt to fit individuals to programmes setting out predetermined values, but to transform situations where we must manipulate and indoctrinate children 'in their own interests'. Occasionally, he says we feel that we can allow children to test values for themselves, but that for most of the time our task as teachers is 'prudential' (35), that is, determining what the child needs and structuring his education accordingly.

Because of the nature of education, only those situations where the child is allowed to come to decisions for himself are 'truly educational'. In the structured situations where we act prudentially, we are caretakers rather than teachers.

It may seem that at this point we have played into the hands of the advocates of naturalism in education and of progressive educators who advocate 'learning by discovery'. But Wilson anticipates this and says that in 'schooling' (which Lodge defined as the narrow interpretation of education) there is room for caretaking as well as for educating.

AWARENESS IN HIGHER EDUCATION

We have discussed in previous sections some of the dangers inherent in the term 'child-centred'. Yet another danger is that it tends to make people think that the principles implied by the term apply to children only, and that they have implications only in the primary school. But needs exist and awareness of people and their needs exists far beyond the narrow limits of the primary and even of the secondary school. One of the places where such principles are required is Higher Education.

The university is perhaps the most 'traditional' of all institutions of learning. The lecture method of teaching is to be found in the Middle Ages and, in much the same form, in twentieth-century universities. Moreover, it is sometimes the custom to make attendance at lectures compulsory. Not surprisingly, in an age in which students call into question many of the accepted customs and values of tradition, the lecture method has suffered some severe criticism. The main point of the attack is that there is frequently no worthwhile communication between the lecturer and his audience. We have, in this situation, an exact parallel to that situation which we deplored in the primary school, namely of the teacher using a form of language which is outside the experience of the learner and consequently meaningless to him. It was against this, we saw, that Rousseau protested so vigorously.

The problem is partly due to lack of awareness on the part of those who lecture. There is an assumption that the highly academic man or woman requires no training in teaching skills. If a man is brilliant in the field of Classics or Nuclear Physics, how can he fail to master the elementary skills of communicating his experience to others? Yet this is often what he fails to do. More, he often remains *unaware* of his failure to communicate. Again we return to our most important point that if child-centred or even 'learner-centred' education means anything, it means an awareness of the matèrial taught, the person learning it, the best way of making what is taught intelligible to the learner, and whether we are succeeding in doing this. Teaching at university level is not something bestowed as a 'postgraduate gift' (36).

The first awareness, then, in higher education is that the advancement of knowledge is not more important than the communication of knowledge. Learned research is most valuable, but only if its findings are both communicated and applied. There is little value in my carrying on a twenty-year research into methods of teaching if my findings are never communicated to teachers, or if, after they are communicated, they are never used to improve teaching methods.

It has been suggested that before the nineteen-sixties, few teaching problems had been detected in higher education, and that such problems as arose were not thought worthy of attention. It has even been suggested (37) that the term 'lecturer' for a University teacher (or even a teacher in a College of Education) shows complacency about a long-established technique of communication.

But whatever the name given to the teacher, the art of teaching is a process which has certain vital characteristics. It is an activity in which an individual, aided by certain material resources, initiates students into 'mastery of selected knowledge, or skills, or attitudes'. Therefore (and concept analysis ought to have taught us this above anything else) careful attention must be given to all the components of the process: communication, material resources, the student, and the body of knowledge, skills, and attitudes, which is constantly changing. In particular, the problem of the universities is how to remain centres of intellectual excellence while not becoming out of date in their methods or out of touch with those who attend universities to learn. They must find a balance between being centres of 'innovation and discovery' and centres for the 'communication of learning'.

Even at the level of higher education speech and language are tremendously important. Wise (38) says that everyone speaks because they have been 'exposed to speech' from birth and have imitated it. But because there is no 'coherent speech education' in Britain, we are not entitled to assume in the potential teacher speech powers effective for anything beyond ordinary conversation. If there is no power beyond this, we must ask, 'Is this power sufficient to communicate successfully in the classroom or lecture-room?' If the answer is 'No', the question follows 'Ou we not to discover the "need" of such people and reduce the need appropriate education and training?' As evidence for what he is saying, Wise states that in his own Education Department, thirty-three per cent of the graduates training to teach had speech which was in some way or other unsatisfactory for classroom communication.

Relevant to our present problem is that body of research into 'climates of teaching' which seeks to decide whether 'authoritarian' teaching, 'democratic' teaching, or 'laissez-faire' teaching is most effective (39). Such research shows that a 'power figure' (any authoritarian or doctrinaire teacher, at any level from primary school to university) obtains compliance from the learners; they submit to his 'power position'. But more ingenious forms of control are necessary within his group when he is absent. His pupils become so dependent on his power or authoritarian manner that in his absence they are unable to regulate their own learning behaviour.

If, on the other hand, the teacher does not exert all his power but encourages partial activity from the group, the members of the group may work more slowly and show more confusion, but they become very concerned to learn and they work enthusiastically. As we have seen already in this chapter, the questions here are 'What do they learn?' and 'How far can they be "left to their own devices"?'

The important thing is not to give an answer to this question in this book. Far more vital is to show that child-centredness is not something which applies in the infant school particularly, in the primary school also, much less in the secondary school, and not at all in further and higher education (40). That it does so appear is proof of what we said in Chapter 1, that teachers ought not to wear labels and shut themselves in little boxes. Only by becoming aware (and again we emphasize the word) of wider educational problems will such problems be solved.

NOTES AND REFERENCES FOR CHAPTER 4

1 'Child-centred Education', P. S. Wilson in the *Proceedings of the Annual Conference of the Philosophy of Education Society of Great Britain* (January 1969). This journal offers a useful introduction to concept analysis in article form (see also references in the Bibliography).

2 *Anschauung* is a German word which, as Rusk stresses, is difficult to translate simply into English. This is a frequent feature of language and is nowhere better shown than by the Roman poet Lucretius who complained about *patrii sermonis egestas* (poverty of vocabulary in his native tongue), by which he meant a lack of terms in Latin capable of expressing exactly, and without ambiguity, concepts from Greek science.

In *Doctrines of the Great Educators*, R. Rusk (Macmillan 1957), Rusk translates *Anschauung* as 'intuitive apprehension', and says that it is used to refer to 'immediate experience of objects'. This process eliminates anything which comes between the learner and his experiences in the form of a 'mediating agent', including the teacher and even language (which is symbolism). Readers will find Rusk's Chapter 9 both interesting and useful.

3 Jean-Jacques Rousseau (1712–1778). His main political work, namely, *The Social Contract*, and his main educational work *Émile*, were published in 1762. The subtitle of *Émile* is 'On Education', and it consists of five books. The 'Everyman' translation gives a good introduction to Rousseau, as does Chapter 8 of *Doctrines of the Great Educators*. Students whose knowledge of French is good may wish to look at some of the more famous passages (quoted by Rusk) in the original. Friedrich Froebel (1782–1852), the 'Father of the Kindergarten', famous for his work *Die Menschenerziehung*, which was translated in 1887 by W. N. Hailmann, and published by Appleton. Rusk devotes Chapter 11 of *Doctrines of the Great Educators* to Froebel. It is important to note that, although he is associated with 'play' and its educative uses, Froebel said that boyhood was a time for work. This balanced idea is often conveniently missed by the pro-Froebel school. There is a College of Education for the training of teachers in Froebelian methods.

Heinrich Pestalozzi (1746–1827), famous for his book *Wie Gertrud Ihre Kinder Lehrt* (*How Gertrude Teaches her Children*), sub-titled 'An Attempt to Help Mothers to Teach their own Children'. A well-known translation is that of Holland and Turner, the second edition of which was published in 1894 by Swann Sonnenschein (now Allen & Unwin). Students who are proficient in German may wish to look at the original, to see what the style is like. Rusk devotes Chapter 9 to Pestalozzi, whom he describes as 'a sorry figure' among the great educators. Maria Montessori the only 'great educator' in Rusk, apart from Dewey, who lived on into the twentieth century. Her famous work was *Il metodo della Pedagogia Scientifica* (*The Method of Teaching Scientifically*). The book was translated by A. E. George (with additions by the author) under the title *The Montessori Method: Scientific Pedagogy as Applied to Child Education in 'The Children's Houses'*, published in 1912 by Heinemann. Montessori was famous for devising methods of teaching defective children and then applying these methods to normal children. A feature of this was 'arithmetical apparatus', which has much in common with such modern devices as 'Cuisenaire rods'. Before Montessori little was done for mentally defective children. It is interesting to note that in 1905 the famous Binet (intelligence) test appeared in France, the aim being to introduce a scientific measure of mental deficiency and to ensure that the right children were assigned to 'special schools', the forerunners of the present schools for the educationally subnormal (E.S.N.). Rusk's Chapter 12 is devoted to Montessori.

4 'The Enlightenment', sometimes known by the Latin name *Illuminati* (the enlightened ones). The movement belonged to the eighteenth century (time of Rousseau) and was a group of free-thinkers and literary writers in France and Germany. It aimed to free the human mind from the tyranny of ritualistic religion on the authority of reason. It was a sceptical (even atheistic) movement and numbered in its ranks Hume (see *History of Western Philosophy*), Gibbon (author of *The Decline and Fall of the Roman Empire*), and Voltaire. It opposed the absolutism of the Church and despotism in society.

5 To Piaget, an 'operation' is logical thinking, as accepted by a logician. Thus when he talks about 'pre-operational' thinking, he means that the child can reason in a particular way, but that the way would not qualify for the title 'logical thinking' as adults understand it. This, however, is a great advance

on the old idea that logical thinking did not begin until the age of eleven. Because of this, the philosophy of the Primary School was to cram the mind with information so that the learner would have the necessary raw material on which to exercise his logical thinking at the secondary level. In the period of 'concrete operational thinking', the years from 7/8 to 11/12, the child is capable of adult logical thinking, but requires the help of concrete objects. He is still not able to reason in terms of ideas only, but requires things which he can see and touch to assist his thinking.

6 *Social Class Influences upon Learning*, Allison Davis (Harvard University Press 1948). This is an excellent little book. It is to the point and extremely easy to read, but contains a tremendous number of useful (and often unsuspected) facts. One important feature is the section on 'culture-bias' in intelligence tests, i.e. the extent to which tests of intelligence favour middle-class children and penalize working-class children. All students are warmly recommended to read the book.

7 Johann Friedrich Herbart (1776–1841), famous for his work *Allgemeine Pädogogik* (General Principles of the Science of Education Psychologically Deduced from its Aim). The work was translated by H. M. and E. Felkin as *The Science of Education* (Swann Sonnenschein, now Allen & Unwin, 1904). The thinking of Herbart, who was Professor of Philosophy *and* Education, is a great deal more complex than is that of Rousseau, Pestalozzi, and Froebel. The beginner will find Rusk's Chapter 10 a useful starting point.

8 *An Essay on the Content of Education*, E. James (now Lord James of Rusholme). Although written within five years of the 1944 Education Act, the book poses problems to which complete solutions have still not been found in the realm of comprehensive education and the curriculum.

9 *The Fight for Education; A Black Paper*, ed. C. B. Cox and A. E. Dyson (The *Critical Quarterly* Society 1969). This was followed by a second publication *A Black Paper on Education; The Crisis in Education*, with the same people as editors.

10 The essay was entitled 'Have the Arts and Sciences Conferred Benefits on Mankind', and the competition was held in 1750.

11 *Groundwork of Educational Theory*, J. S. Ross (Harrap 1942).

12 The idealists emphasize the spiritual side of man's nature, and at times verge on the metaphysical world in thinking of the aims and content of education. They are concerned with the infinite potential of man as suggested in Sophocles' chorus 'What a wonderful thing is man. . . .' For a recent work on idealism, see *Idealism in Education*, D. J. Butler, Harper & Row, 1966.

13 This idea was popular with Erasmus, the great Renaissance thinker. It must be remembered that he based his educational work on Quintilian's *Institutio Oratoria*, which gave what was to become a most influential account of the education of the orator, who was to be *bonus orator dicendi peritus* 'a good man skilled in speaking'. There was thus a moral as well as an intellectual tone to the treatise. In the Renaissance, the works of Quintilian became available to the western world, and greatly influenced the thinking of Erasmus.

14 *Text-Book in the History of Education*, P. Monroe (Macmillan 1925). The book is now difficult to obtain, but is a fine one, dealing with education from ancient China to the present day.

15 See also 3 above.

16 *Truth and Fallacy in Educational Theory*, C. D. Hardie (Cambridge University Press 1942).

17 *An Introduction to Philosophical Analysis*, J. Hospers (Routledge & Kegan Paul 1956, 2nd edn 1967). An excellent book for those with considerable experience of philosophy, but certainly not a 'beginner's book'.

18 *A History of Western Philosophy*, referred to in the notes and references for Chapter 1 and on a number of other occasions.

19 *Authority and Freedom in Education*, P. Nash (John Wiley 1966). See also the chapters on these concepts in the present book.

20 See *Plato's Theory of Education*, R. C. Lodge (Routledge & Kegan Paul), p. 10. 'In the wider, or more generic sense, education is used as equivalent to "experience", the experience of a living organism interacting with its normal environment. An insect, such as a bee, an animal such as a horse or dog can learn from experience. . . . So also with human organisms. Falling in love, being stung by mosquitoes, losing money on the Stock Exchange are "experiences", which are, in this wider or generic sense, highly educative".'

21 'Instruction and Learning by Discovery', R. F. Dearden. One of a series of articles in *The Concept of Education*, ed. R. S. Peters (Routledge & Kegan Paul 1967).

22 *Language Teaching; A Scientific Approach*, R. Lado (McGraw-Hill 1964).

23 *Teaching Foreign Languages in Schools*, Caleb Gattegno (Educational Explorers 1963).

24 See R. F. Atkinson Chap. 41, 'Instruction and Indoctrination', in *Philosophic Problems and Education*, ed. Y. Pai and J. T. Myers (Lippincott): '[INSTRUCTION] is essentially a rational process, both at the giving and, in so far as it is successful, at the receiving end. . . . No higher degree of conviction is sought than is warranted by the nature of the support available. Not conviction itself but justified conviction, rational assent is the aim.'

25 'Social Class and Linguistic Development; A Theory of Social Learning', by B. Bernstein, one of a series of essays in *Education, Economy and Society*, ed. A. H. Halsey, Jean Floud, and C. A. Anderson (Free Press 1961). This essay is most interesting, because it again shows how easy it is for error to arise when we use language as a means of communicating ideas. It is further evidence that the emergence of concentration on language in the twentieth century, as exemplified by linguistic analysis, is not accidental.

26 This is John Wilson, and must not be confused with P. S. Wilson mentioned at the beginning of this chapter. John Wilson contributed an essay to the symposium edited by T. H. B. Hollins, *Aims in Education; the Philosophical Approach* (Manchester University Press). The essay is entitled 'Education and Indoctrination'.

27 'Non-Directive Education' by Christopher Jarman, *Education for Teaching*, Journal of the Association of Teachers in Colleges and Departments of Education (Spring 1969).

28 'Needs and the Needs Curriculum', B. Paul Komisar, in *Language and Concepts in Education*, ed. B. Othanel Smith and R. H. Ennis (Rand McNally 1961).

29 *Teaching French; An Introduction to Applied Linguistics*, R. L. Politzer (Blaisdell Publishing Co. 1965). For further discussion of prescriptive and descriptive rules in language, see *Latin by Stave Analysis; A Linguistic*

Approach to Grammar and Translation, H. Schofield (Educational Explorers 1969), with a foreword by Caleb Gattegno.

30 *Half Our Future,* also known as the Newsom Report (H.M.S.O. 1963).

31 There is a great deal of highly technical literature on the nature of human abilities. One of the best books for students in Colleges of Education (but still fairly technical) is *The Structure of Human Abilities,* P. E. Vernon (Methuen 1950). For those who prefer individual articles, there is *Intelligence and Ability,* ed. Stephen Wiseman (Penguin Modern Psychology 1967).

32 'An Essay on the Content of Education.' See 8 above and notes and references for previous chapters.

33 The *Gestalt* school of psychology was originally a school of 'perception theorists'. The word *Gestalt* is the German for 'shape' or 'whole'. The basic belief of the school is that human beings perceive shapes or wholes, not isolated individual lines, marks, etc. We do not, when confronted with what appears at first sight to be a random group of lines, think to ourselves, 'That is a random group of lines'. We find that the lines represent a definite shape or configuration, e.g. a house beginning to collapse. This shows that the sense of sight does not act in isolation. Sense data (in the instance above, the sense data consists of lines) is fed into the brain which 'interprets the data'. In the same way, light which passes through the lens of a camera reacts with the film inside the camera. It is not the light in isolation which is responsible for the negative which eventually becomes a photograph.

The brain interprets the data fed into it in terms of the past experience of the viewer. Thus different people may 'see' different things when they look at the same collection of lines.

Transferred from the province of perception to the province of learning, *Gestalt* psychology says that problems are not isolated stimuli which evoke isolated responses, or even series of stimuli which evoke habituated responses. Instead, when we are faced with a problem, we draw on past experience in an attempt to produce a solution. If this is not readily available, we may indulge in trial and error or random behaviour. Then suddenly we see 'in a flash' the solution to the problem. This flash is insight or understanding. We see the whole problem situation and the solution clearly. Again the emphasis is on 'wholeness'.

Probably the most famous example of *Gestalt* psychology is the series of experiments with apes conducted by Wolfgang Köhler. These are described in a fascinating Pelican book entitled *The Mentality of Apes.* Further information can be obtained from a book already mentioned in a previous chapter, *Theories of Learning* by E. Hilgard. Previously we said that the book was very advanced and difficult to follow. This was partly because of the mathematical concepts involved in behaviourist learning theory. Mathematical concepts are absent from the account of *Gestalt* psychology, which, consequently, is considerably easier to read and understand.

34 *Social Class Influences upon Learning.* See 25 above.

35 The Latin word *prudens* means 'wise'. It is from this that the word 'prudential', as used by Wilson, is derived. The term therefore means 'showing wisdom' and, here, 'showing wisdom on behalf of someone less experienced'. We have argued in this chapter that the child does not know what is 'good for him'; he does not know what his 'needs' are in relation to the 'needs' of society. Consequently the teacher must interpret both sets of needs and

teach each individual so that the two sets of needs are reconciled. In so doing, his behaviour is 'prudential'. He knows what is good for each individual, because of his greater experience.

36 See *University Teaching in Transition,* ed. David Layton (Oliver & Boyd, 1968). This is a useful book and not difficult to follow. It consists of a series of articles and the emphasis is essentially practical. It is written by university teachers who are aware of the problems of communication and the unrest which can stem from faulty communication.

37 See also 36 above.

38 'Talking to Large Groups', Arthur Wise, in *University Teaching in Transition.* See also 34 and 35 above.

39 The classic researches in this area are those of Lippitt and White. Other useful findings are those by Coch and French. Readers who wish to find accounts of both groups of investigations should see *Basic Studies in Social Psychology,* H. Proshansky and B. Seidenberg (Holt Rinehart 1965).

40 Further Education refers to education carried on in Colleges of Further Education (the old technical colleges). Higher education refers to education carried on in Universities, institutes with university status, and Colleges of Education (formerly teacher training colleges).

Link Chapter

AIMS

Chapter 5

The Concept 'Aims'

It is appropriate to make the subject of the first 'link chapter' the concept 'aims' for three reasons:

Firstly, when we analysed the concept 'education' (in Chapter 2) we looked at a number of definitions. Some of these *implied* what the aims of education were, at least for the people who put forward the definitions. The implication was in the wording of the definition. Thus when Plato wrote, 'I mean by education that training . . .' he was really saying that for him the primary aim of education was 'to train'. Similarly when Ducasse gave the etymological definition, he was really saying, 'The aim of education is, by derivation, to "lead out" the powers, capacities, etc. of the young child'. We criticized this aim in the first section of Chapter 4, when we considered 'education according to nature'.

Even when we abandoned the idea of defining education, and suggested Peters' three criteria, we were really implying 'aims' when we stated the criteria. For example, the first criterion stated that 'education implies the transmission of what is worthwhile'. This could be simply expressed in terms of 'aims' as 'One aim of education is to transmit what is worthwhile'. Again, the second criterion, that 'education *must* involve knowledge and understanding', is definitely *prescribing* an aim and could be reworded as 'Education *must have* as one of its aims the imparting of knowledge and the development of understanding'.

Secondly 'aims' link together what we said about the concepts 'education', 'training', and 'child-centredness', in the first trilogy, with what we shall say about 'culture', 'curriculum', and 'liberal education', in the second trilogy. There is a close connection between the aims of education and the content of education. Since the content of education in school is the curriculum, what we say about aims will serve as a bridge between 'education' and 'curriculum'. Two examples will show the connection clearly.

The definition of education by Plato which we have just recalled, shows that he regarded education as having a moral aim: to produce good citizens. The aim affected the content, with the result that children were to be allowed to see only examples of good conduct from their parents, teachers, and nurses. They were to be allowed to read only good literature, that is, literature which showed them examples of good behaviour. A moral aim required a moral content or a moral curriculum.

Education in ancient Japan aimed to produce sound character. It aimed to make the individual respect his father and mother, be obedient, and live an orderly life. Therefore the content which would make the achievement of this aim possible consisted of the Confucian principles of morality and *Samurai* etiquette. Calligraphy (the Greek words mean 'beautiful handwriting') was thought to develop character. Therefore Japanese children spent many hours in school developing beautiful handwriting and developing their character. In 1870 (1) Japan changed the aim of her education, for she now aimed to become a world-ranking economic power. The change of aim brought a change of content. The content of Japanese education is now technological, because the aim of that education is to produce technological supremacy.

Thirdly, the concept 'aims' gives us an opportunity to apply not only concept analysis, but also linguistic analysis. The former analyses the term 'aim' or 'aims'; the latter analyses expressions in which these terms appear. The reader has now had considerable experience of what concept analysis involves, and will be able to deal effectively with the strict linguistic analysis. By applying linguistic analysis to statements containing the concept 'aim' or 'aims', we shall gain greater understanding of the concepts themselves.

FOUR STATEMENTS OF AIM(S) EXAMINED BY LINGUISTIC ANALYSIS

At the start of this chapter we used different expressions containing the term 'aims'. We did this deliberately to produce different emphases. In the first criterion of Peters, we found the expression, 'that education *implies*'. Making a positive statement of aim out of this implication we said: 'One aim of education is ...' But to convey the idea that Peters intended when he used the word 'must' in his second criterion, 'that education *must* involve knowledge ...', we used the word 'must' in our expression of aim. We then said: 'Education *must have* as one of its aims the transmission of knowledge'.

This second type of expression is prescriptive. In Chapter 4, we said that prescriptive statements tell us what *must* be done, just as the doctor when he 'prescribes' tells us what drugs we *must* take in order to become well again. The opposite of 'prescriptive', we remember, is 'descriptive'. We can prescribe the aims of education by using a prescriptive statement; we can describe the aims of education by making a descriptive statement. Again, a simple illustration will help to make this point clear.

In English we endeavour to avoid splitting the infinitive. We say 'to learn quickly' instead of 'to quickly learn'. In the second expression, 'quickly' splits the infinitive 'to learn'. Now, we may say: 'In English we *do not* split the infinitive.' This is a descriptive statement; it 'describes' what people do not do when they speak or write English. But we may also say: 'You *must never* split the infinitive in English'. This is a prescriptive statement. It is a command telling us what we *must not do* when we speak or write English.

Now it is possible that both expressions will achieve the same end. We may convince some people not to split the infinitive by saying that people do not do so. We may have to forbid others to split the infinitive to achieve the same result. This is a very important point. The reader will need to recall it in a little while when we talk about the 'external' and 'internal' aims of education. But before we do that, we must look at four ways of expressing the idea of 'aim' or 'aims'. These are:

THE AIM OF education
THE AIMS OF education
AIMS OF education
AIMS IN education

By examining each in turn, we shall see the significance of the wording. We shall see whether it is more meaningful to use one rather than the others. But because we now know that linguistic analysis examines words only to clarify the ideas which the words represent, we shall find that the examination helps us to understand better the concept 'aims'.

'THE AIM OF education' is prescriptive. It is dogmatic, too. There is a toughness about the expression. There is a 'categorical' air about the statement as there is about the statement, 'There is only *one way* to succeed'.

However, Perry (2) warns us that categorical statements of aim in education are dangerous. They result in education being 'over-directed' and 'over-determined', and cause a narrowness such as that seen in Spartan education, Jesuitical education, and Calvinistic education. We have seen that Plutarch described Spartan education as aiming to produce warriors. The Jesuitical education consisted of *one* content, taught by *one* method, to achieve *one* aim. Calvinism taught that some were born to salvation, others to damnation, and Calvinistic education was correspondingly rigid. We must ask ourselves, in these cases, whether the process which the Spartans, the Jesuits, and the Calvinists called 'education' would match up to the three criteria which we have accepted. In some cases, over-determined education comes close to 'indoctrination'. Nothing is likely to produce over-determined education more quickly than the form of statement, 'THE AIM OF education is . . .'

Monroe, speaking of the aim of primitive education (3), writes: 'The aim of education (if an aim can be spoken of where the process is unconscious) is to adjust the individual to his material and immaterial environment through established or fixed ways of doing things in regard to both work and worship.'

It is interesting to analyse the wording of this statement of aim. In the first place, it appears that it could be expressed in a much shorter form such as:

'The aim of primitive education is to produce adjustment.'

But we now find the same sort of difficulty that we encountered when we tried to reproduce a simple unitary definition of education comparable in simplicity to 'an adverb is a part of speech'. Here, we found that 'part of speech' was an insufficiently clear term. In our shortened form of Monroe's definition of primitive education's *single aim*, the term 'adjustment' is similarly imprecise. To clarify it requires an expansion of the shortened statement to:

'The aim of primitive'education is to produce adjustment to a traditional physical life and a traditional spiritual life.'

Monroe also quotes, as an example of an expression of the single aim of education, Sturm's (4) statement: 'The aim of education is piety, knowledge, eloquence.' Again we can say that the aim is 'to produce adjustment', since all three concepts, 'piety', 'knowledge', and 'eloquence', would be needed in Sturm's day. However, 'piety' again represents a spiritual emphasis which is not necessarily present in the other two concepts. Where primitive education stresses 'physical' and 'spiritual', Sturm stresses 'spiritual' and 'intellectual'.

The highly prescriptive expression of aim results, then, in one of two things, either in two aims masquerading as one, or as one aim expressed in such vague and general terms that it is virtually meaningless. Such an expression might be: 'The aim of education is to prepare the individual for life'.

'THE AIMS OF education', using the term in the plural, is also prescriptive. It is less dogmatic than the first expression, and we are not so aware of any toughness in it. We do not drop the definite article as we shall see happens in the third and fourth expressions. Nevertheless, we imply several generally accepted aims instead of only one. Instead of saying: 'There is *one aim* of education, and *this is it*', we are really saying: 'People generally agree that there are a number of aims of education; *these are they*'.

It is certainly more promising to use the plural term in at least one respect. We have seen that the three criteria which we accepted imply at least two aims. It would not, therefore, be possible to reconcile the three criteria with the prescriptive dogmatic statement, 'THE AIM OF education'. Again, it is possible to see that education everywhere may have one specific aim. It is equally plain to see that this could not be *the only aim* of education everywhere. An example will make the distinction clear.

O'Connor (5) argues that one of the aims of education in all societies is 'to provide a minimum of basic skills'. We can appreciate that this applies as much in a primitive society as it does in our own. The Polynesians, through their education, may aim to provide the young with the skills of fishing, sowing seed, and building huts. In our society, we may regard the skills of reading, writing and counting as the basic minimum. If we use the expression '*the aim of* education' instead of '*the aims of* education', we are compelled to say: 'The aim of education is to provide a minimum of basic skills', which means that there is virtually no difference between Polynesian education and our own. The skills taught may differ, but once we have taught those skills, we have completed 'education' in both communities.

We are at once reminded of the distinction which we made when considering 'education according to nature'. This distinction was between 'the necessary life' and 'the comfortable life'. The necessary life was the life of survival, which is achieved for the Polynesian by teaching him the skills of fishing, sowing, and building a hut. It makes no allowance for transmitting what is 'worthwhile', which is so much a feature of the comfortable life. By accepting the criteria of Peters, we must also accept the form of statement, 'The *aims* of education'. We may then say, in connection with our own society, 'The aims of education are the provision of a minimum of basic skills and the transmission of what is worthwhile'. This is a prescriptive statement. Less prescriptive than either 'The aim of education *is* . . .' or 'The aims of education *are* . . .' would be, 'The aims of education *include* . . .'

At this point it is appropriate to move to the third form of statement: 'AIMS OF education'. At once we are aware that the statement is not in the least dogmatic; it is not prescriptive. It is neither prescriptive nor dogmatic because we have dropped the definite article. This form of expression is the one suggested by 'The aims of education *include*'. Indeed, we can call this non-prescriptive expression 'inclusive'. The use of the definite article in the prescriptive expressions implied 'exclusion'. In the first form of expression, we were saying 'This is the aim of education' to the exclusion of all others. In the second prescriptive statement we were saying 'These are the aims of education' to the exclusion of all others. If we adopt the wording 'aims of education', we can expand it to 'Some of the aims of education are a.b.c.d.e.', or 'A.b.c.d.e. are aims of education'. In neither case is there any toughness in the statement which makes it impossible for the listener or reader to suggest other aims which are not given by the writer or speaker.

We must now return for a moment to part of Monroe's statement about the aim of primitive education. He said in parenthesis 'if an aim can be spoken of where the process (of education) is unconscious'. This is a very important statement. It is so easy to confuse 'aims of education' and 'what people seek to achieve by education'. Let us take two simple examples. We often hear people talking about present-day education and saying: 'Education nowadays aims at equality of opportunity'. This implies that something in the process called 'education' is directed to bringing about equality of opportunity. But in Chapter 2 we said that education was a process of initiation, and that some individuals benefited much more than others from this initiation. This suggests that education cannot be said to aim at equality of opportunity. What the speaker really means is: 'People wish to produce equality of opportunity *through* education' or, 'People with particular ideas and beliefs in our own time are anxious to give greater equality of opportunity in education'. This means that such people want everyone to have an equal chance to obtain and benefit from education.

The second example is similar to the first. We often say that 'education produces social mobility'. This again implies that there are certain characteristics in the process to which we give the name 'education' which result in social mobility. These characteristics of education enable a working-class boy to obtain entrance to Oxford, to obtain a first in Classics, to join the administrative grade of the Civil Service, and to move from working-class to middle-class status. As in the first example, what the speaker really means is that we have made social mobility possible by throwing open educational opportunities to all those who have the ability to profit from them. These opportunities depend on the person's academic ability, not on the ability of his father to pay the fees to buy him an education.

We have given these two examples for a very good reason. Such loose use of language can result in 'equality of opportunity' and 'social mobility' being described as 'aims' of education, whereas in fact they are 'results' of education. They may also be an indication that 'aims' of *educators* have been fulfilled; they cannot be described as 'aims of education'. Although we have ceased to use the tough form of expression seen in 'The aim of education' and 'The aims of education', we must be no less rigorous in our thinking and in our analysis of statements. Because a process (in this case, education) produces certain results when used by certain people in a certain way, it does not mean that these results are what the process *aims* to achieve.

If we go back for a moment to Sturm's statement of the aim of education, we can see clearly the importance of what we have been saying. He said that 'The aim of education is piety, knowledge, eloquence'. If we match up a process which has this aim with the three criteria, we see at once that the only term which will unquestionably remain is 'knowledge'. The other terms will remain only if they can be shown to come under the heading of 'worthwhile activities'. A moment's thought will show that except in a very narrow sense for a small section of modern society, they do not. We have seen the strengths and weaknesses of three of the four expressions. At the same time we have been obtaining a clearer understanding of the concept 'aim' or 'aims'. There remains only the fourth statement.

'AIMS IN education' differs significantly from the other three forms of expression. In this form alone, the word 'of' is replaced by the word 'in'. When we analysed the first two expressions, we suggested that the use of the definite article was the reason why they were prescriptive and even dogmatic. Furthermore, this feature was increased by the use of 'of' in combination with the definite article.

There is another important consequence of using the word 'in'. In the first three expressions, there was an implication that 'aims' were something outside education, something even towards which education was directed. Aims gave direction to education.

Peters suggests that aims are only 'external' to education, because certain people have seized on things which education 'does' and have made them things which education 'must do'. If we talk about 'aims in' education, we are making a descriptive statement ('We *do not* split the infinitive when we write or speak English'). When we take these things outside education, we make them aims by saying that education *must do* them. This is a prescriptive statement ('You *must not* split the infinitive when you write or speak English'). We said, when we first examined the two forms of telling people that splitting the infinitive was not the 'done thing', that both forms of statement might result in people not splitting the infinitive. What we now wish to know is, can we achieve what we want to achieve in education only by prescribing the aims?

Peters goes on to say that 'externalizing' the aims of education and expressing them in the form of a prescriptive statement is merely another way of saying: 'The aim of education is to educate'. For different reasons, because he did not believe in absolutes, Dewey (6) makes a similar statement when he says: 'The aim of education is to enable individuals to continue their education'. It is interesting to note that Dewey uses the first of our four expressions, the highly prescriptive, dogmatic one, but 'to continue their education' is very vague and general.

EXTERNAL AIMS OR INTERNAL PROCESSES?

The answer to our problem is that the situation is different for the experienced and the inexperienced teacher. When experienced teachers educate their pupils, they do it automatically. In the same way, the experienced car-driver drives automatically, and the expert golfer swings his club automatically. To educate, to drive a car, to swing a golf club has become second nature.

But for the beginner in any of these situations, the problem is very different. The teacher, the driver, the golfer, has to be aware of what he is trying to achieve. For him the aims must be *explicit*.

On the other hand, Peters may be saying no more than that the aims of education can be implied from the criteria for education. We have seen this for ourselves, when we made definite statements of aims out of the criteria and their implications. Again, it is useful for inexperienced teachers to make explicit statements of aims rather than to leave them implied in the criteria. By externalizing them, the inexperienced teacher reminds himself of the nature of aims.

The real danger of externalizing aims is that the term 'aim' is then used in a metaphorical sense. The first idea that the metaphor suggests is a 'distant point of aim'. It suggests some point at the very end of a process, and few teachers are involved with the end of the process called 'education'. To help us solve this problem, we must undertake analysis of yet another type of statement commonly found in education – the metaphor.

ANALYSIS OF THE METAPHORICAL IDEA OF AIM AS A TARGET

Scheffler (7) tells us that statements about education may take one of several forms. They may appear as definitions, as slogans, or as metaphors. In careful hands, the first and third types of statement are used deliberately to achieve different purposes. Metaphors can contain educational truths, but it is also possible for them to hide a number of weaknesses. For example, a metaphor must be relevant to the area in which it is used. Metaphors from politics may not be relevant to 'art'. Similarly, and this is most important for our present purposes, all metaphors referring to situations outside education are not necessarily appropriate in an educational context. When we meet a metaphor, we must first recognize it; then we must examine its details to see how many of them match up to the situation under discussion and how many do not. The reader will see that we are here using the same technique that we used when we asked: 'Does this process match up to one, two, or all three criteria for education?' In Chapter 7, we shall ask: 'Does this subject match up to one, two, or three of the criteria which James uses for deciding what shall be the content of the curriculum?'

The metaphor which concerns us here is that of 'aim', which reminds us of a 'target', of a 'rifle range', of a 'marksman' who shoots in an effort to hit the target. The target is always 'one target' and 'at a distance'. If we analyse the details of this rifle range situation, we shall be able to decide

whether it is full of educational truths or whether it h
fallacies.

The marksman aims at a distant target. The target itself is
In the centre is the bull's-eye. The next circle is the 'inner', the
'magpie', and the last one the 'outer'. The quality of aim is determin
the number of shots which land in the bull's-eye. A man who lands all
shots in the bull's-eye is a first-class shot. If he lands in the inner, the
magpie or the outer, or, if he misses the target altogether he is not a
first-class shot. In addition, the shots which miss the bull's-eye may be
'scattered' or 'grouped'. If they are scattered, it means that the aim is
unpredictable, any given shot may land anywhere on the target or miss the
target entirely. If the shots are grouped, they may have missed the bull's-
eye, but their direction is predictable. If they are grouped in the top left-
hand corner of the target, the rifleman can easily correct his aim. He must
aim lower and to the right. The random shot does *not* know how to correct
his aim.

The act of firing sends a bullet towards the target. Once the marksman
has fired, that is, lined up the rifle and squeezed the trigger, he ceases to
have control over the bullet. It is directed towards its destination because
it and the rifle have been manufactured in a specific way. The marksman
has nothing to do with this manufacture. He merely accepts that the bullet
and the rifle in combination will produce the required results, provided
that he can aim straight.

Furthermore, the bullet obeys natural laws while travelling towards the
target and when it hits the solid material behind the target. The fact that
it is flattened and distorted on impact is no concern of the marksman.
His sole concern is where it leaves a mark on the target. This mark enables
others to assess the quality of his aim and shooting and to communicate
this to the marksman. His success is not measured in terms of what he
achieves *for* the bullet but in terms of what he achieves *for himself by
means of* the bullet.

That is, briefly, the picture that the rifle range metaphor brings to mind.
We must now examine the details to see what light, if any, it throws on
the problems posed by the four expressions containing the word 'aim' or
'aims'.

First of all, the target on the rifle range suggests that the expression
'The aim of education' is appropriate. There is only one target and only
one aim However, because this target has different circles on it, the
suggestion is not of a single aim but of a number of aims. This suggests
that the expression 'The aims' is appropriate. It is also in keeping with the
difficulty which we encountered in statements beginning 'The aim of'. We
saw that we either have a very vague single aim – 'The aim of education
is to enable individuals to continue their education' – or else we abandon

he aim of education is piety, knowledge,
l is between 'aims' and the circles of the
n' and the single target. It can be said that
our thinking about aims. The idea of a
r, is somehow not appropriate. Does the
ample, have no aim other than to pass on
school teacher, who achieves the aim for
teen or eighteen, but never knows, except
former pupils, whether those who continue
through higher and further (8) education ever achieve the aim or reach the
target? Again, is it reasonable to say that the aim of education (or the
aims of education) are the same for all these groups of pupils, but that the
process which enables them to achieve the aim is either different, or longer,
or both? It is for this reason that it is, perhaps, less appropriate to think
of 'aims' in the target sense than of 'aims' in terms of 'purposes', 'intentions', and 'focuses of concentration and attention'. Here 'aim' is connected with 'role'. The teacher in the infants school has a specific role.
She is the first person the child meets when he begins formal schooling.
Society, as well as junior and secondary teachers, expects certain things of
the child when he leaves the infants school. Therefore, society and junior
and secondary school teachers expect certain things of the teacher in the
infants school. These expectations largely determine her role. They also
determine the things on which she concentrates attention. Thus, they
determine her 'aims'.

But few teachers in the infants school would think of their aims in
terms of a distant target, of what the child will be when they hand him
on to someone else to receive the next stage of his education. Rather do
they concentrate their attention on day-to-day tasks, and in this way
achieve their aims. In this way, too, the aims can be said to be *intrinsic*
as Peters has suggested.

It now seems as if the 'target' part of the metaphor has only limited
usefulness. The rest of the metaphor seems even less useful. No teacher
can afford to neglect the child passing through his hands as the marksman
can neglect the bullet as it passes through the air. A few children (for
example, delinquents) may reach the end of their schooling 'distorted',
like the bullet at the end of its flight. These, however, are in the minority;
they are rarely the direct result of the teacher neglecting what happens to
them.

Or again, pursuing the same line, the teacher cannot refuse to handle a
child who is not perfect, as the rifleman will refuse to use a bullet or a
rifle which is defective in manufacture. The marksman refuses because he
cannot achieve his 'aim' with defective material. The teacher nearly always
has to achieve his aims with pupils who are less than perfect intellectually,

emotionally or socially. The teacher may be classified as first-class if his pupils are successful in some specific way. But this is not the reason why he is a teacher. He aims to achieve success *for*, rather than *through*, his pupils. Some teachers choose to do this for the most unpromising pupils, such as the emotionally disturbed, the physically handicapped, or the mentally subnormal.

It is possible to argue that education is only narrowly interpreted as what happens in schools, colleges, and universities. According to this argument, no teacher, even at university level, ever sees whether the target is reached by any of his pupils. Each individual embarks on a job or a career, and continues to receive 'education' in some form or other. To this extent the target metaphor is appropriate.

However, we said at the start of this book that our philosophizing would always have some practical implication or application. We have been aware all the time that our readers would be intending teachers or already practising teachers. Consequently we must attempt to arrive at some conclusions about 'aims' for such people.

In the first place, we take Peters' point that aims can be intrinsic to the process of education. But we must remember that Peters is thinking first and foremost as a philosopher. It may well be that experienced teachers, as in our imaginary process described previously, regard aims as intrinsic. However for the beginner it is helpful to take these intrinsic aims out of the process and have a look at them. The experienced teacher has such command of the material of his subject that he teaches it 'automatically'. The beginner often likes to take out the book and refresh his memory. So it is with the aims of education. When the young child learns to read, he first reads aloud. Then he 'internalizes' the sounds and the process, and reads silently. So the young teacher first 'externalizes' the aims of education so that his teaching shall not be 'aimless'. As time goes on, he is not conscious that he is trying to achieve specific things every hour of every day. It is at this stage that teaching becomes more natural. It is natural to read silently, artificial to read aloud. But the natural only *follows* the artificial. It may be philosophically artificial to externalize aims of education, but it is often necessary, as a prelude to internalization and natural teaching.

O'CONNOR'S FIVE AIMS OF EDUCATION

For this reason, we shall attempt to give some definite guidance by closing this chapter with O'Connor's 'tentative' list of aims. The list is *tentative* (9) to avoid the dogmatism which we mentioned earlier. O'Connor is not saying: 'Here are the aims of education'. Because he offers a list of five aims, he is still less saying: 'Here is the aim of education'. Instead, he is attempting to give aims in terms of general agreement. If we took a number of educational experts and showed them O'Connor's list, we would not expect them to disagree violently with any of the expressed aims. At least they give direction and a framework for our thinking. They may represent things which the inexperienced teacher accepts that he *must* do. They may also represent what the experienced teacher finds himself doing, without being consciously aware of striving after external aims. O'Connor's list is:

> To provide men and women with the minimum of skills necessary for them to take their place in society and to seek further knowledge.
> To provide men and women with vocational training that will enable them to be self-supporting.
> To awaken an interest in and a taste for knowledge.
> To make people critical.
> To put people in touch with and train them to appreciate the cultural and moral achievements of mankind.

An examination of these aims refers us back to ideas already mentioned and prepares the way for ideas which will be developed in the next three chapters.

In the first aim, the first half could apply as much to education in a primitive society as in a civilized society; the second half has more direct application in a civilized society. The second aim is not only limited to civilized society; it is also a development of the first aim. When we talked (in Chapter 4) about the need to earn a livelihood, we defined this as an 'acquired', or 'second-order' need of civilized man. Primitive man grows his own food to keep him alive; civilized man earns money with which to buy his food. The primitive boy learns to farm and fish by the old apprenticeship process of 'association, imitation, and practice' (10). In civilized society, the skills of vocational training are so many and complex that the school becomes the agency for supplying them. Not every child follows his father into a job or profession. Civilized society is so complex that we cannot leave the imparting of survival skills to such a chance process as handing on from father to son. In addition, technological skills change so rapidly as to make this impossible, even if it were thought desirable. Furthermore, there is implied in the second half of the first aim Dewey's claim: 'The aim of education is to enable individuals to continue their education'. Education does this by enabling them to obtain further knowledge beyond what they receive in school. Education not only requires individuals to learn; it also teaches them *how to learn*.

The third aim is definitely connected with this. Again it is specific to education in civilized society, 'to awaken an interest in and a taste for knowledge'. At this point we come close to what we said in Chapter 4 about 'motivational needs'. We are also reminded of Peters' warning (in the criteria), that knowledge which is transmitted must not be inert, but must be understood and must enable the learner to develop 'cognitive perspective'. At this point, too, we are reminded that there is a suggestion of deliberately doing these things, which is at variance with the advocates of 'education according to nature' who believe that a taste for knowledge will 'happen' in the normal course of events. Their aim is to see that education does not stifle the development of this interest and this taste, rather than ensuring that they *do develop*.

The fourth and fifth aims both express definite processes: 'To *make* people critical', 'To *train* people to appreciate'. Again we are made aware of the weakness of the naturalist educators who assume that these qualities will develop of their own accord. We are reminded by the aim of 'making people critical' of a specific need. The individual in our society is subjected to so much propaganda, indoctrination, and persuasion that it is in his own interest to make him critical. It is also in the interest of society. Here we have an example of the matching of the need of society and the need of the individual. Finally, when we speak of 'training the individual to appreciate the cultural and moral achievements of mankind', we not only mention concepts to be dealt with in later chapters, we also remind ourselves of that weakness of naturalism, the concentration on the 'necessary life', the fulfilment of 'basic needs'. O'Connor, in his fifth aim, reminds us of Plato's idea of the comfortable life, which has features over and beyond the bare necessities. Education must aim, in our society at least, to cater for both the necessary life and the comfortable life. Teachers at all levels in the educational system contribute in their different ways to the ultimate achievement of these five aims.

Education takes place within society. We shall become even more aware of this after examining the concept of 'culture'. But, the fact that people criticize education for failing shows that they regard it as having external targets as aims. They also have definite views about what these targets should be. Thus education is said to have failed if, as it becomes increasingly available, delinquency increases. We must accept, in the terms of O'Connor's aims, that it has failed to provide delinquents with skills to enable them to fit into society. On the other hand, education is said to have failed when students rebel; yet we have said that one aim of education is to *make* people critical.

Again, while the public at large rarely criticizes education, because people have little aesthetic sense, it does criticize education when people, especially adolescents, appear to lack moral sense. If we accept the fifth aim of O'Connor, we must accept the criticism also.

These factors, and the linguistic analysis of expressions which formed so large a part of this chapter, show just how difficult is the apparently simple concept 'aims' in education. Philosophers may deny that aims should be externalized, and many teachers may not externalize them in their daily teaching. But external critics may not only externalize the aims for the philosopher and the teacher; they may also require them to 'face up to them'. Nor do these external critics necessarily accept that to speak of the 'functions' or the 'characteristics' of a process alters the practical issues. They argue that processes can function badly and that this is the same as failing to achieve their aims. They can also argue that the characteristics of a process can be undesirable characteristics. By accepting criteria for education we must accept that if this is true of the process we call education, it cannot justly be given the name 'education'. If education fails to achieve its aims, it may be said by its critics to have failed. If certain functions are not apparent in the process, the philosopher claims that the process ceases to be education.

NOTES AND REFERENCES FOR CHAPTER 5

1 In 1869, Yukichi Fukuzawa wrote *Seiojijo, The State of Things in Western Countries*. Japan realized the great gulf between her society and education and the society and education of the West. In 1872 there followed *The Code*, and drastic changes took place in Japanese education, which is now highly technological.

It is interesting to note that the first English Education Act with the idea of 'Elementary Education for All' was in 1870. The state had first made itself responsible for education in 1833, replacing some of the efforts of private enterprise (including the Church and individual philanthropists). It is also interesting to note an even quicker educational transformation than the one in Japan. This was in Russia. At the time of the "October Revolution" in 1917 and the overthrow of the old aristocracy and its ideals, three-quarters of the population were unable to read and write. Only in 1930 did 'elementary education for all' seem even remotely feasible in Russia.

2 'Education and the Science of Education', Ralph Boston Perry, of Harvard University, in *Philosophy and Education; More Readings*, ed. Israel Scheffler (Allyn & Bacon, Boston 1966).

3 *Text-book in the History of Education*, P. Monroe (Macmillan 1925).

4 John Sturm (1507–1589), sometimes latinized in the text-books to Sturmius (as Kominsky was latinized to Comenius), was Rector of Strasbourg Gymnasium (our Grammar School) for forty years. R. H. Quick, author of *Educational Reformers*, Longmans Green, 1902, writes that although Sturm had great influence on the classroom, he did a great deal of harm to education. This is an interesting distinction between the two concepts. The reason for Quick's condemnation is that Sturm attempted literally to revive the Roman idea of eloquence, as exemplified by Quintilian in his *Education of an Orator*. Thus Sturm contributed greatly to that 'verbalism' which Rousseau, among others, condemned. This emphasis on Latin prevented boys from learning the mother tongue.

5 *An Introduction to the Philosophy of Education*, D. J. O'Connor (Routledge & Kegan Paul 1957). See also notes and references for Chapter 1, Section 22.

6 John Dewey (1859–1952) lived through a remarkably long and interesting period of history. His life actually spanned the American Civil War, the Crimean War, the Boer War and the First and Second World Wars. He was born only twenty-six years after the first state grant to education in this country and lived to see the Education Acts of 1870, 1902, 1918, 1944. His lifetime almost embraced the Great Exhibition of 1851 *and* the Festival of Britain a century later.

Dewey graduated in philosophy and psychology in 1879. He gained his doctorate in 1884 at John Hopkins University, for a thesis on Immanuel Kant. He was influenced by the thinking of Herbart, who, as professor of Philosophy and Education, said: 'Pedagogy as a science is based on practical philosophy and on psychology'. He was also influenced at this time by Morris, a follower of the idealist Hegel, Torrey, a 'realist' in philosophy, and G. Stanley Hall, an American experimental psychologist who became famous for his writings on 'adolescence'.

In 1886 Dewey became Assistant Professor of Philosophy at the University of Michigan. In 1894 he was offered the chair of Philosophy at the University of Chicago. He accepted only on condition that he be allowed to cover in his research and teaching the fields of education and psychology as well. He now abandoned the idealism of Herbart and Hegel, and came under the influence of the American 'pragmatists' Peirce and James. *Prasso* in Greek means 'I do', and the noun *pragma* means 'a doing'. This school believed that 'what works (when we *do* something) is right'. They believe in 'empirical values' (values determined by 'doing'), not absolute values as do the idealists. For Dewey, education was philosophy, and philosophy was education.

His two most famous educational works were *The School and Society* (1899) and *Democracy and Education* which he wrote during the First World War. Russell agrees (in 1946) with the assessment of Dewey as the greatest living philosopher in America. A professed atheist, he was a gentle and kindly man who influenced political as well as philosophical and educational thinking.

7 *The Language of Education*, Israel Scheffler (Thomas 1960). See especially Scheffler's advice on how to analyse educational metaphors.

8 See notes and references for Chapter 4, Section 38.

9 Remember that Russell uses the word 'tentative' as the opposite of 'cocksure' p. 26, No. 28.

10 The terms 'association', 'imitation', and 'practice' are used by Plato to refer to two things: firstly, the method of supplying the artisans in the Republic with their vocational training; secondly, the method of supplying the Guardians with their early 'moral sense' and later their 'civic knowledge'. In the latter case, the youths of the Guardian class were to be spectators in the assembly or parliament.

In the same way in this country, before the expansion of technical training and the introduction of such measures as the Industrial Training Act, 1964, apprentices used to sit next to the skilled worker and pick up' his skills during their apprenticeship, by association, imitation, and practice.

The Second Trilogy

CULTURE
CURRICULUM
LIBERAL EDUCATION

Chapter 6

The Concept 'Culture'

'CULTURE' : 'EDUCATION' : 'THE CULTURED MAN' :
'THE EDUCATED MAN'

'Culture' is a term which is used almost as frequently as the term 'education' itself, and with as little precise meaning. It is a word which conveys to most listeners a general impression rather than a precise idea. This general impression is of 'doing the done thing', although we are never really clear who determines what is 'the done thing'. Thus we connect the term 'culture' with such activities as reading Shakespeare, listening to Bach and Beethoven, eating and drinking the right sort of things, and always behaving in an 'acceptable way'.

We can see already that there is justification for linking culture and education, since both, to some extent, involve 'doing the done thing'. Moreover, education, as we have seen, is concerned with what is worthwhile, and the examples which we gave in the first paragraph can be described as worthwhile activities.

We can say that the person who performs these worthwhile activities is frequently referred to as 'the cultured man', and also as the 'educated man'. There is a third idea, common to both the others, namely that of the 'gentleman', since the characteristics of the cultured and educated man are also characteristics in the make-up of the gentleman.

We can now see that all three ideas have developed through history. The 'done things' to which we referred have become traditionally accepted. Examination of the past shows that generation after generation has attempted to match up to the vague requirements of the two vague ideas of the educated man and the cultured man. The thing that all such people have in common is the fear of *not* doing the done thing, which they believe will result in public disapproval, or at least in disapproval by that section of the public which sees them doing things that 'are not done'.

Our line of thinking has now led us to see a connection between education, culture, the idea of a gentleman, and the public. We may, if we wish, use the more technical word 'society' instead of 'the public'. From what we have said, it appears that society, at least in part, determines what is culture, and that there is a connection between culture and what is worthwhile. This reminds us that Peters said that 'education implies the transmission of what is worthwhile'. The word 'implies' is interesting here. What Peters is really saying comes very close to what we have said: 'When you think of education, you think of some people handing on values to other people'. This makes even more emphatic the interconnection between education and culture, both of which appear to involve values and transmission.

CULTURE AND EXCELLENCE

There is historical support for the ideas which the word 'culture' brought to mind. In the nineteenth century Matthew Arnold (1) defined culture as 'the best that has been thought and spoken in the past'. Here is evidence that an eminent thinker also considered that culture (like education) involved the handing on of values. He also saw that culture was a cumulative thing. Each generation, when it thought or wrote something that was worthwhile, added something to the existing culture. The idea of 'values' and 'excellence' is equally clear when we think of Newman's (2) definition of culture as the 'pursuit of perfection'. If the reader thinks for a moment of what he has learned about Plato, he will recall Plato's educational ideal for his Guardians. The ultimate aim of their education, which Nettleship (3) describes as the 'ascent to truth', was 'the contemplation of the Good'.

The connection between *élites* and excellence and culture is emphasized by Sir Richard Livingstone (4). After making the point that the spread of democracy will not help 'standards', whether democracy is interpreted in social or educational terms, he writes: 'To call the masses into power is to dilute the existing culture'. We can see in Livingstone's words a reflection of the ideas of Plato. Livingstone later continues this idea by saying that 'life without standards is the most barren life of all, sweet in the mouth but bitter in the belly'.

Matthew Arnold also emphasizes the important connection between culture and right standards. He condemns the upper class members of the public schools of his day as 'barbarians', because of their obsession with sport and physical prowess. At the same time, he condemns the middle class as 'Philistines', because of their concentration on the material aspects of life.

THE SOCIOLOGICAL DEFINITION OF 'CULTURE'

In marked contrast to what we have seen, so far, to be an 'aristocratic' interpretation of culture, is the 'sociological' definition. Allison Davis illustrates this in the following passage (5):

'In its generic sense, culture includes all behaviour which the human being exhibits in conformity with his family, his play-group, his social class, his church and all other human groups.'

Later, Davis writes:

'It is granted, of course, that all inhabitants of the United States learn certain behaviours in common. There are relatively few such common American cultural traits, however, in comparison with the great variety of cultural acts, beliefs, and values which have been differentiated by various social strata in the United States.'

We have now reached a very interesting position. From what has been written above we can see that both concepts – the aristocratic and the sociological concepts of culture – are not necessarily so different as they seem to be at first glance. For example, both interpretations stress behaviour. Davis actually uses the expression 'all behaviour'. When we let our minds think of the ideas which the word 'culture' triggered off, we mentioned specific forms of behaviour such as 'doing the done thing' and 'behaving in a gentlemanly, cultured, or educated way'. Both interpretations refer to a 'way of life'.

Moreover, we talked of values when we thought of the implications of the term 'culture', and Davis also uses the term 'values'. We implied that there is a set of values which determine a type of behaviour known as 'doing the done thing'. Davis says that there are different sets of values, and that these vary according to which social class a person belongs to.

In both interpretations, standards are implied. If we have standards, we demand that people's behaviour measures up to these standards. In exactly the same way we demanded that a process must measure up to certain criteria if it is to be called education. Standards form the basis of a code of behaviour.

THE RELATIONSHIP BETWEEN THE TWO INTERPRETATIONS OF CULTURE

We are now able to distinguish between what used to be called 'Culture' (with a capital C) and 'culture' (with a small c). The first interpretation is that made by Plato, Arnold, Newman, Livingstone, and others; culture (with a small c) is what Davis is describing when she talks about values which vary according to social class. In both cases, culture is linked with a form of behaviour, and with a way of life.

In fact, sociologists now distinguish between the two concepts by using the terms 'culture' (our 'Culture with a capital C') and 'sub-cultures' (our 'cultures with a small c' and Davis's 'cultures which vary with social class'). In education we are often concerned with the basic problem of how to bring the two interpretations together. How do we convey to a slum child the 'gentlemanly' idea of 'the done thing', when his 'culture' gives him an entirely different set of values?

Again, we are reminded of what we said about public language and formal language in Chapter 4. Culture and formal language go together; the sub-cultures and public language go together, at least at the lower end of the social class scale. It seems that we are not very far from an idea which has become familiar to us during the course of this book – the difference between the necessary life and the comfortable life. We can, therefore, extend our combinations of ideas and say that the necessary life, public language and working-class values go together; just as we can say that the comfortable life, formal language and middle-class values also go together. In school, where we try to educate by initiating pupils into knowledge, ideas, and beliefs, we encounter two groups of children. In the first group, there is little difference in their home life between the necessary life and the comfortable life. The values are the same in their necessary life as in their comfortable life, and these values correspond with those generally accepted by society. In the other group, the only level of life in the home is that of the necessary life; there is no time for 'refinements'. Indeed, there is often no money for refinements; and sometimes there is complete ignorance of what refinements are.

We have suggested that standards guide our behaviour. If we behave in accordance with certain standards, then our behaviour is stable and predictable. If we meet a situation today and again tomorrow and then a month hence, we shall react to it in the same way. We react in this way because the standards which we accept demand that we act in one way rather than another. Regularly reacting in this way produces a habitual reaction.

For this reason, it is interesting that Davis, in her definition of culture and extension of the idea in her discussion of behaviour, uses the word 'trait'. In psychology there is a definite connection between habitual responses and traits; a trait can be defined in terms of habitual responses. Peck and Havighurst (6) illustrate this when they talk about 'character traits'. Among the character traits which they list are 'attitude to parents', 'emotional maturity', 'responsibility', and, most important of all from our point of view, 'consistency of personal values'.

It is really this last trait that Culture is trying to transmit. A feature of the cultured man is that he behaves consistently. The behaviour of an 'officer and a gentleman' is in accordance with rigid standards. There may be occasions when an 'officer and a gentleman' would like to strike a lady, eat peas off a knife, or brawl in public, but his code of values will not allow such behaviour. He therefore refrains from indulging in it.

It is also interesting, in the light of our own argument here, that Peck and Havighurst say that the '*primary* source' of character traits is one's family and neighbours. From these we learn our first standards on which our code of conduct will be based. The '*secondary* source' for character traits is institutions. These include first and foremost the school in all cases, the church in some cases, and clubs and similar places where people intermingle and behave in specific ways. In addition, character traits are determined by respected figures. These may be universally respected figures of history, or current idols with less general acceptance, and teachers. In terms of what we have already said, Peck and Havighurst are saying that the first values come from the home and family. Certain values and standards, a certain 'culture' are learned long before the child arrives at school. His character is formed in accordance with these standards and values; his behaviour is determined by these standards; his success or failure is judged by his family in terms of how well or how badly he measures up to the culture of their social class.

The necessary life, then, provides each individual with 'learning patterns' and 'behaviour patterns' before the 'comfortable life' does. The standards of the necessary life include personal cleanliness, eating habits, conduct towards other people, attitudes to authority. These differ with different groups. In some cases the standards which the child brings to school with him help him to settle in school and to learn. In other cases, the behaviour patterns and standards which the child brings with him to school prove a definite hindrance.

The reader will now appreciate further what we said about needs in the sixth section of Chapter 4. There we said that both society and the child had needs. Society determines what are desirable forms of behaviour in all individuals; the school is one of the agencies for producing these desirable forms of behaviour. In some cases no reconciliation is needed between the needs of society and the needs of the child. In other cases there is a tremendous discrepancy. In many cases, the needs of the child are definite lacks or deficiencies. The necessary life has not fulfilled the needs which society imposes. It is then that the school has to 'reduce the needs' by supplying what is lacking.

IMPLICATIONS OF CULTURE FOR CURRICULUM

We can leave this problem for the time being, and concentrate next on those aspects of the concept 'culture' which have definite implications for our next concept, 'curriculum'. We can see at once that the curriculum is the vehicle by which the school communicates elements of the general culture (7). It transmits what is worthwhile; it produces 'awareness of standards'. It does this by reflecting important items of the general culture in the curriculum. The content of the curriculum is therefore concerned with knowledge, beliefs, values. If we think back to the ideas of Plato, Arnold, Newman, and Livingstone, we can see why the Classics were the basis of the curriculum for so long. They represented what was most worthwhile. Through the Classics, the school produced the educated man, the cultured man, the gentleman.

Current changes and proposed changes in the curriculum are attempts to reflect in school changes in the culture of society in general. But there has always been opposition to the inclusion of certain things under the heading of culture. What we have termed the aristocratic interpretation of culture for a long time refused to accept that Science, which was very much a part of our way of life, was 'cultural'. This attitude prevented Science from being included in the curriculum. Even late in the nineteenth century, thinkers like Thomas Huxley (8) and Herbert Spencer were not heeded when they claimed that Science was culture. Spencer claimed that the knowledge which was most worthwhile was Science.

Ross (9) shows an awareness of the problem when he declares that culture has grown gradually. It is a process to which many minds have contributed. Changes in culture are not necessarily the substitution of one thing for another. Each generation receives the culture from the previous generation and makes its own modifications.

Once more we are brought face to face with the real connection between the concepts 'education' and 'culture'. Peters asserts that 'education is initiation'; Ross says that 'we are initiated into culture'. Putting these two ideas in a single sentence we can say: 'Education is a process which initiates each individual into the general culture of society.' By this we mean that we introduce him to certain generally accepted knowledge, certain generally accepted ideas and beliefs. When education ceases, it is often replaced by such less desirable processes as indoctrination. As we shall see (in Chapter 9), indoctrination is also a method of bringing people into contact with beliefs. As we would expect from what we have already seen in this book, education does it in a morally acceptable way; indoctrination achieves its ends in a way that is morally objectionable. Education achieves its ends rationally, indoctrination irrationally.

There is, then, a close connection between general culture, education, and the curriculum. Yet the nature of all three poses difficulties which are well expressed by Ross when he writes:

'But, since the successful absorption of the common culture enables, even impels the individual to contribute to it, it is clear that, the more one succeeds with one generation, the greater will be the task with the next. As the body of culture is increased, the task of education in transmitting it and securing conditions for its general enlargement continually grow more complex.'

In that passage, Ross seems to be saying no more than 'the more complicated life becomes, the more items jostle for inclusion in culture and the curriculum'. With culture there is no problem. We can expand culture almost *ad infinitum*. The problem comes only when we have to decide which items from the culture we require to reflect in the curriculum.

The position, however, is not as simple as that. We miss the whole point unless we realize that if we concentrate too closely on the connection between education, culture, and curriculum, we are in danger of becoming hazy about the actual concept 'culture'. We would then be in the same position as Herbert Spencer's contemporaries whom he so severely criticized.

Spencer says that in his day, people were regularly debating whether Classics or Mathematics ought to be studies in the curriculum. Such people thought that they were attempting to clarify the concept 'curriculum'. Spencer is adamant that they were not. He says that to assume that debating whether Classics or Mathematics is better is the same as answering the question 'What is meant by curriculum?', is as naïve as saying that dietetics consists of deciding whether bread is more nutritive than potatoes. He argues that while few would fall into the latter error, many would fall into the former. Today we hear a great deal about curriculum reform, and analysis of this problem which, as we have seen, is central to education, is most valuable. But there is still a very real danger that such discussion misses fundamental issues, and that at least some of the 'problems' posed are merely the type of trivial issue to which Spencer referred, in contemporary guises.

CULTURAL ELEMENTS WHICH INFLUENCE THINKING TREMENDOUSLY

We suggested earlier in this chapter that the values of culture are those things which have influenced men's thinking. A few things influence thinking *tremendously*. In the same way, many teachers have influenced thinking; few have influenced it as *tremendously* as, for example, Christ did.

Russell uses this type of argument when he considers culture. His arguments also give a very definite answer to the perennial issue: Is science part of culture? and, by implication, to the more recent question, 'Is technology part of culture?' Both science and technology are becoming increasingly greater parts of everyday life. Consequently they affect, to a very considerable extent, what we have referred to as the necessary life. But the question 'Are science and technology parts of culture?' is, as we have seen several times, really asking if they make significant contributions to what we call the comfortable life. Russell declares:

'The triumph of science has been mainly due to its practical utility, and there has been an attempt to divorce this aspect from that of theory, thus making science more and more of a technique, and less and less a doctrine as to the nature of the world.'

There are echoes here of the ideas of Plato. The education of the Guardians was to be in the principles, not in the application, of mathematics and science. When mathematics was applied in the education of the artisans, it was 'tolerated' by Plato. He described this type of education as *banausic*, which can be translated as 'menial' or 'fit only for slaves'. We ourselves saw (in Chapter 3) that techniques and know-how are characteristics of training, not of education. Russell is saying that science has become famous for the very reasons which deny 'cognitive perspective'. Culturally and educationally, science, to be acceptable, must contribute to 'cognitive perspective'. We shall have reason to recall this problem in our next chapter on curriculum.

Although there have been various interpretations of culture or cultural emphases throughout history, Russell implies that *genuine* cultural elements are those which have 'dominated the future from their own time to the present'. Culture was interpreted in rational and aesthetic terms in Ancient Greece; in civic and moral terms in Ancient Rome; as Scholasticism in the Middle Ages; as humanism in the Renaissance; as science by Bacon (10), and later by Spencer and Huxley. Indeed, if we read Huxley we find that culture has been used to describe a very complex process in more recent times, while in the Middle Ages it meant 'saintliness'. The relationship between education, culture, and curriculum has seldom, if ever, been simpler than it was when saintliness was culture. To achieve saintliness one studied theology; to study theology one learned Latin. The reader should bear this simple process in mind when we deal with modern curriculum problems in the next chapter.

But few of these emphases have lasted. Fewer still continue to *dominate* thinking. Many people have contributed to culture, few can be thought to have made contributions which are almost synonymous with culture itself. An example will illustrate this.

Ancient Athens produced many great figures. Two in particular are relevant to the present discussion – Solon (11), the law-giver, and Sophocles (12), the dramatist. When he first produced his code of laws, Solon revolutionized life in Athens. When Sophocles wrote his plays, they had no such revolutionary effect. Yet the name of Sophocles is much more generally known, even today, than is the name of Solon. The impact that he has made on the mind of mankind is incomparably greater. Why should this be so? The answer also answers our question as to what dominates the mind of man and why – in other words, what are the real elements of culture.

In the plays of Sophocles, all human tragedy and suffering is mirrored.

Men and women in modern Birmingham still suffer the same torments for the same reason as did the heroes and heroines and even the lesser characters in the pla · of Sophocles. All that mankind could suffer through mental anguish is shown there. Men and women today can recognize themselves and their problems in the Sophoclean characters, because they are outside the confines of time and place.

To take another example: Russell suggests that Greek architecture still dominates the present. Newman declared that 'culture is the pursuit of perfection', and the Greeks reached perfection (or something very near it) in their architecture. Without the advantages of modern knowledge and modern scientific and technological inventions, they produced buildings of which, alas, only ruins remain. Yet in those ruins there is 'aesthetic perfection', which modern man knows will never be surpassed. Thus the buildings of Greece and the plays of Sophocles have the power to make a deep and lasting impression that the laws of Solon can never match. If we think about this in conjunction with what Russell said of science, we begin to realize why there is such an emphasis on the 'humanities' in any interpretation of culture. And it is not surprising to find the same emphasis in the curriculum.

We have strayed a long way from the issues which we raised at the beginning of this chapter. We attempted there to reconcile an apparently aristocratic interpretation of culture, which stressed certain values and standards, with the sociological definition of culture. The lower down the class structure we went, the less possible it seemed to reconcile the values of general culture with the values of particular sub-cultural groups (13). How do we reconcile the value which says that it is the 'done thing' to read Shakespeare, with the value which says that it is the 'done thing' to watch Liverpool play soccer? People with the latter value have frequently never heard of Shakespeare. If they have he is no more than a name to them.

FURTHER THOUGHTS ON ACADEMIC CULTURE AND CULTURE AS A WAY OF LIFE

In fact, there is a great deal of relevance in what we have said in the later pages of this chapter to the problem of which we have just reminded ourselves. For, in Ancient Greece, life was relatively simple compared with modern life. The aristocrats enjoyed almost unlimited leisure; the artisans, being little better than slaves, had little or no leisure; and the ample leisure of the one class depended on the lack of it in the other. Moreover, there was a tremendous gulf between the learning of the aristocrats and the ignorance of the artisans. The artisans accepted the rulings of the Guardians because they had insufficient knowledge to challenge them. As well might one, who did not know what 'astronomy' meant and had only 'public language' in which to express himself, attempt to challenge the views of the Astronomer Royal on his own subject.

Life in the Middle Ages was even simpler. For both classes the aim was saintliness. The *élite* were able to study theology because of their knowledge of Latin, and thus sought to attain saintliness; the lower orders received an education determined by the *élite*, which sought to help them to achieve saintliness and hence find salvation. Because there was only one way of life, there was only one culture – general culture. Because there was only one way of life and only one culture, there was only one set of values for everyone. The *élite* supervised these values; the lower orders did not challenge them.

However, with the passing of time society has become tremendously complex. There is no longer *one* way of life, no longer *one* set of values, *one* general culture. The spread of education is partly responsible for this. At a certain stage of his development, every infant suddenly realises that he does not *have to* obey the orders of his parents. The automatic reaction is to avail himself of the new found power and to defy his parents. He makes it plain to them that he has no intention of obeying *all* their commands. This is what has happened in society. The worker has become emancipated. The 'boss' can no longer employ his workmen as Greek upper-class families employed slaves. The working man has developed his own ideas, and his own way of life. Even the class-structure has become more complex; sociologists now recognize seven class divisions (14), four of which are for 'white collar workers', three for manual workers (15). When society was simple, the single code of standards which determined behaviour was prescriptive; there was no alternative to accepting it. This is illustrated in some of the books describing the plight of the working man before the advent of the trades unions.

However far we move from the idea of a general culture with a set of values and standards, and sub-cultures with their own values and standards, we are bound to come back to it again. But now we can no longer think of the general culture without thinking at the same time of sub-cultures. A warning, however, is necessary. When (in Chapter 4) we discussed instruction and learning by discovery and formal instruction and education according to nature, we saw that we were not dealing with pairs of alternatives. The educator does not simply have to pick one alternative from each pair. In the case of education according to nature, we saw that one interpretation was meaningless because it seemed not to rise above the lowest level of the necessary life. The aim of education, in this interpretation, was to let the development of the child take its course. The child will 'grow' (if we may use that word) mentally and physically if left to his own devices. Education, we decided, would have little value if its sole aim was to leave the child to his own devices.

Exactly the same applies to the two interpretations of the concept of culture. To say that we can no longer think in terms of a culture like the saintliness of the Middle Ages, which was a single way of life with a simple set of rules for all, does not mean that we can go to the other extreme. We cannot abandon the general culture and say to the sub-cultural groups, 'Live according to your own rules, follow your own devices'. In other words, we cannot say that we are faced with a simple choice between two sets of values – those belonging to culture, and those belonging to sub-cultures. To do so would merely be to offer the necessary life as an alternative to the comfortable life. If the choice fell in favour of the necessary life, we could not, by any stretch of the imagination, speak of achieving progress. We may be aware of something without being entirely governed by it. We can accept that the recognition of sub-cultures is a sign of progress; but this is not the same as saying that in future everyone must be dominated solely by his own sub-cultural behaviour patterns.

King (16), in a chapter called 'Culture Conflicts', suggests that in every country there are now problems of 'divided culture', contradictory interpretations of culture. In our own first chapter, we saw that the word 'philosophy' can be used by different people to mean different things. King says that precisely the same thing is true of the word 'culture'. Even within one society there are inconsistencies. To take a single example; in Britain we tend to assert that the Communist state *imposes* a way of life, and that, because of this, it is evil and denies freedom. Yet the Tzarist system, which Communism replaced, was even more restrictive of freedom. It perpetuated a social system which had been destroyed in France by a revolution over a century before. We have already seen that one school of thought, protesting against the existing system, *in education* replaced the education content of the old authority by another. Yet eventually the new authority fell into the bad old ways of its predecessor. In trying to break down barriers, it merely re-erected the same barriers under another name.

In America there is a very definite culture conflict between two ideals, individuality and conformity. The American constitution says that man has certain 'inalienable rights'. Yet if he takes this too literally, he infringes the liberty of others and acts contrary to the democratic ideal.

In the Soviet Union, the Marxist/Leninist ideal is to abolish class and privilege. In theory this would solve the problem which we set ourselves in this chapter, to reconcile the cultural values of the 'gentleman' and the everyday life values of the lower classes. In theory, the Russian idea would bring the two values together by degrees until they merged and became the basis of one culture. But who will bring about the abolition of class?

The answer is 'The Party'. The question is how will The Party differ from any other *élite*? Will it abolish itself, once it has abolished social class?

Culture conflicts may be symptomatic, not of sickness, but of vitality. To have two parties in a government gives a choice to voters which is not there in states where there are no party politics. One party is there to scrutinize and criticize every act of the other. Much the same situation is present when there are two cultures. It is no less logical for sub-cultures to call into question the long-established values of the general culture than it is to say that one aim of education is to make people critical. When one society condemns the cultural conflicts of another society, it is often only condemning by projection the inconsistencies within itself (17). This is another example of assessing problems in terms of preconceived ideas and biases rather than against the criterion of reason.

We conclude the present chapter in terms of our own society, in which we both live and act as teachers and educators. Through the centuries, different authorities have established a body of knowledge, ideas, and beliefs, to which we give the name 'culture'. The most important single characteristic of this culture is worthwhileness. Its content has a lasting value, whether it leads directly to immediate benefits for individuals or not. In addition, the content of the culture may be useful, because the knowledge which it gives enables individuals to follow a career, or because the ideas which it provides enable individuals to guide their conduct in a way that makes them and others happy. This culture is mirrored in the curriculum and is, therefore, transmitted by education. By handing on the culture, education initiates people into knowledge and ideas which are worthwhile. There is a definite historical connection between the culture which has come to us from the past, and past ways of life. Because culture appears in the curriculum, culture must not be thought to be an entirely academic entity; the idea of the gentleman in culture was once a definite way of life.

In modern complex societies different social classes and groups have characteristic ways of life. One group finds religion a dominant influence, another that politics is equally dominant. The problem is not solved by each pouring scorn on the dominant influence of the other. As so often in this book, we come to the point where we are forced to admit that a crucial factor in the problem is awareness. If society as a whole is forced to accept that there are ways of life characteristic of smaller groups, the smaller groups must also refrain from shutting their minds to the wider culture. It may well be that the task of education is to increase this mutual awareness as the first step to resolving apparent or real culture conflicts. Once it has made the 'lower classes' aware of the values of the general culture, it must not attempt to compel acceptance. If it does this, it ceases to be education. Instead, to gain acceptance for these values it must make them acceptable on rational grounds.

NOTES AND REFERENCES FOR CHAPTER 6

1 Matthew Arnold (1822–1888) was the son of the famous Thomas Arnold, headmaster of Rugby, and a considerable poet. From 1851 to 1883, he held the post of Inspector of Schools. In 1859, and again in 1865, he was sent to the Continent to study the educational systems there, and when he returned, he stressed the importance of reorganizing secondary education in this country. It could be said that the study of comparative education began with Matthew Arnold, received impetus from Kandel before the Second World War, and became prominent as a regular area of study after the end of the war, when world problems emerged in politics and in education.

In 1861, Arnold wrote *The Popular Education of France*, followed in 1864 by *A French Eton*. In 1868 he published *Schools and Universities on the Continent*.

In addition to his official duties as an Inspector of Schools, Arnold was very much concerned with culture. He was Professor of Poetry at Oxford from 1857–1867, and published several works on criticism, including his important *Essays in Criticism* in 1865.

In the last phase of his life, he combined his interest in culture and his critical powers in a critical analysis of the society of his day, as well as of religion in England. These activities resulted in his famous *Culture and Anarchy* published in 1869, in which he described the danger of materialism as exemplified in English society. It is interesting to compare his thoughts on culture as a collection of what is truly excellent, with Plato's idea of absolute values as the important bases of society and of education. Plato stressed these values in reply to the more pragmatic ideas of the 'sophists', who gave lessons for money in politics, mathematics, and rhetoric. As time went on, they laid more stress on cultivating the 'persuasive tongue' than on spreading real knowledge. It is interesting to recall that we said that Quick condemned Sturm for over emphasizing rhetoric, claiming that he greatly influenced the classroom but did much damage to education (in notes and references for Chapter 5, Section 4).

2 John Henry Newman was a slightly older contemporary of Matthew Arnold, having been born in 1801. His name is always associated with the 'Oxford Movement', described by Émile Legouis and Louis Cazamian (*A History of English Literature*, Dent, 1926) as one of the 'fervid streams of philosophical thought in an industrial age'. It will be seen at once that such a movement could fairly be described as 'cultural', and also had in it a note of what might be called social protest against the social effects of the Industrial Revolution.

In 1845, Newman left the Anglican Church and became a convert to the Church of Rome. His emphasis in education was always on excellence, on the intellectual and the academic. He was also a great respecter of 'tradition'. He died in 1890.

3 R. L. Nettleship is well known for a series of *Essays on Plato's Republic*, (Macmillan 1938).

4 Sir Richard Livingstone, an eminent classical scholar and writer on cultural issues. In 1944 he published *Education for a World Adrift*, Cambridge University Press.

5 *Social Class Influences upon Learning*, Allison Davies (Harvard University Press). Several references to this excellent little book have been made in the notes following earlier chapters.

6 *The Psychology of Character Development*, R. F. Peck and R. J. Havighurst (John Wiley 1960). The main purpose of the book was to raise questions about the real effect of present educational and religious practices on the development of character. It is difficult in places, but should be read for the main ideas which it puts forward. See also the issues in our own Chapters 11 and 12.

7 What we referred to, previously, as 'Culture (with a capital C)'.

8 Thomas H. Huxley (1825–1895) is said by Monroe (*Text-book in the History of Education* – see also notes at the end of Chapter 1, Section 25) to have accomplished more for the actual extension of the natural sciences in education than any other Englishman. He was a member of the first London School Board, as well as a university professor. He re-emphasizes the points made by Bacon, that education should be 'realistic'. He is famous for his definition of 'liberal education':

> 'That man, I think, has had a liberal education who has been so trained in youth, that his body is the ready servant of his will, and does with ease and pleasure all the work that, as a mechanism, it is capable of; whose intellect is a clear, cold, logic engine, with all its parts of equal strength, and in smooth working order; ready, like a steam engine, to be turned to any kind of work, and spin the gossamers as well as forge the anchors of the mind; whose mind is stored with a knowledge of great and funda-mental truths of nature and the laws of her operations; one who, no stunted ascetic, is full of life and fire, but whose passions are trained to come to heel by a vigorous will, the servant of a tender conscience; who has learned to love all beauty, whether of nature or of art, to hate all vileness and to respect others as himself. Such a one, and no other, I conceive, has had a liberal education; for he is, as completely as a man can be, in harmony with nature.'

This passage was written before the technique of linguistic analysis was as completely developed as it is today. It is interesting, therefore, as an exer-cise in linguistic analysis. At this point in the present book, the reader has gained some experience of the technique and may like to try to analyse it for himself. Some suggested approaches are given below:

1 Is the concept 'trained' (in line 2) appropriate in connection with 'liberal education'? This problem is dealt with in our own Chapter 8.

2 Is the metaphor of the mind as a machine an apt one? To what extent is this concept in agreement with the ideas of the behaviourists? To what extent was Huxley's choice of metaphor influenced by prevailing condi-tions in his own time? Would the metaphor be even more appropriate in our own time?

3 Is the metaphor of the passions and the will appropriate? To what extent is it similar to Plato's idea about the vegetative, appetitive, and rational parts of the soul, and to Herbart's ideas about the mind and the will?

4 What are the possible reasons for the use of the term 'nature' in the last

quarter of the passage, and to what extent are these ideas in accordance with or at variance with the ideas about nature held by eighteenth-century thinkers?

5 To what extent is the language the objective language of the scientist, and to what extent is it emotive? Where do we draw a distinction between metaphorical language which conceals educational truths and is acceptable, and emotive language, which analytical philosophers would condemn (see Emmet on the 'bewitchment of language').

9 *Groundwork of Educational Theory*, J. S. Ross (Harrap 1942). This was at one time a famous work in teacher training colleges. Readers should look at the book and ask themselves what is the difference between Ross's approach and the analytical approach, and to which writers of the present time Ross can be compared.

10 Francis Bacon (1561–1626) substituted a practical and useful aim in education for the old verbal and theoretical one. Speaking of the education of the past he said:

'Philosophy and the intellectual sciences are adorned and celebrated like statues, but, like statues, are not moved from the spot whereon they stand.'

He believed that education should deal with objects and ideas. A similar viewpoint is expressed by Spencer and Huxley.

11 Solon (*c.* 640–558 B.C.) was a member of an aristocratic Athenian family, who became famous as a statesman and a poet. He effected a *seisachtheia* (or 'throwing off of burdens') by making it impossible to exile people or to make slaves of them if they failed to pay back money which they had borrowed as a mortgage on land. He also reconstituted the *boule* (or senate) and set up the Heliaea as the final court of appeal. The Council of the Areopagus (mentioned by St Paul) was allowed to retain its right to try religious crimes and cases of premeditated murder.

12 Sophocles (496–406 B.C.) wrote 120 plays, most of which have been lost. The seven remaining ones are amongst the most famous of all tragedies:

Antigone (441 B.C.)
King Oedipus (date uncertain)
Electra (date uncertain)
Ajax (date uncertain)
Trachiniae (date uncertain)
Philoctetes (409 B.C.)
Oedipus at Colonus (posthumously, 401 B.C.)

He added a third actor to the conventional two in Greek tragedy, increased the number of the chorus from twelve to fifteen, and greatly developed scenery. In his plots, man's will plays a greater part than it did in the plays of his predecessor Aeschylus. Aristotle says that he portrayed people as they ought to be, while Euripides (the third of the famous trilogy of Athenian dramatists) portrayed them as they are. Matthew Arnold says that Sophocles 'saw life steadily and saw it whole'. Racine has exerted a similar influence in more recent times. The classical scholar Richard Claverhouse Jebb produced translations of the plays which are worth reading in their own right.

13 The technical term used by sociologists.

14 The divisions of the 'General Classification Scale' are:

    Class 1 Professional and higher administrative.
    Class 2 Managerial executive.
    Class 3 Inspectorial/supervisory (higher grade).
    Class 4 Inspectorial/supervisory (lower grade).
    Class 5 Skilled manual/routine grade non-manual.
    Class 6 Semi-skilled (manual).
    Class 7 Unskilled (manual).

For further information about these classes the reader is referred to *Social Mobility in Great Britain*, ed. D. V. Glass (Routledge & Kegan Paul 1954).

15 Strictly speaking, the two main classes – white collar and manual – merge in class 5 (see Section 14 of the notes to this chapter).

16 *World Perspectives in Education*, Edmund King (Methuen 1962). This is a very readable book which should be read. It appears from its title to be a book about comparative education, and it is. But it is a *Philosophical* approach rather than the more usual comparison of educational system in a number of countries.

17 'Projection' (and other 'ego-defence mechanisms') is dealt with at some length in *Assessment and Testing: An Introduction*, H. Schofield (George Allen & Unwin 1972). In projection we see our faults clearly in others and condemn them for them, instead of condemning ourselves.

Chapter 7

The Concept 'Curriculum'

CURRICULUM AND SPECIFIC CURRICULA

For all teachers a study of the concept 'curriculum' is essential to a study of education itself. If we had begun the present book with an analysis of curriculum, we would have covered the same ground as we have covered by starting from education. The reason for this is that curriculum implies 'content', 'aims', 'training', 'worthwhileness', and 'culture', all of which we have considered. In addition, a study of curriculum raises other issues – liberal education, freedom, authority, which we shall meet in later chapters.

However the term that comes most readily to mind when the term 'curriculum' is used, is 'content'. This is variously defined as 'subjects', 'projects', 'areas of study', terms which, as we shall see in a moment, raise the issue of teaching method. This, too, is closely connected with the concept 'curriculum'. Strictly speaking, however, if we talk of method and content and their interconnection, we are thinking of a particular curriculum or of different curricula, for example, the primary school curriculum, the secondary school curriculum, and remedial curricula. The concept 'curriculum', however, cannot be so limited. We have already seen an example of this in the last chapter. There, we began by talking of Culture (meaning the general culture and culture meaning sub-culture). In the same way the concept Curriculum is Curriculum (with a capital C). Specific types of curricula (with a small c) develop from the larger concept. Our experience of linguistic analysis tells us that we must be careful always to distinguish clearly between the two.

Specific curricula imply specific content, specific bodies of knowledge. The larger concept Curriculum implies the general fundamental principles which underly all the specific curricula and help to determine their content, and each specific curriculum can be said to have its own philosophy. This idea of fundamental principles and specific bodies of knowledge is indicated by a sentence from the Norwood Report (1):

'Education ... must be ultimately concerned with values which are independent of time or particular environment, though realizable under changing forms in both.'

It is not difficult to recognize the idea of education and general culture in the first part of this sentence, which mentions 'values independent of time or particular environment', a concept very close to 'what is worthwhile', in the sense used by Peters. Nor is it difficult to recognize the connection between the ideas expressed in the second half of the sentence from Norwood and curricula. The reader might also ask himself with what justification we could use 'Curriculum' where Norwood uses 'education'.

What we have so far said suggests that Curriculum is a concept closely connected with knowledge and values and with their transmission. Specific curricula, then, may be said to be the interpretation by different individuals or by different bodies of what is worthwhile and what must, therefore, be passed on from one generation to the next.

This is in keeping with Peters' suggestion that it is not necessary to give a precise definition to 'worthwhileness' as an idea when he says, in the first criterion, that education implies the transmission of what is worthwhile. Worthwhileness is a general idea, to which different people will give different specific meanings. A member of a primitive community may have different values from someone in a civilized community, but there will be certain characteristics in the values of both which imply worthwhileness.

CRITERIA FOR CURRICULUM

Because of this, it is not surprising that James (2) does with Curriculum very much what Peters did with education. He does not give a definition of Curriculum, nor does he give a list of the areas of knowledge and beliefs which constitute it. Instead he establishes three *criteria*. If we ask what shall be included in the curriculum, we find the answer is whatever measures up to the following criteria, which James refers to as three 'broad headings'. The criteria or broad headings are:

1 That an area of study may contain information which is essential to the business of living.
2 That an area of study may inculcate valuable skills.
3 That an area of study may contribute to the spiritual development of the individual.

The word 'spiritual' is one of the vaguest terms in education. So often we lump together as 'spiritual' all those things which do not fit into any other category. Thus we talk of education as physical, intellectual, and spiritual. The word spiritual, however, has a religious as well as a philosophical connotation, and, in both cases, we connect it with the very difficult concept of 'soul'. The more closely we connect 'spiritual' and 'soul', the more we become lost in those metaphysical regions which we mentioned in Chapter 1. Our aim is to avoid as much as possible going beyond the physical.

Yet there is no need for such thinking. We may quite reasonably use the word 'spiritual' to refer to such emotional aspects as aesthetic appreciation. By so doing we move away from the physical but we do not become

involved in metaphysical speculation. We do not begin to ask such questions as 'What is God?'; instead, we enter the areas of art and music. We
do not need to stray outside conventional areas of the curriculum. Indeed,
spiritual values are often said to come from the humanities, or from literature and the arts.

This is very much the sort of thing that James means when he uses the
word 'spiritual'. In fact he defines spiritual as 'the satisfaction of the
highest intellectual, moral and aesthetic capacities'. We may say, with
some justification, that Plato would have agreed with this idea.

JAMES'S CURRICULUM CRITERIA AND O'CONNOR'S AIMS OF EDUCATION

It is also interesting to see the connection between James's three broad
heads and O'Connor's aims of education. The connection should not be
surprising. We have already said that there is a definite connection
between the aims and the content of education. For our purposes the
content of education is the school curriculum, which reflects and is to a
greater or lesser extent determined by the aims of education. What education aims to do determines what we study. Consequently there is also a
connection between James's three broad heads and Peters' three criteria.
We can show the relationships as follows:

JAMES. That an area of study may convey information which is essential
to the business of living.

O'CONNOR. (Aim 1.) To provide men and women with a minimum of
the skills necessary for them to take their place in society and to seek
further knowledge.

PETERS. That education must involve knowledge and understanding and
some kind of cognitive perspective, which are not inert.

JAMES. That an area of study may inculcate valuable skills.

O'CONNOR. To provide men and women with a vocational training that
will enable them to be self-supporting.

PETERS. (No direct equivalent from the three criteria.)

JAMES. That an area of study may contribute to the spiritual development of the individual.

O'CONNOR. To put men and women in touch with and train them to
appreciate the cultural and moral achievements of mankind.

PETERS. That education implies the transmission of what is worthwhile
to those who become committed to it.

James says that ideally whatever makes up the content of the curriculum ought to match up to all three criteria. If anything does match up to all three, there is little or no possible argument against its inclusion. Latin in the Middle Ages could be said to have measured up to all three criteria. It is partly for this reason that it has survived for so long in changed and still changing circumstances. We saw in the last chapter that James's idea was true of Latin when we examined Huxley's statement that the aim of education in the Middle Ages was saintliness. Latin was a 'tool subject', a vocational skill, because it led to an understanding of theology, which was essential to the business of living. Latin, via theology, also satisfied the highest intellectual, moral and aesthetic capacities.

In modern times we can, and do, argue that Latin is valuable. It falls under Peters' heading of worthwhileness. It may thus be argued that it satisfies James's third broad heading. But it can no longer be argued that it satisfies James's first and second criteria. Nor can it necessarily be argued that it has the unique value in the third sense that it is often claimed to have. It is also interesting to see that it satisfies James's first criterion of 'conveying information that is essential to living for the gentleman'. But historically Latin became associated with *élites*, since it did not serve the same vocational purpose for the majority.

James concludes that the subject most likely to satisfy all three criteria at the present time is the mother tongue. It is significant that native language and literature figures in Soviet education at all levels. The mother tongue is a 'tool subject' (in American parlance), or what we should call 'one of the three Rs'. It conveys information necessary for the business of living, because all information is conveyed to the natives of any country through the mother tongue. Consequently, immigrant groups are underprivileged, or culturally deprived (3) since they receive their information through a language which is foreign to them. Finally, the mother tongue measures up to James's third criterion, because it helps through literature to cater for the highest intellectual, moral, and aesthetic capacities of man.

CURRICULUM CONTENT AND METHOD

We said earlier that there was a connection within specific curricula between content and method, between *what* is taught and *how* it is taught. Ministry Circular 323(4) suggests that an illiberal teaching method may prevent a particular area of study from providing cognitive perspective (to use Peters' term), but this does not mean that the subject itself is illiberal.

We shall deal fully with liberal education in Chapter 8, but we must mention it here very briefly. Circular 323 deals with the problem of 'liberal studies' in technical colleges. This term is generally used to refer to the non-vocational aspects of the college programme. The parallel in the Grammar School is to make the Science students study Latin and the Arts students study Science in order to maintain a balance in the education they receive. The Ministry Circular 323 suggests that this is not necessarily the answer to the problem of how to make a balanced curriculum or to give a balanced education. In our view, the problem is to ensure that further education does not become synonymous with vocational training. The Ministry's suggestion is that a vocational subject or area of study can be made liberal by using methods that are stimulating and enlightening – an interesting point which is worth considering further.

In Chapters 2 and 3, we saw that there are important differences between education and training; and because of these differences we use the two expressions 'the educated man' and 'the trained scientist'. A misunderstanding of the exact difference between the two leads to the error of thinking that teaching Latin to the scientist and science to the classicist *automatically* gives balance. James argues that the scientist can develop something like Peters' 'cognitive perspective' far more effectively through science than by studying Latin in a sixth-form 'cram course'. We recall, too, that Russell maintained that science ceased to be cultural when its reputation rested upon its 'applied values' rather than upon its function as an explanation of the world.

We can now see that there is a connection between what Russell and James and Circular 323 are saying. We can teach science in a severely factual and applied manner, or we can teach it as a vocational subject. In neither case does it measure up to more than one of James's three criteria. In that case, it merits inclusion only as much as any other area of study which measures up to only one of the criteria. In terms of Circular 323, the *way* it is taught robs it of any liberal value. It is tied to a vocational idea.

Similarly, it is possible to teach Latin by the centuries-old method which requires the pupil to learn and recite the grammar. In the early stages, success is largely measured by the ability to parrot this basic grammar. The sole aim of the teaching is to enable the child to undertake the academic exercise known as translation. No interest is aroused by the process; the object is merely to enable the child to pass an examination. He seeks to obtain a facility in Latin because certain university faculties demand Latin as an entrance requirement. It will readily be seen that Latin taught by this method is no more liberal than vocational science. It is absurd to argue that it caters for the highest intellectual, moral, and aesthetic capacities. It is in fact little removed from mental training (5).

The realization of this fact prompts people from time to time to seek new methods of teaching. Nuffield Science is a case in point. Unfortunately, there is a belief that by altering the method of teaching we eliminate *all* wrong thinking, whereas the opposite often happens. There is a very real danger, as James warns, that there will be such concentration on method that content will be ignored. Yet we cannot sensibly consider one without the other. It is as meaningless to dress up inert material in a new method as it is to make material inert by teaching it (transmitting it) badly.

Much damage can be done, and has been done in the past, at the early levels of education. It was believed at one time that the child was not capable of reasoning before the age of eleven. The 'curriculum' of the junior school, therefore, consisted of a number of facts which were crammed into the mind and stored until reason should awake at the age of eleven. Reason was then supposed to act like a bricklayer on the bricks which had been stockpiled throughout the primary school years.

By this process of cramming, we rendered the information inert. In history and geography, we taught concepts of time and space, which meant nothing to the child, because they were outside his experience. We used language beyond the child's understanding. The better pupils were able to form what Peel (6) refers to as 'verbal habits' and to parrot the words when required to do so, on a stimulus-response (7) level. The less bright were completely bewildered by the whole process.

This was often followed at the secondary level by teaching, which was sometimes good instruction, sometimes bad, sometimes even doctrinaire ('This is right, because I say so !').

CURRICULUM AND CULTURE

In Chapter 6, we saw that both Culture and culture (sub-culture) could be referred to as a way of life. We also saw that the second interpretation of culture was much more definite and tangible than the first. The first was nebulous, or, as Peters would say, slippery. We saw, too, that one of the problems facing the teacher was how to reconcile these two ways of life for pupils whose home life contained few of the values and beliefs of the general culture. We are in a similar problem situation with Curriculum and curriculum or curricula. Curricula are implementations of the basic principles within the concept of Curriculum, but we must remember that general principles are not the same as dogmatic instructions. We saw that the establishment of criteria of education gave more room to manœuvre than descriptive definitions which said 'Education is . . .'. When Peters speaks of what is worthwhile, he does not give a list of worthwhile activities and say that anything outside this list is not worthwhile. Such an approach would guarantee absolutism. In the same way, the establishment of principles within the concept of Curriculum, or the establishment of criteria against which to test areas of study for suitability, is not the same as saying, 'The following *shall be* the curricula for primary and secondary schools'. Again we are reminded that the task of philosophy is not so much to provide a simple, easily applied solution, as to examine all the avenues of approach. We have still a long way to go in our analysis of the concept of Curriculum.

The primary school curriculum has become, traditionally, the three Rs. Its content supplies each child with the basic skills of reading, writing, and counting. In a previous chapter we have suggested that these may be called 'survival skills'. Naturally they are more sophisticated than the survival skills in primitive societies. Nevertheless, since later they are basic to earning a living, they have a survival characteristic. James remarks that there has been very little change (or talk of change) in the content of the primary school curriculum. It still retains its basic nature. There is much talk of changes of content in the secondary school curriculum; changes related to the primary school are changes of method (8).

King (9), discussing the increasing demands which technological development imposes on the school, questions whether the three Rs are any longer sufficient as the core curriculum of the primary school, and there are others who appear to agree with him. In recent years, there have been suggestions such as the inclusion of French and science in the primary school, which appear to lend support to King's idea. Others have argued that *all* subjects are only elaborations of the three Rs. In this argument, for instance, French and mathematics are extensions of letter and number knowledge.

We may already have touched upon the solution to this problem, when we suggested that the method by which a subject is taught can be enlightened and enlightening, or dull and depressing. The old method of rote learning in the three Rs can be assigned very clearly to the dull and depressing category. If the new methods are to be effective, they should aim at open-ended teaching. Instead of teaching reading, writing, and counting as skills in themselves, they should be taught in such a way that they are easily applied in many more complex areas. Learning to write, like learning the grammar of a language, is not the end of a process. It is the acquisition of a necessary skill which enables the learner to embark on more intellectually demanding processes. Language enables the learner to express ideas, and it is for this reason that he learns it. Learning language, in the traditional sense, is no more valuable than learning to play the violin. Both involve instruction and drill.

Other people argue that the demand which technology makes on education is in the area of higher-level skills, and this affects secondary curricula. Since the Newsom Report, we have been made aware officially that we cannot afford to have large numbers of children of average and below-average ability leaving school to enter the labour market as unskilled workers. The implication here is that, for these pupils at any rate, the content of education and consequently the curriculum, should have more vocational emphasis than in the past. But it must be remembered that even in advanced technological societies the school must continue to transmit the values of that society. We must avoid the tendency to think of the curriculum solely in terms of *knowledge* to be transmitted rather than of a balance between knowledge to be transmitted and attitudes and beliefs to be developed, values to be established, individuals to be made capable of ultimately emerging as useful and valuable members of society.

For this reason, it is well to remind ourselves that Peters, when establishing his three criteria for education, stressed *first* that education involves the transmission of what is worthwhile, and *secondly* that it involves the transmission of knowledge. Similarly, O'Connor (and we must assume that the order in which he states his aims is not accidental) states that the first aim of education is to provide men and women with 'a minimum of the skills necessary to take their place in society and to seek further knowledge'. Only after that does he state that the aim of education is to provide vocational training.

It is possible to argue that O'Connor is, by this order of aims, thinking in terms first of the primary school, then of the secondary school. It could then be argued that the skills needed to take one's place in society are the skills based on that early socialization which the infant school begins and the junior school develops, and the skills necessary to acquire further knowledge would then be the three Rs of the primary school. But if we accept this, there is still a vocational emphasis in the second aim, suggesting like Newsom, that there should be a vocational emphasis at the secondary stage of education.

On the other hand, James's first criterion for curriculum content is more general and, consequently, open to either interpretation. He states that the content of the curriculum must convey information which is essential to the business of living. Secondly, he envisages that an area of study may *inculcate* valuable skills. Again, the wording suggests that the first criterion includes an idea wider than the provision of vocational skills, and that the provision of these wider skills is the more important function of the curriculum. Again, we can refer to the ideas of Peters, especially his suggestion that first and foremost the content of the curriculum should be in those areas of study which are intrinsically valuable, irrespective of any vocational or utilitarian value they *may* possess.

James sums up the problem admirably when he says: 'The primary question to ask is this: for an individual of a given age and intelligence. what is the equipment of knowledge and the attributes of mind and character that we believe *should* be possessed?' This is eminently reasonable. It suggests that in deciding the curriculum, the *individual* is considered because he possesses a certain level of intelligence and has certain needs which the curriculum must fulfil. On the other hand, the individual cannot alone be the criterion which determines the content of the curriculum. When he leaves the school, he has to become a member of society which will make demands of him according to his age and ability. The curriculum therefore must ensure that he is equipped to meet such demands.

Thus James is saying that through the curriculum we *determine* what men shall be, since we cannot leave this to chance. This is the same emphasis that we saw in P. S. Wilson's article, when he said that education as it takes place in school was largely *prudential*. Such education produces teachers whose expertise enables them to determine what individuals will *need* in later life and the provision of a curriculum which will supply those needs. Exponents of 'soft pedagogy', putting forth the sentimental ideas, which in Chapter 4 we saw so severely criticized by Hardie, fail to appreciate this point sufficiently. Moreover, however much we argue at the philosophical level that the aims of education are intrinsic to the process itself and that the content of the curriculum is implied by the process of education itself, at the practical level society *expects* certain things of the school and of the products of the school. If these expectations are not met, society deems that education is failing in its aims and that the curriculum is not meeting the demands made upon it. The main demand which society makes is that its members shall acquire at school a minimum body of knowledge and skills, certain desirable attitudes and modes of behaviour, self-discipline, and a sense of responsibility. These cannot be provided at one specific level of schooling. If society demands these things, the demands must be acknowledged by the infant school teacher as much as by the secondary school teacher. Again we are reminded of the point that we made in Chapter 1 that education cannot be compartmentalized into different levels of schooling. It must be a continuous, evolutionary process to which teachers at all levels make their contribution.

King questions whether the school, in other societies as well as in our own, is any longer the main educative influence. When the Church or the Court controlled education, it decided what it required of its members and provided the curriculum which would produce the type of person required. But as life and society become more complex, the demands made on the school are not always determined by a single body, the Church, the Court, nor even by educationalists. Educationalists are more and more compelled to interpret for the schools the demands which a technological age makes on the curriculum. Moreover, the demands may not only be national; they may be demands arising from international needs. We are faced with the problem whether there must be drastic alterations in the content of the curriculum or merely different emphases, with the content remaining much as it has always been. When King says that there have been greater social advances in the last thirty years than in the past three hundred, but that the curriculum has not kept up with them, we are bound to ask to what extent must revolutionary progress in society produce revolutionary changes in the curriculum. May it not be that the curriculum, while making adaptations to meet contemporary demands, has also to provide an anchor holding to the past? If there is no such anchor, we may well face the situation where changes in the curriculum become purely arbitrary. In this case, by attempting to meet *every* demand made by progress and change, we succeed in meeting none of them.

Once more we are reminded that within education there are many problems, but few easy and obvious ready-made solutions. In addition, we are provided with further evidence of the necessity to clarify every problem and to ask what exactly are we attempting to solve. When debates about curriculum reform occur, there are so many vested interests involved that the problem is often obscured. For this reason Wiseman is able to say that in spite of our professed desires for change, education is largely conservative, and Hollins is able to refer to the 'gaseous clouds of platitudes and lay-sermonizing' which appear in debates on education and the curriculum.

It is not difficult to see why it is so easy to criticize the content of the curriculum at any stage of our educational system. Everybody has the right to make demands of education, but it is not always easy to convince people either that theirs is not the only demand being made and that, if their demand *is* met, something must be excluded to accommodate it. What would have to go may be more worthy of inclusion than the new demand. The greater the number of demands made on the curriculum, the more difficult it becomes to decide what it ought to transmit and achieve. In spite of O'Connor's five aims, Peters' three criteria, and James's three criteria, the answer, when we ask what subjects should be included in the curriculum, *now* is in many instances based on utilitarian considerations. In the past we have erred in the opposite direction. We argued for the inclusion of Latin and supported our demand by vaguely cultural and often totally unjustifiable evidence. Now we tend to go too far in the direction of utilitarian arguments. By so doing, we run the risk of substituting the production of individuals admirably trained in a vocational sense for the development of cognitive perspective. Again it appears that the real need is the one which the Greeks stressed above all others, namely the need for balance and harmony.

Thus by providing relevant arguments, instead of emotional and obscure ones, we could make a case for the retention of Classics. If properly taught, they satisfy both James's third criterion and Peters' first, as well as O'Connor's fifth aim, admirably. Unfortunately, if by Classics we mean Greek and Latin in the original, we meet these criteria only for the very bright few.

It could be argued that for the majority Greek and Roman studies in English would fulfil the same function as Greek and Latin fulfil for the gifted few. There is a growing tendency to initiate more and more pupils into such studies and less and less into Greek and Latin. However, some will argue that the full benefit of Classics lies solely in the initiation into what is worthwhile through Classical literature in the original. In this way, the languages are to the literature what we have seen Latin was to theology in medieval times.

Similarly, it could be argued that philosophy would give overall perspective, would cover many subject areas, and would have a broadening rather than a narrowing effect. But again it could be argued that philosophy is only suitable to certain levels of ability and, more important still, to people with a high level of maturity at secondary school level.

There remain, for the secondary curriculum, those areas which are developing under the names of the social sciences, which include social psychology and sociology. The way has been paved for these subjects to some extent right from the primary school, where there is a growing tendency to abandon definition by subject. We now talk of 'integrated studies' and see no reason to classify things as English, or History, or Geography. By so doing we destroy the greatest traditional barrier, the compartmentalization of knowledge under subject headings. Thus to some extent the traditional and conventional approach to History and Geography disappear, too. It is not unusual nowadays for the stress in history to be on the less academic areas of social history and economic history.

'ACADEMIC' v 'PRACTICAL' : THE PROBLEM OF EXCELLENCE AND CURRICULUM

In using the word 'academic', we are reminded of two other curriculum problems which have been gradually emerging during the last few paragraphs. Let us call them the 'academic *v* practical' problem and the 'problem of excellence'. The two are not unconnected, but we will deal with them in the order stated.

In an earlier chapter we saw that James said there was a tendency for reality to be associated with the factory and the workshop rather than with the school and the laboratory. Those who take this view assess the value of any area of study by its 'relatedness to life'. Now no one denies for a moment that, if we teach a boy at school how to install the electric wiring in a house, we are teaching him something which is not only practical and useful, but is also most directly related to life. There is nothing theoretical or academic about the actual wiring of a house. But if we teach a boy classical physics, we cannot, in the same way, say that this knowledge is practical, useful, and related to life.

Yet James argues that this is not simply a narrow attitude but a definite misunderstanding of the facts. Many of the areas of knowledge which we teach in the secondary school are not directly applicable to a situation such as repairing a burnt-out fuse. But when we talked of culture in the last chapter, we said that culture and curriculum were closely related concepts. We also said that although many contributors to culture make an impression on the mind, few make a permanent impression. We instanced the difference in the impression made by Solon the lawgiver, the practical man, and that made by Sophocles, the academic man according to our present definition. The impression that Sophocles made was at the theoretical level; yet his was the permanent impression.

James argues that the so-called theoretical or academic areas in the curriculum are not less useful than the applied areas. It used to be thought that education consisted of disinterested knowledge, that is, of knowledge which was not directly practical. More recently there has been a tendency to scoff at this idea and to assign it to the limbo of outmoded thinking. Yet James argues that the larger issues of life are those for which preparation comes through the academic and the theoretical. Again we come back to the idea that the academic and theoretical, rather than the obviously practical and useful, are the areas which give cognitive perspective. It can be argued that it is a comparatively easy task to teach the man who has cognitive perspective, the knack or skill necessary to mend a fuse. It is extremely difficult to develop in the purely practical man cognitive perspective from his knack of mending a fuse.

This book has stressed the interrelatedness of concepts, because it is a point which is all too easily overlooked. We have also seen that certain themes recur, one of which is the difference between the necessary life and the comfortable life. We saw it when we discussed the aims of education; we saw it again when we discussed culture. And now we are very close to this idea in our present argument. The severely practical and utilitarian, the non-academic has close associations with the necessary life; the theoretical and academic are closely linked with the comfortable life. But, just as education includes training, just as the man who understands formal speech can understand public speech, so the things that take account of the comfortable life take care of the necessary life also. The point is that the connection is not immediately obvious. Yet the opposite is never true; the man brought up to understand only public speech cannot understand formal speech.

We can see how the other problem, the problem of excellence emerges from the same argument. There is a great deal of talk at the present time about equality and equality of opportunity, a good deal of which is erroneous. It is most commonly at fault because it is based on emotional rather than on rational arguments, appealing to people's preconceived ideas rather than to impartiality and objectivity.

One of the fallacies of the so-called egalitarian argument is the assumption that if we establish a common curriculum we shall achieve equality. What does this argument mean? It may mean, in the first place, that by subjecting all children to the same subjects of study, we prevent some children from excelling academically, and some from not thus excelling, which is demonstrably nonsense. We can make all children practice hurdling every day of every week, but we shall not succeed in making everyone a gold medal-winner in the hurdles event at the next Olympic Games. The psychological concept of individual differences tells us that certain people have greater *ability* than others, to mention only one area of difference. Thus, if you make all children study only the three Rs at primary school, and Mathematics, Physics, and English at the secondary school, you will find good, bad, and indifferent performers at both levels in all three subjects. This is reminiscent of Peters, who is both psychologist and philosopher, when he described education as a process of initiation. He added, you will remember, the warning that not all people benefit equally from the initiation. This argument seems to be a thinly disguised attempt to limit excellence. As Nash (10) argues, there are greater possibilities in a democracy than in a totalitarian state. But there are also greater possibilities for the evil, the base, the shoddy. Because there are possibilities for both good and evil, there is constant conflict between the two. Democracy often means little more than not committing oneself in the direction of either good or evil. In this way, while we pay lip-service to intellectual excellence, we do many things in our educational system to curtail it artificially, for instance, when we say that subjects from which only the very bright can profit shall not be included. Because the mass cannot benefit, the subjects must be eliminated. In most other areas, we deliberately encourage excellence. In education we seem to be afraid, or ashamed, of excellence when we encounter it.

The logical argument for a common curriculum is not an 'anti-excellence' argument at all. It could be called the supporting argument against too early specialization. Let us take the example of the Soviet system, where there is a common curriculum in the secondary school. All pupils who enter the secondary school study the native language and the native literature, a foreign language, Mathematics, Science. The purpose behind this is not to erect barriers to excellence, but to give everyone a chance to show his *degree* of excellence. By allowing no optional subjects, the system does not allow an individual to penalize himself. It does not ask him to choose between Physics and German. Such a choice could mean that, in the later stages of education, a man might be incapable of pursuing a particular career because he did not have the basic knowledge for that career. He lacks the basic knowledge because he chose an irrelevant optional subject at a certain stage in his school career. Russia does not permit to develop the situation where a man cannot be an engineer because, in the third form of the secondary school, he dropped Maths and Science in favour of Biology and German.

The Russian system, however, does not say that, because every child studies the same secondary school curriculum, every child therefore has the same opportunity to become a top-class engineer. Indeed, those who at a certain stage show that they are not gifted with such abilities, are directed into a type of schooling which is suitable for them *and* for the State. This is a much condemned feature of the Communist system, but it is a condemnation based largely on emotional grounds, as we shall see in a later chapter on indoctrination. Yet a moment's rational analysis of the situation will show that this is precisely what Socrates meant when he said that it was the duty of the educator to diagnose the *arete*, the excellence or ability of every individual and then to train him accordingly. In this way the individual would benefit himself and the State to the best of his ability. The suggestion here is more of 'from each according to his ability, to each according to his need' than that the subjecting of all people to a common curriculum at some stage in their school career makes all people equal.

Wiseman (11) makes it very clear that one of the reasons why Curriculum causes so much difficulty is that education must go on. We cannot hold it in abeyance while we consider the reform of the curriculum. He implies this especially when he says that one of the factors which has determined the content of the curriculum of teacher training is 'historical accident'. Yet the best people to alter this situation – those engaged in training teachers – frequently fail to do so because their job does not allow them time to stand back and look at the situation, free from their everyday teaching and administrative duties. He further says that the curriculum can be sensibly reappraised only in the light of the changing aims of education. It is useless, according to this argument, to say that we will change the content of the curriculum, unless we are prepared to add the words 'in relation to the following changes in educational aims'. At this point it can be argued that we are talking about a common curriculum, because one of the contemporary aims of education is to produce equality or equality of opportunity, but in Chapter 5 we saw that this was a false argument. The aim of education can never be equality, since such an aim is irrational. The true statement is that some people wish to use education in the narrow sense so as to *appear* to be making everyone equal, which is an entirely different matter. It is like saying that one of the main defects of the eleven plus selection examination is that it produces anxiety and a sense of failure in children, implying that this is a characteristic of the examination itself, just as a rolling walk was once thought to be characteristic of a sailor. The truth of the matter is that it was a combination of parents' reaction and public reaction which caused the anxiety. The reaction of some parents to any selection process is, '*My* child must be selected'. Tremendous pressure is then put on the child to succeed. The other reaction is the one which regards those who are not selected as failures, or second-class citizens. This again is an emotional rather than a rational reaction. In the first chapter of this book we saw for many years there was a similar emotional reaction to the term 'social class', and to the even more potentially unpopular term 'lower class'. The only result was to make educationalists slow to investigate class problems in relation to education. This meant that many people who might have been helped did not receive that help. When a more rational attitude prevailed and we *examined* social class problems, we developed a much greater awareness, which in turn was transmitted into methods for helping children from the lower classes. The shamefulness (or embarrassment) was not characteristic of a particular class of society; it resulted from an emotional reaction of people outside the social class in question. Precisely the same sort of thing happened with the eleven plus examination.

CURRICULUM DETERMINED BY THE 'ELEVEN PLUS' AND UNIVERSITY REQUIREMENTS

The other argument connected with the eleven plus in relation to the primary school curriculum was that the examination determined the curriculum. Again, the argument is fallacious. The primary school curriculum existed long before the selection examination for secondary education was introduced. Apart from the intelligence test (12), the content of the selection examination was based on the three Rs. The ability of the pupil in Arithmetic and written English was tested, together with his general intelligence (13). Later the intelligence test was changed to the 'Primary Mental Abilities' (14).

Once more it is the wording of the argument which is careless. It is not so much the curriculum (or content of primary education) which was determined by the eleven plus, as teaching methods. The teaching for the last two years of the primary school was directed to getting children through the examination which, in many cases, required a certain amount of sheer drill. Children were given three minutes to answer Section A. Then they responded to the command: 'Put your pencils down'. Then they were told, 'You have five minutes to answer the questions in Section B'. This also was followed by the command: 'Put your pencils down'. Some children had been drilled so effectively that they could repeat the instructions word for word on the day of the examination. More problematic still were the after effects of this combined drill and conditioning. It took some children the whole of their first year in the secondary school to extinguish these automated responses and to learn to concentrate on any piece of work for longer than a period of from three to five minutes. But the evil stemmed from the method of approach, not from the idea of selection.

At the secondary level, it was similarly claimed that the curriculum was dominated by the Universities. This was a reference to the old matriculation requirements for university entrance. In the days of the old School Certificate Examination (15), candidates wishing to attend university had to obtain a 'credit' (16) in English language, a language other than English, Mathematics, a science, and either History or Geography. It is difficult to see any substance in the argument at all. A glance at the subject requirements for university entrance shows what is virtually the basis of a desirable common curriculum. In the Soviet system, native language, a foreign language, Mathematics, and Science are all elements in the common curriculum.

Moreover, what do those who protest that this robs the secondary school curriculum of freedom, envisage by the key word, 'freedom'? The requirements of the university not only gave coherence to the secondary curriculum (a point made by James); they also seemed to call for areas of study which, one would have thought, would have been the choice of most people, given the freedom to choose the secondary curriculum. It may be thought more desirable to arrive at a choice of *a*, *b*, *c*, *d*, and *e* for oneself than to have them 'imposed from above'. But, in reply to this it must be said that there is a real distinction between having something 'imposed' and having that thing 'required on rational grounds'. We shall find that this is a very important distinction in the area of morals and morality, which is the subject of analysis in Chapter 12.

CURRICULUM NO LONGER A SACRED INHERITANCE

Much more important is the argument put forward by Monroe (17). His claim is that a significantly different interpretation of the concept 'education' (in the narrow sense of something taking place in school) resulted from the realization that the curriculum was no longer a 'sacred inheritance'. When it was so regarded, the subjects of the curriculum, well established by authority, were accepted as having permanent validity. No one could be thought of as an educated man or a cultured man unless he had mastered these areas of knowledge. This eternal validity principle was one of the main stumbling-blocks in the way of a reappraisal of curriculum.

Monroe continues by saying that, although the curriculum reflects cultural values, each generation must ask itself whether such values are still relevant to its own needs. (It must be said by way of warning that Monroe is an American, and that during the last hundred years there has been a markedly pragmatic element in American philosophy and philosophy of education, and a dedication to 'progressive education' long before it became common in this country.) In Britain, there is still considerable evidence of that absolutism in behaviour, standards, and education which was taken to America in the seventeenth century and rejected by Franklin's demand for 'American education for the Americans!' The main task is to ensure that, whichever point of view is taken as fundamental – the pragmatic-progressive, or the absolute-traditional – it must not hinder progress. It is as easily possible for the apparently liberal process of the pragmatic-progressive educator to prevent progress as it is for absolutism. Progressivism prevents progress by becoming aimless and substitutes drifting for progress. Absolutism prevents progress by stagnation and overprescribed aims. We have already seen Perry's reference to this (18).

In the first chapter of the present book we said that we preferred the analytical method of philosophy to the historico-philosophical approach, because the former began with present problems. Monroe makes almost precisely the same point when he says that any consideration of curriculum must begin from the present. We read such statements as: 'The curriculum is a compromise between tradition and current needs'. The reader may care to exercise his analytical powers on this statement. The important word for us at this point is 'current'. We cannot give historical answers to contemporary problems, if we want them to be relevant and effective.

It may be argued that the present curriculum must offer the child present life in its idealized form. The curriculum must confront the child with present social activities, present ethical aspirations, and present appreciation of the culture of the past. This last phrase is a most telling one. It does not follow that present appreciation of the culture of the past will mean unquestioning acceptance of it. It *may* mean acceptance after critical analysis, because the past stands up to rigorous analysis. In such cases, the impression that the past culture makes will be even deeper than that made by uncritical acceptance, just as religious beliefs which the holder has tested for himself are always stronger than those which are blindly accepted. There is, if this process takes place, no reason why the curriculum should be an uneasy compromise between tradition and current needs. Analysis may show that traditional needs are not very far removed from current needs. We may have to make modification with changing circumstances, but many needs are human needs which, like human values, transcend time and place.

We have not yet answered the question: 'What subjects must go in the curriculum?' Nor is this surprising. To determine some issue on rational grounds is much more satisfying than adopting an authoritarian or doctrinaire solution. Rational solutions are far less rigid; they leave more scope for interpretation. They result from the use of criteria, not from absolute commands and narrow definitions. When the curriculum was established by authority, the items were clearly and rigidly prescribed, and it is against this rigid prescription that the present age protests. The answer was always unanimous because it was based on the same pre-conceptions. In the present day, we are probably freer than ever before to determine the curriculum, and for this very reason there is less unanimity about the content. If we accept the freedom, we must also accept diversity of opinion and differences of beliefs and values. Philosophy is bound to take account of such factors as public demand, sectarian interest and inherited privilege. When it seeks to oust some factors on rational grounds, it is itself strongly attacked and progress is again arrested.

Social demands can spring from two main sources. The first source is those social classes which were never considered before in curriculum-making. Such people constitute the mass, which Livingstone (as we saw) accuses of diluting the general culture, once it is initiated into education. The second source is those who have investigated these same classes of society, assigned a specific definition to their needs, and make curriculum demands on the strength of the evidence they produce. From both sources comes the anti-academic attack, from writers such as Havighurst (19), Rogoff (20), and Rossi (21) who believe that social injustice stems from the old authoritarian, academic curriculum.

But the attack is not solely on the academic in the sense that it tries to destroy the academic entirely. It really makes the same basic point that we made in Chapter 6 on culture. This was simply that the academic approach would not lead the lower classes from the culture of their home and class and everyday lives to the culture of the comfortable life. This is what the Newsom Report was saying, and again we are made aware of the importance of method or approach. The argument of the social reformers is that it is useless to continue the historical practice of transferring a watered down curriculum content from one group to another. In this way, the Direct Grant Grammar School received a watered down Public School curriculum, which was further diluted for the state Grammar School, and further still for the Secondary Modern School. Throughout, it was the academic method of approach to specific subjects which was the common factor in all the situations mentioned.

JAMES'S CURRICULUM IDEAS AND THE NEWSOM REPORT COMPARED

It would appear at this point that Newsom and James were poles apart. But closer examination questions whether they *are* fundamentally different. In both there is a suggested connection between 'curriculum' and 'suit-ability'. James is not arguing that everyone can profit from a study of Greek, or that every child should have an academic education. He is merely arguing that there is no reason to abolish either Greek or the academic approach for those who can benefit from them, simply because there are others who cannot so benefit. James would doubtless agree with the idea of the Newsom Report that every child must find self-respect and self-fulfilment through his education. The point at issue is that, while some may need the academic approach to be removed before they can find that self-respect, others find it through the academic approach. Moreover, it is Newsom, not James, who states that education 'must stimulate more intellectual and imaginative efforts to expand literacy'.

Again, both James and the Newsom Report stress that education, through the curriculum, must convey knowledge and beliefs essential to the business of living. Because Newsom speaks on behalf of the children of average and below-average ability, while James is thinking largely of those above-average, it is natural for Newsom to imply that for his pupils the curriculum may have to 'spell things out'. Thus a Newsom approach will always need to stress basic skills in every part of the curriculum; poor expression will persist in History and current affairs, as well as in English. With the bright child, the mastery of the basic skills long ago led on to more sophisticated and more satisfying uses of them. Number concept presents no problem to the bright child in his satisfying mastery of differential calculus. For the bright child, cognitive perspective may develop naturally and easily through the areas of study themselves. The Newsom child may have to be told again and again before he can develop anything other than a utilitarian knowledge of essentials. For him, cognitive perspective will come only with much more effort. There will be a greater need for direct teaching to bring about desired development in the case of the less than average child.

Thus, it is on rational, not emotional, grounds that the Newsom Report advocates a non-academic curriculum. The Report is not merely another attack on the academic ideal for the sake of attacking it. The bright child may be able to take part in a learned discussion on morals and morality. He may gain the knowledge necessary for such discussion from life itself, and from English, Latin, and French literature. He can see that these areas of study have much to offer in the solution of life's problems. He may even have sufficient understanding of religion to realize that this, too, can help develop a philosophy of life, a code of behaviour, and so on.

It is far different for the dull child. For this reason, Newsom suggests that religious teaching should begin with the personal and social problems experienced by the individual. Then, gradually, the teacher can work outwards from some present problem to the more general principles of religion. An obvious starting point may be: 'Why do we advocate chastity before marriage?'

We ought to be reminded at this point of Piaget's stages of thought development and the development of language which is parallel to it. We remember that at the concrete operational stage the junior school child cannot think logically in terms of abstract ideas. Instead he can think logically (perform operations) only if there is something concrete to assist his thinking. In the same way, we saw that it was necessary in our speech to children at this stage of development to avoid nouns such as 'ruler', meaning 'king'. The children cannot generalize for themselves. We deal elsewhere with the concept of mental age (22). For the moment we will merely say that a child's mental age may be the same as, greater than, or less than his physical age. Thus we may find a dull child in the secondary school, whose age is fourteen, with a mental age of only ten. This means that his thought processes are much more akin to those of a child whose physical age is ten than to those of a child whose physical age is fourteen. We have a child in the secondary school with a primary school mentality. To him, the approaches of the primary school are much more relevant to his need than the academic approach.

Musgrove (23) says that in the last resort, the curriculum must be judged by its end-products. Really this means that the success of the curriculum must be judged by the success in life of those submitted to it, which might appear to be the *élitist* doctrine put forward by Plato. But by adding that we need to develop much more sophisticated and elaborate methods of studying the products of educational institutions than we have at present, he shows that he is far from taking an *élitist* view. The simple method of judging that we have at present, namely, labelling people either successes or failures, must be the least sophisticated technique imaginable. It may be sensible to label roses first- or second-class trees and to sell the second more cheaply than the first; little harm can result from this sort of classification. It is a much more dangerous process when we put the same labels on people. Musgrove makes the point that over the past century the curriculum has grown largely as the result of incorporating in it activities which were formerly 'leisure' activities. He instances literature, art, music. The reader will remember that earlier in this chapter we suggested it is precisely through these subjects that the curriculum measures up to James's third criterion that the content of the curriculum shall minister to the spiritual needs of the individual.

Year by year we gain a greater insight into the concept of individual differences. We learn more about how children learn, what they need to derive from their schooling, and yet, at the same time, we seem less and less able to reach agreement on what areas of study shall be in the curriculum at any given level. Perhaps the paradox of the curriculum is that the more we know about the learner, the less dogmatic we become about *what* he must learn for his own good. When we had to consider only what *must* be in the curriculum to perpetuate the priesthood, the Guardians, or some other *élite*, without worrying about the masses, the matter was comparatively simple. Now we are very much aware of the masses – so aware of them in fact that we are reluctant to dogmatize about what they should study.

It seems that here we come very close to what we said (in Chapter 4) was a meaningful interpretation of child-centredness. In this instance, we mean an awareness that, at the present time, the children of less than average ability present educators with a great problem. They also provide them with great opportunities and possibilities which, if taken slowly, will be of great benefit to the pupils. It is, as we have said before, a question of deciding exactly what the child needs and then of fulfilling that need. Any hasty changes in the curriculum might well merely extend the meaningless interpretation of child-centredness, by deciding upon the content of a curriculum and then justifying it by reference to some preconceived idea of our own about the needs of children.

The interrelatedness of content and people is well stressed by Owen (23), when he talks about 'strategies in curriculum development'. He says that Curriculum strategy, like military strategy, must be worked out against a map. If not, both military strategy and Curriculum strategy will go badly astray. In the case of Curriculum, the map will be made up of principles, problems, and people.

This is a most useful analogy and reminds us of Scheffler's statement that educational truths of great importance may be found in analogies and metaphors, if only we take the necessary care and trouble in analysing them. In demands for curriculum reform, which are frequently more heated than justifiable, it is all too easy to overlook the principles and the people. The demands then cease to be in the interests of children, and become instead a projection of the biases and preconceptions of the people who make them. Secondly, unless some philosophy of the curriculum is accepted, any changes may be too rapid and even arbitrary. At this juncture we return to our earlier distinction between the concept of Curriculum and the implementation of the fundamental ideas of the concept in specific curricula. Any changes which are made must be made in the light of fundamental principles. There must be no substitution of subjects *d, e,* and *f* solely on the grounds that subjects *a, b,* and *c* are not achieving what we hoped they would achieve. Any content which replaces another must be fundamentally more effective, not arbitrarily chosen.

In Chapter 6, our analysis of the concept 'culture' revealed two interpretations of the word, one academic, one sociological. Both interpretations involved a way of life, life at different levels. The problem which faced us then was how to repair the cultural breach which exists between these two ways of life, and it is the same problem which faces curriculum reformers. How are we to ensure through the curriculum which has been described as 'an artificial contrivance designed to accelerate and promote change' (24), that every child will be supplied with what he will need *in later life*, in such a way that he will also understand it *now*?

Musgrove (25) indicates one way in which a solution is being attempted. Like the Newsom proposals for religious teaching, the type of reform to which he refers begins with the mundane and familiar and develops from there to embrace higher ideas and ideals. Subjects which were once merely practical and applied, and which were given such names as 'drill', 'woodwork', and 'cookery', have received a changed emphasis and purpose. They have been deliberately renamed 'physical education', 'technical subjects', and 'domestic science and housecraft'. We saw some of the implications of this type of change in Chapter 3, when we determined the logical geography of the concepts 'education' and 'training'. These subjects are no longer regarded as aiming solely at transmitting a skill to be applied narrowly in a particular situation. Musgrove claims that 'instructors' have disappeared and that 'training' has become a term of abuse. He also adds a warning that in the change of emphasis, subjects are being pressed into service for which they were not originally envisaged. Although this may be a legitimate and effective development, there is also the risk that such subjects are not capable of fulfilling the extra demands which we make upon them.

Yet what Musgrove is saying is very much what we saw was the content of Circular 323. By a more liberal approach to familiar areas of study, we may develop personality and social awareness through subjects which we never suspected could be used in this way. Indeed, this approach may be more effective than the substitution of new and more liberal contents.

The problem of curriculum is capable of being simply stated; its solution is far from simple. But only to discover the fundamental problem takes us a step forward. As Newsom saw it, the problem is: 'A universal, fixed, curriculum ought to be ruled out, if only because of the wide range of capacities and of tastes among the pupils with whom we are concerned.' It has also been said that the Ten Commandments are all the law that man needs to live by. But there are thousands of specific laws implementing the fundamental principles of the Ten Commandments, and every year we become even more aware of the deficiency of many of them. The same can be said of the curriculum, and, just as there appears to be no easy solution to the legal problem, so there appears to be no instant solution to the problem of the curriculum.

NOTES AND REFERENCES FOR CHAPTER 7

1 In 1938, the Spens Report had recommended what came to be known as the 'tripartite system' of secondary education. This meant that at the secondary level there were to be grammar schools, technical schools, and modern

schools. These schools were to have different curriculum emphases, but were to carry 'parity of esteem'. In 1943, this idea was confirmed by the Report of the Committee of the Secondary Examinations Council, known as the Norwood Report (from its chairman Sir Cyril Norwood). This report said that the tripartite system was justified because there are three types of student, the bookish intellectual, the technical, and the practical. The report suggested that the idea of multilateral schooling – the basis for comprehensive education – was inappropriate if we recognized the three groups or types of pupil mentioned above. It accepted the idea that eleven was a suitable age for transfer from primary to secondary school, and also suggested that the first two years in all three types of secondary school should be 'diagnostic'. (A full explanation of this term is given in a companion volume to the present book, *Assessment and Testing: An Introduction,* H. Schofield, George Allen & Unwin, 1972.) In brief, this term means that the first two years will be spent teaching the child specific material and at the same time attempting to diagnose where his strengths and weaknesses lie, in the light of which the best education for the child can be determined. The argument for the comprehensive school is that since a certain number of children in all three types of school will, as the result of such diagnosis, be transferred to a different type of course, they should be in the same school. Thus there. will be no shame in being moved from one sort of education to another, nor will there be the transition problems which occur when a child has to move from one school to another and begin to mix in different social groups all over again.

2 *An Essay on the Content of Education,* E. James. Several references to this book have been made already.

3 The psychological term 'deprived' has many shades of meaning. It has the same basic meaning as in everyday speech, where the word implies a lack or deficiency. The psychologist usually qualifies the term with another. Thus John Bowlby, in *Child Care and the Growth of Love* (Pelican 1953), talks about 'mother-deprivation'. This can be caused by the death of the mother, or the hospitalization of the mother or the child for long periods, especially during the child's infancy. 'Culture deprivation' commonly occurs when immigrant children are unable to understand sufficiently the language of the country to which they come to benefit from the schooling they receive. They fail to become initiated into the culture of their adopted country.

In the same area is 'culture bias', a feature of intelligence tests. Not only do tests favour children in the country of their origin (e.g. English children have an advantage over Indian children on an English test), but certain classes also have an advantage over certain other classes (e.g. middle-class children have an advantage over working-class children). This subject is also dealt with in our companion book (see above). Philosophically, culture bias is associated with such concepts as 'equality of opportunity'.

4 A circular from the Ministry of Education, dealing with the problem of liberal studies. Much of what we say in Chapter 8 about liberal education is relevant to this problem of liberal studies, which are sometimes referred to as 'general studies'. We can see here the distinction often made within secondary education between 'general' and 'vocational' emphases within the curriculum.

5 For a description of mental training, the student should refer back to Chapter 3 of this book.

6 *The Pupil's Thinking*, E. A. Peel (Oldbourne 1960, 2nd edn, 1967). This book is an attempt to summarize Piaget's writings on the development of thought processes in the individual from infancy to adolescence. Although it is sometimes described by students as difficult, it is worth remembering that it is much simpler than Piaget's own writings, even in their English translations.

7 Stimulus-response learning has already been mentioned in the notes on Chapter 3, Section 2, under the heading 'Behaviourists'. The stimulus-response level of learning is the most elementary of all. In language learning, it consists of giving an equivalent in one language (response) for a given word in another (stimulus). Thus we might have 'station' (stimulus), *'la gare'* (response). Similarly, in the old-fashioned mental arithmetic, the stimulus 'two twos' would evoke the response 'four'. Such parroting does not show that the child has any insight into, or understanding of, the material parroted.

8 There is more concern with changes in teaching method in the secondary school at the present time than there was when James wrote. However, the general truth of his remark remains unaltered.

9 *World Perspectives in Education*, Edmund King (Methuen 1962); already referred to and recommended as useful reading for philosophy as well as for information about comparative education. It must be stressed that comparative education is not merely comparing the structure of educational institutions in a number of countries. Nor do we study other countries' educational systems with a view to importing them, as we import Dutch cigars and American shirts. A country's educational system is the product of the history, the general culture, the economic climate, and the customs and tradition of that country. The real purpose of studying comparative education is to find how these factors influence the way in which different countries solve those educational problems which are common to all countries at a given time. It is interesting, to take a single topical example, to compare what the Scandinavian countries, the United States, and we ourselves, mean by 'comprehensive education'. This is more fundamentally important than the actual school system to which it gives rise. In this example, we have the same parallel that we discussed in the present chapter between Curriculum (the concept) and curricula (the embodiment of ideas implied in the concept).

10 *Authority and Freedom in Education*, P. Nash (John Wiley 1966).

11 *Aims in Education; the Philosophical Approach*, ed. T. H. B. Hollins (Manchester University Press). There is a foreword by S. Wiseman.

12 The term 'intelligence test' is an omnibus term, which is insufficiently precise for many purposes. We use it to mean many things, whereas strictly speaking it should refer only to a test of general intelligence. The problem is further discussed in *Assessment and Testing: An Introduction*.

13 See also 12 above. Spearman believed that intelligence consisted of a general factor, g, and special (or specific) factors, s.

14 The seven Primary Mental Abilities are those areas of ability which Thurstone believed ought to be tested by those wishing to measure intelligence. They are:

Verbal ability
Verbal fluency

Numerical ability
Spatial ability
Perceptual ability
Memory
Reasoning.

15 The old School Certificate examination was the predecessor of the present General Certificate of Education. School Certificate was similar to the 'O' level of the G.C.E. The equivalent of the present Advanced level of the G.C.E. was the Higher School Certificate. There was also a level between School Certificate and Higher School Certificate, known as the 'Subsidiary' level. In School Certificate subjects, one could reach a pass grade with $33\frac{1}{3}$ per cent, a credit grade with 45 per cent, and a distinction grade with $66\frac{2}{3}$ per cent. Matriculation, which was a university entrance requirement, demanded credit grades in Mathematics, English Language, a language other than English, a Science subject, and either History or Geography. If a candidate failed in one subject in the School Certificate Examination, he had to resit all subjects. He could not, as with failures in 'O' level, sit only for the subject in which he had failed.

It is interesting to note that it is frequently stated now, when one applies for specific jobs, that passes in subjects are required not only at 'O' level, but on the same certificate. This approximates more closely to the old School Certificate requirements and was introduced because many candidates gained passes in six subjects spread over a number of sittings of the examination.

16 See 15 above for the meaning of the term 'credit'.
17 *A Text-book in the History of Education* to which there have been frequent references in the notes on earlier chapters.
18 See notes on Chapter 5, Section 2.
19 'Education and Mobility in Four Societies', Robert J. Havighurst, Chapter 11 of *Education, Economy and Society*, ed. A. H. Halsey, J. Floud, and C. A. Anderson (Free Press 1961). It should be remembered that this is the Havighurst of Peck and Havighurst – see notes on Chapter 6, Section 6.
20 'American Public Schools and Equality of Opportunity', Natalie Rogoff, Chapter 13 of *Education, Economy and Society* (see 19 above).
21 'Social Factors in Academic Achievement', Peter H. Rossi, Chapter 22 in *Education, Economy and Society* (see 19 above).
22 The subject of mental age is dealt with at some length in *Assessment and Testing: An Introduction* (see previous references). It is a method of expressing intellectual level devised by Binet. The I.Q. (Intelligence quotient) of a child, which is the more usual way nowadays of expressing mental level, is calculated from the following formula:

$$\text{I.Q.} = \frac{\text{Mental age}}{\text{Physical age}} \times 100$$

Thus, if a child is ten years old and his mental age, according to the Binet test, is twelve, his I.Q. is:

$$\frac{12}{10} \times 100 = 120.$$

23 'Strategies of Curriculum Innovations', J. G. Owen, in *Journal of Curriculum Studies*, Vol. 1, No. 1 (November 1968), published by Collins. This is a most useful new publication from the School of Education, University of Birmingham. It deals with contemporary investigation of contemporary problems of Curriculum and is a good way of keeping abreast of current thinking.

24 See 25 below.

25 'Curriculum Objectives', F. Musgrove, *Journal of Curriculum Studies* (see 23 above).

Chapter 8

The Concept 'Liberal Education'

Any analysis of the concept 'liberal education', involves us in etymological considerations (that is interpreting the present meaning of the word in terms of its derivation). In Chapter 2, we found that, in the case of the concept 'education', this could be a dangerous approach. It was dangerous, however, for two specific reasons; first, our subsequent discussion showed that defining education was not a profitable procedure; secondly, we saw that it was by no means certain from which word 'education' was derived There were the alternatives *educere*, 'to lead out', and *educare*, 'to train'. The result was that an etymological definition could result in educations being given two opposite meanings.

With the word 'liberal' we are on much safer ground. We know that the Latin word *liber* meant 'free', and that the plural, *liberi* meant 'free men', as distinct from *servi*, or 'slaves'. Moreover, the verb *liberare* meant 'to free', and the abstract noun, *libertas*, 'freedom'. Consequently, there is no possible interpretation of the word 'liberal' which means anything other than something to do with 'freedom'.

It is also necessary to gather some evidence in our analysis by the historico-philosophical approach, which we discussed in Chapter 1. In using this approach we are not being untrue to our claim to examine current issues by applying the technique of linguistic analysis. As we saw when we examined naturalism in Chapter 4, present misunderstanding, which results in unsound practices, often stems from the retention of the meaning which a term had originally but is no longer appropriate.

The Greeks were primarily concerned that human personality should develop freely, guided by reason rather than limited by artificial constraint. They thought in terms of individual rights and individual responsibilities, of moral responsibility and moral freedom, and they believed that the latter should exist in life quite apart from legal obligations. By contrast, the minds of the early peoples of the East were fettered by superstition, which caused timidity in the individual who was not free to develop as was his Greek counterpart. In the Western world throughout the Middle Ages, the doctrine and dogma of the Church were constraints on individual thinking and freedom of thought, and, because the constraints dominated thinking, they also determined behaviour. The individual acted out in blind obedience, not because he was guided by reason. The Greeks, on the other hand, were concerned to free the mind from error. They believed that intellectual freedom would result in rational behaviour.

These last two ideas, in combination, are basic to the idea of *philosophia*, love of knowledge *for its own sake*. This was quite distinct from that applied knowledge which was prone to error. Intellectual freedom enables us to follow the argument wherever it leads, and to reach conclusions in the light of reason. For the Greeks it was reason, not the dictates of the Church, which directed behaviour. Thus Socrates was able to make his two famous statements, that 'Virtue is knowledge' and that 'No man does wrong willingly'. By this he meant that reason frees the mind from ignorance, so that, provided that a man knows the difference between right and wrong, he will automatically do what is right, because to do wrong in this situation would be irrational. In the present day, we would accept that education aims ultimately to enable the individual to make free choices on, for example, moral issues, rather than to habituate him to make correct responses without really understanding the reason for his choices. In this respect, education is a liberating agent for the individual.

When the universities began (2), there was virtually no freedom of learning. For centuries, the Church, which succeeded the Roman Empire as the stabilizing influence after the sack of Rome (3), dominated all thinking and provided such education as there was. There was no distinction between religious doctrine and dogma and education. The elders of the Church possessed a great deal more knowledge than they were prepared to allow the masses to acquire. At times, there were deliberate attempts to suppress (4) the pagan literature of the classical writers, which was still available in limited quantities in the Western world. The reason for such repression was the fear, among the Church leaders, that the writings of the ancients would destroy Christian faith. It would reveal mode of life other than the one which the Church prescribed.

Nor had the individual any rights except those which were granted by some institution. In the later Middle Ages there were only two sources of such rights – the Church and the State. If the State decided to suppress individual rights in its own interests, it frequently did so.

The rise of the universities was partly due to a protest against this control of rights and individual thinking. It represented an attempt to free the mind from the error of thinking that all knowledge was based on theology or on the doctrine and dogma of the Church. There developed the study of Law and Medicine, both of which were accepted as knowledge. The body of scholars and teachers in the earliest forms of universities was known as the *studium generale*, a name which implied freedom in two ways. It meant that students were free to study general areas of knowledge instead of those narrow areas prescribed by the Church. It meant also that people from many places were free to come to study these subjects.

Two other features of the early universities are most important for our concept of liberal education. Firstly, they were in freely accessible areas of population. The monasteries, which had been the centres of medieval learning, were always in remote places. Secondly, the body of staff and students was a democracy. In time, the universities became free to try their own members, just as the priesthood had done previously.

The revival of Classical learning in the Renaissance (5) also contained the idea of liberation. Medieval education was condemned for its extreme narrowness of outlook and content. The Renaissance thinkers attempted to broaden both in two ways; first, by replacing ecclesiastical Latin by the Latin of the best Roman authors, and second, by making Greek and Latin literature more generally available, thus revealing the free life lived by individuals in those two civilizations.

For this reason, Classics subsequently became synonymous with liberal education. The more true this became, the greater the gulf which developed between the concepts of liberal education and vocational training, as we hinted in Chapter 7 when we contrasted vocational training and liberal studies in modern technical colleges.

The contrast originated in *The Republic* of Plato. He defined real knowledge as that knowledge which is acquired for its own sake. Thus real knowledge is not acquired because it is directly useful, or directly applicable. It is often called 'disinterested' knowledge. Peters refers to this sort of knowledge as 'intrinsically valuable', i.e. valuable *in itself*, quite apart from any utilitarian considerations. Plato described knowledge acquired because it was useful or directly applicable (e.g. arithmetic, for the banker) as opinion rather than knowledge, and as *banausic* (fit for slaves) as distinct from being worthy of free men. Plato despised opinion, because it had no philosophical content. It lacked the power to produce what Peters calls 'cognitive perspective'. The true concern of real knowledge, which frees the mind from error, is universal values. To emphasize this difference we must further realize that the word 'technical' is derived from the Greek word *techne*, which means 'skill'. What Plato refers to as *banausike techne* (mechanical or menial skill) is very similar, in most cases, to what is acquired in vocational training in a modern technical college, especially in apprentices' courses.

The passing of time merely emphasized the distinction which Plato made. Studies which were valuable in themselves, especially the Classics, became associated with the privileged class or *élite* in society. They were directly related to the concept of a courtier, a gentleman, a man of affairs, and later the public schools. Liberal education always carried with it a suggestion of privilege and privileged position, of not needing to work for one's living. Finally, in the nineteenth century, the difference was further emphasized when technical skill was added to minimum literacy in a form of education which was used to keep certain elements in society 'in their place'. In the twentieth century a grammar school education, also linked with the concept of disinterested knowledge, became highly desirable, while a technical education remained something of a necessary evil, although, increasingly, a necessary element in our educational system.

Similarly, the Colleges of Advanced Technology, which became Technological Universities, were regarded by many students as somewhere to go if you could not obtain a place in a traditional university. Similarly, it frequently happens that employers regard the man with an engineering degree from a technological university as a less desirable employee than one who obtained the same qualifications at a traditional university. Such thinking is not objective, nor justifiable in the light of available evidence. It is coloured by preconceived ideas, the origins of which are centuries old.

The result of these traditional preconceptions is that instrumental knowledge, which possesses largely vocational characteristics, is distinguished from what is respectfully termed disinterested or instrinsically valuable knowledge, but which is also referred to by the less respectful as useless knowledge. This disinterested knowledge has specific associations with the general culture and helps develop what James termed the 'spiritual' nature of the individual, producing such traits as sensitivity, aesthetic appreciation, and moral sense through a study of literature, languages, music, and the arts. It induces cognitive perspective, which produces a good citizen as distinct from a good plumber. The Arts rather than Science are regarded as liberal and basic to the general culture, since it is only in the sense that it provides an explanation of the universe that science can be called liberal. In its more usual role, science is regarded as applied and vocational.

Nash (6) questions whether the distinction between liberal and vocational, as we have drawn it in this chapter, is really valid. His argument is that education must produce both the man and the worker. This is further evidence to support the theory that the term 'liberal' is not only irrelevant when used with 'education', but is also a potential source of error. We have seen that education includes training, so that, when we speak of 'educating the man', we are implying 'training the worker'. But, once we use the terms 'liberal education' and 'vocational training', we are liable to think of *opposing* concepts rather than of related processes.

Nash says that to draw a clear distinction between 'the man' and 'the worker' implies that they are two different beings. We appear to be dealing with a compulsory choice of either one or the other, as was Rousseau when he said that we must choose between developing the individual and the citizen, since we cannot do both at the same time. Exactly the same division is suggested by the separate ideas of liberal education and vocational training. Instead, Nash stresses that the man and the worker are ultimately two roles played throughout life by the same individual, although sometimes there is greater emphasis on one role than the other. He will probably be more the man when at home with his family; he will almost certainly be more the worker at his place of employment. But in neither situation does he completely abandon the other role. This is an important point which we would do well to remember for the remainder of this chapter. For the moment we must emphasize Nash's point that, once we try to separate the ideas of liberal and vocational, both ideas suffer in the attempt.

We can see the importance of this last point if we think for a moment of the concept of social mobility. This is a term meaning the ability or opportunity to move upward within the social structure and to become a member of a class higher than the one into which we were born. In Victorian times, a woman could achieve social mobility only by 'marrying above her station'. The rich man by marrying his housekeeper afforded her social mobility. Modern social mobility, which frees the individual from the confines of a particular social class, is achieved by acquiring acceptable 'socio-economic status' for the class into which one moves. Thus, social mobility is provided by becoming a member of a certain occupation – usually a profession, which is commonly the direct result of receiving the appropriate vocational training. To receive such training may necessitate reaching a certain standard of education, but this is not the same as saying that one achieves the appropriate socio-economic status to acquire social mobility through that disinterested knowledge which has become synonymous with liberal education. If this is not evidence that vocational training is the liberating agent which *produces* social mobility, it is certainly an argument that vocational training can be a contributory liberating element. It is, moreover, further indication that by using the term 'education' rather than 'liberal education', we avoid the hard and fast distinction between liberal education and vocational training.

It is still possible to use vocational training in the same way as vocational skill was used in the nineteenth century, that is, to keep people 'in their place'. Myrdal (7) emphasizes that this is done in the southern States of the United States by training Negroes in obsolescent skills (i.e. skills which are dying out). For a similar situation in this country we would need to envisage a situation where most country children were trained for the vocation of thatching. The need (again we meet this term) of the negro child is something that will liberate him from the confines of the occupation which his forefathers followed when they were slaves. They are no longer slaves in the technical sense, but they are enslaved to their present status through lack of social mobility.

Nash also shows how the interpretation of liberal education which has developed over the centuries can be dangerous for emerging nations, if it results in those who are freed from the traditions of their underdeveloped country to study in universities abroad interpreting liberal education as demanding that they do not 'soil their hands'. The result is that they 'hang about' (Nash's expression) the major cities of the world, refusing to return to their own land until it can offer them a liberal occupation. But the present need of their country cannot be met by having people in such occupations, so they become slaves of the traditional interpretation of liberal education and fail to help either themselves or their fellow country-men. Moreover in an emerging nation there begins to develop, right from the outset, that distinction between liberal and vocational, between Guardians and artisans, which such nations can least afford to foster.

FREEING THE MIND FROM ERROR

When we come to our second interpretation of liberal education as a process which frees the mind from error, we find again that there is no single error from which the mind of man needs to be freed. We have just seen the error in the minds of those who have come from an emerging nation to receive university education in a country where the comfortable life is long established. Their error is to think that they can go back immediately to the comfortable life in their own land, while the masses work hard to ensure that the necessary life is available to all.

One error in the minds of many members of our own society at the present time is that by rejecting the past totally, we ensure the solution to all present problems. This idea may manifest itself in a general lowering of standards of behaviour throughout society, or in student rebellion against the traditional structures of higher education and the traditional content in higher education courses. We shall discuss freedom fully in Chapter 13; for the moment we will merely say that even permissiveness and complete freedom may themselves be forms of constraint. It can be argued that any form of extreme is liable to imprison the mind. To sub-stitute one extreme for another is often, at best, a temporary release, at worst merely a change of constraint or prison.

So far in this chapter we have not reconciled the apparently contradic-tory ideas of liberal education and vocational training, but we have indicated some aspects of the problem. We have shown not only that it is by no means a simple one, but also that cognitive perspective above all things is needed in any attempt at a solution. At this point, we will turn to a recent concept, namely that of a liberal occupation.

LIBERAL OCCUPATION – A MODERN INTERPRETATION

Havighurst (8), in an interesting research with important implications for our argument, divides society into two groups. These he calls people with 'ego-involving' occupations and those whose occupations are not 'ego-involving'. We can see when we read his findings that the latter class has something in common with Plato's artisans, since 'non-ego-involving' occupations may be called 'society-sustaining occupations', which comprise the many routine jobs on which society depends for its continued existence.

The difference between Plato's interpretation of society and Havighurst's is that the latter says that all are *workers*, but that there are two types of work – that which is intrinsically interesting and that which is not. The latter is only extrinsically interesting, interesting for what it leads to, namely the acquisition of a certain amount of money. Beyond that the job has little or no real interest. One society-sustaining occupation is much like another, provided that it pays as much. Thus, a doctor or a teacher may be described as having an ego-involving occupation, a dustman or a bus-driver has a society-sustaining occupation.

Havighurst's arguments suggest that it may be more meaningful in our present society to transfer the term 'liberal' from 'education' to 'occupation'. An ego-involving occupation would then be a liberal occupation. Such occupations free the individual from boredom and frustration, and from the error which both can produce. Thus, the modern equivalent of the *élite* who received liberal education are those people who derive interest and satisfaction from their occupation, quite apart from any monetary rewards which that occupation might bring. In some ego-involving occupations the monetary rewards are high; in others they are smaller than those in society-sustaining occupations. In spite of this, many people continue to pursue them.

For all these reasons, Havighurst envisages one of the main tasks of the educator as enabling as many individuals as are capable of doing so to enter ego-involving occupations. The error from which he will have to free many minds is thinking that 'what was good enough for dad is good enough for me', or 'why should I worry about getting a satisfying job, when I can have one that pays more and demands less responsibility?'

Here again we are faced with the task of encouraging more people to aim for the comfortable life, not only in terms of physical comforts, but also in terms of emotional satisfaction. Such a task will involve initiating men into the general culture to help free the mind from the confines of the sub-culture, which in some respects is inhibiting and stultifying. It will involve encouraging people to make the best use of their abilities and not to think that occupation is solely determined on a class basis.

But there is an important point here, a point, moreover, closely related to freeing the mind from error and to liberal education. Many people have society-sustaining jobs because of parental attitudes to education (9). Ability has to be freed from parental prejudice. There are figures available to show that the advice of teachers is not always heeded (10). The minds of some parents have a specific error which is difficult to eradicate. The error lies in thinking that if a child can leave school at fifteen and earn £x per week, there is no point in his staying on at school for another three years, earning nothing, only to enter an occupation which pays less in the initial stages.

Here we can see that the teachers' attitudes are geared to the concept of liberal, ego-involving occupations, and to the comfortable life. But the parents' attitudes are determined by illiberal ideas, by material as distinct from spiritual considerations, and again we are faced with the problem of the culture rift.

It is often said that as education becomes more widely available, this materialistic attitude will disappear, and this is possible. If we recall Plato's allegory of the Cave (11), we shall remember that the prisoners in the Cave did not know reality, because they had never seen it. Their vision was limited to shadows of reality, and they had no experience outside this. Similarly, the parent who left school early and whose father and grandfather left school early, has no idea of the satisfaction to be derived from having an ego-involving occupation or of receiving a liberal education. The whole emphasis of his direct experience has been on the illiberal and the vocational. The error which education, as it becomes more freely available, has to remove from these people's minds is the same as that which beset the minds of the prisoners in the Cave. Education has to 'turn the eye of their soul round' and bring them face to face with reality. It has to wean them from the familiar and introduce them to the unfamiliar. But, again, we insist that education, not liberal education, is what must bring this about.

LIBERAL EDUCATION AND THE OUTGOING CURRICULUM

We can relate these developments to what we said about the curriculum in the previous chapter. The Newsom Report advocated an education that was more outgoing in the later stages. In the Soviet educational system, there is a phenomenon known as socially useful work, which begins in the early years of secondary education and to which more and more hours are devoted as the child proceeds up the school. Socially useful work consists of using the hands in the interest of the community, e.g. working in a factory. This is the sort of thing which Newsom recommended, and which is being advocated for the extra year when the school-leaving age in Britain is raised to sixteen.

These ideas may be somewhat surprising to those who have conventional ideas about what a liberal education means. Newsom suggests that the effect of taking the learner outside the school and making him soil his hands will be liberal. It will help to remove the error that all reality is in the classroom; it will help the child develop cognitive perspective. Again we must think of the distinction which we drew in the last chapter between the bright child and the children of average and below average intelligence. We saw that it is more necessary to spell things out for the less bright. The horizons of the bright child may be enlarged through contact with that part of the curriculum which caters for the spiritual side. The less bright may have to go and see for themselves in order to develop overall perspective.

It is interesting to note how often strands re-emerge. At this stage we come very close to the point where the method of teaching becomes the liberalizing agent. In the light of the arguments in the last few paragraphs, it would seem that this is true. An academic method may be liberalizing for the bright child; the less bright may need a more practical and applied approach. The bright children may be able to envisage what life in the factory and human suffering are like, because they are highly sensitive and imaginative. Others may not be able to reach this understanding theoretically.

PHYSICAL FREEDOM FROM WORK : LEISURE AS FREEDOM TO THINK :
MANUAL WORKERS' FREEDOM

Another important point to remember is that all workers are being freed from the necessity of working long hours in order to earn sufficient to feed themselves and their families. In ancient Athens, the leisure of the privileged class, to which both Socrates and Plato belonged, was made possible only by depriving the artisans of most of their leisure. In modern society, the artisan has been liberated *physically* by the machine in more and more sophisticated forms. As the working week is shortened, education time is lengthened. The working man is being given more time to think and more leisure time. But, as we have seen, few working men are engaged in ego-involving occupations. Their leisure time is not catered for by their occupations. The question is: 'May not man, in the course of time, become introspective again, as the Ionian philosophers were?' We are not suggesting that he will ask exactly the same questions. Many such questions have been answered for him. But he may well turn his thoughts to religious, social, and moral issues. He may come to this state of introversion through the education he receives at school or from dissatisfaction with the material trappings of life. The wonder of television begins to pall, the pleasure of motoring grows yearly less. Holidays abroad seemed more attractive when they were out of reach. In this respect, Ferry (12) has written that men will again be brought face to face with such issues as, 'What is my purpose here?' 'Where is life leading me?' and so on. He adds that the experience will be for many an agonizing one. In terms of what we have been arguing in this chapter it would appear that education in the future may have to liberate many people from that agonizing experience.

VOCATIONAL SUCCESS AND UPPER CLASS VALUES : WHITE COLLAR WORKERS FREEDOM

There is a strange contradiction, too, in modern society. As the working man (by which we mean those involved in society-sustaining occupations) is liberated from long hours of work, prestige in the upper classes depends more and more on vocational success. The old social class system of rich and poor has been replaced by a demarcation known as 'socio-economic status'. One's place in the upper strata of society depends less and less on hereditary privilege and more and more on personal achievement. The road to social success and high status is no longer to be found in an education which consists of the pursuit of disinterested knowledge. In Soviet Russia, the consultant engineer stands as high as the general medical practitioner. That particular society needs the engineer as much as it needs the doctor. One does not become a consultant engineer by receiving the education which was once the hallmark of the gentleman. The concept of the 'gentleman' has yielded place to the concept of the 'professional man'. The old disinterested study may no longer liberate; it can, in some conditions, imprison. The gentleman belonged by birth to a high class, into which there was no entry from below. Education produces social mobility, which enables the bright members of the lower orders to enter what was once the gentleman's domain.

Yet still, as King reminds us (13), many of our standards come from the old class of gentlemanly privilege. We still speak of a certain form of desirable behaviour as that of 'an officer and a gentleman'. We still talk of 'Etonian poise and refinement' and of 'Wykehamist manners'. The comfortable life has not been entirely liberated from the values of the old class privilege. Only time will tell what statements of manners and values we shall use a hundred years hence. The expression which perhaps heralds this sort of change is 'professional etiquette'. It at least acknowledges a 'code of behaviour', 'values', and 'standards', a consciousness of what is worthwhile in terms of the new social structure.

It may be that here we have the answer to the question posed in Chapter 6, when we asked how we should reconcile the higher and the lower interpretations of culture, the necessary life and the good life. As members of the group which Livingstone called 'the masses', who, he inferred, would dilute the general culture if they were initiated into it, rise to the top professional group, they will themselves assume the standards of that group. Those in the lower classes may themselves accept the standards of the comfortable life, because members of their own group or class who have got on accept them. By this process, their minds will be freed from that error which divides society into 'Us and 'Them', and sees these as representing two ways of life which shall never meet.

In this respect, the teaching profession is particularly important. Perhaps more than any other group of people it is generally regarded as being concerned with values and standards. The teaching profession is concerned with transmitting these standards from one generation to the next. One of the ways in which the two levels of culture could be reconciled is by members of the lower classes entering the teaching profession and themselves transmitting the values of the comfortable life to others.

There are statistics to indicate that this process may well be taking place. One set (14) shows that over three generations the percentage of teachers recruited from the top two classes of the general social classification scale has fallen considerably in the case of men recruited to the profession. In the case of women entrants, the figure has remained the same. More important for our present consideration is the fact that the percentage of men entering the profession from the classes of manual workers has risen from 29 per cent to 64 per cent, and the percentage of women from 23 per cent to 57 per cent. It is from these lower-class entrants that the healing of the cultural rift can be expected to come.

The healing may not be all in one direction. We have seen (in Chapter 5 of this book) that one of the aims of education, according to O'Connor, is to make people critical. If education succeeds in achieving this aim, those who, through increased social mobility, enter the professions concerned with the transmission of values, may not accept all the standards which they find on arrival. They may, in their own transmission of values, modify them to some extent. This may appear most undesirable, yet, paradoxically, it may be the most effective step to getting the values accepted by the lower classes.

HAS THE ADJECTIVE 'LIBERAL' ANY MEANING IN LIBERAL EDUCATION?

Earlier in this chapter, we asked if we were justified in qualifying the word 'education' with the adjective 'liberal'. The unnecessary use of a word is called tautology: the two words are saying the same thing, conveying the same idea, and one of them is unnecessary. In this case, the argument would be that, since we continually find that education achieves exactly what liberal education achieves, there may be only one concept involved and not two. We could argue that the word liberal merely underlines the word education, especially when we contrast liberal education with vocational training. We could equally effectively contrast *education* and vocational training.

Peters develops a similar argument (15). He says that education involves the transmission of what is worthwhile; that education picks out no one process or method; that education does not merely instruct, but develops understanding through the giving of reasons; that education puts the learner in positions where he is able to develop his own critical powers. Then, after discussing the difference between the broad concept 'education' and the narrow concept 'training', he concludes that liberal education is virtually indistinguishable from education itself.

Peters, in support of his claim, examines a number of fallacies which lurk under the heading of liberal education, and which are implied by the use of the term. The arguments are very similar to the ones which we have used throughout this chapter. Stating them is therefore a good way of gathering together the points which we have made.

Peters argues that the contrasting of liberal education with vocational training applies not only to knowledge (mental concept) on the one hand, and manual skills on the other. It applies also to those areas where the mind and the hand combine to produce vocational knack, skill, or expertise. The tenable idea is not to demand the exclusion of vocational training from the process we call education, but to show that education is not the same as vocational training. We freed our minds from this error in Chapters 2 and 3.

Sometimes an area of study has intrinsic as well as extrinsic value. It is valuable in itself (like an ego-involving occupation) and also has 'utilitarian' value, which means that it can be applied in a vocational situation. The area of study known as psychology is an excellent choice for our purpose.

In Chapter 3, we considered the significance of distinguishing between the two concepts 'teacher education' and 'teacher training'. It can be shown that psychology contributes to both, and it can easily be shown that, for the teacher in training, psychology has a utilitarian value. It provides him with information which he will use when he comes to teach children.

It can also be argued that psychology helps to provide overall perspective. In this sense, it tells us more about human behaviour in general. It also makes intellectual demands on us; it helps us to understand ourselves as well as other people. It thus enables us to assess ourselves in relation to other people. This is not the same sort of use that the teacher makes of psychological knowledge in the classroom, where he applies it to specific situations of teaching method, motivating pupils, etc. The use of psychology in the second sense contributes to teacher education as distinct from teacher training.

The fact that psychology has intrinsic value does not prevent its having utilitarian value. Nor does the fact that it has utilitarian value prevent its having intrinsic value. The two are different features of the same area of study. We are really saying about psychology what we said about science when we discussed curriculum (in Chapter 7). Science can provide either vocational skill or overall perspective.

The liberal argument also says that the mind should be liberated from one area of study only, which is one way of condemning narrowness. It is possible to pursue a narrow path and to pursue it illiberally, by which we mean that we can not only concentrate on one area of knowledge, but we can also acquire this knowledge by methods which are little different from drill. By stressing *liberal* education we are really saying what Peters says in the second criterion, that education must not merely provide knowledge which is inert.

This problem often appears in the controversy over specialization and when specialization ought to begin. The fact that there is a controversy at all indicates an awareness of the danger of narrowness of study and of drill methods. It shows an appreciation of the fact that, in the aims of education, we saw aesthetic emphases as well as the acquisition of vocational skill. It is seen also in the criteria established by James to determine whether certain subjects shall or shall not be included in the curriculum. It will be remembered that his criteria emphasized the academic, the vocational, and the aesthetic. It will also be remembered that James says that, ideally, a subject should qualify by matching up to *all three criteria*. Again, there is no suggestion of choosing the non-vocational at the expense of the vocational. Instead there is a reminder that knowledge is not necessarily valuable merely because it has no obvious application, any more than it is valuable merely because it *has* some specific application.

The third interpretation of 'liberal' is connected with the third criterion of Peters. Education rules out some procedures or methods because they rob the learner of wittingness and voluntariness. This appears to apply to such methods as indoctrination. Indeed, it would apply most relevantly to indoctrination. But education could also rule out those less emotionally-toned methods such as drill and parroting. These are illiberal when they do nothing to create insight (or understanding) in the mind of the learner. They rob him of the opportunity to make what he learns meaningful to him. Uncritical acceptance cannot be liberal. Reason and the use of reason liberate the mind from unthinking acceptance. We have agreed that, when we use the term 'liberal education', we are really only underlining the term 'education'. In the same way, we suggested in Chapter 5 that when we talk of aims we are not necessarily referring to external targets towards which education is directed, but to characteristics of the process called education. Our statement of aims is, in this sense, merely an underlining of the essential characteristics. The addition of liberal studies to vocational training in technical colleges may not achieve either the development of insight or even a balanced curriculum. If the content of liberal studies is not appropriate, or if the content is taught by methods as unenlightened as those in vocational classes, there is merely a reinforcement (16) of a faulty technique. No cognitive perspective will result. To say that the young apprentice *ought* to listen to Bach is no way of liberalizing him. It merely *prescribes* something of which he has no understanding and, because he has no understanding, he lacks the motivation to learn, without which no learning can take place. It may be far more liberal to begin from pop music, which the apprentice understands, and move gradually by stages to Bach. He may then even see flashes of Bach in pop music, and vice versa. The uninspired method of teaching liberal studies copies the old illiberalizing technique of saying, 'You will learn this because it is good for you'. As we saw (in Chapter 1) with the child and his cabbage, the result of this illiberal method is rejection of what is prescribed.

Finally, and the point has great relevance for us, Peters concludes the chapter by saying that the process of concept analysis is itself liberal, because it takes an overall view of the problem. It is not the tool of a particular faction or party, nor does it seek the implementation of specific content and method in education. It cannot result, if properly conducted, in partisanship and bias, because it will always be guided by reason. It is not the medium through which a certain school programme will gain acceptance and popularity. All these things may result from particular people applying the findings and data of concept analysis. But this is not the primary aim of the analysis.

On balance, it seems that the term 'liberal' in 'liberal education' is indeed tautologous. We can, however, see reasons for its being there, some of which indicate a misunderstanding of the terms. Once the noun 'education' is clarified, the necessity to use the qualifying adjective is removed. When we considered aims in Chapter 5, we suggested that the young and inexperienced teacher might find it useful to externalize the aims of education, even though Peters says that they are internal to the process itself. In the same way, it may be useful to use the term 'liberal education' periodically as a means of underlining 'education', to remind us of the logical geography of certain terms which are within education but which are not themselves the same as education.

NOTES AND REFERENCES FOR CHAPTER 8

1 In *The Republic*, Plato stressed that the main studies in the curriculum should be music and gymnastic. Music, in this context, meant much more than 'music lessons', but music as we understand it was to be part of the curriculum, to produce harmony. Alongside music, in this sense, was literature, which was to give moral guidance. Physical education was to produce bodily harmony, for Plato believed that intellectual and emotional harmony needed physical harmony as a complement. Later, Locke (1632–1704) stressed the need for a sound mind in a healthy body (*mens sana in corpore sano*), while the Jesuits also laid great stress on the importance of physical fitness. Rousseau demands that Émile shall be a 'strong, well-made, healthy child', because a strong and sound body is essential not only for a healthy mind (Locke's point), but also for sound moral character. Hence his expression: 'All wickedness comes from weakness'.

2 In the latter part of the eleventh and twelfth centuries, a number of schools connected with the monasteries sprang into prominence. The most significant of these was that of William of Champeaux (died 1121) at Paris. A number of eminent 'debaters' drew very large audiences of students; one such scholar, Abelard, was said to have attracted 30,000 students to Paris. In order to be able to take part in disputations with such masters as Abelard, the students had to be prepared by minor teachers. Thus came together the basic elements of university teaching – the equivalent in modern times being professors and teaching staff of lower status.

The resumption of east-west trade and expansion in other fields outside the Church prompted interest in *secular* affairs. The method of the investigation was usually dialectic or logical debate, applied first to doctrinal issues, then to secular problems. This was especially the case in France and England. However, in southern Italy, the reason for the rise of the universities was somewhat different. There had always been Greek influences at work there and in Sicily; there was always an interest in Greek literature, and, through this, in Greek ideas on medicine. The interest in the theory and practice of medicine in the Middle Ages centred on the monastery of Salerno. Although Salerno never received a charter to make it a university, it fulfilled many university functions and became virtually what we should now call a medical school.

In northern Italy, the chief study at the universities was law, which again was due to local circumstances. The University of Naples received its charter from Frederick II in 1224. Charters were granted either by the Pope or by the Emperor. The modern Chancellor of a University is a reminder of the presence of a representative of the Church in earlier times.

3 The date A.D. 410 is traditionally associated with the fall of the Roman Empire, because in that year Alaric sacked Rome, the capital of the Republic, and of the Empire, too, until A.D. 330, when the Emperor Constantine adopted the city of Constantinople as his capital. The way for the collapse was paved over a period of years. As the imperial frontiers grew in size, the task of keeping out the barbarians became greater and more difficult. In addition, corruption within was a weakening factor.

Christianity spread within the Empire. It preached the idea that all people, including slaves, who possessed no rights in the Roman Empire, were before God equal to all others. Rousseau's ideas (and their culmination in the French Revolution) were the later social equivalent of these religious beliefs.

The Christian Fathers were established figures before the Empire fell. The early Fathers included Origen (A.D. 185–254), Basil (A.D. 331–379), Gregory (A.D. 325–390), Chrysostom (A.D. 347–411), Jerome (A.D. 331–423), Augustine (A.D. 354–430).

4 There was a very marked culture conflict between Greece and Rome on the one hand and Christianity on the other. We have seen one reason for this above. The intellectual and aesthetic content of the Greek world had little appeal to the Christians; the degeneracy of the later Roman empire had even less. The latter was thought to set a bad example, the former would do little to strengthen faith. Greek became the 'language of heresy' and survived only in such isolated pockets as Iona and north-eastern England. There were, however, Greek influences on Christian thinking. One example is Augustine's use of Plato's 'Theory of Ideas' (his metaphysical doctrine of reality) to explain the Christian doctrine of the Trinity. The Nicene Creed (A.D. 325) shows Greek-based Christian ideas, while the Sermon on the Mount shows Semitic-based Christianity.

5 The Renaissance, although it means 'revival', was no sudden phenomenon. The ground was paved for it by the expansion of travel and trade in the period after A.D. 1000.

After the fall of the Roman Empire, many of the works of the classical writers were lost to the West, the manuscripts being taken into the Arab world. There the mathematical and scientific ideas of the ancients were developed, while in the West the Church determined areas of thinking. The *Institutio Oratoria* of Quintilian, on which Erasmus based his educational thinking, was lost to the West until the fifteenth century, when Poggio discovered a complete manuscript of the work. This appeared in printed form in 1470. Understandably, the invention of printing gave great impetus to the Renaissance. It was subsequently no longer necessary to rely on a single manuscript in the hands of a teacher and his exposition of the contents to his pupils.

Some of the most famous names of the Renaissance come from Italy and Germany. These included Petrarch (1304–1347). who had an incomplete manuscript of Quintilian's educational work, Boccaccio (1313–1375), Barzizza (1370–1431), Vittorino da Feltre (1378–1446). Among the German Humanists were Wessel (1420–1489), Rudolph Agricola (1443–1485), Alexander Hegius (1420–1495), John Reuchlin (1455–1522), Jacob Wimpfeling (1450–1528).

Perhaps the most famous of all names connected with the Renaissance was Erasmus of Rotterdam (1467–1536). He wished to use the Classics to improve the social, moral, intellectual, and religious climates of his time. His early education had been designed to prepare him for the life of a monk. He became a wandering scholar visiting England, France, Switzerland, and Italy, and lived the last twenty years of his life at Basle, which became one of the main centres of printing. He corresponded with eminent scholars in many countries. He became famous for his educational works and for his attacks on the metaphysical works of the Humanists. Erasmus reminds us of Aristophanes, the Greek writer of comedies, who satirized Socrates in his play, *The Clouds* (423 B.C.). In this play, he depicted Socrates falling into a well because his mind was on higher things which completely took his mind off where he was walking. The satirical works of Erasmus included *The Praise of Folly, The Colloquies,* and *The Adages.* He also wrote *The Liberal Education of Children.* His basic educational philosophy may be summarized as follows: All the necessary guidance for education is to be found in the Classics, the writings of the Church Fathers, and the Scriptures. But, to obtain the full benefit from these writings, one must be able to read them in the original. Risk of corruption and misinterpretation creeps in if the works are presented in translation. Therefore, the schools must teach Greek and Latin in order to study these works. Grammar forms the basis of all school work, but it is only the means of entering into the riches of literature.

The English Renaissance educators included Roger Ascham (1515–1568), who wrote *The Schoolmaster* and was tutor to Queen Elizabeth I; John Colet; Linacre; Grocyn; Cheke; and Lily, whose *Latin Grammar* was still in use at Eton in the nineteenth century.

6 *Authority and Freedom in Education,* P. Nash, has been mentioned on a number of occasions in the notes and references for previous chapters.

7 'The War on Poverty', Gunnar Myrdal, in *New Republic* (February 8, 1964). It should be noted that President Johnson subsequently gave an address with the same title. *Challenge to Affluence,* Gunnar Myrdal (Random House 1962).

8 'Youth in Exploration and Man Emergent' Robert J. Havighurst, in *Man in a World at Work,* ed. Henry Borrow (Houghton-Mifflin, Boston, Mass. 1964).

9 Elizabeth Frazer, conducting a research in Scotland, found that at the secondary school level there was a high correlation between the attitude of parents to schooling and the degree of success achieved by the child. In this respect, the appendices to the Robbins Report are important. They show that children from the lowest ability group in the grammar school tend to achieve better results, to stay on at school longer, and to stand a greater chance of continuing to university, if they come from 'white-collar' homes than they do if they come from manual workers' homes.

The figures also suggest that the white-collar workers' children in the bright and very bright categories have a greater chance of obtaining five 'O' levels, two 'A' levels, and a university place, than do their working-class counterparts in the same groups. Not unnaturally, the biggest difference in educational opportunity between the two classes comes at the lowest level of ability. Those children in this latter group would find success at secondary school level difficult even with parental encouragement. Without such encouragement, chances of success would be slim indeed.

10 See the ideas expressed in 9 above.

11 The Allegory of the Cave. See Plato's *Republic* (Cornford's translation), Book 7.

12 *Caught on the Horns of Plenty,* W. H. Ferry (Centre for the Study of Democratic Institutions, Santa Barbara, Calif., 1962). 'Further Reflections on the Triple Revolution' W. H. Ferry, *Fellowship,* Vol. 31, No. 1 (January 1965).

13 'Recruitment to Teaching in England and Wales', J. Floud and W. Scott, in *Education, Economy and Society,* mentioned on several occasions in the

notes and references for previous chapters. *Teachers in England and America*, G. Baron and A. Tropp, op. cit.

14 See notes and references for Chapter 6, Section 12.

15 *Ethics and Education*, R. S. Peters, referred to on several occasions in the notes and references for previous chapters.

16 'Reinforcement' is a psychological term used in different learning theories (see also references to Behaviourists, notes for Chapter 3, Section 2). In trial and error behaviour, the learner attempts one solution after another until he stumbles on the correct one by chance. In order to increase the probability of the correct response being made on subsequent occasions, the teacher 'reinforces' it. In the case of rats in the Skinner box, the re-inforcement is in the form of food. Correct answers by children may be reinforced by a tick, a word of praise, or by an actual reward.

Chapter 9

The Concepts
'Conditioning' and 'Indoctrination'

Certain words in our language have a pleasing effect on the hearer because they represent acceptable ideas and even, in some cases, ideals. Other words have the opposite effect, since they have unpleasant connotations for the hearer. The ideas which these words bring to mind are unpleasant, even terrifying. For this reason, once the listener hears them, he tries to dismiss both the words and the ideas from his mind.·

We shall discuss a word of the first type in Chapter 13, when we analyse the concept of freedom. In this chapter, we shall consider two words with unpleasant connotations – 'conditioning' and 'indoctrination'.

CONDITIONING

'Conditioning' rouses unpleasant thoughts for a number of reasons. First of all, those who associate it with animal learning, e.g. rats running in mazes or cats in puzzle boxes (1), feel that such a technique, transferred to human learning, robs the learner of dignity. At other times, the word arouses fear, because we realize the terrifying possibilities of conditioning in the hands of unscrupulous men. The conditioning of children to hate flowers in Huxley's *Brave New World* is an example of this type. Watson's (2) conditioning of the infant Albert to hate his favourite toy is a similar example from real life. Thirdly, we think of examples of rats conditioned to discriminate between black and white boxes because they receive an electric shock each time they enter the black box, and none when they enter the white box. There is no point in the experiment for the rat; the only satisfaction is felt by the experimenter who proves his point by the results he obtains.

This last type of conditioning had a parallel for many years with human learners. In the name of education, knowledge, which adults considered suitable for children was beaten in; if the learner was unable to acquire it by other means. Hardie (3) shows the limitation of such a method of making humans learn when he says that if all we required of children in the context of school was that they behave like circus animals, there could be no better method of achieving success than by flogging them.

This statement, together with what we have said about the meaning of education, about the transmission of values and about the elimination of morally unacceptable methods of transmission shows at once that this is *not* all that we require of children in school. Consequently, it shows the extreme limitation of conditioning.

CLASSICAL AND OPERANT CONDITIONING

For psychologists, the word 'conditioning' has two primary meanings. In both cases it is qualified by an adjective in the terms 'classical conditioning' (linked with the name of Pavlov (4)), and 'operant (or instrumental) conditioning' (linked with the name of Skinner).

In classical conditioning, the stimulus is completely under the control of the experimenter. The dog was shown food (stimulus), and, because he was hungry, he salivated (response). The dog was not a free agent in the matter, and his salivation did not indicate learning. Salivation, in a dog, is like the eye-blink or knee jerk in human beings. All three are reflex actions controlled by the autonomic nervous system, which is *not* under the control of the conscious mind of the individual. Consequently he has no control over his reflex actions as he has over such actions as eating, talking, and walking. If we cross our legs and the doctor taps our knee with a hammer, our leg jerks automatically. In exactly the same way, the dog salivates automatically when it is hungry and has food shown to it.

The learning which Pavlov's dog acquired was simple association. Because various stimuli were paired in turn with the original stimulus, meat, the dog associated each with the meat, and salivated to each as if it were meat. This effect is the result of a very limited technique. The most important point for human learning is that similar stimuli evoke the same response, provided that the learner recognizes that they are similar. At a certain stage in a multiplication sum, we 'add', because we recognize a stimulus similar to the one which evokes the response of adding in an addition sum. With the Alsatian, the conditioning did not lead to anything; it was an end in itself, the end being the proof of Pavlov's theory. In the case of the child responding to stimuli in addition and multiplication sums, however, the mere response is not an end in itself. We shall have more to say on this point later.

In operant conditioning, the stimulus is not completely under the control of the experimenter, and the animal has a considerably greater freedom of response than in the classical conditioning experiments. Although Pavlov's dog could perform some irrelevant responses (from Pavlov's viewpoint) such as wagging his tail, he was strapped in a harness and unable to roam. The white rat in the Skinner box (5) has freedom of movement. He is made hungry, put in the box, and his actions are observed. His actions consist of trial and error behaviour. They are chance (6) or random actions, and do not conform to a discernible pattern. Eventually, again by chance, the rat presses the bar of the food-hopper at the end of the box and a pellet of food is delivered to him. The conditioning has now begun. The next time the hungry rat is placed in the box, he is more likely to press the bar than he was on the first occasion. He is also more likely to press it in a shorter space of time, since the arrival of the food pellet after the pressing of the bar reinforced the bar-pressing. It caused the rat to associate receiving food when hungry with pressing a bar when hungry. The stimulus is not completely under experimental control. We are not even sure what it is.

The most significant findings from such experiments have been in the field of programmed learning or, as it is also called, programmed instruction. Information is given to the learner in very simple forms and in small amounts. After each piece of information has been given, a question is asked. The learner, immediately he has answered the question, is able to look up the answer. If he has answered correctly, his response (the giving of the correct answer) is reinforced. This means that he is likely to remember the information and to give the correct answer next time, just as the rat is more likely to press the bar the next time as a result of the reinforcement.

ANIMAL CONDITIONING AND INTELLIGENT (HUMAN) LEARNING

However, the situations are not exactly parallel. If we accept that there is some similarity between classical conditioning and rote learning, we cannot justifiably claim that there is exact identity. The moment one begins to use the word 'conditioning' with rote learning, one becomes aware that the use of intelligence is not necessarily entirely eliminated. In the rote learning of, for example, French vocabulary-lists, the pupil learns a list of French equivalents to English words. When tested, the stimulus is the English word and the response the French equivalent, or vice versa. The reader will probably recall unhappy occasions when he learned his vocabulary-lists in one direction, expecting the stimulus each time in the test to be the English word. When the French word was suddenly made the stimulus, he made mistaken responses.

But this does not prove that the method of learning had eliminated intelligence from the act of learning. It merely meant that the pupil had not behaved very intelligently when he learned his lists. Moreover, the reason for setting the rote learning was not to prove that, if you gave the English word as the stimulus for the first five questions and the French word as the stimulus for the sixth, a significant number of pupils would make the wrong response. The teacher's real intention in setting his pupils the task of vocabulary learning was to provide them with necessary tools for understanding the language and, through such understanding, to develop in them insight into French culture. The pupils knew also that they would be required to do other things with the words than parrot them or write them down as responses to stimuli. But, for the moment, the rote learning test becomes a convenient method of assessment for the teacher, and a way of earning marks for the pupil. However, only a very poor teacher would allow his pupils to think that this was the only purpose of learning the vocabulary. Only a completely illogical teacher would deliberately try to obscure the fact that the words would subsequently have to be used intelligently in French contexts.

At this point it would seem that there is a connection between classical conditioning and rote learning, but not identity of content or method. There is also a connection between the two processes and instruction, although again there is no identity. We have seen that in instruction, the instructor's role is to impart information. The learner, too, has a definite role, namely to acquire the information. But the learner is at liberty not to acquire the information. He can, for instance, refuse to listen to it, to show that he is a free agent; may subsequently forget it, because he is not motivated to remember it. He may forget it, or refuse to learn it, because he fails to see any usefulness in the information; on the other hand, he may appreciate that the information is basic and that it will lead on to other information and the solution of problems. Two things are immediately apparent; the first, that the person instructed is still a free agent; secondly, that intelligent behaviour is not eliminated by instruction. It is because it is so difficult to eliminate the use of intelligence from even apparently elementary teaching or learning situations, that Peters (7) doubts if much genuine conditioning takes place in human learning.

The applications of operant conditioning principles to human learning are not identical with the application of such principles in animal experimentation. Primarily, Skinner applies the principles to human learning for the benefit of the learner. A closer analysis will assist our understanding.

When the rat is placed in the Skinner box, it is placed in what is, for it, an unnatural environment. A rat would not from choice seek out Skinner boxes to explore. It would behave in the same inquisitive manner outside the Skinner box as inside, if it were equally hungry. It behaves in a particular way not because it is in a Skinner box, but because it is hungry. The bar-pressing is an incidental, even an accidental, act. If the rat is released from the laboratory after a period of time and returns to its natural habitat, it will not, we believe, go seeking bars to press when it is hungry. In short, the rat learns an unnatural mode of behaviour which will not help it in any situation other than the experimental one (8). In this situation, the act is performed for the benefit of the experimenter, not of the rat.

We said in an earlier chapter that the classroom is an unnatural environment for a child, just as learning a foreign language in a classroom in one's native country is an unnatural or artificial or structured situation. We also saw, however, that enlightened teachers introduce new methods of language teaching which reduce the artificiality of the situation. Moreover, the child is not made to perform useless acts in the classroom merely to satisfy the whim of the teacher. If this were so, the teacher would be guilty of using the individual as if he were a circus animal. What is learned in the artificial situation of the classroom may well be, and is intended to be, useful in natural life situations. It is not a skill to be acquired in a vacuum without the application of intelligence and to be performed on countless future occasions without the application of intelligence.

CONDITIONING AND DRILL

We are at this point reminded of our earlier discussion of drill and coaching. We can coach a pupil to make certain moves with chessmen, and we can subsequently drill him in these moves. At first the aim is to habituate him to moving specific pieces, e.g. a knight in one way, a pawn in another, and the queen and a bishop in yet other ways. We may perhaps use only the white pieces for such drill, and not play a game of chess at all.

But Skinner claims that in operant conditioning the response is 'under the control of its own consequences', which is why he considers it to be so important educationally. However, the moving, for example, of the white knight one square forward and one square diagonally to left or right, without the black pieces on the board, is not making the response under the control of its own consequences. This can be so only if, for example, the black rook can take the knight after it has been moved. The habituated act of moving the white knight in a particular way is essential as one of the basic moves of chess. But in a game of chess, the pleasure lies not in making such habituated moves, but in applying intelligence to outwit an opponent. For example, we may sacrifice the knight to make our opponent move his rook so that we can take his queen. Only by applying intelligence can we say that the response is under the control of its consequences.

The problem of the relationship between habituated responses and the use of intelligence is also demonstrated in chess by what are known as gambits. In a gambit, the moves which white makes are little more than stimuli which black easily recognizes and to which he has become habituated, through drill, to make automatically certain counter-moves. But it is easy for the expert chess-player to reveal the flaws in this stimulus-response play by making a move to which his opponent has not learned the response. In this situation, the player who relies solely on habituated responses falls an easy victim to the skilful player who possesses insight into the moves, that is, to the player who applies intelligence to the moves he makes.

Returning to the teaching-machine, we can see that although there are similarities between this situation and the Skinner box, there is not an identical situation. This would be possible only if the teacher confronted the child with the machine and, without a word of explanation, allowed him to discover by trial and error how it worked. In this way, the child might learn by discovery the mechanics of working the machine, but not the purpose of it.

Few, if any, teachers would adopt this attitude to teaching by machine. Instead, they instruct the learner in the method of using the machine. If the teacher is making correct use of the machine he is benefiting the child by allowing him to learn at his own pace, because he believes that this is beneficial to the child. There are some who object that this robs learning of dignity, and that no genuine effort can be required on the part of the learner, that treating learning as a mechanical process is illiberal, and that, because the teaching takes the form of conditioning, it denies rationality and robs the individual of freedom of choice.

Undeniably, life involves choices. But to be able to choose effectively, we must have learned something; we must have acquired information, have been drilled and instructed. Such instruction may have been in learning arithmetical tables or in following rules as part of our moral training. But the aim of all these processes was not to *eliminate* intelligent behaviour. Rather was their aim to make intelligent behaviour possible by providing the individual with the necessary basic tools. If we set out to build a wardrobe in an alcove in our house, and the job necessitates drilling and plugging the wall, we do not set ourselves the task of making the drill and plugs. We take these along as the basic tools for the job. Using a drill and putting plugs in holes are two habituated acts, but such acts do not eliminate the need for intelligence in deciding where to drill the holes, what size of bit to use, and so on. Similarly, habituation to rule-obeying behaviour need not be mere conditioning. There is no reason why the rules which are automatically obeyed, should not be both reasonable rules and also understood by those who obey them. Habituation of this sort is dangerous only when it *deliberately* seeks to eliminate the application of intelligence from the acts which lead to habituation. If we do not understand the acts themselves, we at least understand in what circumstances the acts can be usefully performed. Similarly we saw in an earlier chapter that instruction does not necessarily seek to eliminate understanding of the knowledge which is given. Teaching-machines often provide basic essential information for subsequent intelligent use.

Peters (9) stresses that the conditioning of rats is characterized by two main features: firstly, the action performed is invariably trivial; secondly, it is invariably unrelated to anything that the rat is required to do in its everyday life or is likely to be required to do subsequently. The act of pressing a button in a teaching-machine is trivial. Many of us press buttons in everyday life. But the button-pressing is only the means to the end of acquiring some information. Nor is the information an end in itself, since it is only a link in a chain leading to further information or material necessary for the solving of a problem.

Two questions which are frequently asked are: 'Is conditioning teaching?' and 'Is being conditioned learning'? We are now in a position to attempt to answer both these questions. Vessey (10) defines learning as 'the acquisition of something by a process other than maturation', and maturation as 'the developing of "readiness" to perform certain actions without being taught'. Thus maturation enables the infant to crawl and later to walk and climb stairs. Later still it enables him to begin to talk. Again Skinner and others would have us believe that vocabulary in the infant comes as the result of operant conditioning, but this is extremely doubtful. The child utters a word and parental praise 'reinforces' it. This is true, but the child does not utter the word in the same random way that the rat presses the bar in the Skinner box. The child has heard others utter the word. He has listened to the sound and then attempts it himself as a deliberate act. Something, the desire to communicate, the desire to please, or a simple need, causes him to imitate a sound he has heard. Imitation, however, is not the same as being conditioned. He has, in Piagetian terms, carried out a number of important processes, none of which show that the application of intelligence has been eliminated.

CONDITIONING AND TEACHING

There are times when teachers require their pupils to form habits; at other times they require them to respond to stimuli, and sometimes they require them to be drilled in certain actions and skills. But few teachers limit their endeavours to these activities. If they are good teachers they are all the time seeking to develop understanding in their pupils. Good teachers are aware of the potential dangers of such activities as drill and habituation. Advocates of modern methods often go too far the other way in their attempt to improve on traditional methods. Believing that what was bad in the old methods was drill and habituation, they attempt to eliminate these elements from teaching and learning. Both teaching and learning are deliberate acts. Because we cannot teach anyone anything, but can only cause them to learn, and because learning and teaching imply the development of understanding, conditioning cannot be synonymous with teaching any more than being conditioned can be synonymous with learning.

However, in the early chapters of this book we saw that within education there is a whole family of interrelated concepts. One of these was training, and investigation of this concept showed that there were other concepts within training, such as instruction and drill. None of these was the same as training, nor was training the same as education. But this was not the same as saying that there must be no training, instruction or drill within education. By the same line of argument, teaching may involve drill, habituation and conditioning, but no single one of these is teaching.

To believe that conditioning is the same as teaching is to take the environmentalist view of the extreme behaviourists. Like Watson, we would have to believe that environment was all-important in determining intelligence and personality. We should as a result believe that, by placing any individual in a specific environment, we could make him 'rich man, poor man, beggarman, thief'. Such a belief is so irrational that it is not surprising that there are no longer such extreme behaviourists.

Conditioning is a very limited and limiting technique. The least complex thing that it produces is the single response; the most complex form of behaviour possible by conditioning is habit. There are those like Hull (11) who claim that even language is merely a series of habits. This argument is retrospective. It develops a learning theory, and then examines language and attempts to explain it entirely in terms of the theory. One of the areas where intelligence is most clearly shown is in the true usage of language. Since conditioning eliminates intelligent behaviour, it cannot explain language learning, nor can it figure prominently in human learning of any kind. Scheffler (12) says that knowledge is not achieved through a standard set of operations which process sense data. Instead, knowledge results from applying a 'conceptual framework' to such data. By this process, we develop ideas (complex process) from the sense data (simple raw material). The use of language figures largely in this conceptual framework, since ideas are developed from sense data in terms of language. In the course of this book, we have frequently reminded ourselves that terms in themselves are unimportant. Their only importance is that they represent concepts or ideas. Thus, the analysis of such terms as 'education' or 'conditioning' is not the analysis of words, but an attempt to develop a clearer understanding of the ideas which the words are used to convey. Just as mere linguistic analysis of the *terms* without concern for the concepts behind them cannot result in clearer understanding of such ideas, so conditioning, as a process, can play no part in the formation of ideas.

INDOCTRINATION

The layman frequently pairs in his mind the terms 'conditioning' and 'indoctrination'. Both convey unpleasant ideas which make him unwilling to come to grips with them and define the precise logical geography of each term. It is for this reason that Wilson (13) is able to say that, to many people, the term 'indoctrination' is a nebulous (14) one.

Why, then, did we (in Chapter 2) quote a statement by Ducasse connecting education, which we have come to accept as a liberalizing process, with indoctrination, which most people feel is a process which in some way denies liberty. Ducasse, after defining 'education' etymologically as a process of 'leading out', states that the process of education takes place through instruction, training, and *indoctrination*. Although the first two terms scarcely suggest the act of 'leading out', our own analysis has shown us that they are both concepts within the larger concept of education. Indoctrination, however, appears to be totally out of place, since it would not appear at first glance to measure up to the three criteria (in our view of education) nor to be in keeping with the 'leading out' idea of Ducasse.

The answer to the important question whether indoctrination can play any part in education depends on the answer to another vitally important question: 'Is the process which we call "indoctrination" given that name because of its content, its method, or its aim or intention?' If we look at the implications of this question, we shall see why it is vital to answer this second question before we can be in a position to answer the first.

It can be argued that the content of education can be divided into two parts, usually called 'facts' and 'beliefs'. If we were to ask someone what was the essential difference between these two terms, he would doubtless say that facts can be proved, beliefs cannot. When we deal with facts, we are dealing with certainties (we are in the realm of 'going and doing'); when we deal with beliefs we are dealing with uncertainties (we are in the realm of 'sitting and thinking' or 'theorizing'). However, Hospers tells us that there are very few things which are absolutely and undeniably true, while Wilson warns that few of the things which we teach are absolute certainties. Moreover, he suggests that we should be well advised to worry less about teaching only absolute certainties, than about giving evidence to support the things that we do teach.

This last statement brings us to the second problem: whether indoctrination is so called because of the method which is used to transmit a particular content. No one would suggest that true teaching could ever be confused with brainwashing (a technique associated, even by the layman, with indoctrination). But there are certain areas where, it is suggested, indoctrination can take place as part of teaching. One of these is the area of religious teaching. It is often suggested that there should be no religious teaching in school because although parents are given the option of removing their children from religious teaching lessons, some children who remain will be *indoctrinated*. But is it fair to say that the teacher who, as a committed Christian, attempts to tell the pupils of his or her religious experience is *attempting* indoctrination? We must, moreover, distinguish between the teacher who, out of religious fervour, puts forward beliefs *emphatically* without rational justification, and someone whose sole intention is to *suppress* rational argument. One can argue that the teacher who relies on personal fervour leaves himself open to criticism for not supporting his fervour with rational argument. But this is not the same as saying that merely omitting to support one's beliefs with evidence is indoctrinating.

This brings us to the last point, namely that indoctrination may be so called because of the *aim* or *intention* of the person carrying out the process rather than with either its content or method. However, the fact that we use the terms 'content', 'method', 'aim', and 'intention' shows that it is not as surprising as at first appeared that we have to distinguish carefully between indoctrination and teaching.

INDOCTRINATION AND TEACHING

White (15) also suggests that, historically, there has been some failure to distinguish clearly between indoctrination and teaching:

'The word "indoctrination" was often used in the past to refer to teaching generally; to indoctrinate a person was merely to get him to learn something. In this century the word has taken on more precise meanings. It now usually refers to particular *types* of teaching, distinguished by the different intentions that some teachers have in mind, e.g. to get children to learn by rote, or without reasons, or in an unshakeable way, intentions that were not clearly distinguished in the past, when the word was used more widely.'

This passage is most interesting. It is firstly another piece of evidence not only that philosophy has only in the present century used linguistic analysis to distinguish clearly between apparently similar terms, but also why it uses this method. Secondly it seems that, in the past at least, indoctrination and teaching have been *equated*, although from White's remarks it appears that what was referred to as indoctrination would be much more accurately described as instruction, albeit often unimaginative instruction. However, as we have already suggested, unimaginative instruction is not necessarily indoctrination, if 'intention' is the criterion.

Moreover, even if we accept that unimaginative instruction is indoctrination, we are only admitting that in the past indoctrination, or something akin to it, has played a part in teaching. In the same way, in the first half of this chapter, we suggested that conditioning might play some part in teaching without being the same as teaching, just as being conditioned might play some part in learning without itself being learning. We saw the same sort of confusion when we were discussing education and training in Chapters 2 and 3.

Peters makes a useful and clear distinction between conditioning and indoctrination, when he says that conditioning is concerned with reactions while indoctrination is concerned with beliefs. Yet for our present purpose this distinction tends to confuse the issue, since we have seen that teaching is also concerned with beliefs. Consequently, to say that both indoctrination and teaching are concerned with beliefs, does nothing to distinguish one from the other. It is rather like saying that Arithmetic and Algebra are both concerned with calculations, which does nothing to distinguish between the two.

However, it does suggest that, since the distinction between teaching and indoctrination does not seem to depend on content, and since we have already suggested that to use method as the criterion for deciding what is or is not indoctrination is little better, the answer seems to be that it is the *intention* which decides whether a process is indoctrination. Brainwashing is a form of indoctrination, but the *intention* to close the mind to reason is taken first and the method of brainwashing used only after the intention has been decided.

Such an intention is missing from teaching by rote, instructing unimaginatively, and teaching fervently from conviction. In these, the teacher fails to make his teaching interesting and rationally based. He does not *deliberately* intend to *eliminate* interest and rational evidence. We may say that such teaching is 'dogmatic', 'doctrinaire', 'prejudiced', or 'rigid', but these are words describing the method of the teaching, not its intention.

The above defects regularly characterize 'poor' teaching, and some readers will no doubt have had experience of it. We have given historical examples in this book. It is therefore interesting to note that Hare (16) says that we can detect the indoctrinator by watching the expression on the teacher's face when his opinions are challenged by his pupils. Again, there is the suggestion that it was not the teacher's *intention* that what he said should be questioned. We can sum up the main points made so far in our attempt to distinguish between teaching and indoctrination as follows: both teaching and indoctrination seek to achieve preconceived ends. Teaching sometimes seeks to transmit facts, sometimes to communicate beliefs. Indoctrination is not concerned with facts, but *only* with beliefs. Moreover, while 'good' teaching seeks to use reason and evidence to achieve its ends more effectively and convincingly, 'bad' teaching may omit both without this being its deliberate intention, in order to bring about the desired aim. By contrast, as we shall see in a moment, indoctrination deliberately suppresses both reason and evidence to achieve its aim, which is the inculcation of beliefs. Teaching, when it is 'good', aims to produce insight; it is an inherent characteristic of indoctrination to deny insight deliberately and by all possible means. Teaching may resort to unimaginative methods which are open to criticism. Indoctrination deliberately resorts to methods which are reprehensible and morally objectionable to all save the indoctrinators themselves. Thus while teaching measures up to the third of Peters' criteria for the educative process, indoctrination does not.

INDOCTRINATION: RATIONALITY: JUSTICE

The one word which we can use to describe the characteristic of indoctrination, then, is 'irrationality', a deliberate attempt to remove understanding. Far from encouraging the use of evidence to substantiate, it actually suppresses all evidence which is in any way likely to undermine the beliefs and ideas it is attempting to inculcate. Suppression of evidence, the doctrinaire approach and the authoritarian manner are all *deliberate*, and it is the intention of the indoctrinator that all these features shall be characteristic of the process. His aim is to *suppress* all possible criticism of the beliefs he transmits. One line of argument will be put so forcefully, so repeatedly, so uncompromisingly, that the victim of the indoctrination will never be able to consider an alternative because none appears to be available. The object of establishing these beliefs is simply to establish someone in power, or to increase the existing power of the person for whom the indoctrinators act as agents. Just as one of the aims of education which O'Connor tentatively listed (see Chapter 5) was to produce critical thinking in the individual, so in indoctrination the *sole aim* is to suppress it. Indoctrination is never undertaken with the well-being of the individual in mind. The individual is sacrificed to the interests of the system or the establishment. Thus the Nazi doctrine of racial superiority was not for the benefit of the average German at the expense of the average Jew. The only beneficiaries were Hitler and the hierarchy of the Nazi party, since they had the blind devotion of the average German members of the master race.

The idea of injustice (especially the injustice which is not seen to be done) enters the discussion at this point. The injustice to the Jews was obvious; the injustice to the Germans was none the less real, although it was much less apparent. In the first place, they were deprived of the right to think and decide for themselves. In the second place, and this was closely linked with the first 'injustice', they were coupled with Hitler as the perpetrators of horror. The masses who swaggered and screamed after their leader were thoroughly indoctrinated, but many did not distinguish between their actions and the action of those who behaved that way from free choice. Finally, the indoctrinated were involved in the same eventual catastrophe as their indoctrinators, although they deserved a different fate.

Indoctrination on this scale (and any indoctrination is, by its very nature, likely to escalate) is a total process. In its attempt to suppress freedom of thought, speech and action, it takes control of all those media through which the minds of free men express themselves, the 'cultural forces', as

Perry (17) calls them. These include art, literature, music, science, philosophy, and religion, and they are either converted into actual instruments of indoctrinati , e.g. the repeated roaring of racial songs on the radio, or suppressed entirely, as in the case of religion. Total indoctrination also includes the control of the media of mass communication such as television, press and radio.

The result of this is what Perry (18) describes as an 'irrestible spell' which binds the minds of the indoctrinated and reduces them to a state of 'hypnotic fixation'. A way of thinking is *inculcated*, and this in turn manifests itself in a total way of life. Every available force that will help bring about the preconceived aim is harnessed in the cause of suppressing alternative ways of thought and life. Every distracting force, every opposing influence, is eliminated, if it cannot also be indoctrinated. Acceptance is demanded and obtained simply by making rejection impossible. Rejection is even made undesirable through the blandishments of the indoctrinator, and through ceaseless propaganda. The process is almost frighteningly simple – aims are established, a course of action is decided and relentlessly pursued, the aims are achieved.

INDOCTRINATION: EDUCATION: OVERPURPOSIVE EDUCATION

Indoctrination aims to close the mind; education aims to open and develop it. Education aims to put forward beliefs, but at the same time to make the individual critical and to provide him with the opportunity of being critical. Indoctrination puts forward doctrine and dogma and sets of beliefs so authoritatively that they appear beyond the reach of normal investigation. Consequently, the task of the indoctrinator allows no respite. We have seen elsewhere (19) that the human mind pushes the memory of painful experiences into the unconscious, and seeks to keep them there. But there are times when the conscious mind is so beset by pressures that it cannot retain its hold over the experiences banished into the unconscious. The moment the hold is relaxed, the experiences come into the conscious mind again and cause emotional breakdown. There is a direct parallel between the individual and the indoctrinator here. Once there is any relaxation of the process, people begin to think for themselves. Thus, in spite of the domination of human thought by the Church in medieval times, the stranglehold could not be maintained indefinitely. Once it was relaxed, people began to think and to ask questions, to demand proof of those things which earlier they had taken on trust.

Thus, although genuine education (and by this we mean a process that measures up to our three criteria) can never become indoctrination, we can see that processes which are loosely called education can be indoctrination. It is these processes which Perry called 'overpurposive education' (20). In the counter-Reformation, the Church of Rome attempted to regain its hold over men's minds after this had been loosened by the Protestant Reformation. The result was one of the most systematic attempts to harness education to a cause in the whole of history. Education, from the cradle to the university, was to be controlled by the Jesuits. There was to be 'One aim, one content, one method'. There was to be a close hierarchy of supervision to ensure that no individual deviated by an inch from the decided line. Jesuit education at that time showed all the characteristics which we have just assigned to the process of indoctrination.

A most important point is raised here. It is all too easy to see indoctrination in other people, sects, or countries and to miss it, or its equivalent, in ourselves, just as it is easy to see our own faults in other people through a process of psychological projection (21). We can now see the danger of imposing on education categorical aims from without (see Chapter 5). This is precisely what the Jesuits did when they established their 'over-determined' education. Examples from familiar contexts, on which many look with favour, will show how subtle deception can be.

American schoolchildren are required every morning to swear allegiance to the Stars and Stripes. This is a secular ceremony, the counterpart of the religious assembly required by statute in British schools. American schools are not allowed to provide religious instruction, since this may offend some people. The provision of religious education is regarded as the task of the church, rather than the public school (22). The swearing of allegiance to the flag, however, is accepted. It is a mark of patriotism which conforms with an ideal cherished by the American people. It is a highly purposive, emotional experience to which, over the years, the child becomes habituated. It is difficult to distinguish between this ceremony and indoctrination. It occupies only a small part of a long and busy school day, and it arouses little comment or criticism because it is not alien to American ideals. Nor was the Jesuit education alien to the ideals of the Catholic Church. Yet both have the same aim: to plant certain ideas in uncritical minds to secure a predetermined purpose.

The fact that many people in Britain object to the religious assembly and that few American parents object to the swearing of allegiance to the flag can be used as an argument in favour of the flag ceremony and against Assembly. In fact, it ought to be an argument on the other side. If some British parents object to religious assembly, it must mean that they are, at any rate, thinking about it. One cannot protest against something unless one is aware of it. The fact that American parents do not object to the swearing of allegiance could be no more than a sign that they too have been thoroughly indoctrinated. It may be that, in the country where a famous behaviourist psychologist talked about the 'stamping in' of response (23), a thorough job of 'stamping in' or indoctrination has already taken place!

To Western minds indoctrination is frequently synonymous with Communism. As a result, it is doubly out of favour; it itself is an unpleasant process, and it is practised by a people whose ideals are very different from our own. But, to the Communist mind, indoctrination is synonymous with religious teaching. The Church of Rome and the Communist state have nothing in common ideologically, but they accuse each other of using exactly the same process to achieve their very different ends. Although the expressed aims are different, the common aim may really be the total control of the minds of their respective followers.

INDOCTRINATION: ROTE LEARNING

It seems a far cry from such total indoctrination to the so-called 'indoctrination' implied by such processes as rote-learning. Again we are concerned with two aspects of the process: content and intention. It is possible to argue that if we allow unquestioned learning, stamping in, and reinforcing of a factual content, it is but a short step from this to the inculcation of· unacceptable beliefs. But, as in our consideration of conditioning, we must ask ourselves what is the aim and intention of the teacher? When he requires his pupils to learn the first declension in Latin grammar by rote, is he attempting to pave the way for indoctrinating their minds with the ideas of, say, Maoism? Is he attempting to preclude rationality from their learning? Is he deliberately attempting to habituate his pupils to be unthinking? It is difficult to believe that any of these is the real reason for the teacher's setting his class the task of learning Latin nouns by rote. He requires them to do so because he considers that such rote-learning is essential for a meaningful study of Latin, and because he believes that this is the most efficient way of enabling the pupils to obtain the basic required knowledge.

The teacher is more obviously an indoctrinator and his conduct reprehensible when he attempts to inculcate into the minds of his pupils his own beliefs and attitudes, and also ideas which are by no means certain without the suggestion of possible alternatives. This does not mean that no teacher should teach anything unless it is one hundred per cent certain. Wilson (24) tells us that few things fall into this category, while Hospers shows that even propositional knowledge (25) can very rarely be said to be 'absolutely certain'. The intentions of the teacher, as distinct from the indoctrinator, are based on reason. He puts forward an idea and adduces evidence from his own experience and from that of other people to show what can be said in favour of the idea and what must be said against it. Finally it is often best not to come to a conclusion, but to leave the pupils to make up their own minds. In some cases, and at certain age levels, they may do this immediately. In other cases, and at other age levels, they may not make up their minds for some years. But the leaving of the mind open is a hallmark of education, the deliberate closing of the mind, especially in face of strong evidence that it ought to remain open, is a characteristic of the indoctrinator.

INDOCTRINATION AND MORALITY

The issue of morals and morality which, like the issue of religion, is one which often raises the cry of indoctrination, will be dealt with in Chapter 12. But at this point it is important to introduce the question of teaching morality, to demonstrate something of great importance in our present analysis. It is often said that it is wrong to indoctrinate children of pre-school age in morality. They should not be told what to do and what not to do, because to do so would be to *impose* adults' ideas on their minds. This is muddled thinking. If we ask what is the intention of the average parent who gives such imperatives to his child, the answer will be, 'to protect the well-being of the child'. If we were to ask this same parent, 'Will you expect your son (or daughter) as a teenager, to obey your moral imperatives?' the answer would frequently be, 'Good heavens, no! I would hope that by then he (or she) will be capable of making up his (or her) own mind'. The intention of the indoctrinator in this situation would be to establish such a powerful hold over the mind of the child that he would never be free of it. The purpose of these early commands is to lay down behavioural guidelines which will enable the child to avoid physical and moral danger when the parent is not there to supervise. The content of the commands is also useful when the child is capable of exercising critical thinking on the content of the precepts. We have stressed more than once that method without content is impossible. An adolescent cannot make up his own mind on moral issues if he has no content to criticize, to accept, or to reject on rational grounds.

The teacher, as Peters stresses, and as we shall see later, is an 'authority figure'. He has tremendous influence because of the knowledge he has acquired and because of the power vested in him by those who accept him into their society as a teacher. This authority can be used for good or ill. It can make harmful content harmless or harmless content 'potential dynamite' as Mussolini realized. He said that subjects such as Geography, Mathematics and Statistics were not in themselves politically dangerous, but that the professor from his elevated position could, by a look, a word, a gesture, 'turn them into political dynamite'. The teacher must, therefore, if he is to be worthy of his authority, examine his motives continually to ensure that they are laudable.

The danger is that in a society which behaves irrationally, as our own does for much of the time, educators may also begin to behave irrationally.

The next step is to condemn rationality in others, and the final step is to attempt deliberately to suppress rationality. At this point we cease to teach or educate, and begin to indoctrinate. Although society behaves irrationally, withholds and even suppresses evidence, and acts in an arbitrary manner, the teacher must always build his work on a foundation of rational thinking and open-mindedness.

CONCLUSION

The weight of evidence in this chapter shows that there is a good deal of loose thinking about both the terms 'conditioning' and 'indoctrination'. Because they are seldom assigned their appropriate logical geography, they are frequently confused with each other and, almost as frequently, with other terms, such as 'instruction', 'drill' 'teaching', and even 'education' itself.

Consequently our first task must be to establish in our own minds exactly what both terms imply, how they differ from each other, what they have in common with the related terms, and in precisely which areas and characteristics they differ. When we have done this, we find that, in education, there are processes which bear superficial resemblance to conditioning and to indoctrination, but the instances of *real* conditioning and indoctrination are very much fewer. Neither conditioning nor indoctrination is educationally acceptable, since both fail to measure up to the third of Peters' criteria and must be classified as morally objectionable, since they rob the learner of wittingness and voluntariness. In the instances where certain processes are mistaken for conditioning and indoctrination, it can be said that they achieve little which is genuinely educational and that on these grounds alone they must be condemned. But we must be very clear why we are rejecting a process. It is one thing to reject it because it is inefficient; it is quite another to reject it because it is morally objectionable, just as we must distinguish between sacking an employee because he is not efficient, and sacking him on the grounds that his moral character leaves much to be desired. Our last word must be that conditioning, in the sense acceptable to behaviourists, has little part in human learning and teaching, that there is much more potential danger from the introduction of indoctrination, which is concerned with beliefs rather than reactions. To ensure that it does not become mistaken for teaching we must remember always that education involves:

1 The transmission of knowledge and beliefs, and the justification of both by the teacher to the learner, as well as the understanding of both by the learner.
2 The intelligent use by the learner of the knowledge and beliefs acquired.
3 Wittingness and voluntariness on the part of the learner.

4 The development of cognitive perspective in the learner.

5 Consideration by the teacher of the well-being of the learner in all that he undertakes to do with the learner.

NOTES AND REFERENCES FOR CHAPTER 9

1 Cats in puzzle boxes were used by a number of behaviourists in their experiments. Among these was E. R. Guthrie. The puzzle box had a pole in a vertical position in the centre. The cat was placed in the box, and the door, which could be opened only from inside by pressure on the pole, was closed by the experimenter. The trial and error behaviour of the cat leading up to the final (correct) response of brushing its body against the vertical bar was filmed by the experimenter. On subsequent trials, the behaviour was again filmed. Thus the behaviour of any cat on any trial could be compared with the behaviour of the same cat on any other trial, or with the behaviour of any cat on any trial in the same puzzle box. Thus Guthrie was able to look for 'stereotyped responses'.

2 The infant in question was given a white toy rabbit to which he became tremendously attached. Watson showed that, by making a most unpleasant sound every time the infant went near the rabbit, he could be conditioned to hate and avoid it. This type of behaviour is known technically as 'avoidance conditioning' and is similar to the example of giving the rat an electric shock when it entered the black box, to condition it to avoid it in future trials. Similarly, in the situation quoted from Hardie where children used to be flogged to make them learn, 'avoidance conditioning' was also at work. The children remembered the material they were taught in order to avoid the flogging.

3 *Truth and Fallacy in Educational Theory*, C. D. Hardie (Cambridge University Press 1942).

4 Pavlov was a Russian physiologist who experimented with Alsatian dogs. Knowing that dogs automatically salivate when hungry and confronted with meat, Pavlov, by pairing certain objects, e.g. an electric bell, a light, a metronome, with the meat, conditioned the dog to salivate to these objects. (See also notes and references for Chapter 1, Section 3.)

5 A Skinner box is illustrated in the diagram below:

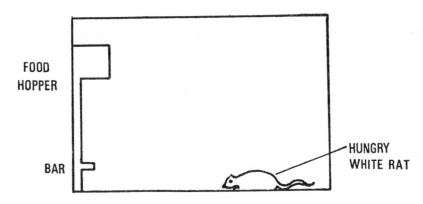

FOOD
HOPPER

BAR

HUNGRY
WHITE RAT

6 The term 'chance' appears in statistical works. If some event occurs by chance, it occurs without any particular reason. Thus if we throw a penny in the air, there is no particular reason why it should come down 'heads' rather than 'tails'. Some events, however, occur too often for chance. Such events occur for some significant reason. If a child who has never learned to do addition sums is given ten sums and gets one right, he does so 'by chance'. If a child who has learned to do addition sums gets ten out of ten right, he does not do this by chance, but because he has learned the process of addition correctly, which is the significant reason for his success. If the child who had not learned addition got all ten right, this would not be merely by chance, nor because he had learned addition correctly, since he had not been taught it. All that we can say is that he obtained the right answer 'too frequently for chance'. In this case, we are not immediately able to isolate and define the significant reason. A fuller discussion of 'chance' and 'significance' and other elementary statistical terms is undertaken in: *Assessment and Testing: An Introduction* H. Schofield, op. cit.

7 *Ethics and Education*, R. S. Peters (George Allen & Unwin 1966).

8 Note: Rapaport writes in *Emotion and Memory*, D. Rapaport (Science Editions Inc., New York 1961): 'Conditioning limits the freedom of reaction and thus is *not comparable to life situations* in which the emotional effect on memory is palpable.'

9 See 7 above.'

10 'Conditioning and Learning', Godfrey Vesey, in *The Concept of Education*, R. S. Peters (Routledge & Kegan Paul 1967).

11 See notes and references for Chapter 3, Section 2.

12 'Philosophical Models and Teaching' Israel Scheffler, in *Philosophy and Education*, 2nd edn., ed. Israel Scheffler (Allyn & Bacon 1966).

13 'Education and Indoctrination', John Wilson, in *Aims in Education; the Philosophical Approach*, ed. T. H. B. Hollins (Manchester University Press 1964).

14 The Latin word *nebula* means a 'cloud'. Consequently when Wilson describes 'indoctrination' as 'nebulous', he means that people's ideas about its meaning are 'cloudy' or 'unclear'. Using a similar meteorological metaphor we often say that people's ideas are 'hazy'.

15 'Indoctrination', John White, in *The Concept of Education*, op. cit.

16 The classic work, by R. M. Hare, is *The Language of Morals* (Oxford University Press 1952). This is by no means an easy book to read, but it is such an important one that those who have some experience of philosophy will find it tremendously helpful.

17 'Education and the Science of Education', Ralph Boston Perry, in *Philosophy and Education*, op. cit. See also notes and references for Chapter 5, Section 2.

18 See 17 above.

19 *Assessment and Testing: An Introduction*, H. Schofield, op. cit. See also 17 above.

20 See 17 above.

21 In the 'ego-defence mechanism' known as 'projection', we see our own faults most clearly in other people. We criticize other people for these faults to avoid feeling guilty at possessing them ourselves. The process is an unconscious one. Also, by projection, the 'bad workman blames his tools'. This is a common phenomenon in everyday life. Instead of giving the real

reason for our behaviour, we invent one. For example, if we sit an examination and fail, we pretend that we never really wished to obtain a pass. We only went because our friends went, and we are not the least concerned that we have failed. We take this line to protect our pride, and again the process is unconsciously inspired. Discussion of this and other 'ego-defence mechanisms' is undertaken in *Assessment and Testing: An Introduction*, op. cit.

22 The term 'public school' in the United States educational system, is what we call a 'state school'. It is called 'public', as distinct from 'private', since it is the school to which everyone is entitled to go. Originally the term 'public school' in our educational system had a real meaning, since it was the intention of the founders of our 'public schools' that poor boys should be educated there free of charge.

23 The term 'stamping in' applies to a successful response to a stimulus which is subsequently repeated whenever the stimulus appears. Each performance of the response 'stamps it in' more deeply. This particular term is used only by E. L. Thorndike (see our Chapter 3, notes and references, Section 2).

24 See 13 above.

25 See notes and references for Chapter 4, Section 17.

The Third Trilogy

VALUE JUDGMENTS
VALUES
MORALS

Chapter 10

The Concept
'Value-Judgments'

We make value-judgments every day of our lives, both as private individuals and as teachers (1). As private individuals we say, for example, 'I prefer coffee to tea with my breakfast', and as teachers, 'Smith is better at English than Jones'. In both capacities we make more general statements, which are still classifiable as 'value-judgments': 'War is a terrible thing'; 'Peace is most desirable'; 'Education is valuable'.

VALUE-JUDGMENTS AND OPINION (SUBJECTIVITY)

The one thing that all these statements have in common is that they express an opinion about the comparative merits of two people or things, or the desirability of something, or the undesirability of something else. Another feature common to all of them is that there is no method of measuring the truth of the statements against an outside criterion. We may find a large number of people who share our subjective view about the relative merits of peace and war, or of coffee and tea as a breakfast drink. We may also find some people who support our view that Smith is better than Jones at English. However in the latter example, we could just as easily find someone who disagrees violently with our judgment. If the person who disagrees with me does so as the result of impressions which he has gained from the work of Smith and Jones in English, he is as entitled to his point of view as I am to mine, because he uses the same grounds as evidence for making the statement. If I say that the man who contradicts me about the respective merits of Smith and Jones in English is wrong, I am guilty of using the word 'wrong' incorrectly, because I am virtually saying that he has no right to make his statement.

Because both statements are based on personal, subjective impressions, there is no proof that either party is right or wrong. All that is clear is that the other person disagrees with my assessment of the merits of Smith and Jones in English. Far from being entitled to say that the other man is wrong, I am entitled only to say that his opinion differs from mine.

VALUE-JUDGMENTS AND EVIDENCE (OBJECTIVITY)

I may, however, be saying that our opponent is wrong because of the evidence on which he bases his statement. But, since he is using the same evidence as I am, I must also be wrong, if this type of evidence, namely the impression which people's work makes on us, is wrong. I may feel that my opponent has got the wrong impression, but this again is only saying that he has not formed the same impression as I have. Consequently since there is no proof that I am right, I cannot condemn as wrong somebody who differs from me merely *because* he differs.

There are other occasions when we *may* be entitled to say that those who disagree with us are wrong. I may have in the school where I teach two boys who are 'good quarter-milers'. A colleague and I have each watched Brown and Robinson running against other boys round the quarter-mile running track. Both boys have won every race which we have watched. But the distance by which Brown beat his opponents was always much greater than the distance by which Robinson beat his. I, therefore, make the statement that 'Brown is a better quarter-miler than Robinson'.

By this I mean that, if the two boys were to run a series of quarter-mile races, Brown would beat Robinson every time, or in the majority of cases. The evidence on which I base this statement is that, whenever I have watched them running in separate races, Brown has always beaten his opponents by the greater margin. But this is not necessarily *reliable* evidence. It is possible that Brown has always run against weaker opposition. In this case, any judgment that I make which depends on Brown's opponents is invalid. Again, it is possible that I have always seen Brown win when all the conditions were in his favour, whereas, whenever I have seen Robinson win, it has always been in conditions adverse to good running.

My colleague and I can attempt to resolve our differences about the respective merits of Brown and Robinson by requiring them to run a quarter-mile race against each other. We now attempt a more objective appraisal of their respective performances as quarter-milers. Both my colleague and I are about to put our opinions (our judgments) to the test. The conditions are acceptable to both, and we try to eliminate every possible source of error.

In the first place, we insist that the school groundsman must measure the running-track to ensure that it is exactly a quarter of a mile in circumference. We also decide that there shall be no other competitors in the race, since one of the boys might have an advantage over the other if he had boys to 'pace' him. We do not insist that both boys wear spiked shoes, because we know that Brown prefers to run barefoot. To make him wear spikes would appear to make the situation fairer; in actual fact it would only make the boys' footwear similar, which would prove a severe handicap for Brown. We ensure, as far as possible, that conditions before the race are as ideal as possible – for example, making sure that neither boy is subjected to situations which might upset him emotionally.

The race is run and Brown wins. I am about to claim victory for my judgment over that of my colleague, when he says: 'But that was only one race. You cannot be sure, on the evidence of one race, that Brown is a better quarter-miler than Robinson.' I am forced to agree, and we stage a series of races, twenty in all, over a period of time, and Brown wins sixteen of them, one is a dead heat, and Robinson wins the remaining three. I am now *convinced* that Brown is a better quarter-miler, but my friend is not so sure. I am convinced, despite the three defeats, because of the sixteen victories. My colleague has reservations because of the three defeats. He reminds me of what statisticians say about the danger of basing conclusions on a small sample, in this case on a small number of instances. He tells me that if we throw a penny in the air, there is as much chance of its coming down heads as tails He tells me further that if we toss a penny twenty times and it comes down heads sixteen out of the twenty times, this does nothing to alter the original statement that there is as much likelihood of its coming down heads as tails. He supports this statement by tossing the coin another twenty times and obtaining sixteen 'tails'. The result of the first twenty throws is exactly reversed by the next twenty, and we have evidence to support the original statement that a penny is just as likely to come down heads as tails. He now argues that if we made Jones and Robinson run another twenty quarter-mile races, we might be just as likely to reverse the results of their first twenty attempts.

But what of our two boys Smith and Jones, and their respective ability in English? From our example of attempting to prove my point about the superiority of Brown over Robinson as a quarter-miler, I might say: 'Why not set the same English test to both boys, to discover who is the better?' There are immediate objections to this. My colleague, who supports Jones, suggests an 'objective test', in which the answers to questions consist of single words placed in blank spaces. I object to this on the grounds that this is not a test of English. I suggest that both boys be set an essay and a comprehension test. My colleague refuses this, since he claims that the essay plus the comprehension test is not as fair a test of English as the objective test. One of his reasons for this is that essays are marked subjectively, or by impression, and that this is an invalid method of marking. The objective test, he argues, has a mark scheme which does not leave room for personal interpretation. I still object that this argument is nullified by the fact that what my colleague claims to be an 'objective test of English ability' is not a real test of 'English ability' at all.

The situation is now very complicated. My last statement that 'an objective test of English is not a test of English ability at all' is another value-judgment. Furthermore, it attempts to contradict my colleague's value-judgment that 'an objective test of English is a fair test of English ability'. Neither of us has, in fact, determined exactly what we mean by the term 'ability in English'. The fact that we both strongly support different methods of testing such ability suggests that we have different ideas about its nature. Consequently, when we claim to be more objective, or more scientific by using the same sort of test for both boys, we are suggesting only that we apply the same measure to different things. This would have been like seeing whether Brown or Robinson climbed a thirty-foot rope faster in order to decide which was the better quarter-miler. When we made our original value-judgments about the ability in English of Smith and Jones, we assessed different things (ability in English, according to two different interpretations) by the same technique (value-judgments, which are really personal opinions). Now we attempt to assess two different things (ability in English, according to two interpretations) by the same method (objective test of English). However, since I do not accept that an objective test of English measures ability in English, we use two different techniques to test two different things, and there is no greater likelihood of our agreeing than there was originally.

The only realistic conclusion, which we can reach is that it is a great deal more difficult to decide whether Smith is, in fact, better at English than Jones, than it was to determine whether Brown was a better quarter-miler than Robinson. By 'decide' we mean produce some form of measurement which will prove to the man who originally disagreed with us that he is wrong and we are right.

KNOWING AND BEING SURE: EXPRESSIONS OF OPINION: STATEMENTS OF FACT

We have been concerned so far with the problem which we encountered in the first chapter of this book, namely of finding ourselves in a situation where we pose a question and arrive at an answer without being 'absolutely sure' that we are right. We asked a question about the origin of the universe and found that it was possible to give answers and to find a body of supporting opinion. Much of this opinion could be described as 'expert' and, because the people who expressed the opinions were experts or authorities in this particular area, we felt that it was meaningful to accept their opinions although there was no means of proving that they were correct. This is an important point, and one to which we shall return later.

The danger in the statements which we considered at the beginning of the present chapter is that they have the same grammatical structure as statements of fact. They are 'is' statements. Hospers (1) embarks on a very lengthy discussion of the nature of knowledge, and, after reading all of it, we come to the conclusion that we are seldom, if ever, entitled to say 'I *know*' if by this we mean 'I am *absolutely certain*'. But this is a much finer philosophical distinction than we require for our purpose. What we must appreciate is that statements of fact (which, supposedly, relate to knowledge) must not be confused with expressions of opinion (which do not, and cannot, in the same way relate to knowledge). If we accept that it is possible to know, we can say, as a statement of fact: 'London is the capital of England'. If someone says that Birmingham is the capital of England, we are entitled to say that he is wrong. But when we say: 'Peace is better than war', we are *not* stating a *fact*; we are expressing an opinion. It is, because of the nature of the subject, an opinion with which many would agree, and it is expressed in exactly the same way as our statement of fact that 'London is the capital of England'. But it is not a statement of fact.

People come to accept expressions of opinion as statements of fact for three reasons; firstly, because they agree with their own opinions, biases and preconceptions, secondly, because many other people, often 'authority figures', support them; thirdly, they are stated frequently and often persuasively. This is nowhere more true than in the case of the indoctrinator. In Chapter 9, we saw that indoctrination has as its content not facts, but beliefs. The beliefs are repeated over and over again, until they become unconsciously accepted as being true. We are now in a position to appreciate that many beliefs are really value-judgments which have gained wide acceptance.

We must distinguish between value-judgments which gain wide acceptance, and those which those making them *expect* to gain wide acceptance, often on no stronger evidence than that they have wide application. When the pound was devalued, the Government expressed a value-judgment, in the same form as a statement of fact, which had wide application. They stated that devaluation was in the interests of the country. Such a statement is emotive, since it seeks to convince. It is not a statement of fact, and could more accurately be expressed in the form: 'In the opinion of the Government, devaluation is in the interests of the country'. In the light of available evidence, the Government had formed an (expert) opinion.

But many people found through experience (empirically) that they were worse off financially after devaluation. Prices rose and their wages bought less than they had done before. Their problem was to reconcile the discrepancy between the idea that devaluation was 'in the interests of the country' (meaning that the *country* would be better off) and their own experience that they personally were worse off. Yet they were, surely, part of 'the country'. For most people, evidence from their own experience, which they can acquire by direct sensation, carries more weight than theoretical (but more general) evidence offered by someone else, although that someone else may be an acknowledged expert. Wider application of the value-judgment does not automatically bring wider acceptance.

We can see a similarity here between the problem of devaluation and the problem posed by the concepts of culture and curriculum (Chapters 6 and

7). There we saw that there was a general culture which had wide application resulting in a general curriculum which, again, had wide application. But at the same time we saw that there were many people from sub-cultural groups, both adults and children, who did not accept the general cultural values or the subjects of the general curriculum merely because they had wide application. We saw that the teacher was often placed in the difficult position of having to heal the breach between the general culture and the specific sub-culture from which their pupils came.

In this case, a body of experts, like the government in the devaluation example, decided what was good for everyone. They expressed a value-judgment in the form of an 'is' statement: 'a, b, and c are good for children', from which they produced an 'ought' statement: 'Therefore, all children *must* study a, b and c.'

We may combine 'ought' and 'is' statements, when the 'is' statement is a statement of fact, but not when it is merely a value-judgment with the same syntactical form as a statement of fact. In the latter case, we shall not be challenged, because the fact is widely accepted as well as widely applicable. In the former instance, we may well be challenged, because the statement, although widely applicable, is not automatically widely accepted.

Thus we can say: 'London is the capital of England' (an 'is' statement of fact), therefore 'All children *ought* to learn that London is the capital of England' (an 'ought' statement based on an 'is' statement of fact). But there is no exact parallel between this justification and the justification for basing an 'ought' statement on an 'is' statement in the situation where we say: 'x, y, and z are good for children' (an 'is' statement-value-judgment), therefore 'Children ought to learn x, y, and z' (an 'ought' statement based on a value-judgment).

These ideas may come as something of a surprise to the reader. They may also prompt him to ask, and indeed they ought to prompt him to ask, 'How great a part do value-judgments play in education, and how great a part have value-judgments played already in this book?' The answer is that value-judgments have played a considerable part, and nowhere more than in the discussion of the aims of education in Chapter 5. In that chapter we undertook a lengthy analysis not only of the actual aims which various people put forward, but also of the way in which the expression of aims became *the* aim or *the* aims. We saw that some of these expressions were prescriptive, like 'ought' statements, telling us what we must do. Others were descriptive, like 'is' statements.

But however the ideas were expressed, they remained only ideas or opinions. They were not facts. Even when we said that Huxley defined the aim of medieval education as saintliness, we were not stating a fact. We were giving an opinion of Huxley. We are not saying that it was not an informed opinion, but we are saying that it was an opinion as distinct from a fact. It was based on an interpretation of the evidence available, and interpretations are not the same as facts. It was an expression of belief or conviction, but expressions of belief or convictions are not the same as facts, any more than education (in Chapter 9) was the same as indoctrination, similar though they appeared to be in certain contexts. Two things may be *superficially* very similar without being *essentially* the same. Nowhere is the truth of this shown more clearly than in the realm of factual judgments and value-judgments.

The fact that O'Connor put forward a *tentative* rather than a categorical list of five aims showed that he appreciated very clearly the distinction between value-judgments and facts. He was not saying: 'These are *the* five aims of education' (statement of fact), 'Therefore everyone ought to accept these as the five aims of education' ('ought' statement based on an 'is' statement of fact). He is merely saying: 'I have considered the evidence for what constitutes the aims of education. I have studied education very carefully and have gained considerable expertise in education. As a result of this, I have prestige when I speak on education. Many accept me as an authority on education. Yet in spite of all these things, the following are the five aims of education *only in my opinion* (and in the opinion of other people qualified to speak on the subject). O'Connor is doing no more than expressing an informed opinion.

INFORMED OPINION

The danger now is that having made ourselves aware of the difference between fact and opinion and even between opinion and *informed* opinion, we shall go about rejecting almost everything. This would not be wise at all. Throughout our lives we regularly seek informed or expert opinion. Moreover we often make momentous decisions involving many thousands of pounds as the result of such opinion.

Let us take a simple example. We wish to buy a house. After looking round a particular area, we find just what we have been looking for. We tell our friends that we have found a 'dream house' (value-judgment, not a statement of fact). One friend being wiser than we are, or at least thinking more clearly because he is less emotionally involved with the house, asks if we have had it valued and surveyed. We ask the reason for his question and he says: 'You are so thrilled at finding the house that you want that you have not stopped to ask yourselves whether the price which is being asked is too high, and whether it is structurally sound, free from dry rot, woodworm, etc.'

Our friend has a certain amount of evidence on which to base the opinion that we have not made such inquiries. It is quite likely that the price is too high, because a seller often asks more than the house is worth, knowing that a purchaser will generally try 'to beat the price down'. But we were so carried away by the sight of our 'dream house' that we never thought of trying to 'beat the price down'. Similarly, we were so delighted at finding this 'dream house', that we never for one moment thought logically enough to imagine that there could be anything in it so ugly and destructive as dry rot.

At our friend's insistence, because we have always valued his '*opinion*', we approach both a valuer and a surveyor. We seek the informed (or expert) opinion of the valuer about the price being asked for the house, and of the surveyor about the structural soundness of the house. We give greater weight to the opinions of the valuer and the surveyor than to the opinion of our friend because they are better informed in these areas. They are experts; he is merely a well-informed layman.

When the valuer and the surveyor make their reports on the price and structure of the house, each indicates that his report is an expression of opinion. They write '*In our opinion* the price which is being asked is rather more than the current market value of the property', or, '*In our opinion* (sometimes 'As far as we are able to tell from our examination') the house is generally structurally sound'.

No one appreciates more than a surveyor the importance of distinguishing between fact and opinion. If he were unwise enough to make a 'statement of fact' – 'This house *is* structurally sound' – and within the first week of our occupying it, the front wall fell down, we could take him to court. We could produce the written evidence of his statement of fact, and say that it was on this evidence that we had bought the house, and the surveyor could well suffer heavy damages.

Surveyors have been known to be wrong, but we do not, for this reason, refuse to have a house surveyed before buying it. We feel that we can rely on the expert opinion of a surveyor much more than on our own uninformed opinion. In other circumstances we even pride ourselves on relying on informed or expert opinion. If we go into an expensive restaurant and are given a large and complex menu, we may turn to the waiter and ask: 'What do you recommend?' The way we phrase our question shows that we are seeking an expression of opinion, not a statement of fact. If we required the latter, we would ask, 'Which dish is best?' But even then we would receive only a value-judgment, but the emphasis in our question is different. We pride ourselves, for some reason, on seeking expert opinion in this situation. A possible reason is that we feel that it is 'the done thing' to ask the waiter for his opinion when we dine in expensive restaurants. By 'doing the done thing' we impress both the waiter and the guests who are with us. (The importance of 'doing the done thing' was considered in Chapter 6.) We consulted the valuer and the surveyor before purchasing a house, because we thought it was the sensible thing to do.

But, in such matters as the curriculum, we are not so concerned with doing 'the done thing', or doing the sensible thing, or even with consulting expert opinion. In such cases, we are often governed by those biases, prejudices, and uninformed preferences, which we have mentioned throughout this book. Herbert Spencer recognized this, when he wrote (2):

> 'Men read books on this topic and attend lectures on that; de˅ le that their children shall be instructed in these branches of knowleage and not in those, and all under the guidance of mere custom, or liking, or prejudice; without even considering the importance of determining, in some rational way, what things are really most worth learning.'

This sentence is a crucial one, since it again raises the problem of curriculum content and how that content shall be decided. In the early part of the quotation, he reminds us of a point we have stressed frequently, that many decisions, including momentous ones, can be and often are made as the result of prejudice and bias or through unthinking acceptance of tradition. He ends by reminding us of a point that we have frequently stressed with equal force, namely, the importance of making decisions on rational grounds if they are to be accepted by others and justified by ourselves.

INDIVIDUAL AND GENERAL VALUE-JUDGMENTS

We have thus reached a most interesting point in the development of our ideas about value-judgments, a point at which it is important to draw together the main threads of the argument before proceeding further. Firstly, there are two basic types of value-judgment; those which affect only a particular individual, and those which affect a large number of people. In the first category comes the individual preference for coffee rather than tea at breakfast-time. Whether we have coffee or tea is of little concern or importance to anyone else. In the other category come those statements which say that devaluation will ultimately be good for the country's economy and similar pronouncements.

In the first type of value-judgment, we do not trouble to bring evidence to substantiate our choice. Indeed, the judgment is so personal that the only individual really concerned is the one who makes the judgment. There is no reason why he should attempt to convince himself. He has in the past tried both coffee and tea as breakfast drinks, and, as a result of, or on the evidence of this experience, he prefers coffee.

In the other type of value-judgment it is usual to give reasons or to present evidence to support it. It is not always possible, however, to convince all the people affected by the results of the value-judgment of the correctness of the judgment or of the advisability of the measures taken as a result of that judgment. The evidence of experience may convince some individuals that both the value-judgment and the measures based on it are wrong.

But this is not strictly true. Neither the highly personal and unimportant value-judgment, nor the general and highly important value-judgment is a 'fact'. Consequently we cannot say that it is wrong in the same way that we can say that the statement $2 + 2 = 5$ is wrong. We can only say that the evidence of our own experience does not support the idea that coffee is better than tea as a breakfast drink, or that devaluation will ultimately benefit the country's economy.

The third step in the argument is that, although we can allow individuals to decide for themselves whether they drink coffee or tea for breakfast, since there will be no general harm or general good depending on their decisions, we cannot allow any individual to decide whether devaluation should or should not take place. In this type of situation, the opinion must be informed opinion. The decision must be made by people in authority, whose opinions are well informed, so that there shall be uniformity. If individuals are allowed to wrangle over the point among themselves, putting forward individual value-judgments which are little more, in most cases, than *uninformed* opinion, the result will be a decision which is certainly arbitrary and possibly even dangerous for a great number of people.

VALUE-JUDGMENTS AND THE CURRICULUM

If we relate these factors to Spencer's statement, we can see he is saying that we cannot afford to have our curriculum decided according to the whims and fancies of individuals, some of whom may be well-informed and some not. It is bad enough to have decisions made for us as the result of informed opinion, but far worse to have them made as the result of uninformed opinion.

Moreover, if we look at the history of education and curriculum content, we find that many 'authorities' have, in the past, dogmatized about the content of the curriculum. They have delivered value-judgments as if they were factual statements, and have often made 'ought' statements without giving any more evidence than that 'we, the Authority, say so'. When people are allowed to do this sort of thing, education possesses a stable curriculum but often ceases to be education because of rigidity, narrowness, and dogmatism. In Chapter 9, we saw that the last three words may be characteristic of indoctrination rather than of education. They are certainly characteristics of poor teaching.

The truth is that, even in the most authoritarian times, for example the Middle Ages or the time of the Jesuits, the content of the curriculum was never decided by anything stronger than informed opinion. We do not say that: 'These subjects *must* be the curriculum because they are, *in fact*, the most important.' We can only say that 'these subjects are (according to informed opinion) the best'. When value-judgments in this particular area become confused with facts, there is always a predictable course of events. For a long time there is stability in the curriculum. Then something happens outside education of great importance, such as the Industrial Revolution or the rise of modern science, and people begin to think for themselves. They begin to see weaknesses in the curriculum content and flaws in the arguments which support the inclusion of those subjects. There is then a violent protest and a new content is produced. Alternatively, the revolution may be in teaching method rather than in curriculum content. We have recently seen a bitter attack on 'formal, traditional methods' of teaching and the substitution of 'progressive', or 'non-directive', methods. More recently still, there has been a severe onslaught on non-directive methods by eminent authorities capable of expressing extremely well-informed opinions (3).

Value-judgments, then, are the only things on which curriculum content can be decided. But this does not mean that there is no justification for saying that 'this and this shall be the curriculum'. If we made invalid all decisions taken on the strength of value-judgments, life would come to a standstill. We ourselves have stressed (and we have seen that Spencer also stresses it) the need for rationality, for the weighing of evidence as objectively as possible. The traditional curriculum became established when certain authorities decided in their own interests what that content should be. The 'child-centred' protest against this traditional curriculum was equally devoid of balance and rationality. It exaggerated the importance of the child in order to make its point. The rational approach, and the one which Peters uses as his criterion for the inclusion of an area of study in the curriculum, is the intrinsic value of the subject itself. The things of the 'academic interpretation of culture' are the things which have intrinsic value, and are worth studying for their own sake. They have a usefulness, but it is an indirect one, namely, of developing sensitivity, appreciation, and rationality in those who study them, as distinct from that direct usefulness which equips one for a certain trade or profession. Such areas of study enable the individual to develop cognitive perspective, and to live a more balanced and beneficial life both for his own ends and in the interest of other people.

The value-judgment which says that these things are intrinsically valuable or good is not an arbitrary one, even if it is not a unanimous one. It is not made to further the interest of the people who make it, but is made in the belief that it will benefit those who follow it. The evidence available to the informed minds capable of interpreting it is that these areas of study are the ones best suited to benefit those who study them. Within these areas, other informed minds are entitled to say that, with certain sections of society, one method of teaching these subjects is better than another. For this reason, the Newsom Report (4) suggests that with the average and below-average ability groups, less academic approaches to the areas of study which figure in the academic curriculum are better. By its very wording, such a value-judgment indicates that the interest of the learner is uppermost in the minds of the people who make it. They are attempting to strike a balance and maintain a harmony between the teacher and the learner, between the teacher and what is taught and between the learner and what is learned, so that the claims of none of the three is exaggerated at the expense of the other two. The value-judgments are not made in a vacuum. They are made as the result of experts weighing the evidence available, and are thus made on rational rather than on arbitrary grounds. Because of this, the decisions about curriculum content and teaching method in the most important cases resemble the value-judgments made by the valuer and the surveyor in our imaginary house-purchase situation.

It is this argument that should be put forward when people ask by what right authorities 'impose' a curriculum content. It is much more sensible for informed opinion to decide what is good for sub-cultural groups and the best method of teaching them that content and *showing them how and why it is good*, than it is to allow the sub-groups to decide arbitrarily what is good for themselves. In this case the opinion on which they would base their value-judgments is singularly uninformed. If the individual feels – value-judgment – that he would be better off not studying mathematics and English literature, there is no guarantee that he is right. It is not the same thing to say that A feels that such a study is useless for him, as to say (as a statement of fact) that it is useless for A to study so-and-so. In the area of the curriculum, as in the area of choosing food and wine for a meal or buying a house, there is a greater probability of informed opinions being right than there is of uninformed opinions being right, or (if we wish to avoid the word 'right' in view of what we have already said) being better or more convincing.

INFORMED OPINION AND EDUCATIONAL PHILOSOPHY

At this point, we can assemble further evidence of the usefulness of educational philosophy for the practising teacher. In terms of what we have said in this chapter, it appears that educational philosophy may, in some respects, consist of a body of informed, educational opinion. In its speculative role, it looks at society and at the needs of society and the needs of the individual in relation to the needs of society. It looks at the factors which contribute to culture and sees which of these ought to be represented in the curriculum. Because it does not have facts of its own but processes the facts of other disciplines, it is not given to pontificating but to expressing opinions, not given to laying down rules but establishing guide-lines.

In its critical role, philosophy, and consequently educational philosophy, examines the data it gathers on rational grounds, sifting it and deciding what is valuable and what valueless. Acting in the present, it assesses the past and attempts to look into the future to present a unified picture. Then, in its normative role, it attempts to establish norms or standards in the best interests of all concerned.

For this reason, it is often appropriate to express the function of educational philosophy (or educational theory) and the relation of theory to practice in the form of a metaphor. Metaphors, by their very nature, cannot be categorical factual statements, for the simple reason that they must not be taken literally. Thus, we find such metaphorical expressions as: 'Educational theory (or philosophy) is a lamp which guides the feet of practice' or 'Practice without theory is blind, theory without practice is lame.' We cannot take these as factual statements or act upon them as categorical imperatives. (So-and-so is true, therefore, everyone must . . .) Instead, we must examine the appropriateness of each metaphor and decide why it is used. At once we are required to behave rationally. By not expressing an idea directly, the metaphor makes it impossible for us, if we are thinking people, to confuse it with a statement of fact.

VALUE-JUDGMENTS AND AUTHORITATIVE FIGURES

Value-judgments, then, play a very large part in our lives. They also appear frequently in education. They entail opinions and beliefs, even beliefs fervently held by large numbers of people. If we can show to our own satisfaction that there is substance to the opinion or the belief, there is no harm in our accepting the value-judgment. But we must beware that we do not use value-judgments in the way that the religious fanatic, eager to make 'doorstep conversions', attempts to use scriptural texts, taken completely from context and repeated dogmatically and categorically. So often, by behaving in this way in education, we not only hide the truth of the value-judgment, we also turn people, perhaps for all time, against the idea contained in the value-judgment. Such a value-judgment as 'A cultured man reads Shakespeare' may be stated with such bigotry that it turns the hearer against both the idea of a cultured man as well as against Shakespeare. Value-judgments can be cryptic and forceful, as this one is, but the more cryptic and forceful they are, the more carefully they need to be handled. The best way to use value-judgments, and especially the most dogmatic, is to give convincing reasons in support of the statement. We must not believe, like the Bellman in the *Hunting of the Snark*, that 'what I tell you three times is true'. If one is entitled to make the value-judgment 'Shakespeare is good' others are entitled to remind the speaker of what a king of England (5) said to the contrary: 'Shakespeare is pretty poor stuff, really, but it is not "the done thing" to say so'. Both sides have made value-judgments; neither side has stated a fact. Each side has phrased its value-judgment strongly. It is the duty of both sides to bring evidence in support of their claim. The fact that the person who makes the first claim is one who is vested by society with the authority of a schoolmaster, does not automatically make him an authority on Shakespeare. When he makes his claim, he may be doing no more than passing on to a group of children something which *his* teachers passed on to him. He may have accepted it as a statement of fact and may be handing it on similarly as a statement of fact. He must be prepared to defend the statement if there are those in his audience who do not accept it as readily as he did at the same age.

Conversely, the fact that the contrary value-judgment was made by an English monarch, a figure of great authority, does not automatically make it any more justified than if it had been made by the man in the street. Neither is necessarily an authority on Shakespeare. Consequently, each, if he is to be convincing, must give reasons for his opinion.

In an earlier chapter, we saw the important contribution of Leibniz to philosophy. Leibniz found flaws in the syllogistic reasoning of Aristotle (6) but, because Aristotle was so venerated as an authority (even in some quarters as the supreme authority) in matters of logic, Leibniz refrained from exposing the flaws. Subsequently other people showed that Leibniz was correct, and that, in spite of Aristotle's authority and his undeniable eminence in logic, there were flaws in his system.

Blind acceptance of value-judgments because of the eminence of the person making them, often weakens that person's position and robs the statement of its importance. Unthinking people turn the judgment into a slogan which is bandied about to no other effect than to bring it into discredit. For similar reasons, many words in the English language, such as the adjective 'great', cease to have any meaning because they are misused so frequently. Similarly many important statements lose their force because they become clichés. Nowadays, if we quote the old saying, 'To teach John a subject, we must know John as well as the subject', we are unlikely to receive any response but laughter. Yet many eminent writers have written, and are currently writing at great length, without saying anything more profound than the writer of this apophthegm, which frequent and thoughtless repetition has made hackneyed.

We have stressed a number of points in this chapter because they are important in themselves, and also because this is the first chapter in a trilogy. The points at issue have an important bearing on the concepts analysed in the other two chapters, namely values and morals. The fact that these same points have thrown further light on the concepts in previous trilogies is further evidence of the interrelatedness of concepts within the family of education, and of the folly of attempting to study any one in isolation from the rest.

NOTES AND REFERENCES FOR CHAPTER 10

1 *An Introduction to Philosophical Analysis*, J. Hospers. For other references to this book see notes and references for Chapter 4, Section 17 and Chapter 12, Section 4.
2 *Education, Intellectual, Moral and Physical*, Herbert Spencer. (See also notes and references for Chapter 1, Section 20.
3 The reference here is to the *Black Paper*; see also notes and references to Chapter 4, Section 9 and the subsequent articles in such papers as the *Daily Telegraph*, expressing the views of such eminent educationalists as Sir Cyril Burt and Stephen Wiseman.
4 Entitled 'Half Our Future'; see also notes and references for Chapter 4, Section 28.
5 The statement is attributed to George III after reading *King Lear*.
6 Those who are interested in learning more about Aristotelian logic should consult the appropriate chapter in Bertrand Russell's *A History of Western Philosophy*, to which numerous references have been made throughout this book. Those readers who undertake such a study might care to assess whether they find the content of philosophy easier to understand now, after gaining more experience in the subject, than they did when they were referred initially to Russell.

Chapter 11

The Concept 'Values'

Throughout this book there have been many implied references to values in education as well as explicit mention. In Chapter 2, when we considered Peters' three criteria, we found that education involved the transmission of what is worthwhile, or what a particular society values so highly that it finds it important to pass it on to each succeeding generation.

Since education is the medium through which society transmits what it finds valuable, the content of education can be defined as 'a set of values'. Thus, when we examined the curriculum, the content of that formal education which the school, acting on behalf of society, transmits, we were again involved in a discussion of what is valuable. We found that education is concerned with beliefs as well as with facts, with norms or standards as well as with training.

But we have also seen throughout this book that many of the terms which represent concepts within education are nebulous. We specifically said this about indoctrination (Chapter 9). There, the term was nebulous because many people do not wish to come to grips with it, because of the unpleasant connotations which the word has for them. In the case of education and, indeed, in the case of values, the terms remain nebulous because we know 'vaguely' or 'roughly' what they mean, and, as a result, never discipline ourselves to ask what *exactly* they mean.

ABSOLUTE VALUES

We found it useful, in Chapter 3 where we analysed 'training', to add certain adjectives to the term which, by qualifying it or limiting it, gave us a clearer starting-point for our analysis. It was much easier, we found, to grasp the idea of 'vocational training' or of 'physical training', both of which are fairly specific activities, than to understand the general concept of training. Similarly, with values there are two limiting adjectives which we can add, one of which is familiar, the other less so. Most readers will have heard of '*absolute* values', some may have heard of '*pragmatic* values'. By contrasting these two types of values we shall begin to think more clearly about the general term 'values'.

In Chapter 5, we contrasted externally imposed aims of education, illustrated by the metaphorical use of 'aim' as a 'target', with the intrinsic aims of education. By intrinsic we meant characteristic features which were *within* the process of education itself. Because the transmission of what is worthwhile is intrinsic in education, we are fulfilling one of the main aims of education when we do just that. We do not think, here, in terms of aiming at a distant target. Indeed, we are not consciously aware of having and fulfilling an aim.

If we understand the above distinction, we have gone a long way towards understanding the terms absolute and 'pragmatic' (sometimes replaced by the word 'instrumental'). Again, if we think about what we said on the subject of conditioning in Chapter 9, we shall eventually find that the distinction which we made there between classical conditioning, where the situation was completely under the control of the experimenter, and instrumental conditioning, where the stimulus at least was not under the complete control of the experimenter, will help us to understand the difference between our two types of values.

The word 'absolute' is derived from Latin (1). The ideas of Plato were absolutes, because they represented true reality, had universal validity, and were unbounded by time and space and all the limitations of the finite physical world. These ideas were the ultimate reality from which applied knowledge was derived. Thus a bed on which people sleep in the physical world was based on an ultimate idea. It becomes clear immediately that we are speaking about that world which we described in Chapter 1 as metaphysical, that world which lies outside what we can perceive through our senses. The ideas in this metaphysical world were the source of all true knowledge for Plato.

These views of Plato are presented in the famous *Allegory of the Cave* (2). Here Plato contrasts reality, or true knowledge, with opinion, or applied knowledge, which is used in a particular situation and which possesses no universal validity. Only his Guardians (the philosopher kings) were able, through their education, to penetrate this metaphysical world and comprehend reality. For the rest of the citizens (the artisans) there could never be any understanding of reality but only 'shadows' of reality. Their understanding of reality was to be nebulous, hazy, imperfect. But, just as there can be no shadows without light, so there can be no shadows of reality without reality itself. Reality was the light of the mind that was capable of understanding it (the philosophical mind) and the provider of approximations to reality for those whose minds could not accept the light itself.

This may seem far removed from everyday life, but we can illustrate the idea by a very simple example from schooling itself. We do not think that it is very remarkable if a child in school draws a triangle. The infant school child is able to do this free hand, although the finished product is not very impressive by adult standards. Later, in the junior school, he uses a ruler and produces a much more impressive-looking triangle. The sides are now straight, the ends of the lines meet neatly, and so on. But, the best that we

206 | *The Philosophy of Education*

can say is that the child, to improve his drawing of a triangle, has mastered the elementary skill of using a ruler. This is no more impressive than his mastery of a number of other physical skills. But, later still, at the secondary school level, this same child shows tremendous promise in mathematics. He is able to solve complex problems in Algebra and Geometry. To do this he must clearly have developed mathematical concepts or ideas. Among these there will be the concept or idea of triangularity, of the properties of triangles, and so on. All that he achieves with pen on paper in mathematics is the result of the mathematical ideas or principles which he has developed. These principles are absolute; they are not bounded by space and time. If our budding mathematician goes to China, the same overall principles will apply. When he uses Euclidean Geometry, he is applying principles many hundreds of years old (3). Even when he comes to those areas of mathematics which are compaatively new, he is still dealing with absolute principles derived from the earlier basic principles.

We can see at once that this is much more impressive than his earlier free hand drawing of triangles, or his subsequent improved drawings of triangles with a ruler. The reality for the mathematician is not the physical skill of drawing triangles, or of writing numbers on a sheet of paper. For him reality is understanding the absolute principles of mathematics and subjecting all his mathematical behaviour to those principles. The good mathematician never abandons his (mathematical) principles, or seeks to behave independently of them. If he does so, disaster (in a mathematical sense) results.

It was this connection between absolute ultimate reality and education which we saw was responsible for the development of the idea of liberal education. We have already said that absolutes are infinite, unlimited, and unbounded. Therefore, the mind that is capable of understanding absolutes must be unbounded; it must be unlimited; it must be free. The mind which comes to understand absolute principles of reality has received a liberal or liberating education. It has come to know those values which are eternal and which, Socrates claimed, are the unfailing guides to right conduct. Absolutes, in the philosophy of Plato, are called ideas and possess philosophical content, which is devoid of the shadows of reality, the best that is available to the masses. The *élite* (the Guardians), by firmly pursuing these ideas and subjecting their whole life to this pursuit, become free. Principally they become free from error, especially that error of mistaking the shadow for the substance. Similarly the Christian faith teaches that subjection to the will of an Absolute Being liberates men from the chains of sin. This idea is summed up in the phrase 'Whom to serve is perfect freedom'.

Kant (4) believed in an absolute as the guide to morality. His categorical imperative, e.g. 'Do good', demanded absolute obedience, because to do good is absolutely reasonable. Socrates had said that 'virtue is knowledge' and that 'no man does wrong willingly'. By this he meant that if a man knows the difference between right and wrong, because he is a rational creature he will choose to do right. To do right is rational, to do wrong is irrational. Therefore all that we need to do to ensure right conduct is to ensure that all men know the difference between right and wrong. Kant's justification for the idea of the categorical imperative is similar. We do good for its own sake, because to do good is eminently reasonable.

The Ten Commandments were also categorical imperatives. After beginning with a positive imperative, 'Thou shalt love the Lord thy God . . .' they continue with a number of negative imperatives ('Thou shalt not kill, steal, commit adultery'). It is possible to argue that we ought to obey these Commandments or categorical imperatives because to do so is absolutely reasonable. The Children of Israel, however, were constrained to obey them because the Voice of God had spoken them to Moses.

We shall see later that there is an important difference between the authority of Absolute Reason, and the Voice of God, which has great significance for the teaching of morality and for the answer to the question: 'Can we separate religion from morality and teach morality in those schools where it is not permitted to teach religion?' We shall see that, in such schools, it is possible to justify moral imperatives by reference to the authority of reason (secular authority) but not by reference to religion, God, punishment in the hereafter, and similar ideas (religious authority). We may use natural authority or give physical reasons, but we may not give supernatural (5) reasons.

The philosophy of Plato and the Christian religion are forms of idealism. Both postulate that man's life is an upward striving. The Christian looks towards God, the Greek towards the metaphysical ideas (or absolutes) of Goodness, Truth, Justice, Beauty, etc. Both Plato and Christians share the belief that reality is beyond the confines of time and space. Both believe that man has a physical and a metaphysical self, the Christians in a strictly religious sense. The idealist, as an educator, believes that the metaphysical or spiritual element in man's make-up is more important than his physical self or body. There is a great deal in common between the idealist educator and St Paul. St Paul talks of the 'prison of the earthly body' which temporarily encloses the soul, while the educator asks such questions as 'why does the mind have a body?'

We have already seen the connection between absolutes and authority (a concept which we shall examine further in Chapter 13). For the idealist, absolute values are the supreme authority, because they represent the ultimate reality. The authority of absolutism plays a large part in establishing tradition. It does so in the following way: Absolutes control all our behaviour. They are as far removed from criticism, from being defied or denied, as they are from our physical surroundings. These absolutes are the authority for all that men do, and consequently control all men's lives. They make the same demands on all, and all who respond to those demands do so in the same way. We therefore begin to see the emergence of behaviour patterns in conformity with absolute demands, and these patterns are perpetuated by generation after generation.

In education, the absolutes determine the content. In the case of the absolute authority of the medieval church, the content was narrow and the purpose single and simple. Because of the absolute control of the absolute authority, there is neither change nor apparent reason for change. The method of transmitting the content is highly formal and inflexible. Formalism (6) is the name given to that process of transmitting a set body of knowledge and a set system of values which stresses form rather than content – rules in mathematics, and grammar and syntax in languages. The development of the individual depends on the preservation of this traditional content and value system.

In Chapter 6, we saw that a body of people determines this content and value system. Their right to do this rests on their possession of informed opinion, in the light of which they make value-judgments. These become accepted as values because of the authority which this body of people of informed opinion possesses. The few with informed opinion determine the values for the majority. It is this idea which has reslted, from the days of Plato, in the establishment of the authority of an *élite*. Their control is absolute, and the only method of change is rebellion against their absolutism.

ABSOLUTES AND METAPHYSICS

The basic difficulty posed by absolutes existing in a metaphysical world is that the majority of people are unable to understand them. As Ayer (7) reminds us, Kant said that the understanding which human beings possess, even when they are intellectually gifted, becomes confused and contradictory once it ventures beyond physical human experience in search of reality.

If the intellectually gifted become confused, the less gifted must experience greater confusion. Like Plato's artisans, they cannot pass beyond the boundaries of opinion, and they have to rely on the *interpretation* of reality which is provided by authority. They cannot experience reality for themselves. But authority can only convey 'ideas of reality' to the masses by the use of language, and we have seen throughout this book that this very process has caused untold difficulty throughout history. Unable to understand the reason for what authority says, the average man can only accept and follow, as long as he remains submissive, or reject and rebel as soon as he ceases to be submissive. He then begins to demand reasons for what authority says. In the early Middle Ages, people accepted religion through faith; for long they remained submissive to the authority of the Church. But by the time of St Thomas Aquinas (8), men had begun to ask questions, and the 'logic' of Aristotle was required to justify the claims which had previously been made in the name of faith.

The problem of a metaphysical world and of absolute values, thus is familiar in structure and content. It involves what is possible in terms of logic and what is possible in terms of language. But there is a further difficulty which involves both logic and language. Not surprisingly it was recognized by Wittgenstein, whose development of linguistic analysis we have already considered (9). He said that while it is all very well to say that we cannot understand what lies beyond the 'sense world', and that we must limit our investigations to that world, how do we know where the line between the sense (or physical) world and the metaphysical world lies, if we do not know and understand the metaphysical? This is similar to asking how a man, who has no idea of the meanings of the words 'land' and 'water', can say that the land ends here and the water begins here.

We need not pursue this argument further. However it was most important to state the problem for a number of reasons. We needed to show, for instance, that in the problem of values, at least as far as absolute (metaphysical) values are concerned, we are once more confronted by a problem of terms and their use and meaning. Again, if we require people to accept absolute values, and they refuse to accept them *on authority*, there are then only two ways of convincing them of what we believe to be the truth. The first way is by reason or logic. But logic also involves the use of words. The second method is to convince them, as we convinced ourselves (in Chapter 1) that the sea was warm by testing it. In the field of values we must let people test values for themselves and come to their own conclusions. This is a most important point to which we shall return in a moment when we examine 'pragmatic values'.

ABSOLUTES AND CLASSICAL CONDITIONING

Earlier in this chapter, we said that by understanding the essential difference between classical conditioning and operant or instrumental conditioning, we should receive some help in understanding the difference between absolute and pragmatic values and the basic ideas underlying them. We can, therefore, conclude this consideration of absolute values by reminding ourselves of the nature of classical conditioning. We are not saying that the two are identical, but we are looking for basic similarities.

In the Pavlovian experiment, the stimulus was completely under Pavlov's control. As the stimulus determined completely the dog's response, we can say that its behaviour was completely controlled by Pavlov. To ensure that the dog's attention became riveted on the stimulus, Pavlov strapped it in a harness so that the dog could not roam about the experimental laboratory and ignore the stimulus merely because it did not see it.

The dog could make typical responses other than salivation when it saw the food. It could wag its tail or it could bark, but Pavlov regarded these reactions as irrelevant. He was solely concerned with what he could measure. He was concerned only with the drops of saliva, which the dog emitted *automatically*.

Finally, what the dog was conditioned to perform was extremely limited. It first associated the meat with a bell. On a number of occasions the dog heard the bell at the same time that it received the meat. After a while, it began to respond to the bell as it had previously responded to the meat, i.e. by salivating (10). The response did not vary; it was the same response. Pavlov would not allow such words as 'think' and 'learn', so we cannot say that the dog behaved 'thinkingly' in either situation or even that it 'learned' to salivate at the sound of the bell. In Chapter 9 we saw that, although conditioning may be a part of teaching and being conditioned may be a part of learning, we cannot equate teaching with conditioning or being conditioned with learning.

The behaviour of the dog, then, is limited and stereotyped. If the bell to the dog appears as nothing more than another form of meat there is no reason why the dog should respond differently to it. If the dog is not a free agent when the meat appears, he is not a free agent when the bell rings.

In the course of this book, we have learned sufficient about language to know that we must be very careful how we use it. We have also seen, through Scheffler (14), that metaphorical statements and analogies are not the same as simple, straightforward statements of fact. We are now going to draw an analogy between classical conditioning and the acceptance of absolute values. This does not mean that we are trying to *prove* that 'accepting absolute values' is another expression meaning 'being conditioned'. If it did, we would not need to use two different expressions to convey a single idea. Nor are we saying that those who support absolute values are deliberately setting out to condition those whom they require to accept them. We are doing no more than using one situation, with which we are familiar because we have studied it, to throw light on a less familiar area which we have just begun to study.

Absolute values, as we have seen, are often connected with an authority. The authority, sometimes an *élite* has prestige and status. It is in a position to command and demand respect and obedience. In the hands of an absolute authority, absolute values can become like the stimuli which Pavlov controlled so completely. We can require a person to associate certain courses of action with certain absolute values. We can require someone to behave or respond in a certain way, because that way is determined by absolute goodness. Once this response to a stimulus has been established, it is only necessary to show that absolute obedience, or any other absolute, is similar, in order to obtain a similar response or form of behaviour. Once the individual has become accustomed to responding in a particular way to one absolute, he can, by simple association, respond in the same way to all absolutes. He will respond *automatically*, in much the same way as Pavlov's dog responded *automatically*, first to the stimulus of the meat, and, later, by association, to other stimuli. We must remember that the dog had no control over the act of salivating, since it was a reflex action. In order, however, to concentrate his attention on the stimulus, he was strapped in a harness and denied his normal freedom.

As we have seen earlier, the ideas and edicts of indoctrinators are equivalent to absolutes. The individual has little alternative but to respond to them in the required way, since all alternative responses have been rendered almost impossible by the process of indoctrination. The nature of the authority which puts forward the edicts is sufficient to remove from all individuals both the ability and even the desire to act spontaneously. Their behaviour becomes what we called earlier an 'inculcated automatism', performed unthinkingly. In terms of the third criterion of Peters, the subject of the indoctrination is denied both wittingness and voluntariness. It is for this reason that the process of indoctrination is not educational. Instead, it is morally objectionable.

ABSOLUTES AND TRADITION

We have already suggested a connection between absolutes and tradition. Absolutes result in a conservative way of life characterized by 'stability', and a conservative way of life characterized by stability is a traditional way of life.

While Socrates and Plato were anxious to maintain stability in a state which was threatened by instability from outside, a threat to stability appeared inside the state as well. This came from the sophists (12), who, for payment, undertook to teach, a task usually entrusted to slaves, or to leisured people who took no payment. Moreover, what they undertook to teach for payment was practical, applied, vocational *training*, to meet the changing demands of the times. As Athens became an imperial power, she was compelled to learn 'imperial skills' which could not be provided by disinterested (liberal) education. The old, conservative, traditional, absolute, aristocratic outlook, typified by Plato, could not deal effectively with changed demands. Innovation was dangerous and Plato, in the *Laws* (13), makes every effort to prevent innovation in education. It is for this reason that innovation became synonymous with a dangerous threat to social stability, just as, in the Middle Ages, Greek became the language of heresy, a threat to the absolute authority and traditional stability of the Church (14).

Moreover, Socrates believed that if *one* absolute was challenged, all could and would be challenged. Thus absolute morality would be replaced by the 'morality of expediency'. Men would do right, not in accordance with the demands of a criterion of absolute right, but because it was expedient (15) to do so. They would do right, because they found that in certain circumstances it was more to their advantage to do right than wrong. But if it was possible in some circumstances to find it more beneficial to do right than wrong, it was also possible to find circumstances where it was to one's advantage to do wrong. We have now moved from an absolute criterion which applies in the same way to everyone, to a criterion which is peculiar not only to particular circumstances but to particular individuals in those particular circumstances. It is possible for my neighbour and me to find ourselves in the same problem situation. He finds it to his advantage to do wrong; I find it to my advantage to do right. We both act in a way advantageous to ourselves without any regard for the interests of the other. Neither of us has the least concern for other people. It appears that we are passing from a situation where there is one set of rules which applies simply and rigidly to everyone, to a situation where each individual discovers one set of rules which, because they work for him, are the ones he accepts as governing his behaviour. It is not difficult to see that, to Plato, this appeared to be little better than anarchy.

ABSOLUTES: IDEAS: REALITY

Plato believed that ideas are reality, that reality resides in generalizations in a metaphysical world. But another famous Greek philosopher took the opposite view. Aristotle believed that *particulars* represented reality. To take a simple example: Plato would say that the word 'cat' represented reality, and that 'the black four-legged animal with a shiny coat and green eyes which walks about my garden purring' is only a very imperfect representation of reality. It is a shadow of the real thing. Aristotle, a biologist, maintained that 'the black four-legged creature with the shiny coat and green eyes, which walks about my garden purring', which I, and everyone about me, calls a 'cat', is reality. It is tangible. We can know it through our senses; we do not require logical proof of its existence. If I say, 'That is a cat', no one is so bewildered by my verbal subtlety that he fails to understand what I mean. Moreover, I can even say 'Cat' out of the blue to anyone who has ever seen a cat, and, provided he speaks my language, he knows quite clearly what I am talking about.

For Aristotle, the *term* 'cat' is merely a generic term (16). It does not have any real meaning in isolation from individual members of the cat family. It is used to refer to lions and tigers, to Persian cats and Siamese cats, to leopards and cougars. It is much easier to say, 'The cat family' than to say, 'Persian cats and Siamese cats, and tigers and leopards and cougars and . . .' For this reason (namely convenience of reference), says Aristotle, man has invented such generic terms as 'cat'.

During the Middle Ages, controversy raged as the result of the differences in interpretation of the word 'reality'. The Platonists said that the term 'cat' represented the reality. These people were called 'realists', because they believed that the terms were reality. They were also called 'universal-ists', because they believed that universal ideas (the term 'cat' is one) represented reality.

Their opponents, the Aristotelians, followed Aristotle's interpretation of reality. They were called 'nominalists' (17), because they believed that the term 'cat', far from representing reality, was merely a *name* given to a particular animal. They were also known as 'particularists', because they believed that reality lay in particular objects, not in universal ideas.

We can now see which sides the two schools of thought would take. The Platonists would defend absolutes, being 'universalists' and 'realists'. The sophists would accept Aristotle's ruling, defending individual objects and particular instances. They would be 'nominalists' and 'particularists'. The man who came to a sophist saying that he wanted to build a ship, would see no connection between his request and an idea or universal concept of a ship. Nor would the sophist. He would say to himself: 'Here is a *particular* man with a *particular* need. He wants to build a ship, of which there are different types and different sizes, and ships which serve different purposes.' Of the man, he would ask: 'For what purpose, my friend, do you wish to use your ship? To carry cargo? Splendid. Will your cargo be carried along the coast or across the open sea, for the same boat will not serve both purposes?' By such questioning the sophist would determine exactly what this particular man's needs were, and then satisfy them. The next day, another man might come along for a boat, but with vastly different needs. His individual requirements would also be attended to by the sophist.

In morality, too, the sophist would accept individual differences. He might, when putting forward his ideas, be at cross-purposes with Plato. Plato might, for example, be maintaining that there was absolute truth, and that one of the demands of absolute truth was that no man should ever tell a lie. The sophist might pose a hypothetical problem to show how difficult it is for everyone to accept that. He might say: 'We are at war with an enemy. One of our soldiers is captured by the enemy and is asked to tell where our forces are positioned. He says that he does not know. The enemy brutally beat him in an attempt to compel him to divulge the location of his fellow soldiers. He refuses, in spite of all the pain the enemy inflict on him.

214 / *The Philosophy of Education*

Did this man not tell a lie, when he said that he did not know where his fellow soldiers were, and has he not offended against the principle of absolute truth? Yet men would regard that soldier as a hero.'

We could argue that although the soldier had not acted in accordance with absolute truth, he had behaved in accordance with the demands of absolute loyalty. In spite of the fact that it would have been beneficial to him to divulge the whereabouts of his friends, he acted in the general interest although it entailed terrible personal suffering. All that occurred was that a *particular* individual in *particular* circumstances was compelled to make a choice. He was compelled to choose between a respect for absolute truth and absolute loyalty, when it became impossible to show regard for both in the same situation.

Alternatively, we could say that the soldier exercised rational choice, and that it would be acceptable if, in similar situations, all people made their decisions by rational choice. Again we encounter difficulties. We show elsewhere (18) that people have different personalities, that one person may show 'high aggression', another 'high persistence'. Other people might receive a low rating on both counts. A person with a high rating in both aggression and persistence would be more likely to behave in the manner of our brave soldier than one with a low rating in both traits. The possession or absence of a certain trait necessary to endure long enough to make the rational choice might well, therefore, determine whether the choice is made or not.

PRAGMATIC VALUES

Pragmatism is a very different idea of values than absolutism. Pragmatism (derived from the Greek word *pragma*, a deed or doing) was envisaged by the American philosopher William James as a method of settling metaphysical disputes that otherwise might be interminable. It was an attempt to trace and relate all notions to their practical consequences, and became the foundation of the later philosophical thinking of John Dewey. Pragmatism is concerned with means rather than ends, which are the concern of absolutism. It is, as a result, also known as 'instrumentalism'. Therefore pragmatic values are values which the individual develops as a result of *doing* something, in particular doing something in a *particular* situation. If we cast our minds back to Chapter 1, where we talked about theoretical answers and empirical answers to questions, we recall that empirical answers were obtained as a result of 'going and doing'. Theoretical answers were obtained by 'sitting and thinking'. We can now see that absolute solutions, or solutions in terms of absolute values, are theoretical. Ideas themselves are theoretical; they 'exist in thought'. Since absolute values are ideas, the answers resulting from ideas must be theoretical. Empirical

values are those values which emerge as a result of experience, of trying
things in problem situations, of 'going and doing'.

EXPERIENCE AND VALUES

Dewey stresses the importance of experience, both in morality and in
education. Indeed, he has described education as the 'constant restructuring
of experience'. He has said that it is not knowledge which is important, but
the uses to which individual people put knowledge which matters most. In
morality, his idea is that what works is right. The test of truth is verification. If we test an absolute and find that it does not work (such as the test
of absolute truth with our hypothetical soldier), we abandon that absolute.
We decide, therefore, whether to tell the truth or not in future in the light
of the circumstances in which we find ourselves. There is agreement here
between theory and reality, for Hartshorne and May, in a famous experiment (19) to test the consistency of personality traits, found that a trait like
honesty had different interpretations in different situations, that it was
different in primary school children and in adults, and that it was not fixed
and absolute.

For Dewey, the supreme authority was not an *élite* like Plato's Guardians,
or an institutional body like the Medieval Church, but Experience. All our
decisions are made in the light of our *personal experience*. This sort of
thinking is not inconsistent with the historical development of the United
States, and Dewey was an American. In the pioneering days of the frontier,
there was no realism in attempting to observe such absolutes as 'Thou shalt
not kill'. The truth, which emerged through verification was that you either
killed or were killed. Since the object of being a pioneer was to make your
contribution to the development of your country, and dead men cannot
make contributions, it became 'right' to kill Indians. A dead idealist, in
these conditions, obeying the dictates of absolutes, is less useful than a
pragmatist who comes to rapid decisions in the light of present and personal experience. For the pioneer, what was right was what worked.

Unfortunately, the pragmatist soon becomes the victim of his own arguments. It may be desirable to have 'emerging values' when your country or
society is emerging. But what happens when it actually becomes established.
Pragmatic values may be good or at least useful in a constantly changing
environment, but those who found that these values worked in a pioneering
environment might not find them so useful in a settled environment.

The pragmatist would argue that, in peaceful, stable situations, you still
develop values according to your experience. But where are the guide-lines?
Is the individual always competent to make his own decisions in the light
of his own experience? When there is a conflict of interests between one
section of the community and another and both come to hold their views,

attitudes, and beliefs in accordance with their own experience, who is the final arbiter?

This is where such things as faith and belief cause such concern and difficulty. One person, because of his experience, is deeply religious; he even claims that his faith is the result of *religious experience*. He wishes to communicate this to another but fails and may be called an indoctrinator because the experience of the person he wishes to teach does not allow him to accept the belief and because he persists in spite of this in trying because religious experience is so rewarding for him that he feels it must be equally rewarding for others. Moreover, the person who holds the belief feels that it is 'his duty' to communicate his ideas to others.

We can now see why absolute values gave rise to the philosophy of idealism, while the non-absolute interpretation of values gave rise to the philosophy of naturalism. Absolutism is connected with the metaphysical world, with man striving after perfection, with man as he will ultimately be. Non-absolutism is concerned with the natural world, with man as he is. Both have their own interpretations of reality and both interpretations are 'right' in view of the assumptions made. The two ways of thinking are self-consistent, but this is not to say that both are right, or that either is 'right' ultimately.

We can see, too, the connection between instrumental values and instrumental conditioning. The rat in the Skinner box finds itself in a strange situation. It has never been in a Skinner box before, since it is not part of its natural habitat. The only similarity between this situation and previous situations is that the rat feels hungry. This is a physiological state; there are stomach contractions which 'set up a need' which the rat seeks to reduce. The American pioneer surrounded by Indians also found himself in a strange situation. All that there was in common between this situation and those experienced previously was an urge to live. This sets up a need which the pioneer sought to meet.

The rat performs 'trial and error' behaviour. He runs about, sniffing, in an attempt to meet his need by finding food. He performs many actions without succeeding. Suddenly, and quite by accident, he presses a bar and a pellet of food is delivered at his feet. He has never before obtained food by pressing a bar, but this time pressing a bar worked.

This necessitates a certain amount of relearning. In one situation, that is, when the rat in its natural habitat feels hungry, running about sniffing eventually enables it to locate food and meet the need imposed by hunger. In the Skinner box, running about sniffing does not meet that need, since it does not enable him to locate food. But the accidental pressing of the bar, which he has never done before, produces food. The more often he presses the bar in the Skinner box when he feels hungry, the more likely he is to press it on successive trials, because the response has been reinforced. He learns by experience that pressing the bar works. The truth lies in the verification. Consequently, even when the experimenter has structured the experiment in such a way that the bar, when pressed, does not deliver food the rat continues to press it for a considerable number of trials. Eventually, the response to bar-pressing when hungry is extinguished, and the rat has now learned not to press the bar when hungry. He must adapt his behaviour to the changed circumstances that bar-pressing does *not* now work.

BELIEFS AND VALUES

Conditioning, as we have seen, is far from being high-level behaviour. Developing beliefs, accepting and rejecting values, are both forms of high-level behaviour, the importance of which far exceeds the bar-pressing behaviour of the rat. We have also seen that neither the idea of absolute values nor the idea of pragmatic values is entirely satisfactory. The question is not simply of balancing one theory against another in terms of values. There is the problem of individual emotions and individual personalities. Moreover, as Stephenson (20) has emphasized, disagreement over values may not be a unitary thing, but two things, essentially different although not unconnected. We have become used to this basic idea by considering related concepts which are not the same, because each possesses its own logical geography.

DISAGREEMENT IN BELIEF V. DISAGREEMENT IN ATTITUDE

Stephenson (20) distinguishes between 'disagreement in belief' and 'disagreement in attitude'. It may appear that, since the wording of the terms is similar, we are required to find a 'logical' connection' between the terms in order to appreciate their respective meanings and relationship. Stephenson stresses that the connection is *psychological* not logical.

When we appear to disagree with someone over a matter of fact, we often do no more than express a different opinion. We say, for example, 'You are wrong to buy that carpet'. The reader will no doubt recognize this as a 'value-judgment' loosely stated as if it were fact (see Chapter 10). What we really mean is that in these same circumstances, this is not the carpet we would have bought. Matters of choice and aesthetic values (which may enter into the choice of a carpet) are emotionally determined. Thus if I say, 'That is a good picture', I am making a judgment on the basis of the picture's appeal to my emotions. I am not stating a fact. We also saw in Chapter 10 that such subjective ideas cannot be proved to be right or wrong, since there is no standard measure applicable to them.

Stephenson says that in many so-called 'debates' over educational issues, we never progress beyond disagreement in attitude to the essential and central issues. The real concern of genuine educational debates are disagreements in belief. This was clearly shown when we referred to the curriculum issues considered by Herbert Spencer (pages 348–9). In the passage referred to, Spencer states that one of the tragedies of the education of his day was that many parents made the important decision about the content of their children's education not on logical grounds, but as the result of whim and fancy. He also stresses that even greater confusion arises, often at higher levels, when the so-called 'experts' believe that debating whether Maths or Latin is more important is the same as debating major curriculum issues.

However, Stephenson shows how such disagreements in attitude can be the bridge which we cross into areas of disagreement in belief. If we retain our example of debating whether Latin or Mathematics is more important, we shall see the difference between the two *levels* of disagreement and the essential difference between them.

I may have *felt* for many years that Latin is more important than Maths. This is an attitude, since it is emotionally based; it is something which I feel without applying logical analysis to the situation. However, I find that the school in which I teach requires children to choose between studying Maths and studying Latin. I am now very much concerned and I state as my belief that Latin is more important than Maths, and I attempt to persuade my headmaster of my belief. I say: 'Latin is more important than Maths. Therefore, all boys must study Latin'. My headmaster now demands reasons for my belief. I tell him that Latin is more 'cultural' than Maths and that the school exists primarily as cultural influence. My headmaster brings convincing arguments that this is wrong. I now say that Latin is a better mental discipline than Maths and that it ought to be retained on those grounds. My headmaster then produces evidence, from researches, to show that Latin is not a better mental discipline than Maths. Again and again I produce arguments to support my belief, and each time my headmaster demolishes them with more convincing arguments. I can now do one of two things. I can either abandon my belief, because the logical arguments which I have heard show that it is not logically tenable, or I can become dogmatic about it. I can say: 'I know that his arguments are very clever, but they don't really convince me. If I really tried, I could produce arguments which would destroy his. I shall continue to hold my belief that Latin is more important than Maths'. In this case, I continue to hold both my original belief and my original attitude. Moreover, I still differ from my headmaster in both belief and attitude as to the relative importance of Latin and Maths.

On the other hand, I may accept that my headmaster's arguments are so conclusive that I must abandon my belief. If a belief is worth holding, we must be able to say two things about it: one, that it can be logically justified, two, that we can *persuade others* to accept it by producing the logical evidence necessary to substantiate the belief and convince them.

However, I need not necessarily change my *attitude*. Thus while I cease to differ in belief from my headmaster, I continue to differ from him in attitude, when both the belief and the attitude relate to the respective merits of Latin and Maths. I now *know* that my belief was wrong, but I still have a feeling that Latin is more important than Maths.

VALUE AND STAGES OF CHARACTER DEVELOPMENT

We can now appreciate that, at least in the context of education, it is not practical to discuss the concept 'values' entirely in isolation. Whenever we are concerned with values (and we shall see more of this in the next chapter on morals), we are concerned with standards and with human behaviour, with the nature of the standards which guide the behaviour, and with the ways in which the behaviour is determined by the standards. What we have just said suggests that people may behave emotionally or rationally in relation to the values which they hold or which society holds.

It is also important to remind ourselves at this point of what we said in Chapter 6 about culture, and in Chapter 7 about curriculum. In those two chapters, we made the point that general culture can be associated with a way of life – indeed, with what we chose to call the 'comfortable life'. We also saw that sub-cultures too are ways of life. Some of these we distinguished from the first way of life by calling them 'the necessary life'. Subsequently, it became clear that the school is an area where conflict between the two ways of life and the two sets of values may need to be resolved.

What we have said in this chapter suggests that absolutism is unlikely to provide the solution. Indeed in the past, absolutism, which refrains from giving, or refuses to give, rational explanation and evidence for what it says, has done a great deal of harm to education, and to large numbers of people in the name of education. We saw absolutism at work in the traditional, formal teaching of bygone days.

On the other hand, the non-directive, pragmatic, instrumental approach has been tried, and, while hailed at first with great enthusiasm because it was 'different', is now undergoing considerable reappraisal and criticism. The first approach is over-determining, the second is often insufficiently definite and determining.

For these reasons, and because we have seen throughout this book that psychology and philosophy frequently cannot be separated, we shall end this chapter by showing the five stages which Cronbach claims (24) the human character passes through in its development. This is a similar evolutionary concept to that of Piaget's five stages of thought development between infancy and adulthood. Cronbach further claims that, in certain individuals, character development is arrested at a particular stage and never goes beyond it. The character is never fully developed subsequently.

Even before we have seen the stages, it is not difficult to believe that this arresting of development may arise from the way in which the individual is taught, and in particular from the way he is required to respond to certain values. It is also possible to see that, once the character-development has been arrested at a certain point, the attitude to value, and the beliefs centring on this attitude adopted by the individual, will be in keeping with the level of character-development which he has reached. By examining the stages and relating them to what we have said about values, we remind ourselves once more that the problems of value-judgments, values, and morals can be sensibly undertaken only in relation to individual people, just as educational philosophy is only a useful area of study if it gives us a better understanding of education in relation to people.

Cronbach defines character as 'the way an individual makes choices, which affect the welfare of others'. In Chapter 12, when we analyse the concepts 'morals' and 'morality', we shall see more clearly the importance of this definition. Subsequently, he gives the five stages of character development (22) which follow. The chief characteristics of each stage are given, and it is a useful exercise for the reader, as he goes through them, to relate them to the absolutist and non-absolutist positions which we have already described at some length.

THE AMORAL STAGE

This is the state of the infant at birth and for some time afterwards. At the physical and intellectual level, he is described by Piaget as being at the 'sensori-motor stage' of development for the first eighteen months of life. This means that during this period he develops 'gross muscular co-ordination' (23), followed gradually by 'fine muscular co-ordination' as his brain assumes increasingly greater control over his body.

At the amoral stage of character development, the child does not know the difference between right and wrong. If his brain is only just gaining sufficient control over his bodily movements during the first eighteen months to allow him to develop 'fine' as distinct from 'gross' muscular control, it is not surprising that his 'mind' has as yet no concept or idea of right and wrong. As a result, the child has no idea whether his actions or choices have a good effect or a bad effect on the welfare of others. His choices and acts are the result of physical wants (rather like the hungry rat in the Skinner box) and of impulse. He gradually learns not to touch at the physical level and to assume some control over his emotional expression at the intellectual/emotional level.

It is important to note that the psychological declaration that the child is *amoral* at birth resolves the philosophical controversy about 'original sin' (24) and 'innocence'. The absolutist doctrine of the Medieval Church was that the infant was 'born evil', and that the task of education (which the Church controlled) was to *re*-form the child's 'fallen nature'. This resulted in a concentration on salvation in the hereafter rather than on welfare in the present environment. This, too, is in keeping with a belief in metaphysical absolutes which govern all conduct for all men.

The 'child-centred' thinkers, from Rousseau onwards, believed that the child's nature at birth was 'good' and that as a result education was not a process designed to *re*-form a fallen nature, but to permit a 'good' nature to develop without let or hindrance. In more than one chapter already, we have seen how these conflicting beliefs resulted in very different educational ideals, content, and method.

THE SELF-CENTRED STAGE

By the time the child has reached the age of two years, the psychologist says that he is 'self-conscious'. This is not the same as the lay use of the term, although there is a connection (25). The psychologist means that the child is aware that he is *a self* and not an extension of his mother. This awareness is shown in such behavioural acts as tantrums, disobedience, and the use of the word 'No' with emphasis, because the child is aware that he does not *have* to obey parental commands. Parental commands (moral imperatives) are given throughout these two years, firstly for the child's own safety (e.g. 'Don't touch the fire') and secondly, so that he begins to develop some sense of right and wrong (what 'pleases' and what displeases parents). An adult is able to weigh the consequences of his actions, partly because he has developed a concept (or idea) of time. The young child lacks this concept and is governed by immediate desires which must be fulfilled. Thus, although in some situations he can be excused for not behaving morally, i.e. making the choice which is 'good' for himself and others, in other situations he knows what is right and chooses not to do it. Immature adults can also behave in this self-centred way.

THE CONVENTIONAL (OR CONVENTIONAL CONFORMING) STAGE

Freud referred to the period from seven to eleven years as the 'latency period' (26). He believed that it was a period of tranquillity between the sexually disturbed and disturbing periods of infancy and 'puberty adolescence'. The child is at his most amenable and conforming during this stage, which begins with conformity to the demands of his parents' moral imperatives. Now, it develops into an uncritical acceptance of what the

222 / The Philosophy of Education

group does without asking himself whether such behaviour is good or bad. Thus if a child falls in with 'good company' and is 'conventional conforming', he is described as 'good'. If, however, he falls among 'bad' companions and is 'conventional conforming', he is described as 'bad'. The standard or criterion against which such judgments are made is that of rigid adult assessment of 'good' and 'bad'. On the other hand, in his intellectual development, the child, Piaget says, is at the 'concrete-operational stage' of development. Consequently, he can perform logical operations, provided that he has visual assistance, such as arithmetical apparatus, to assist his thinking. He conforms, to some extent, to what he sees. It is more difficult to act logically in relation to right and wrong in the moral field, and many children tend to do what they see others doing, or to accept the demands made by adults without question.

There are, again, some adults who never progress beyond this stage of character development. They display lack of insight or understanding, and often lack of initiative. It is easier to follow than to take the lead or make a decision.

At this stage, too, the expediency of the sophists (and even of Kant, who admitted that more people behave in accordance with the demands of expediency than the commands of the 'Categorical Imperative') governs behaviour. A conventional morality develops, based on pious platitudes such as 'Crime doesn't pay' and 'Honesty is the best policy'. On the credit side, the conforming conventional person is no longer self-centred, since his behaviour exhibits great concern about 'what the group thinks'. However, it is 'What does the group think of *me*?'

THE IRRATIONAL CONSCIENTIOUS STAGE

Conscience is a guide in the making of a choice, or a state of internal self-criticism. As a result of choice or criticism, some modes of behaviour are rejected, although they would achieve certain ends which would appear to be expedient to the individual. In Freudian terms, the 'ego' (or natural self) knows that bribery achieves ends. The 'super-ego' (or better self) condemns bribery on principle. Conscience, therefore, *can* be equivalent to absolutes in governing conduct.

At the irrationally conscientious stage of development, people act as a result of values held emotionally rather than rationally. Behaviour is often guided by anxiety and there is a connection here between behaviour and something akin to being conditioned. The rat, which receives an electric shock when entering the wrong box, avoids that box in future. When a need is created (i.e. it is starving), the rat attempts to meet it because it causes tension. The irrationally conscientious person often acts merely to avoid the anxiety which an unacceptable mode of behaviour would induce.

But such behaviour is characterized by rigidity. If there is a conflict of modes of behaviour, the irrationally conscientious person cannot adapt to the situation. The choice itself may result in anxiety and culminate in neurotic maladjustment. Again, the irrationally conscientious person may be inefficient, because of a desire to drive himself to the limits of perfection and attention to detail when neither of these is required. Finally, the irrational conscientious person, in certain areas, may become bigoted.

THE RATIONAL CONSCIENTIOUS STAGE

At this stage, the individual initially encounters values in the same way as the irrationally conscientious man. But he examines them in the light of reason. When confronted with a choice which seems to involve demands of equal weight or strength, he becomes neither anxious nor rigid. Instead, he takes stock of the situation rationally, first asking himself whether he was right to regard the demands as being equal. He examines the consequences of his action for himself and for others on as wide a basis as possible. He attempts to see the rival values within a conceptual framework (a framework of rational ideas).

Here there is a parallel with the acquisition of knowledge. We have seen that the teacher can instruct the learner, i.e. he can supply information, facts, etc. without wondering whether the learner understands them or troubling to discover whether the learner understands them. Similarly, the learner can accept the information uncritically, without asking himself what use he can make of it. But the wise teacher and the 'insightful' learner make sure that any facts or information are incorporated into an overall picture, to fit into their rightful place within a conceptual framework. What happens at the cognitive (intellectual) level happens also at the emotional level of moral choices. Plato says that the rational part of the soul has the task of guiding the irrational part. The rationally conscientious man uses reason in much the same way.

The rationally conscientious man realizes that all people, at some time or other, are confronted by a clash of values. He has come to know his values thoroughly because he has examined their nature and the consequences of acting in the light of such values. He has heard the absolute value expressed in the moral imperative, 'Thou shalt not kill'. The irrationally conscientious man, acting on principle but displaying bigotry, argues that war is never justified. When asked for evidence for the statement, he merely repeats the categorical imperative. He substitutes the absolute for reasons. Such substitution saves him from taking a decision or making a rational choice.

By contrast, the rational, conscientious man condemns war in general because it seldom produces a lasting answer to problems of real magnitude and because it involves tremendous human suffering, especially among innocent people such as children. On the other hand, there are wars of oppression where more suffering would result from people standing back and condemning war on principle than would result from active opposition offered to the oppressor.

Choice is not necessarily easy for the rationally conscientious man. He may be required, as Wilson warns, to make rational choices against a background of irrational behaviour by members of an irrational society. His behaviour may put him into an uncomfortable minority, whereas irrationally conscientious or even conforming conventional behaviour would place him in the secure and comforting ranks of the majority. Either of the latter two resembles the man who shies away from philosophical analysis of concepts, or the man who accepts every concept-based slogan that he hears as possessing validity (27).

We can sum up the behaviour of our five stages in terms of the reaction of the individual at each stage to values. The amoral individual (and psychopaths are examples of adults who are permanently at this stage of development) have no values. They react entirely out of self-interest, knowing nothing of right and wrong or of other people's feelings. They act in terms of their own pleasure or pain.

The self-centred individual is aware of ethical values (values relating to 'good' and 'bad') and of group norms or standards. But he chooses to ignore both. The conventional conforming man wants to act according to the example of the company he keeps. Ethical values involve abstract ideas of good and bad, and he is either unable or unwilling to work at this level. His conformity may not even result in consistency, which is often useful since it in turn results in predictability (28). If the group changes its mind or way of behaving, he suffers a similar change of mind and shows similar changes in behaviour. The irrationally conscientious man has ideas and values, but is emotionally attached to them. He may even defend them emotionally when to abandon them rationally would be in the interests of all.

The rationally conscientious man has few rigid standards, since reason has shown him the need for adaptability. He has some basic guidelines for his behaviour and certain basic goals. But he may have to abandon entirely, or at least modify, some strongly held views in the light of events. He never runs the risk of becoming an indoctrinator or of being indoctrinated.

STAGES OF CHARACTER DEVELOPMENT: ABSOLUTISM: PRAGMATISM

We have examined, now, five stages of character development (29), or even five types of character. The five stages are those through which the rationally conscientious man passes, just as the adult who is fully developed intellectually passes through all the Piagetian stages of thought development. But some people can experience arrested development at any one of the five stages.

The result of our analysis shows that the problem of deciding between absolute values and pragmatic values is by no means an easy one. We are tempted to say that absolute values are not acceptable as guides to human conduct or as the foundations of standards within education, since they are liable to produce rigidity, fixation, irrationality, dogmatism, immaturity, indoctrination and bigotry, all of which are out of keeping with the three criteria of education. Yet the three criteria contain one which says that education involves the transmission of what is worthwhile. When absolute values prevail, there is little doubt about what is worthwhile in the society where the absolutes prevail. There may be no room for interpretation, there is likewise little room for misinterpretation. There is the risk of stagnation; there is also the certainty of a type of stability, although not necessarily of equilibrium.

Non-absolutism may have different consequences. Plato believed that only few people were capable of understanding reality. The majority were not, and as a result, required their education and their lives to be largely determined by those who could and did understand reality. All people are not the same. In the twentieth century we have reports, like the Newsom Report, which stress this point, the particular need of those people of average and below-average ability. At a very rough estimate, this means something like half the population (30). The pragmatic values may seem ideal, since there is an absence of dictation by minorities, and consequently less likelihood of enslavement of the minds of the majority.

We have seen a similar idea in relation to non-directive methods of teaching. At a superficial glance, it may appear that discovery methods are best suited to those of average and less than average intelligence, since they cannot benefit from the academic approach. Yet the Newsom Report does not condemn the academic approach out of hand. We have also seen that those of average and below-average intelligence may need more direction than the very bright, who may be better able to discover for themselves.

Whether children are very bright, average, or below average in ability, they must live as members of a society. This society is first the home, then the school, then the adult community. If each individual were left to discover 'what worked for him' and was allowed to equate this with 'what is right', we would no doubt find that groups of people would share common experiences and come to common conclusions about what was right. There would not, as some people suggest, necessarily be complete anarchy. Anarchy is not the alternative to absolutism.

But we have already seen on numerous occasions that the result of this group agreement on 'what works' and consequently on 'what is right' does nothing more than to produce those units of society which the sociologist calls 'sub-cultural groups', and those codes (or methods) of behaviour which the sociologist calls 'sub-cultures'. We cannot merely produce an aggregate of all the sub-cultural behaviours and say that this is the Culture of society, the content which education seeks to transmit. Over and above all the approximate behaviours, degrees of morality, and interpretations of duty, there are the abiding standards, the framework of values within which society exists.

Now a framework may be large or small, broad or narrow, and it may do no more than set the outer limits which no one wishes to reach, much less to transgress. A schoolboy can write a very good Latin prose without ever approaching the skill displayed in the fair copies of Richard Shilleto (31). Yet, the fact that the schoolboy is never likely to reach the standard of Shilleto's Latin is not considered sufficient reason for withholding these fair copies from him, for pretending that they do not exist, or for abandoning the writing of Latin prose by schoolboys because few of them are ever likely to become Shilletos.

Nor is there any guarantee that the pragmatically determined values are better than the externally imposed values. It may be that some discoveries made by researchers are accidental. But this does not mean that every researcher, when asked what he is looking for, will say, 'I don't know until I find it'. Progress in research would be very limited with this basic rationale. There are some structured researches which produce *nothing*, if by nothing we mean failure to substantiate the hypothesis which was tested. But there are many more which not only substantiate the original hypothesis, but also suggest the next line of investigation, and ultimately result in the solution of a major problem. Socrates was vividly lampooned by Aristophanes (32) because he fell down a well while contemplating the metaphysical truths which lie behind the physical universe. But we could equally well ridicule the seeker after pragmatic values falling down the same well because his eyes were focused such a short distance in front of him that he was at the bottom of the well before he saw the edge of it. His eyes were on the ground all the time, but he met the same fate as he whose eyes were in the air.

The criticism of Dewey and the pragmatists is that they are victims of 'the dominance of the foreground'. They become so obsessed with being involved in problem situations, with sharing experience, and with re-structuring experience, that they never stand back from their involvement to ask precisely when and how they are to obtain an 'overview of the total situation'. It is true that those who acquire their values pragmatically are not the victims of values imposed, not only from without, but also from above. But it is not easy for them to deny, and to support the denial with convincing arguments, that they are not just as much dominated by present experience. The absolutist determines what is right and communicates this very clearly to others. The pragmatist runs the risk of finding what he verifies as 'right' because it works, but of not being allowed to communicate this to someone else for fear that his experience may not lead him to the same view of 'rightness by verification'. Dogmatism is an attitude, and is, therefore, not limited to one group of people. The pragmatist may be just as dogmatic about what has worked for him and follow it as slavishly as the absolutist follows by what is right for everybody.

In the very first chapter of this book we stressed the importance of reason and of giving reasons of producing evidence, and of critical appraisal. It is fitting to conclude this chapter with a passage from MacIntyre (33). In our inquiries we have so often found that extremes of view are seldom acceptable, that we no longer find it surprising that the truth often lies somewhere between two extremes and contains fragments of truth from both. Thus we were not able to separate instruction entirely from learning by discovery or conditioning entirely from teaching. In much the same way we have implied that reason and criticism are the 'bridge concepts' between absolute and pragmatic values, between values which apply to all individuals and those which are determined by individuals, of the relationship not only between tradition and current needs but also of the relationship between society and the 'individual'. MacIntyre writes:

'But there is something more important about critical activity. It is not the activity of isolated individuals. It is always exercised inside an academic tradition which is the tradition of some particular society. Unless critical standards claim social recognition, criticism is untrue to its own claim to universal allegiance. But a condition of this is precisely the refusal to make criticism the prerogative of an *élite*. For, to create an *élite* is to allow a debasement of standards for everyone else. And to allow this is to make criticism the instrument of one part of society against another. But to claim such a prerogative for some special class is precisely to restrict the moral openness which critical activity requires. We are all equal before the impersonal standards of reasons. . . . Thus, intellectual standards and democratic community need each other.'

NOTES AND REFERENCES FOR CHAPTER 11

1 The Latin verb *solvere* means 'to unloose', 'to free'; its past participle is solutus. The Latin preposition ab means 'from', so that *absolutus* means 'freed from', 'unrestricted by'. For this reason, absolute values are those metaphysical values, which are not bound by the physical world perceived through the senses, nor by time and place. Readers who studied Latin at school will remember a grammatical construction known as the 'ablative absolute'. The meaning of 'absolute' here is again 'free from', since the ablative absolute is detached from the main sentence: (The city having been captured), the enemy fled. The ablative absolute is in brackets.

2 See also notes and references for Chapter 8, Section 11.

3 Euclid was a Greek mathematician, whose date and place of birth are alike uncertain. He was at the height of his powers, at the ancient seat of learning at Alexandria, about 300 B.C., i.e. twenty years after the death of Aristotle. His major work was called *The Elements* and dealt with the theory of numbers and geometry. The first six volumes dealt with plane geometry and were authoritative works until the end of the nineteenth century.

4 Immanuel Kant (1724–1804) was the author of two famous philosophical works – *The Critique of Pure Reason*, and *The Critique of Practical Reason* The 'categorical imperative' ordered men to do right on the grounds of pure reason, which is highly idealistic. Practical reason suggested that men do right, because it pays them, or because it is expedient, or because it is useful. Because of this, the categorical imperative results in absolute morality, while practical reason results in what we nowadays call the 'morality of expediency', or 'utilitarian morality'. Those who wish to read more about Kant are referred to Chapter 20 of Russell's *History of Western Philosophy*.

5 The Latin word *super*, like the Greek word *meta* (already seen in the word *meta*physical) means 'beyond' or 'outside'. Thus the supernatural world, like the metaphysical world, is one outside or beyond the limiting factors of physical objects, time, and place. It is the world perceived by the intellect, while the natural world is perceived through the senses.

6 For an account of formalism and other theories, see *Theories of Education*, J. P. Wynne (Harper 1963). Wynne relates each theory to the curriculum content it produces, and to its 'axiology'. The Greek word *axios* means 'worthy of', and the neuter plural *axia* means 'worthy or worthwhile things' or 'values'. 'Axiology' is, therefore, a system of values.

7 *The Problem of Knowledge*, A. J. Ayer (Pelican 1956). This is not a book which every student will feel impelled to read in its entirety, but it is worthwhile reading the first introductory chapter, where Ayer gives criteria against which to measure information which we claim to 'know' with certainty.

8 St. Thomas Aquinas (1225–1274) in his work *Summa Contra Gentiles* examines the 'meaning of wisdom' and the 'aim of the universe', in an attempt to provide a declaration of 'truth' as professed by the Catholic Church in its doctrine and dogma. In the work he examines the real relationship between these religious truths, faith, and rational proof. He accepts Aristotle's argument, known as the argument of the 'unmoved mover', as proof of the existence of God. For those who do not wish to delve into all the philosophical intricacies of this proof, the basic ideas are listed below:

    1 At the lower end of the 'existence order' is formless matter.
    2 Higher up the existence order is matter which has form.
    3 The universe and all that is in it is matter. The universe and all that is in it is matter which has form.
    4 Within the universe there is 'movement'.
    5 We know that formless matter cannot produce matter which has form, neither can matter move matter.
    6 Therefore, something outside matter must produce matter which has form from formless matter, and movement.

7 Because in neither case can matter be the creator or mover, the creator or mover must be 'mind', the only alternative to matter.

8 Because this mind controls the universe, it must be universal mind or intelligence (*nous*).

9 But if this mind or intelligence is itself capable of being moved itself, it cannot also move matter. Therefore the mover must itself be unmoved.

10 This 'unmoved mover' is God.

Readers should note that Aristotle's God contains no 'religious ideas'.

Aquinas also deals with the problem, seen earlier, of Universals and Particulars. God, he says, knows both universals and particulars, because he knows everything. He knows the things which the mind of man can know because they exist, and things which the mind of man cannot know because they have not yet come into existence. God is *absolute*, not bounded by time or space. He therefore sees the past, the present, and the future. He also sees into the minds of men.

Catholic philosophy today (known as Neo-Thomism) represents an attempt to reinstate the basic ideas of St Thomas Aquinas.

9 See Chapter 1.

10 Behaviourists talk about 'functionally equivalent stimuli'. If two stimuli are functionally equivalent, it means that they are both capable of evoking the same response. Once the bell had become associated with the meat, it was a stimulus functionally equivalent to the meat and was just as capable of evoking the response of salivation as was the meat itself. The popular saying 'A wink is as good as a nod to a blind horse' is an example of functionally equivalent stimuli. In this case, both are equally useless; they are functionally equivalent because neither is capable of evoking a response from the blind horse.

If we relate this to absolute values, reaction to one absolute is very much like reaction to another. This is why we are able to say that we do things 'on principle'. Principle, in this case, is a generalized attitude or generalized response, unthinking, uncritical behaviour governed by the demands of one or another of the (functionally equivalent) absolute values. This sort of behaviour is stereotyped, because all who act 'on principle' act in the same way.

11 *The Language of Education*, Israel Scheffler (Thomas 1960).

12 The Greek word *sophos* means 'wise', and the original meaning of 'sophist' (the Greek word was *sophistes*) was 'one learned in some art or craft'. It was also used to mean a wise man in general, and the 'Seven Sages of Greece' were known as *sophistes*. But it is with the former, meaning that we are concerned in this chapter.

From the middle of the fifth century B.C., the sophists gave lessons for payment, largely in the areas of Rhetoric (oratory) since this skill was necessary to sway an audience as a public speaker. Politics (necessary when the people were active participants in a democracy), and Mathematics (necessary in trade and commerce as well as in shipbuilding, etc.). Originally, they were useful because they popularized knowledge and made it available to those from whom it had previously been kept. However, as time went on, they concentrated not only on 'Rhetoric', but on 'specious arguments'. Thus they gained the reputation for being able to prove that black was white or that the better cause was the worse, and the worse the better. In this way, they were destructive of the traditional values, replacing absolutes, and even the rational, by expediency. Some of these sophists became very famous and some appear in the dialogues of Plato. The most famous names include Protagoras (the name is the title of a Platonic Dialogue), Gorgias (the title of another Dialogue), Hippias of Elis, and Prodicus of Ceos. Later, after Rome subjugated Greece, the sophists figured prominently as teachers of Rhetoric in the University of Athens. It should be noted that the Romans, too, found oratory important, and that Quintilian's main educational work was *The Education of an Orator*. However, this education was designed to develop moral responsibility, of which Plato would have approved, and Erasmus subsequently did approve.

13 *The Laws* was the last dialogue written by Plato. The best known translation of the work is that by Benjamin Jowett, reprinted by Oxford University Press in 1953. In *The Laws*, Plato presents his revised views on politics, society, and education. Instead of proposing the ideal educational system, as in *The Republic* – the absolute best – he proposes 'the best in present circumstances', or a modified idealism. He sounds a very definite note of conservatism, a fear of innovation which would add further to the decline of the old ideals. Even innovations in children's games were to be banned. 'The plays of childhood have a great deal to do with the permanence or want of permanence in legislation; he who changes sport, is secretly changing the manners of the young.'

14 One of the most famous heresies of the Middle Ages was the Manichaean heresy. Manichaeus was a teacher of Rhetoric (really a sophist). (See 12 above.) He read philosophy written in Latin and was addicted to astrology. St Augustine became a follower of Manichaeus, but later rejected his teachings. The rejection, Russell tells us, was not primarily on religious grounds after his conversion, but on scientific grounds, because the best writings of the eminent astronomers made nonsense of the claims of Manichaeus.

15 The Latin word *expedit* means 'it is advantageous, or useful'. One of the best illustrations of its connection with the word 'expedient' in the present text, is a line written by the Latin poet Ovid (Publius Ovidius Naso, 43 B.C.–A.D. 18: *Expedit esse deos et, ut expedit, esse putemus.* ('It is expedient (or convenient) to believe that the gods exist, and, since it is expedient, let us believe.')

16 The third declension Latin noun *genus, generis* means 'race', 'type', or 'species'. Thus, a 'generic term' is a term which classifies types and species. Generic terms are frequently found in Biology.

17 The Latin word *nomen* means 'a name'. Thus a 'nominalist' is one who says that the generic term 'cat', far from representing reality, is merely a name given to a particular species of animal. We often talk about a nominal payment. By this we mean a payment so small that it hardly constitutes a 'real' payment at all. It is a payment 'in name only'.

18 *Assessment and Testing: An Introduction*, H. Schofield.

19 The experiment by Hartshorne and May to determine the precise nature of such personality traits or characteristics as honesty, was a large scale one which became famous. Accounts of the findings appear in: *A Study in Deceit*, H. Hartshorne and M. A. May (Macmillan, New York 1928). *Studies in the Organization of Character*, H. Hartshorne and M. A. May (Macmillan, New York 1930).

20 'The Scientist's Role and the Aims of Education', C. L. Stephenson, in *Harvard Educational Review*, XXIV (Fall, 1954).

21 *Educational Psychology*, Lee J. Cronbach (Harcourt, Brace and World Inc., 1954).

22 The reader should compare these stages with the four levels of morality defined by the social psychologist McDougall: (1) PRE-MORALITY – concern with self-controls pleasure/pain. (2) EXTERNAL MORALITY – controls reward/punishment. (3) EXTERNAL/INTERNAL MORALITY – concern for own reputation – controls social praise/blame. (4) INTERNAL MORALITY – controls self-praise/self-blame.

23 When the human infant is born, its brain is much better developed than its body, since the brain must, right from the moment of birth, direct and control all bodily movements. The fibres of the brain are partially insulated at birth with a substance called myelin. Complete insulation does not occur until the age of five or six years, i.e. roughly the time at which the child begins formal schooling. As the insulation improves, the control over bodily movements increases. The 'gross muscular movements' of the infant are random movements of the whole body. He 'reaches' with his whole body. Gradually these overall, and inefficient, movements are reduced, and the child's 'reaching' comes to resemble the adult act more closely. In a similar way his 'overall scribblings' (gross muscular act) are gradually replaced by finer, more controlled movements of drawing and colouring. The co-ordination is the result of the control of the bodily activities by the brain.

24 The doctrine of Original Sin is that every individual is 'born evil' because Adam sinned. Thus mankind, by its own actions, estranged itself from the love of God, which can be recovered only by the act of redemption performed by Christ in dying (for the sins of the world) on the cross. The idea is illustrated in the following verses from Cardinal Newman's hymn, 'Praise to the Holiest in the Height':

> O, loving wisdom of our God!
>   When all was sin and shame,
> A second Adam to the fight
>   And to the rescue came.
>
> O wisest love! that flesh and blood,
>   Which did in Adam fail,
> Should strive afresh against the foe
>   Should strive and should prevail.
>
> And that a higher gift than grace
>   Should flesh and blood refine,
> God's presence and his very self,
>   And essence all-divine.

25 In the psychological sense, a person is 'self-conscious' when he is aware that he is a self. In the lay sense, a person is 'self-conscious' when he is too aware of himself. In company, he feels that all eyes are looking at *him*, he becomes embarrassed, and his actions become gauche and often absurd. It can be seen that the second (lay) sense derives from the first (psychological) sense. It is also a good example of how words which remain the same take on slightly different meanings when used by different people.

26 The Latin verb *latere* means 'to lie hidden'. It has a present participle *latens* which is used as an adjective, 'lying hidden'. This adjective is used in the scientific term 'latent heat'.

The significance of the term 'Latency period' is that, during the period from seven to eleven years, the sexual conflicts of infancy lie hidden and thus a period of stability and calm results. This is broken by the re-emergence of sexual conflicts in puberty and adolescence.

27 The term 'validity' and its accompanying term 'reliability' have been discussed at some length in *An Introduction to Assessment and Testing*, op. cit.

Briefly, if a psychological test (e.g. an intelligence test) is valid, it does what it claims to do. Thus, the intelligence test tests intelligence, and not some other characteristic of human beings.

If a slogan is valid, it means what it claims to mean. However, we have seen throughout this book that words, and even whole statements, do not always mean what they say or what they claim to mean. It is for this reason that linguistic and concept analysis are so important.

28 In *Assessment and Testing: An Introduction*, we showed that individuals display certain traits of behaviour. Hence a man is '*generally* honest' or '*consistently* unreliable', or '*usually* anti-social'. If we know that the individual possesses such traits, we can predict the way in which he will behave. This does not mean that we shall be right in our predictions every time, but it does mean that we are more likely to be right than wrong. It was said that the old 'eleven plus' examination had 75 per cent success with its predictions of the suitability of pupils for grammar school education. Thus, when the examination predicted that a child was suitable for grammar school, there was a good chance that the prediction was right. If, however, the predictive accuracy of the examination were only 25 per cent, we could not feel happy in using it. There would be insufficient consistency in the predictions to produce confidence.

29 Note also Piaget's stages: ANOMY from a Greek word meaning 'LAWLESS'); HETERONOMY (meaning controlled by or obeying someone else); SOCIONOMY (controlled by or obeying Society's demands); AUTONOMY (meaning 'self-governing', 'self-controlled' or 'self-disciplined').

30 If the population of the British Isles were measured for intelligence, the distribution of their test scores would follow the normal curve of distribution shown below:

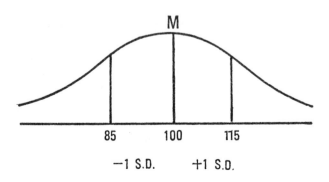

Two out of every three people lie between the vertical lines marked '+I.S.D.' and '−I.S.D.', or, in other words, two out of every three people have an intelligence quotient somewhere between 85 and 115, with 100 as the mean. See also *Assessment and Testing: An Introduction.*

These people are stated to be of average intelligence. But, it will be appreciated that to apply the word 'average' to someone with an I.Q. of 85 and a person of I.Q. 115 is making a very general expression of 'average'. We can subdivide this average group into 'upper average' and 'lower average'. Upper average would include those whose I.Q. is between 100 and 115. Lower average would include those whose I.Q. is between 85 and 100. Thus, if we define 'average and below' as those of I.Q. 100 and under, we embrace half the population in our definition. If we set the upper limits somewhere between 100 and 115, we alter the percentage to whom the definition applies again. Consequently, any figure quoted must be an approximation.

If we define as 'average and below' those who fail to obtain grammar school places, we may come nearer to our stated figure of two out of every three. The percentage of the population in any given area varies, because of the availability of grammar school places in relation to the population of the area. It could thus be as low as 20 per cent or as high as 30 per cent.

31 Richard Shilleto was a fellow of Peterhouse and Trinity College, Cambridge, in the nineteenth century. An eminent classicist, he was the author of numerous works, but the one specifically referred to in this chapter is: *Greek and Latin Compositions*, R. Shilleto, Cambridge University Press, 1901.

32 Aristophanes (448–380 B.C.) was the great comic dramatist of Athens. The following is a list of his plays which remain extant:

The Knights	424 B.C.
The Clouds	423 B.C.
The Wasps	422 B.C.
The Peace	421 B.C.
The Birds	414 B.C.
Lysistrata	411 B.C.
Thesmophoriazusae	410 B.C.
Ecclesiazusae	392 B.C.
Plutus	388 B.C.

33 'Against Utilitarianism', A. C. MacIntyre, in *Aims in Education; The Philosophical Approach*, ed. T. H. B. Hollins (Manchester University Press 1964).

Chapter 12

The Concept 'Morals'

The term 'morals' implies behaviour, and the adjectives 'moral' and 'immoral' suggest behaviour which is acceptable and unacceptable. There is also a suggestion of 'social criteria', because when we talk about moral behaviour being acceptable and immoral behaviour being unacceptable, we think of the acceptance, or non-acceptance, *by society*. Society has established norms or standards against which to measure different modes of behaviour to determine their acceptability or otherwise. In much the same way, Peters established three criteria against which to measure different processes, to determine whether they merit the term 'education'.

Because norms or standards are established by society, there is a link between all three concepts in this trilogy – value-judgments, values and morals. When society establishes its norms of good and bad behaviour, it is making a value-judgment. It is saying that some forms of behaviour are more socially acceptable, more in the interest of the majority, than others. It makes these judgments not arbitrarily or in isolation, but in relation to the values which it holds. We can take a simple example of this. A given society defines sexual promiscuity as immoral behaviour. The definition is based on the value judgment that sexual promiscuity is not in the interests of society. The value on which the value-judgment is based is called 'chastity'. Thus a society which accepts chastity as a value among other values cannot permit promiscuity. It is compelled to make the judgment that 'lack of promiscuity' is better than promiscuity.

MORAL RULES

This suggests that the values which a society holds and in the light of which it makes its value-judgments result in the formulation of moral rules or, as they are sometimes called, a 'moral code'. These rules are prescriptive. Prescriptive statements are 'ought' statements, and prescriptive statements about behaviour state that 'Behaviour *ought* to be . . .'. Consequently, we can see a parallel between morals and morality and laws and legality. The laws of any society are a set of prescriptive rules which determine what is legally acceptable behaviour. The laws are there to protect the interests of .he society against those whose behaviour is anti-social or criminal. The legality or otherwise of any form of behaviour is determined by reference to the legal rules. Similarly, the morality of any form of behaviour is determined in the light of the moral rules. Infringement of either legal or moral rules has certain consequences for the offender. If he infringes the legal rules, he is punished by imprisonment (segregation from society) or by fine (payment of money to society). If an individual breaks the moral rules, he is punished by social disapproval or social ostracism (1), and by being made to experience a feeling of shame.

MORAL RULES: ABSOLUTES: THE SOCIAL CONTRACT

In the light of what we said in Chapter 11 about different types of values, we can see that moral rules may be absolute, as in the case of the Ten Commandments. These are ten categorical 'ought' statements, which Moses claimed were given to him by God himself. Thus we see that there is a connection not only between absolutes and morality, but also between religion and morality in this instance.

But in Chapter 11 we also saw that the pragmatist rejects the idea of absolute values and categorical imperatives which tell every individual, regardless of his personal experience, what he *must* do or *must not* do. The pragmatist argues that each individual's own experience will provide him with the necessary guide to right and wrong conduct. 'Right' is what works, 'wrong' is what does not work.

But we are faced with a problem here. What works for me is right for me, according to the pragmatist. But what is right for me, because it works, may not be right for someone else, because for him it does not work. It may not be right for a large number of people. How then can we reconcile the different interpretations of 'right' of different individuals so that we do not have a chaotic society in which each has his own values and modes of conduct according to self-interest?

At the end of Chapter 11, we suggested that reason was helpful in making such decisions. It was suggested that critical thinking, based on reason, was not the prerogative of any *élite*. Its aim was not like the aim of absolutism, to close the mind of every individual and merely to require him to conform to some set of rules, but to keep the mind open until generally (or socially) acceptable evidence could be produced.

Sometimes this evidence is at the very elementary level of common sense. Lucretius (2), the Roman poet, in the fifth book of his *De Rerum Natura*, gives one of the first instances of men entering into a 'social contract' (*nec laedere nec laedi* – 'neither to harm nor to be harmed'). This type of social contract is a form of pragmatic morality. Men found that if they harmed someone, that person was likely, if the opportunity arose, to harm them in return. The opposite of the social contract is the 'eye for an eye and a tooth for a tooth' principle. Men found, *by experience*, that by refraining from harming others they themselves remained unharmed. Because refraining from harming others 'worked', it was 'right'. The fact that men openly came together suggests that they pooled their experiences and produced an elementary rational argument on elementary rational evidence to support the making of a contract. Once the contract was made, a simple code of moral behaviour was established.

The essential difference between the 'Ten Commandments' situation and the 'Social Contract' situation is simply stated. In the first situation, the code of behaviour was imposed from without by a Supernatural Being working through the agency of a chosen individual. Ideas from the metaphysical world were transmitted to the natural world, and the behaviour of natural men was in future governed and determined by these absolute ideas or ideals.

In the second example, the moral rules are the outcome of the experience of men in the natural world. There is no reason for any *élite* to interpret the absolutes for the rest, or to impose them on the rest, because no absolutes are involved. Any difference of opinion or interpretation must be settled internally, within the natural world. There is no opportunity to determine how people will behave by threatening them with punishment and loss of rights in the hereafter, or with failure to obtain salvation. In the social contract, behaviour is regulated from within society; in the case of the Ten Commandments, behaviour is regulated by reference to external absolutes.

These two approaches have led to such questions as, 'Can we have morality without religion?' From this develops the important question, 'If morality' and religion are inseparable, how can we teach morality in secular schools?'.

The absolutist in morality, who believes in absolute values and the voice of God, denies that religion and morality can be separated. God is the Supreme Being; God is infinitely wise. When God gave the Commandments to men, therefore, he gave a set of rules infinitely more wise than any which man could devise by applying his own finite wisdom. Because these infinitely wise rules came from God, we have the right to impose them on men. They are in the best interests of all. Man-made moral rules can be based only on personal preferences, preconceptions, prejudices, faults, to which, as we saw earlier, even keen intellects are prone.

Those who do not accept that religion and morality are inseparable bring forward a number of arguments. In the first place, they argue that there are, in any society, those who do not accept the existence of a Supreme Being, and, to them, the Ten Commandments *are* man-made moral rules. Moses, they argue, attributed them to God only to ensure their acceptance. By bringing in the justification of absolutism, he was saved the difficulty of obtaining rational acceptance of his code in the light of rational arguments and the presentation of evidence.

Secondly, those who refuse to accept that religion and morality are inseparable, may use the arguments which Hospers (4) uses when he attempts to answer the question, 'What is knowledge?' They would ask, 'When Moses claimed that the Ten Commandments were given to him by the voice of God, how did he *know* that it was God speaking to him?' He may well have 'felt intuitively' or have 'believed' that it was the voice of God, but 'feeling intuitively' or 'believing', even 'believing strongly', is not the same as *'knowing'*. Now Hospers would not argue that because of this Moses was not entitled to act in accordance with the Ten Commandments, because he did not *know* that the voice of God had given them to him. He would only argue that the element of uncertainty might be used as a reason for other people to challenge his right to impose them on his people.

This question of certainty is a most important one. In an educational context, we cannot be as particular about what constitutes certainty as an epistemologist (5) (one who is an expert on the meaning of knowledge) can. If we were, we would have to accept, with Hospers, that scarcely anything can be described as 'absolutely and undeniably certain'. If we accepted this, there is very little that we would feel entitled to 'teach', very little instruction that we could justifiably give.

BELIEFS AND MORALITY

However even in the realm of information, which is only one area of teaching and education, we must exercise care. In the area of belief (and what we have said about morality so far, indicates that it is in this area rather than in the area of fact or information) we must exercise even greater care.

Wilson (6) says that it is all too easy for the teacher who holds certain beliefs to indoctrinate his pupils with these beliefs. He may, because he holds these beliefs so strongly, teach them as if they were incontrovertible fact. He may support them not with generally acceptable evidence, but with emotional fervour. It is for this reason that there is so much discussion about the right to offer religious teaching in schools.

Wilson continues by saying that there is no necessity for a thing to be one hundred per cent certain before it is taught. What we must do is to support what we teach with evidence which people can accept because it is rational. Rational evidence is free from bias, personal preference and prejudice.

If we return to our original problems – whether it is possible to separate religion from morality, and whether we are entitled to use, as a moral code, such a set of absolutes as the Ten Commandments – we can now make the following observations. It is one thing to claim that the Ten Commandments must be the basis of any moral code because they were given by the voice of God, and another to say that they must be the basis of any moral code because on rational grounds they can be shown to be the most suitable basis for such a code. The devoutly religious person and the person who does not accept the existence of a Supreme Being, as well as the person who neither accepts nor denies the existence of a Supreme Being but claims that there is no way of knowing if the Commandments were given in this way, may all accept the Commandments as the basis of their moral code, but for different reasons.

The first man accepts them for religious reasons, as a result of his religious conviction. Because of this, he is more likely to impose his beliefs on those whom he teaches than are the other two. They accept the Commandments because they seem to be rationally justifiable. Because of this they are more likely to justify them to the people they teach. They see 'rationality', not 'divine inspiration' as the source from which the Commandments came.

Later in this chapter we shall have cause to see that the reason given for accepting and teaching certain ideas is very important, and nowhere more so than in that situation where we are compelled to give people reasons why they should behave morally or in accordance with a moral code.

There is a very important connection between what we have said about moral rules and the answer to the question, 'Can morality be taught?' If we accept that morality is, by definition, obedience to rules, then there can be only one answer to the question. There is no doubt that morality *can* be taught. If we can teach language by the use of linguistic rules, we can teach morality by the use of moral rules. Even those who will not accept any form of absolute morality or of obedience to absolutes as the basis of morality, will admit that, in the sense we have accepted, it can be taught by habituation. We can, at this point, bring in the pragmatist's arguments about values developing from personal experience. When we are placed in problem situations, certain basic experiences will occur and recur. This is inevitable in any learning situation. Thus, if we recognize an element in one situation which reminds us of a smilar situation, we shall recall how we acted in that situation and act in a similar way. Just as we can become habituated to raising our hat to a lady whether she be old or young, so we can recognize elements in moral situations which are basic and to which we can respond in a way which has become habitual.

TRADITIONAL BASIS OF (MORAL) BEHAVIOUR

Certain habitual forms of behaviour become traditionally accepted and other people in subsequent generations model themselves on these accepted forms of behaviour. Again, they may do this critically or acceptingly. Let us take the example of 'an officer and a gentleman'. This expression implies a particular code of behaviour. There are certain things which it is acceptable for an officer and a gentleman to do, such as escorting a lady, refraining from using obscene language, and displaying courage in the face of adversity. Equally, there are certain things which an officer and a gentleman ought *not* to do. He ought not to strike a lady, use obscene language, or show cowardice in adversity.

Now, *A* may think that he would like to be 'an officer and a gentleman'. He finds the idea emotionally satisfying and, as a result, he accepts quite uncritically the demands of the code of behaviour necessary. *B*, on the other hand, may compare the life of an 'officer and a gentleman' with a different mode of life, and decide in favour of it on emotional grounds, but he may also prefer it on rational grounds. He may see more point in being an 'officer and a gentleman' than in being something entirely different. He may not accept every detail of the demands made by the code as having rational justification. He refuses to regard it as a perfect absolute beyond question or the desire to question. But he may decide that on balance the elements of the code are much more reasonable and capable of justification than are the elements of the alternative forms of behaviour or way of life.

In a similar way, members of a monastic order submit to the strict code of rules which govern the behaviour of all the members. In this case, the word 'order' is significant and indicates that all the members are governed strictly by the same unquestioned demands.

The monk and the 'officer and gentleman' have one thing in common, namely that they submit to the demands made by their respective codes of behaviour *voluntarily*. They exercise free will or free choice in selecting their mode of life. In this way, the life of the monk and that of the 'officer and gentleman' differ from that of the ordinary member of society who has to comply with the demands of that society without having the opportunity to choose, unless he is prepared to accept the consequences if his choice leads to unacceptable behaviour.

JUSTIFICATION AND MOTIVATION IN (MORAL) BEHAVIOUR

This is an important point, since it raises the two new ideas of 'justification' and 'motivation' in morals. Justification, moreover, raises the problems of absolutism and expediency which we have previously mentioned, and the idea of a 'utilitarian morality'. We must consider these terms carefully.

The motive is the internal reason for doing something. We often hear someone say, 'I felt moved to do so-and-so', or 'The urge to do so-and-so came over me'. The choice of form of expression is important in view of our definition of the terms 'motive', 'inner reason', and 'inner urge'. It is easy to see that a man has an inner urge to become an 'officer and a gentleman', or a monk. The inner urge causes him to exercise his free choice and choose to become one of these in preference to many alternative ways of life.

Now one of the strongest motives for doing anything is the desire which human beings have for satisfaction. If we feel that a particular course of action will produce satisfaction, we are prone to undertake that course. If when we have undertaken it, the satisfaction we expected actually happens, we have one of the strongest motives of all for continuing with our chosen course.

We can see now an important difference between the way of life which is the lot of everyone living in society, and the particular and specialized life chosen by an individual, as with the 'officer and gentleman' or the monk. Both the 'officer and gentleman' and the monk obey a code of rules to give stability to the community of which they are members. Society has even greater need of a code of rules governing the behaviour of all its members to ensure stability in that society. It cannot, in the interest of all its members, allow them all to do as they please until they find a code of rules to which they can submit themselves voluntarily, in order to derive satisfaction.

For this reason, the terms 'utilitarian morality' and 'morality of expediency' are important. What we have written about absolutes, in both values and morals, suggests that it is very difficult to maintain an absolutist position in the present age. We live in an age of expansion, and the only examples of life governed by absolutes suggest a very narrow and constricted way of life. Such constriction results ultimately in rebellion and upheaval.

One alternative is the 'morality of expediency', or the 'morality of utility'. We do not do good because we recognize an absolute standard of goodness to which we feel obliged to conform without question. We do good because it is in our own interests. The society in which we live demands that we do good, because it is in the interest of the members in general. The coining of such terms as 'the public good' and 'the public interest' is everyday evidence of the morality of expediency.

We can also use this situation to show the difference between justification and motivation in relation to moral behaviour. If we say to a child, 'you must be honest', he may ask for a reason. The only reason that the absolutist can give is, 'Because being honest is right', which to the child seems no better reason for being honest than the original command.

The non-absolutist may justify the command by saying, 'If you are dishonest, you take an unfair advantage of other people.' This may be a sufficient reason for an adult, since it is logical. He can deduce that, if *his* dishonesty gives him an unfair advantage over others, other people's dishonesty may give them an unfair advantage over *him*. In the end, therefore, it is in the interest of all to be honest. More meaningful for the child is the motivating explanation – 'Because, if you are dishonest, no one will trust you and no one will like you'. Since the child wants to be liked, and, possibly, even to be trusted, he is motivated to be honest. He is not honest because of an absolute standard to which he is forced to conform, nor because he has weighed honesty against dishonesty on rational grounds. He is honest because being honest will bring him satisfaction, and, as we have seen, acquiring satisfaction is one of the most powerful of human motives. We shall have reason to return to this point in the final sections of this chapter, when we consider the role of the teacher and morality within education.

However before we do this, we must draw together the main threads of our argument so far, and then give further consideration to morality as a separate concept from religion, a point which we have already briefly mentioned.

SUMMARY OF MAIN IDEAS ALREADY MENTIONED

Morality is concerned with good and bad behaviour. It is a social phenomenon, since it involves the evaluation of the consequences of our actions for other people and their actions for us.

We have seen that there is an 'absolute morality', but that this is virtually impossible to maintain. It is constricting in an age of tremendous expansion and, in a questioning age, virtually impossible to justify. Because of this, there is no such concept as 'universal morality', a code of behaviour or code of rules of conduct which is applicable to all societies, wherever they may be, irrespective of their stage of development, their history, aims, and values.

Each society, then, develops a code of behaviour suitable to its own needs, to provide itself with stability. One of the most stabilizing elements in any society is tradition, so that there is usually a considerable traditional content in morality, especially in the code of conduct designed for all the members of society, irrespective of any special codes of conduct which they choose to follow, because of the satisfaction it provides.

The general code of conduct designed to ensure stability for society may be supported by justifying explanations or by motivating explanations. The justifying explanation is based on reasons showing that the consequences of obeying the code of rules are in accordance with the requirements of reason. On the other hand, the motivating explanation gives the individual a reason for doing what the rules demand because it is in his own interest to do so. Whether a justifying explanation or a motivating explanation is given, society is using a morality of expediency or a utilitarian morality rather than an absolute morality.

Members of society may follow the rules of morality thinkingly or unthinkingly. If they follow them thinkingly, they do so because, having analysed them, they find that there is justifaction for their existence. Such people understand the thinking which prompted others to formulate the rules. The behaviour of people who follow the rules unthinkingly is a series of habits which have developed from habituated responses. It is easier to obey the code of rules *automatically* than it is to analyse them and determine whether or not it is reasonable to obey them.

But individuals adopt different ways of life within the overall life of society. Some of these, as in the case of a monk, demand a very strict observation of the rules. Participation in such particular ways of life is voluntary, unlike participation in the general life of society, which is compulsory for all members of society. In these particular ways of life, the code of rules may be based on the values underlying the general code of behaviour for society as a whole, but they may be more strongly stressed and allow less variety of interpretation. However, there is compensation for the extra rigour in the fact that those who undertake to live by the stricter code, are motivated to do so by the satisfaction which the way of life provides, and by the fact that they undertake obedience of their own free will. Voluntariness is permissible because the people concerned are old enough to understand the implications of the chosen way of life for them.

But wherever we follow the argument about morals and morality, we arrive at the same idea that morality, morals and moral codes are all concerned with one primary object, namely the establishment of the good life. For the member of the monastic order the interpretation of 'good' may be an absolute one, the living of a life in conformity with the will of God. His code is based on the single command, 'Be ye perfect, even as your Father in heaven is perfect'.

For members of society in general, unless the society is governed by absolute values the moral code will not be based on such a stringent demand. Nevertheless the primary concern is still the good life and which forms of conduct contribute towards it and which do not. The good life may be the Greek idea which we met when we considered the concept of culture, namely the 'comfortable life' as distinct from the 'necessary life'. But whatever the interpretation of the term 'the good life' in the non-religious sense, the key problem is always this: To what extent is it possible to have a good life which is not based on religion? This is really our earlier question 'Can there be morality without religion in another form. Until we have settled this issue, we cannot analyse the role of the teacher in the area of morality.

RELIGION AND MORALITY

In Britain, the question whether morality can be totally separated from religion is not a vital one, since religious education is still retained by statute in state schools. However, as such concepts as Humanism gain wider acceptance and as more and more people in a materialistic age question the right to teach religion in schools, we are becoming more aware of this question.

In a secular educational system, the question is even more pressing. The problem is simply stated. If morality can be totally separated from religion, well and good. It matters little whether religion is taught in schools or not, since the school can still discharge its social responsibility of teaching morality. However, if morality cannot be totally separated from religion, there are very clearly definable consequences for both teachers and pupils in a secular educational system.

In the first place, if the two things cannot be totally separated, the secular school can teach only an 'approximate' morality. Secondly, if they are not totally separable, those children whose parents do not ensure that they receive religious education at home or at church are *deprived* in the area of morality, compared with those children whose parents do. In all other areas of deprivation, the school seeks to redress the balance. In the moral situation, the secular school is unable to teach religion to redress the balance.

Thirdly, the committed Christian, or even those who have 'leanings' towards religion, must suppress their feelings when they undertake moral teaching in the secular school. Consequently, if morality cannot be totally separated from religion, such teachers are unjustly constrained in their moral teachings. In Chapter 13, we shall see that constraint is a denial of freedom.

However we look at the problem, it is a delicate one. We have seen that indoctrination remains a nebulous term, because its unpleasant connotations make any discussion of the concept difficult.

We have seen repeatedly in this book that once we leave the area of fact and enter the area of belief, we are on difficult ground, since it becomes increasingly difficult to bring publicly accepted evidence to support beliefs. Religion is the supreme example of an area of beliefs and also the area where it is most difficult to adduce convincing evidence. On the one hand, it is often argued that there is historical evidence that the 'contemplation of God' is the ultimate end of man. Those who accept this idea argue strongly that morality and religion cannot be separated. Others refuse to accept the idea and back up their refusal with the claim that what the first group of people call 'evidence' is not evidence at all. It is intuition, feeling, subjective impression, even a distortion of the facts by reading into history what we hope to find there.

Again, there are some who argue equally weakly that because morality can be taught in a secular school, it must be capable of total separation from religion. This is a bogus argument, since, as we have already suggested, those who believe that morality and religion cannot be totally separated, are equally entitled to argue that what is taught as 'morality', in the secular school is not really morality at all.

Both sides in this particular argument are at least concerned with the same thing, namely, providing something through education which will result in the good life for those committed to their care. Again, we can see that the situation is problematical, since both sides will define the good life differently. The religious side will say that the good life is that which is founded on *supernatural* virtues, while the non-religious side will claim that it is founded on *natural* virtues. Few, like Aquinas himself and the Neo-Thomists, will accept that there can be any reconciliation of these two groups of virtues. Once a secular educational system is established, the most that will be admitted is that the Church is at liberty to teach super-natural virtues. The school is categorically forbidden to do so.

Again, for those who receive teaching from the Church about the super-natural virtues and from the school about the natural virtues, there is no real problem. Provided with a kind of knowledge by both sides, they have the content necessary for them to make their own decision in adulthood. The real problem is posed by the child who only hears one side of the story, and is, as a result, never in possession of sufficient knowledge to allow him to make the decision whether he can live the good life and behave morally without religion.

The philosophical problem which emerges from this discussion is simply stated. As there are some children who, unless they receive religious education from the school, will never receive it at all and may even never encounter religion, are we justified in creating a secular educational system? Put in a slightly different way, the question becomes: are we entitled to teach religion in schools, with the possibility of offending an unknown number of people, to prevent a similarly unknown number of people from never receiving any religious education or contact with religion at all?

Frankena (7) makes a determined attempt to analyse all the implications, including whether morality and religion are totally separable, what the implications are for the teacher of morality in the secular school, and whether the whole problem does not centre on two different interpretations of the word 'spiritual'. The religious interpretation of 'spiritual' is both emotional and metaphysical, and involves such ideas as 'communion with God'. The non-religious interpretation of 'spiritual' is also emotional, but the emphasis is more aesthetic, such as we saw James give to the term (Chapter 7).

Frankena admits that morality is 'genetically' (8) dependent on religion. By this he means that morality, as generally interpreted in Western civiliza-tions, is an *outgrowth* of Christianity. We often talk of the 'Christian Ethic', which imparts a 'social emphasis' in the good life. Humanism and Chris-tianity are close in many areas, especially in their concern for the individual and his rights. But, while Christianity is concerned for the supernatural man, the soul, and the metaphysical, Humanism is concerned solely with the natural man, the body, and the present, physical existence.

An atheist philosopher such as Hume (9) would argue that the fact that Christianity and morality are genetically connected is no evidence that we cannot have complete morality without religion. If we leave the field of philosophy and turn to the psychologist Allport, we can see a similar argument applied to human 'drives'. Psychologists before Allport had argued that human drives, like animal drives, result from instincts. Instincts govern all our behaviour, and it is only because civilization makes the instinctive basis of our behaviour somewhat less obvious that many people think that man alone is not ruled by his instincts.

Allport, however, argues that there may be an instinctual basis for human drives, and that, although originally instinctual, they ultimately become *functionally autonomous*. Once this happens, the connection is severed and the instinctual and the functionally autonomous drives become totally separate. A simple example of this is the habit of smoking. Some, following the Freudian line, may argue that smoking originates as a substitute for breast sucking, to reduce the need for oral gratification. This is stating the problem at the instinctual level. Later, however, a man may smoke for no other reason than that smoking gives him satisfaction. The drive (or urge) to smoke has now become completely separated from the original drive. The argument for the functional autonomy of morality would be parallel to this. The religious origins of morality, as we have defined it, are no guarantee that morality and religion cannot be totally separated.

It is also possible to argue that morality requires religious motivation. This is a positive approach to motivation and one which says that many people are good only for religious reasons, because they wish to 'obtain salvation'. Again, there may be an element of negative religious motivation in some people's moral behaviour. They may fear that failure to live the good life will result in damnation, which, of course, they wish to avoid. However, we cannot argue from this that *all* people live the good life *only* for religious reasons. We can find people who are motivated to live the good life and to do right because they believe, not in a Supernatural Being, but in such concepts as peace, and social justice.

RELIGION: MORALITY: TEACHING MORALITY

Frankena says, as we said previously, that once secular education is established, we are concerned with two main problems: firstly, whether within such education adequate moral teaching can be given; secondly, what those who teach morality are, and are not, permitted to do.

Firstly, as we have just seen, there are some people who act morally solely for religious reasons. For such people, it is helpful and even necessary to receive religious teaching. But we also saw that not everyone requires religious motivation to act morally. Unless we can say that *no one* acts morally *without* religious teaching, we are not advancing a strong case for condemning secular education.

Secondly (and this is a stronger piece of evidence than the first), *no one is completely* moral without receiving religious teaching. But this is not the same as saying that *few* people, or indeed nobody, can be adequately moral *without* receiving religious teaching. We may in the end be compelled to say that, while perfect morality presupposes definite religious beliefs, everyone *can* be *adequately* moral *without* religious beliefs. In reality, we are saying that *absolute* morality is inseparable from religious belief, but that utilitarian morality, rational morality, morality of expediency – call it what you will – is feasible without religious belief. Since the Church is always available to cater for religious belief, this second reason is not sufficient to condemn secular education entirely.

Thirdly, we can argue that *most* people are only *adequately* moral, if they possess religious beliefs. This is at once the strongest argument against secular schools, but, at the same time, the most difficult to substantiate. Apart from the difficulty of assembling evidence in a non-factual area, we are faced with the problem of defining the term 'adequately'. A dozen people would give a dozen definitions. It could be argued that, as adequate morality is the morality of expediency, this is the best we can hope for, since even an idealist like Kant accepted that absolute morality was unattainable generally.

When we discussed indoctrination in Chapter 9, we had to decide whether content, method or intention determined whether a process was indoctrination or not. We are concerned with similar ideas when we consider the teaching of morality and the interpretation of the term 'spiritual' in secular education. Let us take the problem of content first. The teacher in the secular school system *may not* use the Bible as the content of any moral teaching he may give. He must not define 'spiritual' as 'pertaining to a man's soul', nor use the Bible to show that a man's soul can be saved only by his becoming a committed Christian. Here, we are really saying that the soul and salvation are not one hundred per cent certainties, nor are they ideas for which we can, necessarily, produce sufficient publicly acceptable evidence. Therefore, the secular school forbids this content and this definition.

In the area of method, it is not so easy to be categorical. The secular school cannot forbid a man to behave as a Christian. Nor can it compel him to hide the fact that he goes to church. Finally, it cannot prevent pupils making the deduction that this teacher's exemplary behaviour is motivated *solely* by his religious convictions. His spiritual life shows itself in his physical life, and, since imitation is a method of learning, he may be instrumental in his pupils learning his way of life through imitation.

However, the secular school can forbid this teacher to make any of these things explicit. He may not tell them overtly that he behaves as he does because of deep Christian convictions, that true Christianity makes it essential to separate the spiritual life from the 'life of the flesh'. The teacher in the secular school can base his teaching only on human experience. Teachers must transmit a certain way of life because they can accept, on purely rational grounds, that such a life is desirable and good. They can only show that there are certain areas such as music and art which enrich life, and turn the necessary life into the comfortable life. This is the aesthetic, as distinct from the metaphysical, interpretation of the term 'spiritual'. It is connected with culture rather than with religion. If we heed O'Connor's idea that the fifth aim of education is to train pupils to appreciate the culture of the past, we can only treat religious achievements historically, in a way that can be accepted equally in the presence or absence of religious belief. The work of Michelangelo and Mozart must be accepted as great painting and great music resulting from great artistic talent, not from the religious motivation to paint or create music 'for the greater glory of God' (10).

What we have already stated explicitly has implied what the intention of the teacher in the secular school must be when he undertakes moral teaching. He is forbidden to convert any pupil to his own beliefs through his teaching. He must avoid 'forming the pupil's mind' in a religious sense, as assiduously as Rousseau demanded that the teacher must avoid forming the child's mind in the intellectual sense. He may teach his pupils the desirability of living at peace with himself and his neighbours, in terms of commonsense and human experience. He may not attempt to communicate his experience of the 'peace of God, which passeth all understanding' and the desirability of attaining such peace.

The most that the teacher in the secular school can do is to help pupils work out a 'philosophy of life'. In this, he will subscribe not to the Christian ideal but to the ideal of Aristotle that the ultimate end of human life is happiness. He will show that happiness is most likely to come to all men when they behave morally, and that behaving morally thus leads to satisfaction. Since we have already seen that satisfaction is one of the strongest motives for submitting to non-religious as well as to religious demands in moral contexts, sacred and secular may not be poles apart, except in explicit statements.

THE TEACHER AS SOCIETY'S MORAL AGENT

Although men frequently debate whether morality can be taught without teaching religion, there are few who would deny that morality (defined as 'right conduct') should be taught in school. Society generally agrees that morality not only *can* but *ought* to be taught. It also accepts that the teacher is the one best qualified for the task. Again we encounter the problem of the comfortable life and the necessary life.

In Chapter 7, we suggested that one problem facing the teacher is that of ensuring, through the curriculum, that the gap between the values of the general culture and the values of sub-cultures is narrowed. In the same way, since values and morals are connected, the teacher has to help certain children to reconcile the demands made by the general code of behaviour established by society and the 'sub-codes' accepted by smaller units within society.

The teacher, in the area of morals, is an interpreter. The philosopher is able to describe different types of life. The teacher must determine, in terms of the society in which he teaches and in terms of the experience of his pupils, which type of life it is best for them to lead. This is one example of the teacher having to consider the needs of the child in conjunction with the needs of society, and the demands developing out of them (see Chapter 4). The teacher has to deal at the practical level with material which the philosopher considers at the theoretical level. As Brown (11) says, the ultimate aim of the teacher is to bring his pupils to understand the difference between right and wrong, between good (or socially acceptable) conduct and bad (or socially unacceptable) conduct. We can now see more clearly what O'Connor meant when he placed first in his list of aims of education the task of teaching the individual those skills which will enable him to take his place in society. Unless the individual can accept certain moral demands which society will make of him, and unless he has the knowledge necessary for the making of moral choices and the experience which teaches him which is the right choice, he will not fit into society as a good citizen. If he cannot fit into society as a citizen, he cannot fit into society as a workman applying the training he has received. Making moral choices involves cognitive perspective.

HERBART AND MORAL EDUCATION

The teacher, then, must impart the knowledge of good and bad to his pupils, form moral habits, teach moral skills, and develop moral motives. Teaching morality is not the same as imparting knowledge or training, since morality is neither knowledge only nor a skill only. Moral education is a process best understood in the terms used by Herbart (12), who regarded morality as the ultimate aim of education itself. His expression to describe the process was that 'outer compulsion' must lead to 'inner freedom'. The teacher must ensure that the individual passes from a static state of order (*Regierung*) (13) to a dynamic state of self-discipline (*Zucht*). (14). The latter state is achieved only by the full development of individual personality. The transition from the static to the dynamic state is to be achieved by instruction (*Unterricht*) or teaching. Herbart stresses the vital importance of interest as the intermediate goal of education. The process of instruction or teaching must *involve* the child. He must find satisfaction in his activities.

PIAGET AND THE CHILD'S MORAL DEVELOPMENT

This is not dissimilar to the developmental psychology of Piaget in the twentieth century. He says that the child's moral growth is parallel to his cognitive (intellectual) growth. He starts from a pre-school period of complete dependence on parental absolutes, and on teacher absolutes in the early years of the infants school. The earliest moral demands take the form of categorical imperatives ('Do this'; 'Do not do that') issued by his parents. The child learns that when he obeys these categorical imperatives, his parents are pleased. When they are pleased, he is satisfied. Thus by deriving satisfaction from his earliest forms of moral behaviour (obedience to absolutes), he is motivated to continue with this form of behaviour. Those who advocate that the child should be allowed to develop a pragmatic morality, even at this early age, ignore two main points; how he acquires the necessary experience, and how he is protected from (possibly) serious harm while he learns pragmatically. The 'discipline of natural consequences' (15) can be a hard master in the school of morality.

When the child goes to school, he transfers many of his feelings for his parents to his teacher. Consequently, he is prepared to obey her imperatives for the same reason that he obeyed those of his parents, namely, to please her and to derive satisfaction from experiencing her pleasure. However, the teacher gradually structures moral problem situations, just as she structures other learning situations. Socialization is one of the aims of the infants' school. We saw earlier that morality is a social phenomenon, and consequently social situations are the early contexts for moral behaviour. Gradually, the transition is made from 'all imperatives' to 'some imperatives and some rules', though the rules are often explained by the voice of the teacher. From there, the child progresses to obedience to impersonal rules which are rationally based. He learns that if he obeys the rules as he obeyed the parental voice and the teacher's voice, his behaviour gives pleasure and he still derives satisfaction from pleasing those whom he loves and respects. He also learns that infringement of the rules can lead to his exclusion from the group. His rational understanding of the rules still depends on his actually experiencing the consequences of good and bad behaviour.

When the child reaches the 'formal operational' stage of development at eleven or twelve years, he is able to think gradually in terms of ideas which develop out of his earlier physical experiences. He is now able to think in terms of the concepts 'right' and 'wrong', to visualize the consequences of particular courses of action (without actually experiencing them), just as he is able to formulate hypotheses and test them against available data in the cognitive field of science.

We can see the relationship now between these stages of moral (and cognitive) development, and the stages of character development which we discussed in Chapter 11. But each individual is not merely allowed to develop according to his own whim. The teacher, the practical interpreter for the pupils of the theoretical morality of society, knows what characteristics he wishes to develop in all children so that they will behave in socially acceptable ways. Although he does not wish to stifle individuality, he does not wish development to be purely random.

MORALITY AND CHARACTER DEVELOPMENT

In Chapter 2, where we described education as a process of initiation (into culture, morality, etc., as we now appreciate), we suggested that although all children are initiated, not all benefit equally from such initiation. Consequently, although all children pass through this process of moral education, not all of them emerge as sterling citizens who will behave at all times in a socially acceptable manner.

The connection between moral education and character development is a most important one. Indeed, many would claim that it is as important as the acquisition of knowledge, since it is little use possessing a vast store of knowledge if we estrange ourselves from society by our im-moral behaviour. Peters has emphasized the importance of values as well as knowledge in education, and the transmission of both by morally acceptable methods.

Peters states that if we accept the Freudian point of view, the child begins life with a strange, unruly amalgam of wishes upon which is gradually imposed a code of social demands or rules, which make some ways of gratifying wishes acceptable and others unacceptable. Little by little, life becomes a rule-following process. The particular style of rule-following which the child adopts determines his character. We can see now the connection between what we wrote earlier about the five stages of character development, suggested by Cronbach, and what Peters is saying here. The five stages can be called five approaches to rule-following. The rules are moral rules.

Peters continues by saying that the educator must decide what type of character he wishes to develop in the child, just as we saw earlier that Lord James suggested that the educator must decide what type of individual he wishes to develop through education, using the content of the curriculum to achieve these ends. The important point, in both instances, is that the individual can learn to apply the rules or conform to the demands rigidly, mechanically, and without possessing insight into the demands or the the reason for their being made, or he can perform what is required of him rationally, understanding not only what is required but *why* it is required.

It is this latter state which Peters is concerned to develop, since he declares that his wish is that a person of autonomous (16) character shall be developed, who follows the rules *in a rational manner*. To achieve this, he must subscribe to principles of a high order which enable him to follow the rules intelligently and permit him to modify them objectively in the light of changed circumstances. It will be seen that the pragmatic approach does not cater adequately for the acceptance of principles of a high order as *criteria* for the development of behaviour, and that the true absolutist approach does not encourage the individual to make modifications.

One of the most important of the principles envisaged by Peters is *objectivity*, which has virtually been the theme of this book. At the outset we suggested that all problems ought to be brought to the criterion of reason, to determine precisely how well they measure up to its demands. To achieve this, the individual must, says Peters, go beyond that level of cognitive development to which Plato gave the name *orthe doxa* (17).

The above is the view of one philosopher/psychologist. We shall end this chapter with the definition of morality by another philosopher/psychologist, Piaget (18). It is briefly expressed, but not essentially different from the ideas of Peters:

'All morality consists in a system of rules, and the essence of all morality is to be sought for in the respect which the individual acquires for these rules.'

The method of acquiring respect determines character for the individual.

NOTES AND REFERENCES FOR CHAPTER 12

1 'Ostracism' is a word which came into being with the Athenian government reforms introduced by Cleisthenes ('Father of Athenian democracy') in the sixth century B.C. An *ostrakon* was a piece of pottery on which was recorded the name of anyone whose banishment seemed to be 'in the interests of the state'. Any person whose name appeared on the potsherds of 6,000 citizens, was compelled to go into exile for ten years. His property in Athens, however, was not confiscated. During the whole time that the system was in being, no more than ten people were ostracized. There have, however, been some remarkable finds of potsherds bearing the names of some of the most famous statesmen of Athens in the sixth century B.C., including Aristides (who was actually ostracized), Themistocles, who made Athens strengthen her fleet, and Megacles, uncle of Pericles, the greatest Athenian statesman of the fifth century B.C.

2 Lucretius (full name Titus Lucretius Carus) lived from 99 to 55 B.C. He was a philosophical poet, whose work *De Rerum Natura*, in six books, was an account of creation based on a remarkable 'atomic theory', which remained acceptable into the nineteenth century.

One of his primary motives for writing the book was to remove men's superstitious dread of the gods. He was thus very much a man who believed that moral conduct did not depend on religious belief. His famous line: *Quantum religio potuit suadere malorum* ('What a great deal of mischief superstition can cause') sums up his attitude on this subject. To show how man came to act morally, he describes the making of the 'social contract', an idea which became popular with later political and Utopian philosophers. The term was the title of Rousseau's famous political work published in 1762.

3 The Latin word *saeculum* really meant the period of time known as 'one generation'. In other contexts it also meant 100 years. Tacitus, the historian, uses it to mean 'the spirit of the times', which comes near to our use of the word 'secular'. The real basis for our meaning of the word, to mean the opposite of 'sacred' or 'religious', comes from the medieval writers, who used the word to indicate 'wordliness' in the Scriptural sense of 'the world, the flesh and the devil'. In ecclesiastical Latin it came to mean 'heathen'.

The term 'secular schools', and similarly 'secular education', means a system in which there is no provision for religious teaching. It may be that, as in France, a certain time is set aside when those parents who wish can take their children from the school to the Church to receive religious teaching. In America, those parents who wish their children to receive religious teaching must make provision for it in their own time. In Communist countries the state actually discourages religion and religious teaching, whether in or out of school time.

4 An Introduction to Philosophical Analysis, op. cit.

5 The Greek word *episteme* means 'knowledge' or 'understanding'. An epistemologist is one who is interested in the nature of knowledge. He is, thus, basically, an analytical philosopher who carries out his analysis in one particular area, examining one particular concept in detail and depth.

6 *Education and Indoctrination*, op. cit.

7 'Public Education and the Good Life', William K. Frankena, Chapter 14 of *Philosophy and Education*, ed. Israel Scheffler (Allyn & Bacon 1966).

8 Every human being is connected genetically with his parents and ancestors since he is composed of the same genes (physical material). He has the same physical nature, or belongs to the same type. The analogy holds good for the concepts 'religion' and 'morality'. They both involve ethics – from the Greek word *ethikos*, meaning of or for morals– that is, both are concerned with ideas about what is good (or right) and evil (or wrong) behaviour. They are, therefore, made of the 'same (idea) stuff', and are genetically connected.

9 David Hume (1711–1776) was almost exactly contemporary with Rousseau, but there the similarity ends. As a philosopher, Rousseau was never in the 'first division', whereas Hume is described by Russell as 'one of the most important among philosophers'. He developed the ideas of John Locke (the English empiricist) and George Berkeley (the subjective idealist who denied

the existence of matter) to their logical conclusion. Hume wrote *Treatise on Human Nature* between the years 1734 and 1737. He subsequently wrote *Inquiry into Human Understanding* (compare Locke's essay *Concerning Human Understanding*) and *Dialogues Concerning Natural Religion*. The *Treatise on Human Nature* deals with understanding, passions, and morals. Concerned with reason and experience (empiricism) he writes at one point: 'Generally speaking, the errors in religion are dangerous; those in philosophy only ridiculous.'

10 What amounted to the 'motto' of the Society of Jesus (Jesuits) was *ad maiorem Dei gloriam*, 'to the greater glory of God'. Even today, in certain R. C. schools, the present writer has seen the abbreviaion *a.m.d.g.* at the top of a pupil's work next to his name.

11 *General Philosophy in Education*, L. M. Brown (McGraw-Hill 1966).

12 For an account of the whole structure of Herbart's thinking on education, the reader is referred to *Doctrines of the Great Educators*, R. R. Rusk (Macmillan, 1957 edn, which contains an additional chapter on Dewey).

13 Readers should note how the idea of *Regierung* can be detected through its association with such words as 'Regimen' (strict routine). There is a tendency among teachers to confuse the concepts 'order' and 'discipline'. They talk about 'keeping discipline' when they should really say 'maintaining order'. The poor disciplinarian is often the teacher who, because he never establishes order at the start of a lesson, never has an audience sufficiently receptive to respond to *Unterricht* (instruction or teaching). Consequently, their lack of attentiveness makes it impossible for them ever to become interested or involved in the lesson, and thus to discipline themselves through active participation.

14 Resulting from character training.

15 The 'discipline of natural consequences' is advocated by both Rousseau and Herbert Spencer, although the latter, seeing the potential dangers of taking the idea to its logical conclusion, warns that children should not be allowed to suffer the most serious consequences of their behaviour. For example, it is more sensible to warn a child of the possible danger of climbing trees than to allow him to discover this for himself by falling out of a tree and breaking a leg.

In moderation, the discipline of natural consequences is part of the natural moral education of every child. All children find themselves in social situations where some act of behaviour transgresses what the group finds acceptable and results in the group's showing either mild or serious displeasure. We cannot save children from learning the consequences of their actions if we wish them to become socialized. Socialization is a practical experience. Although theoretical (adult) guidance can help the child, it cannot prevent him from the empirical acquisition of social and moral knowledge.

16 The Greek word *autos* means 'self', and the autistic child is one who withdraws into himself, who refuses to communicate.

17 The three levels of cognitive experience recognized by Plato were:

doxa – opinion
orthe doxa (from which the English 'orthodoxy' is derived) – right opinion
knowledge.

If we relate the term 'orthodoxy' to what we said about the stages of character development (in Chapter 11), we shall see that it often means little more than unthinking acceptance of and conformity to ideas and ideals. An irrational conscientious person is often completely orthodox but has little knowledge of the ideas which result in his conformity.

18 *The Moral Judgment of the Child*, Jean Piaget (Free Press 1948).

Chapter 13

The Concepts 'Freedom' and 'Authority'

Throughout this book we have seen that it is difficult to isolate any concept within the 'family' of education and to study it without discovering that it has important relationships with other key concepts. Thus culture was related to curriculum, training to education, conditioning to teaching, value-judgments and values to morals. For this reason, we presented 'trilogies of concepts. But we also found that concepts could not even be limited to the trilogies in which they were placed. To take but one example, we found that culture in the second trilogy was connected with values in the third.

Consequently, we should not be surprised to find that our final pair of concepts, 'freedom' and 'authority', are related educationally in a most significant manner. At first glance, it appears that they are poles apart, that they are opposites, like the 'bi-polar' personality factors (1) developed by Cattell. Indeed, Nash (2) describes freedom and authority as 'principal polarities', and, because of this, we shall first examine each concept separately. However, Nash continues by saying that they can be broken down into a number of 'sub-polarities', each of which represents an aspect of the main polarity. In the same way, the personality of an individual can be broken down into a number of bi-polar factors, e.g. dominance and submissiveness. But no individual is wholly dominant or totally submissive. Some people may have a predictable tendency in one direction or the other, while others, nearer to the centre of the 'continuum' (the scale between the two poles), are dominant and submissive in approximately equal proportions. It is for this reason that after analysing the two main concepts separately, we shall discuss important interrelationships between them.

THE CONCEPT 'FREEDOM'

To set ourselves the task of undertaking a complete analysis of freedom would be almost as difficult and lengthy as undertaking a full analysis of knowledge. But, as with concepts already analysed, some investigation of the meaning of freedom itself must be undertaken before its full significance in educational contexts can be appreciated. Although we have paired freedom with authority, and Ross (3) paired freedom and discipline, these pairings are important sub-polarities rather than the polarities themselves.

For this reason it is significant that the single word 'Freedom' is the title of Maurice Cranston's book (4).

FREEDOM AND LINGUISTIC ANALYSIS

Cranston begins his work by inviting the reader to consider how much or how little we *really* say when we make the statement, 'I am free!' Syntactically, the sentence is simple (5), and has exactly the same structure as 'I am hungry' and 'I am cold'. But there the resemblance ends. The sentence 'I am hungry' is complex neither in terms of syntax nor in terms of ideas. It simply means that I need or want food. 'I am cold' is a little more complex. Taken literally, it means that I am physically in need of heat. Taken metaphorically, it means that, as a person reacting to other persons, I lack emotional warmth. We understand both these statements because we have tested them empirically. We understand as the result of first-hand experience. But if I say 'I have knowledge', my hearers are not so clear about my meaning. Not only are there many areas of knowledge, but, as we saw in the very first chapter of this book, there are different types of knowledge. Thus my hearers might ask: 'You have knowledge of what?' (area of knowledge), or 'What do you mean by knowledge?' (definition of knowledge). Similarly, after the statement, 'I am free!', we should feel compelled to ask, 'Free from what?' (area of freedom) or 'What do you mean by freedom?' (definition of freedom). We shall return to the problem of 'freedom from . . .' in the final pages of this chapter. For the moment, we would do well to remind ourselves that (in Chapter 3) we found it was meaningless to say, 'I am trained', since the person to whom we addressed the statement, merely asked, 'Trained for what?'. Thus at the outset, Cranston says that freedom is not a 'unitary' concept (we saw in Chapter 2 that we could not find a 'unitary' definition for education), but that there are many freedoms.

Freedom may mean 'absence of constraint', and at once we think of freedom as automatically a 'hurrah word'. No right-minded individual would applaud constraint. Being free from constraint means being free from indoctrination, from unjust imprisonment. But Aristotle adds a warning that freedom from constraint taken as an absolute, may result in little more than a state of anarchy where every man does as he pleases. If this is true, we are forced to modify our automatically enthusiastic reception of the word 'freedom' as meaning 'absence of constraint'.

Constraint ('limiting factor') may be natural or artificial. Rousseau objected to the educational system of his day because it imposed artificial (man-made) constraint on the natural development of the child. This is clearly shown in two statements: 'Nature wishes them to be children before they are men' (artificial constraint of education), and 'Cities are the graveyard of the human species' (artificial constraint of the social system of his day). In a modern psychological context, if a child performs badly at school because his ability is low, his educational attainment suffers from natural constraint. But, if his performance at school is poor because poor environmental factors, such as a poor home, prevent his ability from developing, then his progress is hindered by artificial (man-made) constraint. Similarly, equality of opportunity becomes an important issue only when some are denied opportunities because of artificial constraints. One of these in the past was the irrelevant criterion of wealth for deciding who should be admitted to grammar school, or to Oxford and Cambridge.

Cranston, approaching freedom from the linguistic standpoint, says that adding adjectives to qualify 'freedom', a technique which we ourselves examined earlier (Chapter 3), may only make for greater obscurity instead of greater clarity. For this reason, to think that such adjective/noun expressions as 'economic freedom' or 'religious freedom' make the term 'freedom' clearer is fallacious, since they merely lead us to ask what is meant by 'religious' and 'economic'.

Instead of saying, 'I *am* free', I can say, 'I *feel* free'. The difference here is similar to the difference between saying, 'I *know* that people are cruel', and, 'It *is my experience* that people are cruel', or between 'Bradman *was* the greatest batsman who ever lived' and 'I *always feel* that Bradman was the greatest batsman who ever lived'. In all three cases, the more dogmatic form of the claim is the more likely to be challenged and the more easily contradicted.

In his second chapter, Cranston gives three important interpretations of the statement, 'I *feel* free!'. These can be shown as:

1 The individual is given the opportunity to indulge his desires, preferences, etc., without being debarred by *authority*. Thus, when the medieval universities were founded, individuals were free to pursue secular knowledge of their own choice without being forbidden to do so by the *authority* of the Church. Again, if I cease to be a teacher and become a navvy, I may be able to indulge desires and preferences which the *authority* of public opinion prevented me from indulging when I was responsible in my capacity as a teacher (public servant) for the well-being of children.

2 A person masters a habitual weakness, e.g. the habit of smoking. For many years, unable to break the habit, he reproached himself for being weak-willed. However, when in the end he does give it up, he is free from his weakness.

3 One exchanges one bondage for another. A man completes the decoration of the entire interior and exterior of his house and *feels* released from bondage. But he is really only free to become 'enslaved'

by his garden, which has gone to ruin while he was decorating. The change may appear in the guise of freedom and give a feeling of freedom.

Another important point is that words can be used descriptively, that is in a matter-of-fact manner, or emotively, that is, in a persuasive manner. We made a distinction (in Chapter 10) between factual statements and value-judgments, and issued a warning that it is dangerous to confuse the two. Similarly, it is dangerous to confuse the descriptive and emotive use of words. The descriptive use of words is in the cognitive or intellectual sphere, the sphere of rationality, impartiality, and objectivity. The emotional sphere is the sphere of preferences, prejudices, bias, and subjectivity. Again, we are reminded of the difference between factual statements and value-judgments. 'Latin is a language' is a statement of fact; 'Latin is a language which ought to be studied by all intelligent people' is a very different type of statement. We became aware of a related problem when (in Chapter 2) we saw the importance of distinguishing between descriptive and stipulative definitions. Cranston says that the descriptive meaning of freedom varies with different contexts, but its emotive meaning, for those who value freedom, remains constant.

DEFINITIONS OF FREEDOM

In Chapter 2, we began with a number of definitions of the term 'education' taken from writers throughout history. This was useful for two reasons; firstly it showed whether there was any detectable consistency in the content of the definition, or whether each man found education to be something quite different from the rest; secondly, it was useful as showing that in the end there was no unitary definition of 'education' which we could accept. Instead we decided on certain characteristics of education which were important to all those who receive education and to all those who examine education philosophically. We can centre our own thinking (and acting, in the sense of practical teaching) upon these common areas or characteristics. It is, therefore, interesting to see that Cranston gives a number of definitions of freedom (or liberty) spread over a period of many centuries. These include:

'Liberty is a perfection of the will' – Duns Scotus (6).
'Liberty or freedom signifieth properly the absence of opposition' – Hobbes (7).
'Liberty . . . is the power a man has to do or forbear doing any particular action' – Locke.
'By liberty we can only mean a power of acting according to the determination of the will' – Hume.

'Freedom is independence from anything other than the moral law alone' – Kant.

'Freedom is spontaneity of the intelligence' – Leibniz (8).

'Freedom is necessity transfigured' – Hegel (9).

'A free man is one who lives according to the dictates of reason alone' – Spinoza (10).

FREEDOM: INTELLECT: WILL

Three important concepts emerge from these definitions – will, reason, intelligence. We can now see that freedom implies responsibility, since freedom is the absence of determinism. We are free to act, unlike the Calvinist who is constrained by predestination (11). Therefore, if we are free to act, we are free to do wrong or right. If we are constrained to do right, we lose our freedom of choice and consequently a very important type of freedom. Freedom *of* action makes responsibility *for* action inevitable.

At this point we return to the subject of Chapter 12, namely, morals. If we are to choose between right and wrong in a way which is not predetermined, we must bring intelligence to bear. If we merely conform, either because we have been 'conditioned' to conform (our freedom having been taken from us) or because we do not wish to think about the implications of conforming (abdication from freedom), we lose our freedom.

The next problem is whether the will is the intellectual or emotional agent of our actions. If we act intellectually, we act in accordance with reason. If we act emotionally, we act according to whim or caprice. For this reason Herbart saw the strong connection between the intellectual and the moral content and processes of education. Herbart declined to accept freedom of the will as the possibility of motiveless action and arbitrary choices. They were mere caprice, which could result in the replacement of freedom by licence. It would also deny the educator any freedom to develop desirable characters in his pupils. On the other hand, he wished to avoid the sort of determinism in education which is present in the Calvinist interpretation of human behaviour in life. For this reason, he writes that education would be tyranny if it did not lead to freedom. In a paradoxical statement, defining the task of the educator, he says that 'he must determine the child to the free choice of good', a problem which we considered as central to teaching morality (see Chapter 12).

Herbart saw an essential connection between knowledge and will. Knowledge was that which prevented acts of will from being merely arbitrary. Unless the educator supplies the child with the right experiences in school, he cannot enable him to acquire the knowledge which is basic to the making of right choices. In Chapter 4, we saw that the Naturalist school of educators believe that they, and they alone, give the child freedom, by subjecting him to the negative non-determinist education advocated by Rousseau. If Herbart is right, the Naturalist school and their modern counterpart the non-directive educators, may well be denying the child the very freedom which they seek to give him by failing to provide him with the necessary knowledge on which alone meaningful choice can be based. We shall have more to say on this point in the closing stages of this chapter, where we shall consider the idea that one can only have any sort of 'freedom from . . .' only 'on the authority of' somebody or something.

In view of what we have just written, and because we shall consider his arguments further after we have given some consideration to the concept of authority, it is relevant and, indeed, necessary to close this section on freedom with the definition (stipulative type) which Nash gives in the introduction to his book *Authority and Freedom in Education*. Significantly, because he believes that authority is the 'provider of freedom' (or, as we have said, we can have 'freedom from' only 'on the authority of'), he reverses the order of the concepts in our title for this chapter. After defining authority as 'that which exercises a force or influence over us', he defines freedom as 'the power to achieve, choose, become'. This is a dynamic definition in keeping with Herbart's ideas that 'outer compulsion' in education can lead, and must lead, to 'inner freedom', or the freedom which self-discipline gives to 'achieve, choose, become'.

THE CONCEPT 'AUTHORITY'

In one important way, the concept 'authority' reminds us of the concept 'freedom', analysed in the first part of this chapter. Neither is a unitary concept, and, just as we found that there were different types of freedom, so we find there are varieties of authority.

Moreover, when we examine the term 'authority', we are reminded of the terms 'aim' or 'aims' (analysed in Chapter 5), for it is possible to have 'authority', '*the* authority', '*the* authority *of*', 'an authority'. We shall see, later, that the teacher is 'in authority' 'on the authority' of society.

ETYMOLOGICAL DEFINITION OF AUTHORITY AND ITS IMPLICATIONS

The word 'authority' comes from the Latin *auctoritas*, which means 'presence' or 'bearing', and was the word used to describe the 'demeanour' of a dignitary. This could well be the reason why Peters says that the word 'authority' has an 'aura' about it.

Because of this idea of the 'presence of a dignitary', there is often an association of ideas between authority and power. The early Roman consuls were invested with the supreme power of life and death over the citizens, and the Roman *pater familias* also had similar power over all members of his household. In this respect, his authority exceeded that of even a typical 'Victorian' father, although in many other respects there is great similarity between them. Heitland (12) also tells us that, although the Roman senate (13) did not have the legal authority or power to pass a law, declare war, or negotiate a peace, its moral authority was such that for centuries it did these things without anyone questioning its legal right to do so. Such was the power of its 'presence' or 'aura'.

This brings us to a most important point. Authority can be imposed, in which case there is always, at least in the background, a suggestion of physical power or force to give backing to the authority. There is a parallel here with what we said on page 258 about exchanging subjection to *A* for subjection to *B*, and calling this freedom. Thus, when the Romans rid themselves of the hated power and authority of their early kings (14), they voluntarily accepted the authority of the senate and the supreme authority of the consuls. Such was their relief at ridding themselves of the imposed authority and accepting a different type of authority in its place, that nearly five hundred years later the Romans were still haunted by the fear of a return of the kings. For this reason it is significant that in Shakespeare's *Julius Caesar* the main character rejects the offer of a crown when at the height of his powers.

We can already see why many thinkers pair the concepts of authority and responsibility. A man with the power of life and death even over his own family has a tremendous responsibility thrust upon him. Roman tradition had it that Lucius Junius Brutus, one of the first pair of consuls, put to death his own two sons for attempting to restore the kings. The authority vested in him by the people gave him the power to order that anyone attempting to restore the kings be put to death. He had a responsibility to the people to see that the order was carried out, even if it meant executing his own sons, if they were the ones who disobeyed. The reader should note that this action represents in human terms the ultimate in objectivity of judgment in a situation where subjectivity would be most likely and most easily understood.

TYPES OF AUTHORITY

Our general introductory remarks about the nature of authority are important for an understanding of the different types of authority which is the subject for analysis in this section. The names of the types are assigned by Max Weber (15).

CHARISMATIC AUTHORITY

This type of authority need not detain us long, since it will not be a characteristic of the teacher, as we use the term, although it is typical of some of the *greatest* of the world's teachers. Charismatic authority has the closest ties with the idea of 'presence' or 'bearing' and of the impact made by these characteristics on others. The 'presence' results from the singular wisdom, bravery, or similar virtue, of the individual concerned, and of the norms or standards which such qualities engender.

The most obvious possessor of charismatic authority is Christ himself. Indeed, the word 'authority' is used most significantly in relation to Christ's teaching in the Gospels. It is stated that 'He taught as one having authority and not as the Scribes' (who were the *traditional* religious leaders). The Scribes were authorities on the Mosaic Law on which the Jewish religion was founded. Yet the presence and the wisdom of Christ, and the power of his teaching, were such that they transcended the traditional wisdom of the accepted religious leaders, and so undermined their authority that from that moment they began seeking ways of removing the threat.

The norms or standards which have resulted from this transcendental authority are typified in such absolutes as: 'Be ye perfect, even as your Father in heaven is perfect'. The scribes had the authority to utter such categorical imperatives, but they could not justify them, as Christ could by the perfection of his own behaviour.

TRADITIONAL AUTHORITY

Traditional authority rests on the established belief in the sanctity of tradition and the legitimacy of the status which this bestows. We have excellent examples of this in the moral authority of the Roman senate and the authority of the Scribes. Long acceptance of the legitimacy of the senate's actions gave it a power which was as strong as any legal power until determined individuals challenged it. Indeed, the whole of Roman life for the greater part of the life of the Republic (16) was based on norms and standards established by what was called *mores maiorum* (17), i.e. ancestral tradition. It was an extremely conservative tradition which can be summed up in the expression, 'What was good enough for my father is good enough for me'. Similarly, long acceptance of the pronouncements by the Scribes on doctrinal issues endowed them with tremendous traditional authority and, hence, with tremendous power over the thinking and actions of the Jews.

LEGAL-RATIONAL AUTHORITY

In view of what we have said about the characteristics of charismatic and traditional authority, the reader ought to be able, with the aid of the term itself, to state the characteristics of legal-rational authority. Like all 'authorities', this makes claims and issues commands. But the *right* to make those commands rests not on the singular qualities of those who issue them, nor on the traditional acceptance of the individuals and their rights, but on the legitimacy of the demands they make. The legitimacy is not based on acceptance as it is in the other types of authority, but on the rational basis of the demands themselves. Moreover, the people subjected to the demands must understand and accept the rational justification. Thus while St. Augustine could demand religious obedience through faith, St. Thomas Aquinas was required to present the rational basis for belief in God and the right of the Church to demand specific forms of behaviour, through its doctrine and dogma.

Rulers and teachers possess legal-rational authority. Both have to make laws or rules to guide conduct. Both are backed by authority. At certain times, both have been able to make *absolute* rules and demands which the present day does not accept as part of their authority. The arbitrariness of the teacher's absolute command is no longer regularly or automatically tolerated by the learner. If the rules which learners are expected to obey are to be acceptable and meaningful, they must be rationally justified. Then their reasonableness will be seen and the demands which they make accepted. At this juncture we can see the connection between authority and what we said about values (Chapter 11) and morals (Chapter 12). It is a type of freedom (namely) 'freedom from absolutes', which gives people the right to demand rational explanation and justification when legal-rational authority makes demands. The monarch whose authority was vested in him by the Divine Right of Kings was in the absolutist position, and far different from the king who rules by legal-rational authority.

HISTORY OF AUTHORITY: RULES OF DIFFERENT AUTHORITIES

All three types of authority introduced above make rules and require them to be obeyed. Moreover, each requires them to be obeyed for different reasons; that is why it is so important to distinguish one type of authority from another. When charismatic authority, so much above and beyond the reach of other authorities, makes its demands, they are obeyed just because they come from such an authority. Christ's rules were so far in advance of anything that the Law of Moses demanded, that their very uniqueness commanded respect. The sayings of Confucius stand in a similar relationship to conventional wisdom.

ae history of educational thought is really the history of one traditional authority after another establishing its rules which become embodied in the curriculum. For a time the authority is accepted, then it is overthrown and another tradition, another authority, is established. Thus when Rome fell, the world lost its stabilizing element. Stability was completely dependent on the authority and power of Rome.

The next authority was the Church. This took over the task of bringing unity and stability. It did so by controlling the thoughts and minds of men by the establishment of doctrine and dogma. Men exchanged the freedom to think for themselves for the stability of a newly-established authority which became traditional and remained so for a thousand years.

The traditional authority of the medieval Church was challenged by the Renaissance, the revival of classical learning. The authority of the Classical scholars rested on the works of Greek and Roman writers. Their ideas were accepted because the breadth of their thinking freed men's minds from the constraint of the teaching of the Church. Classical Latin replaced ecclesiastical Latin and became the traditional authority in the curriculum. Ultimately this new authority became a form of constraint, since the rote-learning of Latin grammar was as deadening as the constricting doctrine and dogma which the Church had imposed.

The Reformation was a religious protest against the dominance of the Church through the priesthood, parallel to the secular protest of the Renaissance. The reformers, who were subsequently known as Protestants, denied the right of the priesthood to interpret Scripture for the laity. Their slogan, 'Every man his own priest', was a demand for freedom made on the authority of the Scriptures themselves, since nowhere in the Scriptures could the reformers see any justification for the establishment of an *élite* to interpret the Bible for the masses. The meaning could be given to individuals through 'revelation', which was the prerogative of God, not of the priesthood.

But the Reformation degenerated into sectarian rivalries, and education became little more than the learning of sectarian creeds, or the same basic process as the one against which the reformers protested.

The eighteenth century was important, since its authority, after man had tired of the various forms of Church authority which seemed inseparable from ritual and dogma, was *reason*. The 'enlightenment' was a demand on the authority of reason for freedom from ritualistic religion. Joining the protest was another source of authority, the appeal to Nature, the protest of Rousseau against artificiality and man-made differences, and all unjust constraints on the individual. In religious matters, too, Rousseau attempted to substitute the authority of nature for the constraint of ritual and dogma. The two authorities were alike demanding freedom from artificiality, one predominantly in the religious sphere, the other predominantly in the social and educational sphere.

From this time, we can trace the rise of the individual. The individual, once he has won rights from authority, is obviously much less bound by the constraints of that authority. However, he is given freedom as distinct from licence. If an individual denies the right of authority to control him in his own interests and in the interests of the rest of society, he assumes the responsibility of acting in the best interests of all concerned.

It seems, then, that on the one side there is absolute authority which, when backed by force, becomes authoritarian, and even when not backed by physical force becomes dogmatic, while, on the other hand, there are individual freedom, rationality and responsibility.

VOLUNTARY ACCEPTANCE OF AUTHORITIES AND THEIR PRONOUNCEMENTS

Less dogmatic than the expression '*the* authority', which has undertones of absolutism, is the expression 'an authority', which, as we shall see in a moment, has much more in common with reason and responsibility. Just as we found it less dogmatic and less prescriptive to talk about 'aims *in* education' than '*the* aims *of* education', so it is less absolute and authoritarian to talk about '*an* authority *on*' rather than '*the* authority *of*'.

There is, too, an essential difference (difference in nature or type). '*The* authority *of*' results in rules which must, for one reason or another, be obeyed. Even reason can become, and did become historically, an *absolute* authority. If we are 'an authority on', we specialize in pronouncements of a learned nature, rather than in rules to be obeyed. However, our pronouncements may result in rules which a man accepts voluntarily. Our pronouncements help him without demanding that he sacrifices freedom of action. He can see the reasonableness of acting in accordance with the pronouncement of the expert. A simple example will illustrate this.

I am a very keen gardener. An authority on gardening writes an article, in which he says that those who grow cabbages would be wise to spray them, at an early stage in their development, with a liquid which is lethal to caterpillars. Another authority writes that roses in the south of England, because of the small amount of sulphur in the atmosphere, are prone to 'black spot', a disease which kills the leaves, and, since roses 'breathe' through their leaves, this can be very dangerous for the rose trees. Each article ends, not with a categorical imperative, but with a 'good tip' which is based on informed opinion (see Chapter 10). One says: 'A good tip' for all gardeners is to spray cabbages in early Spring with x'; the other: 'A good tip for rose-growers in the south of England is to spray your roses with *Y* in early Spring, to lessen the likelihood of their being attacked by black spot.'

We have freedom of choice in both matters. Basically, if we wish to grow healthy cabbages or healthy roses, we should accept the good tips as rules and obey them. But they are not stated categorically. We are likely to obey them because we can see the reasonableness of the contents, and because the wording is calculated to win acceptance.

Again, there are authorities on Shakespeare. These people do not state facts but express informed opinions which, because of their acknowledged expertise, are accepted by those less expert. But such authorities have no right to *demand* acceptance. Certain of them become traditionally accepted. For example, for the layman, Cornford's translation of *The Republic* of Plato is accepted as 'the best'. If one expert so outstrips all others in a given field, he may even be accepted as '*The* authority'. In this case, he has what amounts almost to charismatic authority, which gives him an aura of traditional acceptance. But the pronouncements of all such experts are 'authoritative' as distinct from 'authoritarian'.

The main responsibility of the expert is to give factually correct information, or to base his tips on verifiable evidence. The expert's responsibility is to free the mind of the non-expert from error or to prevent his mind falling under the constraint of error. Thus in terms of what we said about 'liberal education' (Chapter 8), we can say that the 'authoritative pronouncements' of the 'authority on . . .' frequently have a liberalizing effect. Since liberalizing, in this sense, is providing freedom from the constraint of error or erroneous thinking, we see another connection between our concepts 'freedom' and 'authority'.

AUTHORITY: RESPONSIBILITY: FREEDOM

The transition from the absolute authority of the Church, which was itself backed by such authorities as the Bible and the Pope has given way to authority backed by rational justification. The bridge between the two, Peters claims, is science. Man has been released from the constraint of edicts, from absolutes, as unchanging and unchangeable as the Laws of the Medes and the Persians (18). At the same time, he has submitted to the responsibility which the change demands. He has sought reasons for obedience to authority. Now, the authority of reason demands that he give reasons for his actions. If a man acts only in ways which he can justify when called upon to do so, then his behaviour is responsible. He is freed from accepting a course of action, because there is no alternative, as when the course of action is ordained by some supreme authority. But he is faced with the responsibility of recognizing choices and making a responsible decision. He must accept the fact that since his choice will affect others as well as himself, it must be a wise one. Once more we are back in the realm of rational morality.

But desirable though the freedom from absolutes may seem, it has been bought at a price. Absolute authority and unquestioning obedience to that authority provide individuals and societies with a tremendous feeling of security. Because the power of Rome was absolute, the Apostle Paul could claim before the Emperor: '*Civis Romanus sum*' (I am a citizen of Rome). He was *secure*, because he owed allegiance to this supreme civil authority.

Man has rid himself of the absolute submission to the religious demands of the Church and accepted the responsibility of moral behaviour, which can be justified in the light of reason. Yet Jung could say that of the patients who came to him with mental disorders, all those over the age of thirty-five had one thing in common; they lacked any religious belief, the recognition of any religious 'father-figure' or 'authority-figure' to provide *security* in their lives. Jung attributes their mental disorders to the so-called freedom from such allegiance which progress and advances in civilization had claimed for mankind. It is for this reason that many claim that there is truth in the statement about the subservience of man to God, 'whose service is perfect freedom'. For this reason also, the Jesuit writer Lafarge was able to say: 'The highest form of liberty is a response to the ultimate love which is the source of the world's being, and is the finality of the world's development.' For this reason also, Erich Fromm (19) is able to speak of man's 'fear of freedom'. Release from the constraint of authority is most attractive, while one is seeking to obtain it. Once it is obtained and the corresponding responsibility assumed, a man often wishes to return to his former state. The adolescent wishes to be free from parental authority, and the law has recently said that he may now be so free at eighteen instead of twenty-one. Yet, once free, he finds that he enters a strange world of uncertainty for which he is ill-equipped. He seeks escape not from the constraints of society, but from the responsibility which society demands as the price of his freedom.

What is true of the individual is true of the race. Emerging nations, wishing to free themselves from foreign domination, frequently turn and rend one another in their perplexity after freedom has been obtained. The hated authority goes, but the stability of government which produced a desirable security goes with it. It is one thing to claim that reason is a much better master than absolutism. It is quite another thing to be sufficiently responsible to regulate one's life strictly according to reason. Once the constraint of ultimate authority is removed, all those preferences, biases, and prejudices, which are part of our 'irrational self', take over, often with disastrous effects.

Nor does having authority as a teacher absolve us from responsibility both to our pupils and to society. Society recognizes that, as the result of specific training and education, certain people are worthy of the status of teacher. But, in return, the society which awards the status makes strict demands about the way the teacher behaves. There are those who claim that, in these terms, the teacher has very little real freedom, that he is 'socially conditioned' to act out a certain role (20).

The teacher has a responsibility, too, towards those whom he teaches. Under an absolute system, a set body of knowledge is to be taught to all learners. The aim is merely to expose every individual to the same corpus of knowledge. They are not required to interpret it, only to accept it. But when the educational reformers demanded freedom for the individual child to receive teaching which was appropriate for him, a demand made on the authority of the psychological recognition of individual differences, the role of the teacher was changed. Once it was accepted that some children were culturally deprived, deprived of mother love, or deprived of material necessities and emotional stability in the home, the responsibility for filling these gaps was laid firmly on the teacher.

For this reason, the transition from the authoritarian role to his new role must be made in accordance with the demands of reason. Many (alas, too many) new approaches and new methods are not so justified or even justifiable. It is not sufficient to allow the child to 'do as he pleases entirely' because he was once compelled to 'do as he was told entirely'. To adopt a policy of *laissez-faire* in education may be to abdicate as an educator (21).

AUTHORITY AND FREEDOM

Earlier in this chapter we said that we would examine the concepts 'freedom' and 'authority' separately, and then consider the relationship between them. We also suggested, when we began our analysis of authority, that it had at least one thing in common with freedom, namely that there was no single meaning which could be assigned to it, nor was there one particular type of authority or one particular type of freedom. We soon found that it was difficult to talk about either concept for long, without making reference to the other. Moreover, once we had interrelated them, we found the third concept of responsibility occurring more and more frequently.

We should not, therefore, find it difficult to decide why Nash (22) chose the words *Authority and Freedom in Education* for the title of a book of which the sub-title is 'An Introduction to the Philosophy of Education'. Nor should we find it difficult to envisage some of the freedoms which Nash discusses, and to decide in relation to what authorities these freedoms are justified. However, we shall close this chapter with brief mention of some pairs of authorities and freedoms, since they well illustrate points which we ourselves have made.

DEPENDENCE OF MAN ON AUTHORITIES

Discussing the 'authority of work' and the 'freedom to play', Nash makes a number of important points. He states that every man is remarkably dependent on many authorities. One who goes into a liberal profession, such as medicine or teaching, has been dependent on his parents, his teachers, the state, or some other person or body of people for a quarter of a century, or one third of the normal human life span. Moreover, man in general has a much longer period of individual and social infancy than any other species. As 'infancy' can be defined as 'a period of dependence on various authorities', man is *dependent* for a much larger proportion of his total life than is any other creature.

Even when man reaches adulthood and the independence of parental authority and constraint which earning a living and marrying provide, he is not completely free. He is constrained to submit to the authority of work in order to provide for himself and his wife and children the necessities of life. Only after making such provision, if he is responsible, is he free to indulge in leisure pursuits of his own choosing and for his own satisfaction.

The more a man or his family desires in the way of material prosperity, the more he must earn. The more he must earn, the more he must submit himself (thus sacrificing freedom) either to the work bench, if he is a manual worker, or to the demands of increased responsibility, if he is a white-collar worker. We have already touched on this basic problem when we discussed 'ego-involving' occupations in relation to liberal education (Chapter 8).

In underdeveloped countries, the individual is even more dependent than his counterpart in developed societies on providing the necessary life. He still has to obtain the security in this area which, in other societies, advances in science and medicine have produced. In advanced societies, the individual is more inclined to be able to submit himself to the demands of the comfortable life.

In the area of schooling, Nash suggests that we must make the process a truer combination of dependence and independence not only by what we teach, but by the *way* we teach it. He believes that it is the duty of every school to see that both work and play are truly liberating for the individual learner and for the total society of the school. By his so doing, the pupil will be enabled to submit to the authorities and avail himself of the freedoms which society provides, when he leaves school. We see in this statement yet another interpretation of *liberal* education.

However, we cannot dispense with the authority of institutions in society. Only *on the authority* of the Church and the school can we develop the freedom for individuals to think, teach, and learn. These institutions are part of the unifying influence of society. They are the things which give society that basic stability which is necessary, if we are to be able to feel free to explore, to make innovations, to try new experiences. Only because of the security provided by past knowledge and past cultural achievements can man experiment and develop new experiences in the present. Unless there is a basic framework within which to operate, innovation becomes trial-and-error behaviour. Without a clear purpose to the teaching and learning of the past, there can be no clear aims and purposes in present experiment. Without the stability which established values give, it is futile to seek to discover new values. The authority of the past sets a framework of security for the freedom of the present.

For these and similar reasons, we must appreciate that, just as there is a connection between authority, freedom, and responsibility, so there is a connection between authority, freedom, and discipline. The important point to remember is that the authority must come first. We must have discipline in order to have our freedom, since freedom develops out of and through discipline. Discipline is not a constraint placed upon freedom.

The importance of this last sentence cannot be too strongly emphasized. When there are protest movements, such as the one of child-centred education against formalism, there is often a feeling of resentment, a belief that, if men had only thought aright years or even centuries ago, there would have been no need for protest now. It was the very fact that men did think wisely, at that particular time, that allows the carping critics to make such remarks now.

AUTHORITY BEFORE FREEDOM: UNIFYING AND STABILIZING ROLE OF AUTHORITY

Consideration of the remainder of the pairings of freedoms and authorities which Nash undertakes, will illustrate this point. In each case it will be clear that to have attempted to use authority as the 'unifying agent', after years of free activity in any of the areas mentioned, would have been disastrous. There would have been little progress made if, for example, freedom had preceded discipline. But, if men had attempted to curb freedom with discipline, they would have stifled the prospects of progress. Instead of establishing discipline, they would have imposed order, a static condition from which no progress is ever possible. But, within the framework of discipline, each individual is free to develop his own interests without danger to the rest.

So it is that on the authority of the group, each man is granted the freedom to become himself; on the authority of excellence, men are granted the freedom to enjoy the equality of opportunity; on the authority of determinism man enjoys the freedom to choose; on the authority of tradition we enjoy the freedom to create.

AUTHORITY AND FREEDOM – THE BALANCE

The problem in each case is to discover the ideal point of 'balance' between 'authority and freedom'. If we move too far in either direction, we either reproduce the original 'constraining position' of 'authority', or create a situation in which 'licence', not 'freedom', emerges and, with each individual doing as he pleases, a secure, authoritarian state of affairs degenerates into anarchy.

AUTHORITY: LICENCE: LACK OF BALANCE

Plato appreciated this in *The Republic* (23). After describing the perfect state and the perfect man as aristocracy and the aristocrat, Socrates examines the other four states and their equivalent type of man. Each state rests on its own particular authority. Each emerges, reaches its peak and declines, because of faults which are inherent in it. This was a favourite idea with the Greeks. Their great tragic plays are stories of men who, before they became prosperous, submitted themselves with due respect to the authority of the gods and of fate which governed everything and everybody. But, once a man had begun to enjoy prosperity, he began to feel that he was free from such restraining authorities. He became so obsessed with the feeling of power which his material success gave to him, that he felt free to do as he wished. He felt free to avoid that Greek motto (which is a statement of the need for 'balance'), *meden agan*, 'nothing in excess'.

The individual was carried to a high peak of fortune before Nemesis or retribution intervened. 'Pride', as the proverb of a later day had it, 'went before a fall' (24). Because the gods hated the sin of pride, they cast the successful man down from the pinnacle of his fame to the depths of ignominy. From this there grew up a saying: 'Whom the gods wish to destroy, they first make successful'. They freed him from their authority so that he might indulge in licence and anarchic behaviour, and destroy himself.

The only ultimate freedom from authority for the Greeks was the recognition of the ultimate power of authority, which is basically similar to the point which we made about authority coming before its particular freedom, and remaining, even when the freedom is established, as the ultimate 'frame of reference' for that freedom. Such authority is not a straitjacket which denies room to manœuvre and initiative. On the other hand, to assume that one can ridicule authority in the name of freedom is a denial of freedom, because it cannot be justified in terms of reason.

Thus, Socrates saw that aristocracy was the ideal state, but its strength became its weakness and began its decline. In an aristocracy (the Greek word means 'rule by the best') those who were distinguished by birth were the rulers. This state declined when people demanded distinctions other than birth as the freedom to become members of the governing body.

The Greek word for honour is *timē*, and the rule of those distinguished by honour other than birth is *timocracy*. If the type of honour envisaged is academic distinction, one has a 'meritocracy' as in modern society. But, in the Socratic sense, the honours which distinguished the timocratic man were more tangible than intellectual merit.

It is this tangible nature of the honour which is the seed of destruction of timocracy. Certain members of the governing body (the authorities) begin to equate honour with possession of property. Instead of devoting their energies to acquiring the traditionally accepted honours, they expend their energies on acquiring property which becomes the symbol of authority. Those who possess the property become, in their turn, the governing body. The authority has changed its nature and its aims, and the freedom to enter is limited to the few on the criterion of possessing property.

Thus 'oligarchy' (rule by the few) replaces 'timocracy'. Moreover, while the few (the authorities) have been acquiring their property, they have been widening the gulf between themselves and those whom they govern. The state becomes a thing of two classes, the rich and the poor. The rich look down on the poor because they lack the freedom to enter the sanctuary of authority through lack of property qualification; the poor hate the oligarchs, since their criterion of possessing property denies freedom to the masses.

The underprivileged (and lack of privilege is a kind of denial of freedom – the freedom to be the same as other men), unable to challenge the supreme authority in any other way, resort to arms and physical force. By this stage, the actions of both sides have rendered a rational solution impossible. After expelling the privileged few, the 'many' establish themselves as the new authority in which there is equality of right and privilege. In a democracy each man has freedom to act according to his new rights.

But some abuse these rights. In acting according to their interpretation of freedom, they behave in a manner which is characterized by licence. The exercise of freedom by some results in the constraint of others. Exercise of freedom, leading to loss of freedom in one's fellows, brings division as surely as division occurred within the other authorities. The authority of the many is riddled with dissent, as was the authority of the few. Behaviour is arbitrary, irrational, socially unacceptable, immoral. Choices are made purely on a selfish basis.

Eventually, one individual, more licentious, unscrupulous, and perhaps more physically powerful than the others, irrationally imposes his will on the others. Equally irrationally, he attempts to control the behaviour of the rest by constraint. His own position of authority depends on his constraining everyone else's freedom, and the only solution is total submission to his will, to his absolute authority, or the overthrow of his authority by the irrational solution of force. Democracy has now become tyranny.

THE TEACHER AND THE BALANCE BETWEEN AUTHORITY AND FREEDOM

The ideas presented above might almost be called a 'parable' of freedom and authority. It illustrates how easy it is for the authority to become untrue to itself, to move from a tenable position and become authoritarian in order to maintain its authority. It also shows how easy it is for the forces which attempt to modify any authority to fall into the same traps, to be constrained by erroneous thoughts and actions just as the previous authority was. At the very moment when it seems that the ideal situation has been achieved and every man has the freedom to act in accordance with his own choice, we are closest to tyranny, despotism, and the restoration of a single absolute to which all must submit, since all cannot be allowed to behave in a licentious and anarchic way. The only end of such behaviour is total destruction of society and the end of freedom for everyone.

We have said that the balance between freedom and authority, even when the authority is well-meaning, is a delicate one. Nowhere is this more true than in the case of the teacher and the content and method of his teaching. We began this book with a promise that any philosophizing would always be related to the practical task of teaching. It is fitting that we close this section on freedom and authority, and with it the book, with a passage from Nash, in which he applies what we have said about the need for balance and the delicacy of such balance between freedom and authority, to teachers themselves, their aims and methods:

'If the teacher provides too much guidance and leadership, if he tells the pupil everything he needs to know, if he exercises an indisputable and weighty authority, the pupil is liable to find himself on a path with the sun in his eyes, blinding him and preventing him from picking out the route for himself. On the other hand, if the teacher gives no guidance or leadership, if he tells the child nothing, and makes him find his own way unaided, the child finds himself on the same path, this time in total darkness, without even the minimal light necessary to see his way.'

NOTES AND REFERENCES FOR CHAPTER 13

1 For bi-polar personality factors, see *Assessment and Testing: An Introduction*, op. cit.

2 *Authority and Freedom in Education*, P. Nash (J. Wiley 1966).

3 *Groundwork of Educational Theory*, J. S. Ross (Harrap 1942).

4 *Freedom; A New Analysis*, Maurice Cranston (Longmans, Green & Co, 1955, 2nd edn 1967).

5 Sentences can be divided into 'simple' and 'complex'. A simple sentence is one in which the main idea of the writer is expressed in a main clause only. Complex sentences contain subordinate (dependent) clauses in addition to the main clause.

6 Duns Scotus (1270–1308) was a Franciscan, born in the later years of another famous Franciscan, Roger Bacon (1214–1294), who was roughly contemporary with Thomas Aquinas. Duns Scotus attended the universities of Oxford and Paris, where he defended the doctrine of the Immaculate Conception (Virgin Birth of Christ). He entered into dispute with Thomas Aquinas. Most of the Franciscans sided with Duns Scotus rather than with Aquinas. 'Scotus' suggests that he was born in Scotland, but there is an alternative theory that his birthplace was in Ireland.

7 Hobbes (1588–1679) is described by Russell as difficult to classify as a philosopher. He was an empiricist, like Locke, Berkeley, and Hume, but unlike them he had great respect for both pure and applied mathematics. He was also a political philosopher and his famous work *Leviathan* is an expression of extreme royalist opinions. It also contained a bitter attack on the Catholic Church.

8 For reference to Leibniz see notes and references for Chapter 1, Section 16.

9 Hegel (1770–1831), though a frequent critic of the philosophy of Kant, nevertheless developed his ideas. He had a tremendous influence on academic philosophers in America and Britain at the end of the nineteenth century, and many Protestant theologians accepted his ideas. His influence in political philosophy was also considerable, and the young Karl Marx was one of his followers.

10 Spinoza (1634–1677) is described by Russell as being supreme among philosophers in the field of ethics. One of his major works was simply entitled *Ethics*, his others were *Tractatus Theologico-Politicus* and *Tractatus-Politicus*, in which he expressed political theories derived from Hobbes. Readers will find interesting the similarity between the second and third titles and the title of Wittgenstein's early work, *Tractatus Logico-Philosophicus*; translated by D. F. Pears and B. F. McGuinness (Routledge & Kegan Paul 1961).

11 The idea of predestination is a most strange piece of theology. Basically it is a simple denial of the existence of free will, which is something that one can either accept or reject on logical grounds. But predestination (strictly interpreted) predicates the idea that God decides that some shall be born to salvation and others to damnation. Once the decision has been made by God, men cannot, by their own good works, avoid damnation. Jehovah's Witnesses today believe that only a limited number will receive salvation. This 'fixed number' poses problems of its own, as did Plato's plan to limit the numbers in his ideal state to 5040.

12 *The Roman Republic*, W. E. Heitland (Cambridge University Press 1909); *A Short History of Rome*, W. E. Heitland (Cambridge University Press 1911).

13 The senate of Rome was like the American Senate and the English Parliament. Originally, all its members were from the patrician (aristocratic) class, but in the fourth century the plebeians (common people) were admitted to membership. It could not pass laws, but it issued *senatus consulta* (decrees of the senate). It administered finances, appointed provincial governors, supervised the state religion. In later Republican times, it was composed largely of ex-magistrates. Julius Caesar increased the number of senators from 300 to 900, but Augustus subsequently reduced this number to 600.

14 Tarquinius Superbus (Tarquin the Proud) is reputed to have been the last king of Rome. The historian Livy deals with this period. It is thought that Tarquinius was an Etruscan, a member of an Italian people about whom comparatively little is known. Legend has it that Tarquinius was overthrown by his nephew Brutus, who became consul and subsequently sanctioned the death of his own son for attempting to restore Tarquin to the throne.

15 *Theory of Economic and Social Organization*, Max Weber, ed. Talcott Parsons (Hodge 1947).

16 The Roman Republic came to an end with the victory of Octavian in the civil war following Julius Caesar's assassination. Octavian subsequently became the emperor Augustus. He was born in 63 B.C. and died in A.D. 14 and was the Caesar Augustus of the Gospel narrative of the birth of Christ, when he 'issued a decree that all the world should be taxed'.

17 The word *mores* is now a sociological term meaning a pattern of behaviour or living of a given group. This behaviour (or living) pattern becomes characteristic of the group, and is passed on from one generation to the next. It thus becomes virtually traditional for that particular group.

18 This piece of ancient legislation is always referred to as 'The Law of the Medes and Persians, which changeth not', because the authority and power of the legislators was such that it seemed impossible for them to be overthrown. For a similar idea of permanence, see the address to the king in the book of Daniel – 'O King, live for ever'.

19 *Fear of Freedom*, Erich Fromm (Routledge & Kegan Paul 1942). See also *Escape from Freedom* (Holt, Rinehart & Winston 1941).

20 For the idea that human personality is determined by the roles which individuals play out on the stage of life, see *Assessment and Testing: An Introduction*, op. cit. For a discussion of J. L. Moreno's 'role theory' see *Interpreting Personality Theories*, Ledford J. Bischof (Harper International Student Reprint 1964).

21 Russell, speaking of Locke, states that the characteristic which he passed on to the whole of the Liberal Movement (in philosophy) was lack of dogmatism. Locke felt that truth was difficult to ascertain and that the rational and reasonable man could not therefore be dogmatic, since there was in most things an element of doubt. This attitude is the opposite of the authoritarian attitude. It is linked with religious toleration, and with *laissez-faire* (or a policy of non-interference) especially with the right of others to their own views and opinions.

In the nineteenth century, *laissez-faire* was a concept linked with the concept 'socialism' and 'utilitarianism'. Economic *laissez-faire* believed that any artificial interference with the laws of supply and demand must be harmful, a belief accepted by capitalists, since it was in their interests. But socialist thinkers believed that the doctrine was positively harmful to the masses (the workers). Machinery was more efficient than manual labour and could replace it, thus presenting a dire threat to the security of the workers. *Laissez-faire* perpetuated those evils which were eventually stamped out by such measures as the Factory Acts, Trade Board Acts, and Shop Hours Acts, which were aimed at preventing worker exploitation.

In educational terms, *laissez-faire* is dangerous, since it is an underlining of that form of naturalism which we criticized in Chapter 4. It is a belief in non-intervention in the natural development of the child. In later chapters, e.g. when we spoke of freedom and discipline and Herbart's view that the teacher must control the child's experiences in the child's own interests, we had further evidence of the dangers of extreme forms of non-directive education.

22 *Authority and Freedom in Education*. See 2 above.
23 *The Republic* of Plato, Book 8.
24 The sin of pride is represented by a Greek word *hybris*, which has passed into English usage like the word *nous* (the Greek word for 'mind') which we use to mean common sense, or intelligence in its loose, lay meaning. *Hybris* is pride which leads to insolent behaviour against authority.

Bibliography

The possible recommendations in a bibliography at the end of an introductory book on the philosophy of education are almost limitless. Which books an individual reads after an introductory book depend largely on three factors: the amount of knowledge he has gained from the introductory book, the amount of interest he has acquired in the subject, and the special needs which he feels that he has in his course, which further study of philosophy can supply.

It would be strange if no further reading of books on philosophy were recommended, but it would be almost equally strange if *only* books on philosophy were recommended, since we said at the outset and saw throughout this book that philosophy examines facts from many areas or disciplines.

Because of this, a number of general books are recommended at the beginning of the list which follows. After that, the list is subdivided into the concepts examined in individual chapters. Under each concept heading a number of books are suggested, some specifically on philosophical topics, others from related areas.

GENERAL BACKGROUND READING

King, F., *World Perspectives in Education* (Methuen 1962)
This book is generally recommended as a book on comparative education. However, it is much less concerned with factual descriptions and comparisons of educational systems in different countries, than with a philosophical appraisal of the problems which are at the present time common to many nations.
Rusk, R., *Doctrines of the Great Educators* (Macmillan 1957).
This book gives a description of the ideas of all the key educational thinkers from Plato to Dewey. Although it is infinitely less exhaustive than Russell's treatment of individual philosophers, it is eminently readable.
Russell, Bertrand, *A History of Western Philosophy* (George Allen & Unwin 1946).
This provides an excellent introduction to philosophers from the Pre-Socratic period to the twentieth century.

CHAPTER 1. PHILOSOPHY AND PHILOSOPHY OF EDUCATION

Brauner, Charles J., and Burns, Robert W., *Problems in Education* (Prentice-Hall, Foundations of Education Series, 1965).
In the brief introduction, the authors stress that education is a rapidly expanding process which is much less well understood by those engaged in it than it ought to be, a point which we have made in the present volume. They emphasize, as we do, the close functional relationship between philosophy and practice in education, and the need to see, in perspective, the historical, philosophical, social, and psychological foundations of education.
Brown, L. M., *General Philosophy in Education* (McGraw-Hill 1966).
Part 1 of the book is entitled 'Tools of Critical Thinking', while Part 2 is 'Problems in Philosophy Relevant to Education'. The general conclusion is also useful, since it discusses the relevance of general philosophy for education

and attempts to answer the key question, 'Is philosophical inquiry in education of *real* value?' The authors indicate both the strengths and the weaknesses of such inquiry.

Hardie, C. D., *Truth and Fallacy in Educational Theory* (Cambridge University Press 1942).

Although it was stated, earlier in the present volume, that this work is not easy for the beginner to understand, it is worth emphasizing its importance. Now that readers have had some experience of the critical technique used in analytical philosophy, they might well benefit from reading it. Hardie examines data from a number of disciplines in his analysis.

Pai, Y., and Myers, J. T. (eds), *Philosophic Problems and Education* (J. B. Lippincott 1967).

We shall have occasion to refer to this excellent book of articles by distinguished philosophers past and present, in later sections of this bibliography. For the moment, the most relevant portion is Part 1, 'Philosophy and Education'.

Scheffler, I., *The Language of Education* (Thomas 1960).

The book contains an excellent introduction in which linguistic and concept analysis are explained and the difference between the historico-philosophical and the analytical approaches are discussed. There follow excellent chapters showing how different types of educational statements should be analysed. These statements include: descriptive definitions; stipulative definitions; slogans; and metaphors.

Smith, Othanel, and Ennis, H. (eds), *Language and Concepts in Education. An Analytical Study of Educational Ideas* (Rand McNally 1961).

A useful supplement to the above work by Scheffler.

Soltis, Jonas F., *An Introduction to the Analysis of Educational Concepts* (Addison-Wesley 1968).

The title of the book serves as a further reminder of the growing concern of educational philosophers to clarify basic terms which have been loosely used in the past and to determine precisely what meaning they have at the present time of educational change.

Non-analytical works

Throughout the present work, it has been stressed that content and method are inseparable. Even when the analytical approach is used, it is necessary to study the historical background to the present and to venture into the area of other disciplines. Because of this, the four titles which follow are recommended as *complementary* to the analytical approach.

Bayles, E. E., *Pragmatism in Education* (Harper & Row 1966).

Butler, J. Donald, *Idealism in Education* (Harper & Row 1966).

Morris, Van Cleve, *Existentialism in Education* (Harper & Row 1966).

By reading the above works in conjunction with those on linguistic analysis the reader will himself develop overall perspective in his philosophizing. He will appreciate, more and more, that what is ultimately important is his understanding of the *content* of education, and that linguistic analysis, far from being an end, is a method of achieving an end.

Morrish, Ivor, *Disciplines of Education* (George Allen & Unwin 1967).

Philosophy, psychology, and sociology are all considered in this work, again emphasizing the importance of 'inter-disciplinary examination'.

THE FIRST TRILOGY: EDUCATION: TRAINING: CHILD-CENTREDNESS

Education

Peters, R. S. (ed.), *The Concept of Education* (Routledge & Kegan Paul 1967).
  Chap. 1, 'What is an educational process?' (R. S. Peters).
Scheffler, Israel (ed.), *Philosophy and Education*, 2nd edn (Allyn & Bacon 1966):
  Section 1, 'Concepts of Education'.
  Section 2, 'The Study of Education'.

Training

Holmes, B., *Problems in Education: A Comparative Approach* (Routledge & Kegan Paul 1965).
  Chap. 8, 'Teacher Training and the Profession of Education (U.S.A.)'.
  Chap. 10, 'Liberal Education and Vocational Training (U.S.S.R.)'.
Peters, R. S. (ed.), *The Concept of Education* (see above):
  Chap. 7, 'Teaching and Training' (Gilbert Ryle).
Scheffler, I (ed.) *Philosophy and Education* (see above):
  Chap. 8, 'Knowing How and Knowing That' (Gilbert Ryle).

Child-centredness

Archambault, R. D. (ed.), *Philosophical Analysis and Education* (Routledge & Kegan Paul 1965):
  'What is an Educational Situation?' (L. R. Perry).
  'Child-centred Education' (P.S. Wilson).
Peters, R. S. (see above):
  Chap. 5, 'The Concept of Play' (R. F. Dearden).
The Philosophy of Education Society of Great Britain. Proceedings of the Annual Conference 1969:

LINK CHAPTER (5): 'THE CONCEPT AIMS'

Hollins, T. H. B. (ed.), *Aims in Education: The Philosophical Approach* (Manchester University Press 1964).
Jeffreys, M. V. C., *Glaucon: An Inquiry into the Aims of Education* (Pitman 1950).
O'Connor, D. J., *An Introduction to the Philosophy of Education* (Routledge & Kegan Paul 1957).
Whitehead, A. N., *Aims in Education and Other Essays*, 2nd edn (Benn 1962).

THE SECOND TRILOGY: CULTURE: CURRICULUM: LIBERAL EDUCATION

Culture

Arnold, Matthew, *Culture and Anarchy* (John Murray 1920).
Davis, Allison, *Social Class Influences upon Learning* (Harvard University Press 1948).
Eliot, T. S., *Notes Towards the Definition of Culture* (Faber 1950).
Halsey, A. H., Floud, J., and Anderson C. A. (eds) *Education, Economy and Society* (Free Press 1961):
  Part 1, 'The Consequences of Economic Change'.
  Part 5, 'The Changing Social Function of Schools and Universities'.
King, E., *World Perspective in Education* (see above):
  Chap. 5, 'Culture Conflicts'.
  Chap. 6, 'Impact of Technological Change'.

Mannheim, K., *Essays on the Sociology of Culture* (Routledge & Kegan Paul 1956).
Stenhouse, L., *Culture and Education* (Nelson 1967).
Williams, R., *Culture and Society 1780–1950* (Chatto & Windus 1958)

Curriculum
Bereday, George, Z. F., *Comparative Methods in Education* (Holt, Rinehart & Winston 1966):
   Chap. 6, 'Control of School Curricula in Four Countries; the United States, the USSR, France, and England.'
James, E. (*now* Lord James of Rusholme), *An Essay on the Content of Education* (Harrap 1949).
Wheeler, D. K., *Curriculum Process* (University of London Press 1967).
Department of Education, University of Birmingham, *Journal of Curriculum Studies*. Published twice annually by Collins (May/Nov.).
Schools Council, *The New Curriculum* (HMSO 1967).

Liberal Education
Gardner, J. W., *Excellence: Can We be Equal and Excellent, too?* (Harper & Row 1961).
Halsey *et al.*, *Education, Economy and Society* (see above):
   Part II, 'Education, Social Mobility and the Labour Market', Chap. 35, 'British Universities and Intellectual Life' (A. H. Halsey).
   This should be read with the idea of liberal education freeing the individual from class and occupational bondage, and the degree of success which it has in these directions.
Huxley, T., *Science and Education* (New York 1894).
Kazamias, Andreas M., and Massialas, Byron G. "Tradition and Change in Education" (Prentice-Hall, Foundations of Education Series 1965):
   Part 5, 'Conclusions and Generalizations; Tradition and Change'.
Keller, Suzanne, *Beyond the Ruling Class: Strategic Élites in Modern Society* (Random House, New York 1963).
Livingstone, Sir Richard, *Education for a World Adrift* (Cambridge University Press 1944).
Park, J., *Selected Readings in the Philosophy of Education* (Macmillan, New York 1958):
   Chap. 10, 'Liberal Education Reconsidered' (Theodore Meyer Greene).
Williams, R. J., *Free and Unequal: The Biological Basis of Individual Liberty* (University of Texas Press 1952).

LINK CHAPTER (9) CONDITIONING AND INDOCTRINATION
Conditioning
Hilgard, E., *Theories of Learning* (Appleton, Century, Crofts 1948).
   This is the 'bible' on theories of learning. The reader is advised to do no more than read the chapter summaries, to see the different forms which conditioning in animal learning can take, especially the change of emphasis from the conditioning of Watson and Thorndike, to that of Tolman, with such terms as 'reward expectancy' and 'cognitive maps', which thorough-going behaviourists would condemn as subjective.
Peters, R. S. (ed.), *The Concept of Education* (see above):
   Chap. 4, 'Conditioning and Learning' (G. Vesey).

Indoctrination

Bereday, G. Z. F., *Comparative Methods in Education* (see above):
  Chap. 3, 'Indoctrination and Schools in One Country (Poland)'.
Hollins, T. H. B. (ed.), *Aims in Education: The Philosophical Approach* (see above).
  Chap. 2, 'Education and Indoctrination' (John Wilson).
Pai and Myers (eds), *Philosophic Problems and Education* (see above):
  Part 4, Chap. 41, 'Instruction and Indoctrination' (R. F. Atkinson).
Peters, R. S., *The Concept of Education* (see above):
  Chap. 11, 'Indoctrination' (J. P. White).

THE THIRD TRILOGY: VALUE-JUDGMENTS: VALUES: MORALS
Value-Judgments
Emmet, E. R., *Learning to Philosophize* (Longmans 1964):
  Chap. 5, 'Value-Judgments'.

Values

Brodbeck, May, *Readings in the Philosophy of the Social Sciences* (Collier-Macmillan, New York): Macmillan, London 1968).
  Chap. 2, 'Values and Social Science'.
Pai and Myers, *Philosophic Problems and Education* (see above):
  Part 2, 'Metaphysics and Education'.
  Part 4, 'The Problem of Value and Education'.
Park, J., *Selected Readings in the Philosophy of Education* (see above):
  Chap. 21, 'Religion and the Philosophies of Education, (Theodore Meyer Greene).
Scheffler, I. (ed.), *Philosophy and Education* (see above):
  Chap. 14, 'Public Education and the Good Life' (W. K. Frankena).
Soltis, Jonas F., *An Introduction to the Analysis of Educational Concepts* (see above):
  Chap. 1, Section 2, 'Values in Education'.

Morals

Bailey, C., 'The Notion of Development and Moral Education', *Proceedings of the Annual Conference of the Philosophy of Education Society of Great Britain* (January 1969).
Brown, L. M., *General Philosophy in Education* (see above):
  Chap. 8, 'Moral Evaluations'.
Crane, A. R., 'Pre-adolescent Gangs and Moral Development of Children', in *British Journal of Education Psychology*, Vol. xxviii, part iii, p. 201.
Gessell, A., and Ilg, F. L., *Infant and Child in the Culture of Today* (Hamish Hamilton 1943).
Hare, R. M., *The Language of Morals* (Oxford University Press 1952).
Hemming, J., 'Some Aspects of Moral Development in a Changing Society', in *BJEP*, Vol. xxvii, part ii, p. 77.
Holmes, B., *Problems in Education: A Comparative Approach* (see above):
  Chap. 11, 'Individual Freedom and Social Responsibility (Japan).'
Morris, J. F., 'The Development of Adolescent Value-judgments', in *BJEP* Vol. xxviii, part i, p. 1.
Niblett, W. R. (ed.), *Moral Education in a Changing Society* (Faber 1963).

282 / *The Philosophy of Education*

Park, J., *Selected Readings in the Philosophy of Education* (see above):
  Chap. 23, 'An Overview: Existentialism and Education' (Van Cleve Morris).
Peters, R. S., 'Freud's theory of moral development in relation to that of Piaget', in *BJEP*, Vol. xxx, part iii, p. 250.
Piaget, Jean, *The Moral Judgment of the Child* (Routledge & Kegan Paul 1932).
Scheffler, I. (ed.), *Philosophy and Education* (see above):
  Section 5, 'Moral Education'.
Soltis, J. F., *An Introduction to the Analysis of Educational Concepts* (see above):
  Chap. 5, Section 3, 'Moral Education: a Brief Summary'.

Morals and Religion
Hilliard, W. H., 'The Influence of Religious Education upon the Development of Children's Moral Ideas', *BJEP*, Vol. xxix, part i, p. 50.
Jeffreys, M. V. C., *Education – Christian or Pagan?* (University of London Press 1946).
Niblett, W. R., *Christian Education in a Secular Society* (Oxford University Press 1960).
Park, J., *Selected Readings in the Philosophy of Education* (see above):
  Chap. 21, 'Religion and Philosophies of Education' (Theodore Meyer Greene).
  Chap. 22, 'Church-state Separation and Religion in the Schools of our Democracy' (George Hunston Williams).
Scheffler, I. (ed.), *Philosophy and Education* (see above):
  Chap. 15, 'Religion and Higher Learning' (Morton White).

THE CONCEPTS 'FREEDOM' AND 'AUTHORITY' CHAPTER 13
Nash, Paul, *Authority and Freedom in Education* (John Wiley 1966).

Freedom
Ashen, Ruth N. (ed.), *Freedom: Its Meaning* (Harcourt Brace 1940).
Brodbeck, May, *Readings in the Philosophy of the Social Sciences* (see above):
  Part 8, 'Freedom, Determinism and Morality'.
Brown, L. M., *General Philosophy in Education* (see above):
  Chap. 7, 'Freedom and Determinism'.
Cranston, Maurice, *Freedom: A New Analysis* (Longmans, Green and Co. 1st edn, 1954; 2nd edn, 1967).
Lee, Dorothy, *Freedom and Culture* (Prentice-Hall 1959).
Mill, John Stuart, *On Liberty* (Regnery, Chicago 1955).
Miller, Perry, *Religion and Freedom of Thought* (Doubleday 1954).
Pai and Myers, *Philosophic Problems and Education* (see above):
  Chap. 43, 'Causation, Freedom and Moral Education' (Y. Pai).
Williams, R. J., *Free and Unequal: The Biological Basis of Individual Liberty* (University of Texas Press 1952).

Authority
King, E., *World Perspectives in Education* (see above):
  Chap. 10, 'Ideologies and Systems of Control'.
  Chap. 13, 'Barriers in Education'.
  Appendix, 'The Gentleman: the Evolution of an Ideal'.

Peters, R. S., *Authority, Responsibility and Education* (George Allen & Unwin 1959).
Wilson, R. C., *Authority, Leadership and Concern* (George Allen & Unwin 1949).

GENERAL ARTICLES

Just as it is both interesting and useful, for those who study psychology, to keep abreast of current developments by reading the *British Journal of Educational Psychology* (*BJEP*), so, those studying philosophy should read the *Proceedings of the Annual Conference of the Philosophy of Education Society of Great Britain*. This is published each January, and has recently become available in book form through Basil Blackwell, Oxford.

The publication not only provides articles on topics of great importance for education, but it also records debates between the writers of the articles and those who subsequently challenge their views. This is an excellent example of what we said at the very outset of this book, namely, that philosophy is not a process which gives single and simple right answers to problems.

Index